*Cowinner of the Jules and Frances Landry Award for 2026*

# *DEATH OR VICTORY*

## THE LOUISIANA NATIVE GUARDS & THE BLACK MILITARY'S SIGNIFICANCE IN THE CIVIL WAR

*A. J. CADE*

LOUISIANA STATE UNIVERSITY PRESS
BATON ROUGE

Published with the assistance of The Noland Fund

Published by Louisiana State University Press
lsupress.org



Manufactured in the United States of America
First printing

Designer: Michelle A. Neustrom
Typeface: MillerText
Printer and binder: Sheridan Books, Inc.

Jacket illustration: *Assault of the Second Louisiana Regiment . . . at Port Hudson* (*Frank Leslie's Illustrated Newspaper,* May 27, 1863)

Small portions of this text first appeared in the blog post "The Families of the Louisiana Native Guards," *Black Perspectives* (April 2023); and in "A Free Man, Fortiori a Soldier: Corporal John Andrew vs. Archibald Montgomery and the Transformation of New Orleans," *Journal of Military History* 88:3 (July 2024): 660–80.

Library of Congress Cataloging-in-Publication Data

Names: Cade, A. J. author
Title: Death or victory : the Louisiana Native Guards and the Black Military's significance in the Civil War / A. J. Cade.
Description: Baton Rouge : Louisiana State University Press, [2026] | Includes bibliographical references and index.
Identifiers: LCCN 2025045748 (print) | LCCN 2025045749 (ebook) | ISBN 978-0-8071-8550-6 (cloth) | ISBN 978-0-8071-8591-9 (epub) | ISBN 978-0-8071-8592-6 (pdf)
Subjects: LCSH: African American soldiers—Louisiana—History—19th century | United States—History—Civil War, 1861–1865—Participation, African American | Louisiana—History—Civil War, 1861–1865
Classification: LCC E510 .C33 2026 (print) | LCC E510 (ebook)
LC record available at https://lccn.loc.gov/2025045748
LC ebook record available at https://lccn.loc.gov/2025045749

In memory of Zara Ruth Cade,
my little angel who was too sweet for this world

# *CONTENTS*

# *ACKNOWLEDGMENTS*

Many people helped on my journey toward completing this book. First among them are my family: my children, Cordell, Anthony, Peter, and my Angel Zara; and in particular my loving wife of nearly fifteen years, Anne Cade. Great appreciation as well to my loving parents who have always supported me, Anthony Cade and Charon Grady. Their love and support throughout all of my years attending George Washington University and the University of Maryland ensured I could never give up no matter how difficult the process became.

The History Department of GW was an outstanding source of support as I completed this work. Chief among those I wish to acknowledge are Denver Brunsman, Nemata Blyden, Steven Brady, Warren Milteer Jr., and Michael Ross from the University of Maryland. In addition, Angela Zimmerman, Tyler Anbinder, and David Silverman also assisted me greatly. Each individual mentioned guided me along over the years, and all were invaluable in their own way. Additionally, the History Department provided funds and resources for research and conference travel. On a personal level, I met numerous students, especially prior to the pandemic, who were all great shoulders to lean on and discuss my work with. The comradery helped quite a bit during those early years, when I was unsure if I was in the right place. I can state with no exaggeration, without the members of the History Department at GW, I would not have been able to complete this book, and I thank each and every one of them.

Numerous historians and archivists whom I met along the way made me feel welcomed as an academic and historian, and I want to recognize a few of them in no particular order: Jon Sumida, Ned Bedessem, Jon Hoffman, Holly Pinheiro, Kelly Mezurek, Steve Lofgren, Hillary Green, Eric Setzekorn, Lorien Foote, and numerous archivists and librarians at the National Archives and Records Administration, the Library of Congress, the Louisiana State Archives, Louisiana State University, the University of New Orleans, and the US Army Center of Military History. Similar to everyone at GW, each person was invaluable in their own way, from reading early drafts and helping me publish blog posts to simply acknowledging me as an equal and giving advice as needed. For example, Kelly shared sources and Holly helped with early publications. Truly, I thank them all for their guidance and support over the years, and I hope others reading this recognize how welcoming the historical field is to new and innovative research pertaining to military history. Jon Sumida was the first, taking a chance on an undergrad and Marine Corps veteran who submitted a jumbled mess of an honor's thesis when he first fought to get me into graduate school.

Over the years, I had the opportunity to present my research at numerous conferences, which were extremely beneficial toward broadening my knowledge and giving me a chance to better understand my own work. Chris Brick and his team at *Intervals* interviewed me on their podcast for an episode titled "The Sons of Chalmette: The Transnational History of the Louisiana Native Guards." Keri Leigh and Virginia Summey interviewed me for their nine-part Civil War documentary that is still in the publication process. Holly Pinheiro and his editorial team at *Black Perspectives* published two blog pieces titled "Finding Common Ground: Dr. Louis Charles Roudanez and the African American Community of New Orleans during the Civil War" and "The Families of the Louisiana Native Guards." Parts of this book appeared in the July 2024 *Journal of Military History* in an article titled "A Free Man, *Fortiori* a Soldier: Corporal John Andrew vs. Archibald Montgomery and the Transformation of New Orleans." Additionally, I presented papers at the 30th Annual Symposium for the 19th Century Press, the Civil War and Free Expression, the Association for the Study of African American Life and History, The Great Strike: Slavery During the American Civil War, the James A. Barnes Conference, Colloque International, France/Louisiane: une relation Spéciale, the Society for the History of Discoveries, the Society for Military History, the Society of Civil War Historians, and at GW. The opportunity to write and present my research to public audiences resulted in some great feedback and connections to others whom I otherwise would not have met.

The editorial team at LSU Press, chief among them Rand Dotson, were great to work with. There were three anonymous reviewers, and each had suggestions and comments that helped polish a rough manuscript that was nearly one thousand pages into the book you are holding today. Their comments helped to formulate ideas for a follow-on book, so I invite all readers who enjoy this book to look for its sequel.

As many people can attest, completing a book is paradoxically both a solitary challenge and a team effort. Those mentioned by name or simply through their organizations were all part of my team, and their efforts toward building the next generation of historians should be replicated by all to further the growth of the field. I only hope that one day I too can help a junior historian come into their own. Thank you once again, everyone, and I hope you enjoy the book.

★ ★ ★

Any and all information presented in this book is the express research and opinion of the author and not the federal government, the Department of Defense, the Department of Veterans Affairs, or any government agency mentioned in this text or connected to the author. Any statements and opinions herein should be attributed to A. J. Cade.

# *DEATH OR VICTORY*

# *NEVER SURRENDER*

## NEW ORLEANS AND THE LOUISIANA NATIVE GUARDS

"What shall be done with the slaves after they are emancipated?" Frederick Douglass asked this question in February 1862, nearly a year before President Abraham Lincoln's Emancipation Proclamation went into effect. Douglass—a formerly enslaved Maryland man who freed himself, and possibly the most famous African American man in the country at that time—held a meeting at the famed Cooper Institute, where he lectured on the current state of the American Civil War. As he spoke, he recalled the U.S. Army's victories at Fort Henry and Roanoke Island, but he also spoke of defeats at Bull Run and Ball's Bluff. He expressed support for each of these campaigns, describing himself as "standing by the Government." However, he wanted to ensure that federal policy addressed the root cause of the war. He emphasized African American men's loyalty to the Union, reminding those in attendance that "no black man [has been] charged with disloyalty during this war." Pushing his point further, he said, "Black men were good enough to fight by the side of Washington and Jackson, and were not good enough to fight beside McClellan and Halleck."[1] Douglass's belief that Black men should be allowed to serve in the war was inextricably tied to his view of "what should be done with the slaves" after their emancipation: by fighting for their country, he indicated, they would prove themselves worthy of citizenship. The rest of the nation did not arrive at this conclusion as readily. Eventually, an experiment in New Orleans, Louisiana, supplied support for Douglass's view.

The Louisiana Native Guards have a long and misunderstood history in Civil War memory, and because of that, their story has not been fully explored by military historians or fully read by bibliophiles. The story of these regiments began in May 1861 as part of the New Orleans home guards, a local defense force meant to defend New Orleans in case of attack. While part of the New Orleans home guards, the regiment was considered outside the Confederate military, and thus the men in the New Orleans home guards were never Confederate soldiers. In the spring of 1862 the Native Guards were disbanded, then brought back by the Louisiana State Legislature within a few months before the federal government completely disbanded the regiment in May 1862 after liberating New Orleans from Confederate control. However, the commanding general of the Department of the Gulf, the federal command in control of New Orleans, brought back the regiment with the same designation and many of the same personnel in the Union army in August 1862. The first regiment was the foundation for dozens of subsequent regiments in Louisiana, all filled with Black men willing to fight and die for the freedom of all Black people and the promise of what the United States of America could be.

The history of the Native Guards may have begun in 1861, but the system that enabled the regiments to be the first Black regiments in the Union army existed in Louisiana for over a century before the war. Black and Creole men served in the New Orleans militia dating back to French and Spanish control of the region in the eighteenth century. The Louisiana territory was held by the French since 1682, and West Africans from the Senegambia region were kidnapped and forcibly transported to Louisiana as early as 1709 by the Company of the Indies. Enslaved peoples brought their religious practices, agricultural skills, medicine, culture, kinship networks, and military training with them to North America.[2] The French codified their enslavement in *le Code Noir* in 1724, but avenues toward freedom remained, and the French government made allowances for enslaved and free Black men to serve in the military.[3] Because Frenchmen regularly raped and impregnated Black women, dozens of children of mixed race were born during this time, some of whom were freed by their fathers. As early as 1727, free and enslaved men of color served in the French colonial militia, fighting against Indigenous People and members of other European colonies while also garrisoning forts and working the fields.

When Spain took over the Louisiana colony in 1763, it introduced *las Siete Partidas* but kept many of the *Code Noir* laws, allowing Black men to continue to serve in the militia. Spanish colonists were already accustomed to Black men serving in their militias in Europe and the Caribbean, so there was little adjustment needed for the men involved.[4] Spain even expanded avenues for children of white and Indigenous fathers to pursue freedom if they could prove their lineage.[5] However, the new laws also expanded punishments for enslaved people and gave white people absolute authority over all enslaved individuals. Nevertheless, the militia remained one of the few places where Black and Creole men of color could prove their loyalty and possibly gain freedom if they served well enough in combat. When Spain ceded the territory back to France in 1800 with the Treaty of San Ildefonso, the French had already outlawed slavery in France and most of its territories. In the aftermath of the Haitian Revolution—a national embarrassment to the French military—French leaders were keen on selling the North American colony to the newly formed United States in 1803 to get out of the hemisphere and fund the nation's wars in Europe.

Prior to Louisiana's sale to the United States, Congress had already passed the Militia Act of 1792, which defined militia men as white men. All white men between the ages of eighteen and forty-five were to train in their local militias. If needed, the president could call upon those militias to serve the federal government in a time of crisis.[6] Service in the militia, contrary to the twenty-first century definition of the word, was seen as a higher form of service than Regular Army service during the eighteenth and nineteenth centuries. Americans did not want a standing army of regulars who spent most of their lives being paid to train for a war that might never come. Militia men were citizens who trained and prepared for battle, ready to serve and defend their homes, state, and nation, while continuing to train and work to build their local communities. It was often seen as an honorable way for men to give back to their communities. Lax federal control, however, meant that most militias were not enforced, and the men did not train, instead spending their time drinking or doing nothing related to the militia. In the enslaved-holding states, the militia was most often used to quell enslaved revolts. Governors could call upon the state militias for any occurrence they deemed worthy, and only a governor could authorize a militia regiment to exist within their state.

William Claiborne, the first territorial governor of Louisiana, initially wanted to remove Black men from the militia, as did many white Americans, as their presence ran counter to the makeup of militias in other enslaved-holding states. But there were dozens of Black men already serving, some of whom had become wealthy, and they had the support of European immigrants in New Orleans. Black and Creole Louisianans delivered a petition to Claiborne stating, "We were employed in the military service of the late government, as we hope we may be permitted to say, that our conduct in that service has ever been distinguished by a ready attention to the duties required us. . . . Permit us to assure your excellency that we shall serve with fidelity and zeal." The petitioners offered to form "a corps of volunteers" to serve the governor in any capacity.[7] Moved by their petition and bolstered by the support of the white elite, Claiborne authorized their continued service and even called on them in 1811 to assist in suppressing a revolt by enslaved people.[8] Their service was so valuable that, in 1812, the governor authorized the general assembly "to organize a corps of militia" for the defense of Louisiana formed by free men of color.[9] Even Black officers were authorized in the corps. The only required qualification for service was possession of over $300 in taxable property, a high threshold even for white men at the time. The new laws imposed a class dynamic on the unit since only the wealthy and free Creole men of color could serve, alongside white men who could already serve. Nevertheless, military service continued to secure a place in society for Black and Creole men.

Near the end of the War of 1812, when British invaders were stationed on Ship Island, a barrier island off the Gulf Coast, in 1815, General Andrew Jackson was tasked with defending New Orleans from the impending invasion. Knowing he would need more than only wealthy soldiers, Jackson put out a call: "To every noble hearted, generous, freeman of color, volunteering to serve during the present contest with Great Britain, and no longer, there will be paid the same bounty in money and lands now received by the white soldiers of the United States, viz: $124 in money and 160 acres of land."[10] Initially, he wanted only free Creoles and free Black men to join, but after the British promised freedom to enslaved people who aided their cause, Jackson relented and opened the door for enslaved men to serve as well, with his own promise of freedom for those who served. While the commanding officers were all white, Black officers with combat experience, like Joseph Savary—the nation's first Black major—led the charge. Two companies of Black militia men, totaling nearly nine hundred, assisted in defending New Orleans; they were named the Heroes of Chalmette, after the battlefield they were victorious upon. Unfortunately, Jackson did not keep his promise to provide a bounty to free Black Creoles, nor freedom for the enslaved who fought alongside him, though there were occasional instances of enslaved men gaining their freedom on the American side. For example, an enslaved teenager named Jordan B. Noble was later freed by his master, Lieutenant John Noble, in large part because of his actions at Chalmette. In contrast, the British invaders freed hundreds in the aftermath of the battle.[11]

Despite African American soldiers' service, the U.S. government moved to limit Black men in the military again once the war was won, though Louisiana laws circumvented some of these edicts. Between the War of 1812 and the Civil War, Louisiana and the rest of the South took a much more draconian approach to the rights of People of Color, whether they were enslaved or not. Rapes and kidnappings became more rampant. Laws shifted, even in New Orleans, and some white planters pushed to remove all free Blacks from the state to make it easier to retain those who remained enslaved. Militias in the Deep South were being formed explicitly to suppress People of Color, from Indigenous People to enslaved individuals.[12] Some of these militias were only formed to stop enslaved people from rising against their enslavers, making them the antithesis of what other Black groups were doing during the nineteenth century in fighting for the abolition of Black enslavement in America.[13] There were discussions in the Louisiana legislature about enslaving free Creoles after the *Dred Scott* decision of 1857 determined that the government owed no rights to free People of Color.[14] The legislature even stopped the manumission of enslaved people for a time because the state was taking such a hard stance on the issue.[15] Over these decades of change, members of the Black populace knew that the military had been one of the few places they were welcome, and it was also a place they could prove their loyalty and worth to those who believed Black and Creole people were inferior. In 1861, Black and Creole men made plans to secure their place in the politically shifting city with the initial constitution and use of the Louisiana Native Guards in New Orleans's home guards. The home guards was the general name given to all of the local defense units raised to defend the city should an invasion occur.

The *New York Times* published an editorial that disparaged all of the seceding states, while addressing that slavery was the cause of the war and that the federal government had taken no action against it since the country's inception.[16] To the editors, the southern state's actions would end slavery faster than any policy or act the federal government could have taken.[17] However, federal policymakers attempted to separate the issue of slavery from the war effort to placate border states that threatened to secede. Black Americans across the nation spoke out on this issue, reminding citizens that the war was about both slavery and preserving the nation. Even after the passage of the two Confiscation Acts in 1861 and 1862, and General Benjamin Butler's creation of the "contraband policy," military leaders attempted to restrain the flow of enslaved people to their lines. Despite some of the government's efforts, thousands of enslaved men, women, and children persisted in their journey to emancipate themselves and serve in or with the U.S. Army. They worked as cooks and laborers, performed general maintenance, completed fatigue labor for soldiers, built encampments, rebuilt roads and bridges, hauled timber to repair Union ships, drove artillery pieces into positions, and even assisted in repairing public works. Their constant push to enlist forced the army to accept them, and any attempts by the federal government to curtail their efforts fell short. Formerly enslaved men and those who were already free labored extensively to prove themselves and their willingness to work as soldiers if given the opportunity. Eventually, their efforts proved fruitful: both groups trained for military duty as early as June 1862 in Louisiana; then, before the fall, the Louisiana Native Guards were reconstituted in the U.S. Army because of their efforts in New Orleans. If not for the actions of Black people, federal policy might have resulted in African Americans being freed and sent to any number of places, including Liberia, Haiti, Mexico, and Central America.[18] By the end of 1862, the Native Guards opened the door for hundreds of thousands of men to serve in the military, and they proved that all Black people deserved to stay in a nation for which they were willing to fight. This book explores their regimental history to demonstrate the significance of the regiments and their lineal successors in Louisiana during the Civil War.

The argument of this book is that the Louisiana Native Guards were the most significant regiments to form during the American Civil War. With a lineage that dates back to May 1861 and August 1862, the regiments were the first Black units formed during the war. They became the litmus test for both sides, who each held them up as examples of what Black service could look like during the war. By 1863, federal officials theorized that if the regiments did well, then the federal military should dramatically expand Black enlistment, and their successful showing during the summer of 1863 opened the door for more Black regiments in the federal military. The men who served in these regiments continued to affect Louisiana and the Deep South well after the end of the war, and their service contributed greatly to political and social change in the Deep South during the nineteenth century. Unfortunately, their history is not sufficiently well known to cement their story in all Americans' paradigm, but this book will correct that error.

The documented history of the Louisiana Native Guards is scant compared to that of other famous Black regiments that served in the Civil War. For example, the 54th and 55th Massachusetts Infantry Regiments are featured in multiple books and even a movie because of the robust sources in northern archives. The Native Guards, who were serving months before either of those regiments was constituted, have received far less attention. Their reduced attention is attributed to dispersed sources and southern rhetoric soon after the war that attempted to silence their impact on the conflict. A few studies do exist: James G. Hollandsworth Jr. wrote a brief summary of the regiments in

*The Louisiana Native Guards* decades ago; prior to his work, there were only a few articles and biographies about key individuals from the Native Guards who went into politics after the war.[19] Additionally, biographies provide accounts of white officers who commanded the regiments; however, a focus on the careers of commanders in these works means that the Native Guards are often relegated to a single chapter or even omitted. Historiography on the Native Guards is lacking, and the purpose of this book is to fill that gap.

In *Silencing the Past,* Michel-Rolph Trouillot wrote on the silences that affect historical scholarship. The Native Guards are victims of what Trouillot calls the silence of fact creation and the silence of fact assembly.[20] As Trouillot notes, someone has to document a fact when it is created, and another person assembles and preserves those facts. Today, the military employs hundreds of historians and archivists to accomplish this task, but the lack of interested historians and the rampant racism against Black units in the Deep South meant the Native Guards were neglected twice by the archives. The result of these forms of silence, for the Native Guards, is that there are limited sources on these regiments. Although many officers of color were highly literate and educated, letters and diaries of those officers were not preserved like those of their white counterparts. Many of the men who served were important players in Louisiana's history, and yet there is no singular archive where records of their military service have been collected, in part because the men were assigned to multiple designations and commands. Even the high-ranking officers of the original four infantry regiments kept scant records after the war; for example, of the four colonels who commanded the original regiments, only one wrote his thoughts into a detailed diary that survives today.[21]

For these reasons, historians who reveal an incomplete understanding of the history of these units are not totally at fault. A historian might consult one archive, read a letter in which these regiments are briefly mentioned, and conclude that they were not of great historical significance. That misconception could then be repeated through fact retrieval by other historians who encounter the work of the first.[22] However, there is a consequence to over-relying on one or two primary sources, as nineteenth-century narratives could be misleading. Sometimes they contained propaganda that advanced stereotypes and agendas of the North or South.[23]

White historians and other chroniclers of the war's history during the nineteenth century also worked to silence the Native Guards. In his history of the Department of the Gulf, published in 1892, Richard Irwin barely mentions the regiments.[24] Irwin was the paymaster for the command and paid the Black officers in the regiment until he was promoted to the adjutant of the department. Thus he was well informed on the regiments, knew who the soldiers were, and knew their importance to Louisiana and the military. However, he chose to ignore them, almost to the point of erasure from the Department of the Gulf's official history. Other nineteenth-century writers made similar choices. Because they were rarely written about, it can seem as if the Native Guards were not important.

This book strives to overcome these limitations by bringing together multiple sources and archives to tell a complete history of the Native Guards regiments in the U.S. Army. Furthermore, it tells the story of these regiments from both top-down and bottom-up perspectives. Newspaper editorials, personal and official letters, diaries, plantation records, autobiographies, military correspondence, speeches, general and special orders, pamphlets, narratives of the enslaved, official military records, and secondary sources are all brought together to present nearly every facet of the Native Guards and their service in the New Orleans home guards and the U.S. Army's volunteer forces.

While this work is intended to be a complete regimental history of the Louisiana Native Guards and all of their subsequent iterations in the U.S. Army, this is not the end of the story of African American service during the Civil War. As this book is a military history, social and personal aspects of the history of the Native Guards are not fully explored, but they are examined to the degree that they relate to the regiments and the men who served. The families of the Native Guards sacrificed nearly as much as the men who served, and their stories would add a completely different perspective on what it meant to serve. Historians Holly Pinheiro and James Mendez examine that history in both the North and South.[25] Truly, the history of African Americans in the South is much more than a history of enslavement, as thousands of free Blacks were committed to freedom and elevation for all Black people in the nation. Those individuals found multiple ways to reach that goal outside of the army, and their stories deserve to be told.

Outside of the Native Guards, dozens of units comprised of African American soldiers were in the Corps d'Afrique and the United States Colored Troops. They served in infantry, cavalry, engineer, and artillery units for the U.S. Army. Some of those units, which included Black soldiers from Louisiana, served in Texas, Virginia, Florida, Arkansas, Missouri, Mississippi, and Alabama. This book acknowledges the contributions of these units across the Gulf and Deep South, but it focuses primarily on the history and legacy of the

Black and Creole units in Louisiana. Future research should explore the effect of the Native Guards and other units across the southern states and Mexico.

While this work is meant to be a complete military history of the Native Guards, it is not the last word on African American service in Louisiana. Many Black people served on or assisted naval expeditions in Louisiana during the war, and that history remains under-researched. Noncombatant service for the military and the federal government through mutual aid societies, charity organizations, and personal efforts are similarly underexamined in Louisiana Civil War historiography. Black women were an invaluable asset toward Union victory in the Gulf through medical care and other logistical occupations. Furthermore, as this book is a regimental history, there is not enough focus on each individual person who served, and biographies on any one of the men involved would deepen our understanding of the service of all those who fought in the war.

By focusing on New Orleans, this book explores the nuanced social, political, and economic conditions in the city that set the stage for the Native Guards to form and fight in the war. For example, scholars including William Burton and Matthew Jacobson have acknowledged the multiple forms of white identity that existed in the nation during the century. Because New Orleans was a transnational hub, the city's white population was diverse.[26] Rich and poor white Americans lived alongside immigrants from France, Germany, Britain, Ireland, Spain, the Netherlands, Russia, and island nations, among other places. The members of these various white groups did not view one another as equals, and it would not do justice to their history to present them as if they did. The city's African American society was just as complex. It was not simply made up of free and enslaved people; instead, free Blacks and Creoles amassed enough wealth and power that they were generally treated better than poorer whites in the rest of Louisiana. Wealthy, transnational People of Color would not have seen other free Blacks—especially those who had recently been manumitted—as their equals, as those others did not have access to money, education, and networks that ensured their wealth would continue to grow.

The free African American society of New Orleans included those who had been free for generations due to French influence, those who had been freed more recently through American laws, those who had freed themselves by force and lived on the outskirts of society, and the small number of free Blacks who moved to Louisiana voluntarily from places such as England or Haiti.

This nuanced view of free African American society brings the stories of Black officers and noncommissioned officers in New Orleans into relief.

This work further complicates the city's history by drawing forth the perspectives of historical figures who have received relatively little attention. A general's view of the war is very different from a private's, even if they fought in every single battle alongside one another. The same can be said of race: African Americans experienced the war differently than northern and southern whites did. In this book, some big names of the nineteenth-century are shown from a different set of perspectives; because this book is focused on Black regiments raised in New Orleans, many individuals are characterized from the perspective of Creoles of Color in the city. For example, readers will note that members of the Native Guards generally did not see General Butler as an autocrat or General Banks as a strong military strategist or administrator. Some saw President Lincoln as conservative or too moderate. Tracing these perspectives does not represent an effort to rewrite history or influence modern views of historical actors, but instead, to enhance and complicate these stories and show that not everyone saw these individuals in the same way.

This book explores the full history of the Louisiana Native Guards to fill the silences in the history of the regiments. The chapters are organized chronologically, and each follows a theme that is accentuated by the chapter title. The first few chapters strive to correct mistakes in the historiography of the regiments; thus, they are not solely focused on the men who served. Chapter 1 explores what enslavement and freedom meant for People of Color living in Louisiana, and the exigencies that existed around the regiments that caused them to form, including the unit's influence on federal policy. Chapter 2 looks at the regiments in the home guards and liberation of New Orleans, including salient actors from the federal military who later influenced the Native Guards. Chapter 3 examines Generals Benjamin Butler and William Phelps as they spar and constitute the Native Guards in the midst of a rebellious white populace and a loyal Black one. Chapter 4 analyzes the regiments in the federal army, their recruiting and training, and the reaction of white people to Black servicemen. Chapter 5 focuses on the regiments' first taste of combat and demonstrates that the Native Guards were considered an early success from both sides of the Civil War. Chapter 6 looks at the first few months of 1863, the command environment of a new general, and a racist purge of Black officers in the regiments. Chapter 7 is an overview of the Siege of Port Hudson, a well-studied event, but this chapter looks at it from the Native Guards' perspective for its aftermath. Chapter 8 demonstrates that despite purges and racist officers who abused Black troops, the regiments continued to serve well throughout the Deep South. Chapter 9 closes the war and demonstrates that the people who served in the regiments or supported them continued their fight for social and political rights well after the last shots were fired. Taken together, the chapters answer one central question: What was the significance of the Louisiana Native Guards to the Black society of Louisiana during and after the American Civil War? Each chapter answers one facet of that question, exploring how the men in the Native Guards became some of the most important actors in African American history in the Gulf during the nineteenth century.

The language and terminology that appear in this book warrant explanation. To preserve the military history of these regiments, military designations and date formats are used throughout. Instead of Second or 2nd, 2d Regiment is used, as that is how the army formally refers to units below the corps level. Corps-level units use roman numerals; the Native Guards were part of the XIX Army Corps for the majority of their service in the U.S. Army. Generals and high-echelon commands issued orders during the war, aptly named a general order, but if that order contained multiple orders, then sources refer to general orders. This book strives to retain the correct phrasing when appropriate.

The use of language in this book is purposeful. Black men were called "niggers." Some were raised and treated as bastards. As this book is about war and enslavement, many of the actors within die, both in and out of battle. Black women were raped, and many were called wenches and whores for the crime of simply existing as Black women. To sugarcoat these facts of history would betray the lived experiences of millions. While some of this language is painful and offensive to modern readers, it is the language that many heard on a daily basis during the nineteenth century. Direct quotations containing racial epithets are retained to show how soldiers of color were thought of and treated by their fellow countrymen. Thus, terms such as "slave," "negro," and "nigger" are only used in direct quotations throughout and when needed. In all other cases, Black and Creole men and women are referred to as African Americans, Blacks, Black Americans, People of Color, or soldiers of color. Those who were enslaved are referred to as enslaved people, formerly enslaved people, freedmen, freemen, or freed people.[27]

Most importantly, I want to offer a trigger warning for descriptions of sexual abuse, torture, military conflicts, enslavement, and death. This book contains multiple facts of history that make me question how human beings can be so cruel.

The use of the word "Creole" should be seen as shorthand for Creoles of Color. While not all Creoles were of mixed race or Black, those discussed in this book are. Additionally, for ease of reading and to avoid referring to Creoles and Blacks as separate entities when they were working together, only "Blacks" will be used when appropriate. This is not done to de-Creolize an individual but to show the unity and cooperation that existed during and after the war to uplift the Black community of New Orleans. Even the word "Creole" is hard to define, because it has been defined in many ways. It originally referred to Africans born in the New World who were of mixed birth, but French and Spanish immigrants attempted to redefine it to refer exclusively to whites, while Blacks used it to refer to anyone in Louisiana with European ancestry preceding the Civil War.[28] As one European in New Orleans phrased it, "When I say negroes, I wish to avoid the phrase, 'persons of color,' for it is not so easy to find a purely black negro. The colored population, especially that portion of it which is free, is crossed in the first, second or third degree. There are among them persons whiter than you or I, and they suggest a pretty question in genealogy."[29] Such nuanced observations about skin tone, education, and parentage did little to shift the wide use of the label "Black," and many Creoles embraced the paradigm that they were both Black and Creole.

Not all of the men or officers who served in the Native Guards were Creoles. Scholars have overemphasized the experiences of wealthy Creoles of Color, ignoring thousands of servicemen who were not Creole, had no European blood or wealth, and were not even born in Louisiana. In general, terms such as Black people, African Americans, or People of Color will be used to describe the subjects of this book because this study examines them as a group rather than as members of multiple separate caste systems.[30]

"No soldiers can appreciate the final triumph with a keener sense of gladness than those who fought against such odds as the Black Phalanx. Beating down prejudice and upholding the national cause at the same time," wrote Joseph Wilson, a soldier turned historian who served in the Louisiana Native Guards. Wilson argued that "the Negro race . . . is the only race that has ever come in contact with the European race, and been able to withstand its atrocities and oppression," but simultaneously, he argued, Black people in America "multiplied so rapidly in bondage that the oppressor became alarmed, and began discussing methods of safety to himself."[31] As a Black man who came back to the United States to fight in the Civil War, Wilson keenly recognized that ending Black enslavement was at the heart of the war, and he was also aware that Black soldiers needed to fight and win to secure their place in the country after the conflict. To Wilson—and the men he served alongside in combat—service in the Native Guards was the opportunity to truly make their white oppressors tremble at the thought of all the crimes enslavers committed against Black people. It was a fight that every Black man who served in the Native Guards patiently waited to join, and every woman and child who supported them prayed they would win. The martial history of the Louisiana Native Guards is a vast but brief one, and it is the history of the most important Black regiments to serve in the American Civil War.

Chapter 1

# *THE BLACK MANTLE OF SLAVERY*

## THE GENESIS OF THE AMERICAN CIVIL WAR

Henry Louis Rey, one of the great Black spiritualists of New Orleans, conducted a séance in the summer of 1863 to call forth the spirit of a friend and fellow Creole officer of the Native Guards who had died in battle. At the séance, his friend assured him that if People of Color supported the government, even in death, "Equality will come later, it is true."[1] Even today, it is a common refrain of the African American community that service and sacrifice today will bring equality tomorrow, and that sentiment was the foundation for the choices of many Black men and women during the Civil War. The formation of the Louisiana Native Guards in the New Orleans home guards can be understood in these terms. As a unit, the men were used as propaganda—a minstrel show with weapons—by the Confederate state to show that Black men supported the rebellion. However, as Rey and so many others would later attest, soldiers in the Native Guards secured a social and physical place for the African American family their forefathers had spent generations building. The actions of the men in the regiments moved the Union toward arming Black soldiers, and they set the stage for the Native Guards to fight for Black equality in the U.S. Army. By the end of the war, Rey's séance had proven prophetic.

At the outset of the Civil War, Louisiana embraced secession quickly, and the free Black society of New Orleans seemed to commit racial treason when they chose to form the Louisiana Native Guards. Hundreds of men came together and asked the governor to allow them to constitute a defensive unit in support of New Orleans. The following chapter asks why? What transpired in Louisiana that made these men feel as if they needed to join the New Orleans home guards, and just as interesting, why would the governor accept armed African Americans when for decades the idea of armed Black men was feared as a threat to white superiority, as it could foment a revolt among the enslaved? This chapter will prove that—on the whole—they did not serve with any sense of loyalty to the southern rebellion, but rather out of loyalty to one another and the hope they could sustain their identity and society in a new nation while under racial threat from the white society of the city. "The Black Mantle of Slavery" accentuates this point by juxtaposing many of the initial motivations of white men who joined the Louisiana militia with those of Black volunteers to show that the latter's actions should not be misconstrued with a fight for solidifying slavery. An unintended consequence of the choice to form the Native Guards was the publicity it garnered. Children of color who watched their fathers march proudly down the streets began to dream of a future where they could be treated as equals in the South. Additionally, the formation of the Native Guards spurred many in the federal government to question why the U.S. Army was not utilizing soldiers of color early in the war. Unintendedly, Black men who held leadership positions in the Native Guards were able to leverage their experience and networks to garner commissions in the U.S. Army the subsequent year. Thus, the opening of the war and their choice to join the Native Guards initiated the process of changing the Black and Creole society of Louisiana.

The Civil War began when an officer from New Orleans, P. G. T. Beauregard, ordered the bombardment of Fort Sumter in South Carolina on 12 April 1861.[2] Within two days of the surrender of the fort—the event commonly used to mark the beginning of the American Civil War—an editor with the *New York Times* wrote, "The future historian will grope in vain for any adequate causes for such a movement."[3] However, the author recognized that the war began because of southern interests in protecting slavery. When Confederate leaders created their Constitution, they included laws around the issue of slavery. For example, Section 9.4 stated, "No bill of attainder, *ex post facto law*, or law denying or impairing the right of property in negro slaves shall be passed."[4] Various protections for slavery were built into the southern Constitution to protect the right to own African Americans in the Confederacy. Alexander Stephens, the elected vice president for the southern confederation, expressed this intention: "The new constitution has put at rest, forever, all agitating questions relating to our peculiar institution—African slavery as it exists amongst us—the proper status of the negro in our form of civilization. This was the immediate cause of the late rupture and present revolution." Stephens called slavery—and the concept that "the negro is not equal to the white man"—the foundation and cornerstone the Confederacy was built upon.[5] Today's historians do not have to work too hard to understand why only enslaved-holding states seceded. Stephens later attempted to claim the reporter took his words out of context, but in fact he used similar language in other instances as well.[6] Many people knew that if the two sides came to war, a northern victory would result in every "vestige of negro slavery" being abolished.[7] There is some poetic irony in the fact that a New Orleanian began the war to protect slavery, and in doing so set the stage for the downfall of the sacred southern institution in his home city a year later.

Writing on what the South was fighting for in 1862, a correspondent for the *Tribune* noted that its core motivation would be its undoing. To him, there was one thing that held back the South and ensured that the two sides would have to fight until one was completely defeated, an encumbrance he called "The Black Mantle of Slavery." He observed that many southerners "do not now and never have been able to understand how it is that most all our men read and write, while only so few of theirs can." From what he saw of the Confederacy, "The black mantle of slavery is around this country. Slavery benights the people, wastes and desolates the rich soil, breeds nothing but rottenness and ruin everywhere." By this reasoning, slavery would always hold back the South from standing among other successful nations. The *Tribune* correspondent recounted a conversation with a preacher: "So far as he is concerned he knows slavery to be at the root of all our present evils; and not only so, but he knows it to be at the root of all the prevailing evils by which the course of the South has been backward and downward."[8] The black mantle of slavery was a heavy yoke that hung around the necks of both the Confederacy and the United States during the war. The mantle later prevented the South from properly preparing for a northern invasion, and it forced federal leaders to ponder the question of what to do with formerly enslaved people at the end of the war. More than anything else, the mantle gave people across the world a reason to label the United States "the land of the free and home of the oppressed."[9]

Louisiana was led into the Confederacy by Fire Eaters, southern politicians who pushed for secession, in the state legislature and Governor Thomas Overton Moore—all of whom fervently supported rebellion. Moore was born in North Carolina and moved to Louisiana to operate a large plantation in Rapides Parish for his uncle. He learned what it meant to enslave and abuse people through his employment, and when he married a woman whose father left them a large plantation and enslaved people, he became a planter in his own right. Moore engaged in slave speculation prior to the war, regularly purchasing and selling enslaved people as commodities to enrich himself.[10] He entered state politics through the House of Representatives and eventually the state Senate before his run for governor. Inaugurated on 23 January 1860, Moore argued in his first speech that the Republican party would destroy the rights of planters such as himself by fomenting antislavery sentiment. By the end of the year and soon after Lincoln's election, he declared, "I do not think it comports with the honor and respect of Louisiana, as a slaveholding state, to live under the government of a black republican."[11] He believed the South would become a new nation—a slave nation—that would demonstrate to the world that the enslavement of African Americans was the proper way to operate a country.[12] He went as far as telling the international community, a year before the war, that "the election of a republican President is cause for a dissolution of the Union."[13] Many Fire Eaters in the Louisiana legislature shared that view.

Legislators feared enslaved revolts similar to those that occurred in Haiti and Jamaica that led to freedom for many enslaved people, and planters thought Lincoln's election was the impetus for enslaved people to be freed or start a revolution. Within days of Lincoln's election, Moore began drafting a speech for the secession convention that said Lincoln would be "unreasoning and fanatically hostile to slavery." Moore argued that Lincoln's election required the state to leave the Union if it hoped to preserve what he considered vital to Louisiana.[14] He was not alone: multiple militia units began forming in New Orleans within days of Lincoln's election, all pledging to help Louisiana secede if the governor called for it. When Moore received a summons from the U.S. Circuit Court requesting men for the militia to defend federal property, he ignored the requests and began plans to use the forming militias for a new southern nation.[15] Moreover, prominent men in the Louisiana legislature argued that they needed to separate from the federal government to protect their rights in relation to slavery.[16] Many of them petitioned Moore to act, constitute the militia, and separate Louisiana from the United States, and in December the legislature authorized him to select delegates and move toward these goals.

Moore understood the military and political exigencies, and he acted on both quickly. Once the militia was ready, he sent a letter to the commander of the federal arsenal at Baton Rouge: "The safety of the State of Louisiana demands that I take possession of all Government property within her limits." To that end, he ordered all federal troops to leave the arsenal to the state militia.[17] The *New York Herald* reported that "on the 10th day of January, 1861, the rebel troops arrived at Baton Rouge from New Orleans for the purpose of taking possession of the United States Arsenal at that place. This building was supposed to contain at least fifteen thousand stand of arms, which were of course a great acquisition at that time."[18] Forts Jackson and St. Philip were seized the following day, and Fort Pike followed on the fourteenth.[19] Within weeks of these acts of war, Louisiana representatives met to discuss secession, and Moore did not shy from justifying his drastic actions, stating that the federal government "threatened destruction of essential rights and most vital interests of the slaveholding States under the forms of the perverted Constitution."[20]

On 26 January 1861, the Louisiana secession convention met and officially called for secession and an alliance with South Carolina.[21] By a vote of 113 to 17, Louisiana cut all ties with the federal government and the Union.[22] After the vote, Governor Moore and an entourage of Fire Eaters walked the center aisle bearing a Pelican Flag, the banner of an independent Louisiana.[23] The city press declared, "The act is accomplished! The link that has so long bound us to the 'stripes and stars,' has been severed—and in the future, and forever more, the destiny of Louisiana is in her own hands."[24]

Many in New Orleans were thrilled that Moore was leading Louisiana down this path. According to the *New Orleans Crescent*, "The news of the secession was received in this city with a perfect furore of enthusiasm. Guns thundered forth from the foot of Canal street, flags were flung to the breeze in every quarter, and at night, many houses, public and private, were brilliantly illuminated." In an editorial, a writer for the *Crescent* acknowledged the importance of Louisiana to the South, noting that "if there remained any doubt of the disruption and disintegration of the Union, the secession of Louisiana has settled the question. The State which holds the mouth of the great 'inland sea' of the North American continent—the State which contained within its limits the leading commercial city of the Southwest—the State which exports the great bulk of the king of commerce, has given the finishing blow to the Union, and it is now a thing of the past." The author concluded by calling for additional southern states to join the effort so they could protect their rights to slavery, "which have been so cruelly denied them in the late Union!"[25]

The Louisiana legislature even passed a bill approving Moore's order to capture federal property and absolving him of any wrongdoing.[26] A year after the Civil War, a congressional inquiry into the state argued that Louisiana had betrayed the United States "by the choice of her own people," due to the number of political leaders who openly supported rebellion.[27] The same day that Louisiana declared independence, its militia attacked a marine hospital and removed over two hundred injured patients in the name of the South.[28] Louisiana already had many established militias, as the legislature authorized the governor to establish a brigade whenever one thousand men enrolled into a local militia in 1820, and there was a mix of volunteer and established units during the antebellum period.[29] Because of this system, Moore had access to numerous militia and home guard units to attack federal strongholds early in the war. Louisiana officially joined the Confederacy on 21 March 1861, and the governor gave the new government free reign over all seized lands and property. Southerners held a variety of views about how and why the South would win the war. One southern woman thought that justice was on the side of Louisiana, and God would ensure southern victory in the impending war.[30] Meanwhile, a politician from Tennessee believed that the South would win because "every man in the South is a soldier, and even the negroes would fight as they did in the revolution."[31]

By the time of Louisiana's secession, there were already dozens of local home guard units in New Orleans.[32] Some of these units had been created by local orders, and others had been formed through the efforts of small communities of immigrants or philanthropists who had the wealth to pay men to join a unit.[33] Longstanding loyalty to their state meant that their zeal in joining the volunteer military was not surprising; a northern man said that those in the state boasted, "I am not an American, but a Louisianan," even before the war.[34] Thus, most of the forces defending the state were part of the volunteer forces and not regular soldiers. Braxton Bragg was the commander of the military in New Orleans when the war began, but he was assigned a more combative role versus a defensive position in the city. The elderly David E. Twiggs was given command of the Department of Louisiana, later redesignated Department Number 1, and headquartered in New Orleans in May.[35] Twiggs was later replaced by Mansfield Lovell after a tiff with the mayor over his lackluster defense of the city, and the department was charged with using the home guards to defend the state should it be attacked. New Orleans had multiple volunteer units at its disposal. Many southerners attributed the city's readiness for self-defense to the last great battle in New Orleans, when New Orleanians had fought alongside General Andrew Jackson in 1815.[36] While it is true that many of the old units were brought back during this time, the paper failed to mention the Blacks and Creoles who had fought alongside Jackson. In short order, they, too, volunteered again.

In April 1861, Jordan B. Noble—who in his youth had served as a drummer boy and then gained his freedom after the 1815 Battle of New Orleans—

led a series of meetings among free Black people in response to Governor Moore's call for units to defend Louisiana. At the largest of these meetings, held at the Institute Catholique on 23 April, attendees agreed to offer their services to the New Orleans home guards. It was a decision that many would later regret, but it was made to preserve the fragile Creole society of the city in the Confederacy. Cultural shifts in Louisiana during the preceding years had made it clear to Black New Orleanians that they were no longer wanted, and the decision to join the New Orleans home guards was their final attempt to preserve their place in southern society or risk either enslavement or expulsion to Africa or some other colony.

They decided to petition Moore, similar to the petition that was sent to Claiborne in 1803, for the right to serve in the home guards. They also ran an ad in the *Daily Picayune* announcing that they would "be ready to take arms and form themselves into companies for the defense of their homes, together with the other inhabitants of this city, against any enemy who may come and disturb its tranquility."[37] An ad in the *New Orleans Daily Crescent* called upon "all free colored persons wishing to offer their services to the Governor as Vol-

Jordan B. Noble
(Courtesy Historic New Orleans Collection)

unteers as a Home Guard" to attend one of these meetings.[38] The *New Orleans True Delta* noted that "these men whose ancestors distinguished themselves at the Battle of New Orleans are determined to give new evidence of their bravery."[39] On 27 April, Noble published an advertisement calling for additional freemen to join the home guards and asking them to attend a meeting that evening. Within days, Moore was already pondering accepting their organization, aware that their constitution in the home guards would indicate to the world that Afro-descended people possibly deserved a place in southern society other than bondage. While the men petitioned the governor, free Black women volunteered their services as nurses and washerwomen, and offered to work in any other roles available to them. On 1 May 1861, the mayor of New Orleans, John T. Monroe, accepted the service of Black volunteers and praised their sense of loyalty and duty.[40]

After gathering nearly fifteen hundred signatures, a delegation of free Black men met with Governor Moore to officially volunteer their services in the home guards. Aware of the publicity that would result from this offer, Moore accepted their service, and on 2 May 1861 the governor appointed Noble a "Captain of the 'Native Guards' (colored), 1st Division" and directed the division "to serve for the term of the war."[41] The order officially authorized the 1st Native Guards in the New Orleans home guards. Soon after, the *Daily Crescent* declared that free African Americans of New Orleans "are certainly as much attached to the land of their birth as their white brethren" and predicted that they would "fight the Black Republicans with as much determination and gallantry" as anyone else.[42]

Southerners—and a few historians—have incorrectly taken the service of Black and Creole men in the home guards as proof that Black men served in the Confederate military; however, that claim is false. The home guards were a subset of the militia, akin to a deputized police force or a local defense unit, and they were tied to a city rather than the whole state.[43] A militia is not necessarily the same as or part of a military, and few—if any—Black men truly supported the southern military.[44] The few documented cases of Black men supporting the southern military were enslaved people forced to do so under the threat of death.

By the end of May, 440 free Black and Creole men formed lines to begin training.[45] Similar to previous Black units formed since the seventeenth century, the unit was filled with wealthy free men of color. Members in the Civil War unit included barbers, dentists, architects, merchants, farmers, doctors, carpenters, brick masons, artists, dock workers, and a few enslavers. Thanks to militia traditions set by *le Code Noir,* they were allowed to elect their own line officers, and in short order the New Orleans home guards had lieutenants and captains of color serving among their ranks. However, the governor made sure that the regimental commander and his high-ranking staff were all white, giving the command to Confederate colonel Henry D. Ogden, under the direction of the militia commander of the city, Confederate major general John Lewis. They were subsumed under Department Number 1, commanded by Confederate major general David Twiggs. An editorial for the *Daily Crescent* said that the Native Guards contained "our hardest and best fighters," and predicted that, with Jordan Noble at the helm, the men would serve honorably.[46] These men had a proud heritage that went back generations; when the Native Guards formed, the *Daily True Delta* acknowledged that many of the men who were volunteering had "fathers and friends [who had] fought in defense of New Orleans on the plains of Chalmette."[47]

The unit consisted of some of the best soldiers New Orleans had to offer, from all backgrounds and walks of life. André Cailloux was among the first to volunteer to serve in the Native Guards. Captain Noel J. Bacchus, a mixed-race Creole, was a forty-year-old carpenter who owned nearly $1,000 worth of land in the city. Captain Michael Duphart, another Creole, was sixty-two and a shoemaker who owned even more property than Bacchus. Captain Virgil Bonseigneur was a fifty-two-year-old Creole and a plasterer who owned over $2,000 worth of real estate. Less wealthy men joined as well, including Captain Alcide Lewis, a thirty-four-year-old mixed-race mason who owned only $150 in land, and Captain Henry Louis Rey, a local store clerk and spiritualist who was even younger at twenty-nine and owned no property.[48] His father, Barthélemy Louis Rey, was a Haitian refugee who had amassed great wealth from real estate, and he donated quite a bit of it to help create L'Institution Catholique pour l'instruction des ophelins dans l'indigence, a church and refuge for many People of Color in the city. The entire Duphart family joined the Native Guards as well, but they enrolled in different companies to prevent all the males from dying in one battle.[49] Captain Charles Sauvenet was the wealthy and well-educated son of a French lawyer and banker.[50] Others among the wealthy class donated money instead of time; for example, Thomy Lafon reportedly gave $500 to the war effort.[51] According to the wife of one of the former officers, many of them knew each other for years prior to the war, and they even visited the same coffee houses and shops that catered to free Black men.[52]

The men elected officers based on the respect they held among community members and their leadership abilities. Captain Rey was elected because of his multiple forays into spiritualism. While he was not personally wealthy, he was seen as a powerful conjurer and a man who could speak to the dead. For those who believed he held those powers, he was a natural choice to lead men into battle.[53] Rey led the Economy Unit, which was comprised of many members of the Economic Society of New Orleans, a social group filled with Creoles of wealth and education. Captain Cailloux was elected, like most of the officers, because he was economically and politically strong. He was already regarded as a natural leader prior to the war, so men were happy to follow him.[54] As a known public figure in the city, Jordan Noble was perhaps the easiest to elect; he had been selected for service by the governor, and he was among those who had orchestrated the whole endeavor.

The Native Guards were not the only Black men working on the side of the South early in the war. There were allegedly thirty Black men recruited in the Baton Rouge home guards, and a whole company was formed in Pointe Coupée Parish as well.[55] However, like the labor of all African-descended people in the South, theirs was undervalued. Joseph Wilson, a Black U.S. soldier who became a historian after the war, explained that Black southerners contributed to the South by "building breastworks, mounting cannon, digging rifle-pits and entrenchments, to shield and protect his rebelling master."[56] Indeed, there were examples of free and enslaved Blacks in multiple southern states building defenses and fortifications, serving in camps, working as laundresses and nurses, and serving in other noncombatant roles. There were even cases of local commands issuing special orders when cities did not supply their full quota of enslaved labor either due to sickness or truancy.[57] These quotas grew quite large, as the construction of forts sometimes took the efforts of hundreds of people, whom northern writers noted were "forced to work for the rebels against their will."[58] A white northern woman who was teaching in the Deep South was astonished "to see each soldier have a negro along to carry his gun" as soon as the South began to secede, demonstrating that African Americans had sustained the military in the South from the very beginning.[59] However, the closest they came to a battlefield was in their work building defenses. The majority received no compensation for their labor. Rather, the masters of those who were enslaved were paid for their service, and those who were free were paid very little if at all.[60] Those who were not coerced or forced to support southern institutions by the white populace could have their property taken. For example, the plantation of Fannie Richer, a free woman of color, was regularly raided by Confederates in Pointe Coupée for provisions, horses, and anything else they needed to support themselves.[61]

John H. Crowder, a young boy from Kentucky, felt compelled to serve as a laborer for the military, like many in his position did. Crowder's family was extremely poor. His father, Jacob Crowder, was a free Black man living in Kentucky who fought in the war with Mexico in 1846, never to return home. His mother, Martha Ann Spencer, was a free woman of color who divorced Jacob and moved the family to New Orleans. There, she married Thomas Stars—a man who turned out to be shiftless and an alcoholic—before abandoning the family in 1861. Thus, young fifteen-year-old John Crowder was responsible for supporting his family financially. He was working for a jeweler when the war began, but because of the Union blockade, he was forced to take employment under a southern officer in 1862. Crowder had already proven himself highly intelligent; despite laboring in Confederate camps at a young age, he had learned from clergymen and teachers in the city. Crowder's past employment and education later helped him to retrace his father's footsteps into the military, as he eventually escaped his employment with southern white men and joined the U.S. Army.[62]

White southerners loved the idea of African Americans who supported the war, as it reaffirmed the belief that their natural state was that of enslavement. Multiple editorials across the region described how Moore accepted Jordan

*The Plantation Police or Home-Guard*
(*Frank Leslie's Illustrated Newspaper*, July 11, 1863)

Noble's offer to form a militia unit and how the free African Americans of New Orleans formed it "as their fathers did in 1814 and '15."[63] However, many southerners exhibited cognitive dissonance in their understanding of the experience of Black Americans. The white populace was heavily outnumbered, and since many were also outclassed by the free Blacks of New Orleans, whites had a vested interest in convincing themselves that People of Color were loyal to the Confederacy. Yet, as a war correspondent visiting the city noted, "There is one stereotyped sentence which I am tired of—Our negroes, sir, are the happiest, the most contented, and the best off of any people in the world."[64] It was often in the best interest of enslaved people to say whatever was needed to and in front of those who enslaved them. Feigning contentment was a common performance that enslaved people had used dating back generations. This performance convinced many whites that some Blacks enjoyed their lot in life. And during the war it was the best way to assuage whites' nervousness about the possibility of an open revolt.

However, there were signs that many enslaved people did not support the Confederacy. For example, Dianah Watson recalled her aunt being beaten so severely in the city that she collapsed on the ground at the feet of her overseer. When he stopped to confirm she was not dead, she grabbed the whip and beat him instead, and enslaved men carried him to a nearby cliff and threw him off for his cruelty.[65] The same war correspondent who had tired of the southern stereotype of contented enslaved people reported that some whites in the city feared being out at night because "negroes were after mischief."[66] A fascinating example of the varied ways that Black people undermined the Confederacy was the case of Mrs. Welton, a free woman of color who was arrested in September 1861 for selling poisoned pies to Confederate soldiers.[67] Welton was by no means alone in her resistance to the southern cause, as became evident when many supposedly loyal servants fled to federal lines. Some were even thrown in jail for singing:

> We'll fight for liberty,
> We'll fight for liberty,
> We'll fight for liberty,
> When de Lord will call us home.[68]

The Native Guards, like a few other home guard units, were not well supplied or armed—a sign that the local government did not trust them. While some white home guard units were ill-equipped for battle, the city took steps to assist them with equipage and training when possible. The same was not true for the Blacks in the Native Guards. The men drilled with weapons they already owned or purchased new ones. Their wives sewed the uniforms they wore, adding a little French flair through color and style that set them apart from similar organizations in the South. It became obvious that although government officials loved the idea of Black southerners in uniform, they had no intention of actually paying to put them in those uniforms. As the months passed, most of the Native Guards, especially those in the enlisted ranks, were not furnished equipment, weapons, or uniforms. Eventually, their purchase of these goods became an informal test of loyalty, as it proved they wanted to be there. The author of a *Daily Picayune* editorial praised the men who "supplied themselves with arms, without regard to cost and trouble."[69] Those who had the means but refused to do so came under suspicion, so all who had the means purchased some equipage for their drills to give the appearance of loyalty.

Many Americans wondered why free men of color would want to appear loyal when the existence of the Confederacy was predicated on the belief that African Americans were inferior to white men. As there were nearly one thousand men in the Native Guards before their inactivation, the reasons are myriad, but a few stand out.[70] Some may have professed loyalty to the Confederacy for personal reasons, ranging from feeling a sense of allegiance to wanting to preserve their homes. Even more tellingly, though, the few records from men who served show an overwhelming fear of what could happen if they did not serve. Charles Gibbons, a Black Creole in the regiment, later attested that he joined the 1st Native Guards as a private only because he was forced from his home and compelled to join. One of the captains who served gave a similar report, swearing that any who refused to serve were killed and their property confiscated for treason, leaving their families with nothing.[71] Even prominent white people in the city attested later that Black people joined the regiment under duress.[72] It remains unclear whether the majority of Black soldiers volunteered willingly or whether rebellions against the state by free men were not reported in the media. In any case, there are only a few reports of free African Americans being killed, and southern writers after the war used the lack of an archival record to show that Black men supported their cause. Furthermore, Black men had a long history of drilling and parading in military garb to secure their social positions in New Orleans since the French controlled the city. It is no accident that Noble and others who had participated in the War of 1812 were responsible for organizing the unit. They had learned when the United States took over the state that service could equal freedom for some and more rights for others. Decades of experience had shown them that the best way to protect themselves, their families, and all of Black and Creole society was to appear loyal by forming a home guard unit.

The experiences of immigrants and other whites give further clues as to why Black men chose to join. William Howard Russell—often referred to as the father of war correspondence—along with William Mure—the English consul stationed in New Orleans—noticed that dozens of English citizens were being forced into the southern military. They witnessed their citizens kidnapped on the streets of New Orleans, and these immigrants were forced through physical abuse and the threat of death to join the South.[73] Those who refused were suspected of secretly supporting the Union, and they could face any number of consequences. Russell swore that he saw immigrants "knocked down, bound, and confined in barracks, till in despair they consented to serve."[74] Eventually, Mure worked with Moore to free over sixty of his subjects, and Moore publicly denounced the forced enlistment of white immigrants, for fear of European reprisals.[75]

Members of New Orleans's white populace soon realized that demonstrating anything other than strong Confederate loyalty resulted in the end of one's freedom. Whites suspected of harboring sympathies for the Union were assumed to be abolitionists, and an abolitionist was the equivalent of a "black republican," a label that could be deadly in Louisiana. One man claimed that there was only one secessionist in his whole neighborhood, after which thirty guards made a visit to the homes of the others to ascertain whether they were for the Union.[76] Russell described four men who were arrested in a single day for lack of support for the Confederacy, one of whom had only spoken about his beliefs with his own wife. As Russell expressed, "Such is 'Freedom of speech' in Louisiana."[77] He further observed that loyal southerners spied on one another, going as far as watching the letter boxes of those they suspected of disloyalty. Those whom the mob deemed guilty were often deported, jailed, or killed. These were not exaggerations on Russell's part. Charles Ellis was cornered by a mob in New Orleans before he was tarred and feathered for the crime of using "seditious language." Another man in Houma was captured and whipped "one hundred times for being an 'abolitionist of the worst stripe,'" and another mob in the Avoyelles Parish killed one man and injured two others for having Unionist beliefs.[78] One Unionist man felt compelled to join the southern military after a bullet was fired at his mother for his beliefs, in a bid to protect her (and himself) from further violence. Richard Fairchild, a longtime Louisiana resident who fled to the North, attested that he had witnessed two white men hanged for displaying abolitionist sentiment, one from Massachusetts and the other from Ireland, and he said that these were common occurrences throughout the state.[79] A dentist in the city who witnessed and feared this "reign of terror" bemoaned that "many were daily arrested and imprisoned for expressing the Union sentiments of our fathers."[80]

Free African Americans witnessed these atrocities against the white populace, and of course the worst was reserved for People of Color. Even prior to the war, it was not uncommon for a free man who was deemed "too smart" by white leaders to be enslaved because he did not do what a white man wanted him to do.[81] Reverend Jacob Nelson was lynched for preaching about freedom to enslaved people. In Memphis, an African American preacher was hanged for telling his mistress that he and others would be free once the Union arrived, and that, once liberated, he planned to raise a regiment to fight for the North.[82] Free and enslaved Blacks were well aware of the risks of enslavement and death for those who did not display fealty to the Confederacy. One man who avoided service later testified about the men who joined the Native Guards: "It is known to all under what pressure of public opinion, under what threats uttered by the promoters of secession this was done."[83]

Blacks' and Creoles' fear of the white New Orleans populace monitoring them was justified. By order of the governor, the adjutant general of the New Orleans militia created two lists of all men in the city whose age made them eligible for military service. One list included all of the free men, regardless of color, who joined a militia unit, and the other was a "Black-List" that cataloged every man "who shall in any way attempt to evade the performance" in the state militia or home guards. Those on the Black List "shall be marked and designated as suspicious characters and *enemies to the South*."[84] Moore initially threatened to fine everyone on the list.[85] By October 1861, however, the Black List "reached most stupendous proportions," and there were calls by the press to arrest all on the list—including white men—and work them in the fields or on fortifications if they refused to serve.[86] This sentiment demonstrates the societal pressure in New Orleans that compelled African Americans to either get in line and fight for the South or risk their property, their lives, and possibly their families' lives. For free Blacks, arrest could essentially result in taking on the status of an enslaved person. The treatment given to whites who were just suspected of holding Unionist sympathies ensured that free Blacks knew their fate would be grim if they were arrested. For these reasons, many of them chose to preserve their place in the city by volunteering for the home guards.

Free Blacks in New Orleans also had a degree of freedom that did not exist outside of the city, giving them the ability to amass wealth as a class. When the war began, the city's Black residents collectively owned nearly $2 million. Furthermore, many had white fathers or grandfathers who had left behind money and property, which increased their economic standing in the city. It is not surprising that, given these circumstances, some would have felt indebted to New Orleans not only as their birthplace but as a place that allowed them to maintain freedom and economic stability. An editorial published before the war stated, "Our free colored population form a distinct class from elsewhere in the United States. Far from being apathetic to the whites, they have followed in their footsteps, and progressed with them, with a commendable spirit of emulation."[87] A member of the Native Guards later wrote that "The pursuit of personal satisfaction or the persistent acquisition of material things of life occupied" the minds of some of the men who joined. During the war, one white southerner expanded this view by writing, "They [Black southerners] love their home, their property, their slaves, and they are dearly attached to their native land."[88] Thus, many members of the Native Guards were induced to serve for a combination of reasons: they wanted to keep their standing in the city, and they felt a debt to both the state that provided them that standing and members of the white populace with whom many shared familial connections.

The majority, however, were motivated by the belief that service in the home guards would preserve a place for Blacks in the Confederacy. In 1861, nearly everyone in the South believed the Confederacy would succeed and form a new nation based on the continued exploitation of enslaved people. If Lincoln had not been determined to preserve the United States in its entirety, or if events had occurred differently during the war, the South might have achieved its goal. For men like André Cailloux, Jordan Noble, and all those they gathered, being perceived as disloyal would have risked that the new nation would pass laws to further relegate them to an inferior place in society. This was to be expected because of legal shifts in the region. For example, after the *Dred Scott* decision in 1857, legislators in Louisiana debated new laws to remove or enslave free Blacks. Even Black sailors from Europe were subject to arrest and enslavement in a few cases.[89] By the start of the Civil War, it became clear, even internationally, that "the slave-holding part of the American Government has shown a determination to expel the [free] people from their homes, and it can care little or nothing about the choice they make of a place of refuge."[90]

Thus, members of New Orleans's free African American society had two choices when the war began: leave Louisiana and all they had for the unknown, or stay and act loyal in hopes that they could earn a place in southern society and maintain a hope for future equality. As Black men had been forming militias in the city for generations, it is not surprising that they formed a home guard unit once again. Their choice bore fruit: because of their service, the state legislature passed no further laws against free Blacks during 1861.

Serving in the home guards provided a loophole for both white and Black men who had no real loyalty to the Confederacy, allowing them to appear as if they did. Since the home guards could not be ordered out of the state, they had little fear of actively participating in the war because everyone assumed the war would primarily unfold on the East Coast. The units met to drill and train, and that was the expected extent of their service. Thus, men in the home guards could exploit the system by appearing loyal, take advantage of any privileges offered, and never directly support the Confederacy. Those who were seen as loyal to the seceding state were given privileges early in the war; for example, the East Pascagoula Hotel opened its doors to any who were serving, promising "fine accommodation, health, sea bathing," and an overall pleasant experience.[91] One soldier later wrote to his wife that these accommodations were "very comfortable."[92] Even white men—especially immigrants—were known to join a home guard unit in a bid to avoid real military service. Once they joined, they could get away with remaining in service as long as they did not violate any rules. They were able to do this because the call for recruits from the governor made it clear that the home guards would "remain in the parish in which they form, . . . and hold themselves in a readiness at a moment's notice."[93] Thousands volunteered for service, and their units were described in the governor's order as "independent of the Confederacy."[94] Men were assured that they could join a home guard unit and remain in the state no matter what occurred during the war, because they were part of a state militia on a voluntary basis, and not part of the Confederate army. Black and white men who had no desire to serve in combat joined the home guards. The moment they were called on for combat, very few volunteered to serve.[95] The Native Guards functioned in much the same way, and within weeks of their recruiting campaign, two partial regiments were organized for service, filled with men who would never see combat.

The city's military leaders knew that not all of the Native Guards were wholly committed to the Confederate cause, so instead they used the unit for parades, as the Native Guards worked better as propaganda for the South than as a military organization. Within six weeks of organizing, Lewis and Ogden drilled the men and ordered the officers of the Native Guards to engage in the study of warfare and military instruction. It was a public spectacle to watch Black men form lines and drill alongside the white militia units of the city. One white man who witnessed their daily drill reported on their skill and general appearance, recognizing the pageantry of it all.[96] Nonetheless, Lewis continued to refuse to supply the unit with arms and accoutrements.

An unintentional consequence of their publicity was that the Native Guards were venerated by members of the city's Black populace. Students who attended the Institute Catholique regularly followed the unit when they marched, and Black families gleefully attended many of their parades to watch fathers, brothers, and sons walk proudly through the city. Women—many of whom acted as godmothers to the companies—wove silk flags for the units, which were then blessed by the priest at the Institute prior to the parades.[97] These presentations were usually followed by large parties with music, singing, dancing, and food, creating a place of celebration and pride for the free Blacks and Creoles of Color in the city. Whites attempted to quell their zeal: Black churches were monitored and guarded by white home guard units, and free Black men seen socializing with enslaved people were often accused of incendiary sentiments and inciting revolt. City authorities made some allowances, like permitting the minstrel show that the Native Guards performed, but they preserved control over all Blacks in the city. It was a balancing act that never favored the race not in power.

The question of how the men felt during their time in the home guards is not in the historical sources. For generations, African Americans in New Orleans witnessed the horrors of slavery and fought to protect women from white men who wanted to use them, all while attempting to carve out a place for themselves in a state that continued to pass laws to curtail their rights and privileges. With the advent of the Civil War, within just a few months they went from attempting to hold their place in the United States to attempting to hold their place in the Confederacy. Self-preservation must have been paramount for many in New Orleans, as the city was too far south to hope the federal government would soon arrive and liberate them. Governor Moore, the state legislature, and the Confederate government all made it clear that they supported the continued abjection of all Black people. The willpower it took for Black New Orleanians to swallow their pride and march the city streets in a republic founded on the principle they were inferior and deserved enslavement is unfathomable. However, it allowed them to protect themselves and their families from reprisals that were meted out even to white citizens. People of Color in New Orleans knew, from decades of experience, that attempting to act directly against slavery in the city resulted in enslavement for free people and death for those who were already enslaved. Their actions preserved a place for all Black people. As Joseph Wilson later noted, African Americans were the only race to encounter the atrocities of white racism and find ways to flourish, and the choice to join the home guards is an example of Blacks doing what they had to do to survive and thrive.[98]

Enslaved people, too, had a choice to make during these tumultuous times. There were thousands of enslaved people living in and around New Orleans prior to the war, and now they were trapped in a land whose founding principle was their permanent abjection. As early as January, a writer for the *Christian Recorder* recognized that "the enslaved negro population of the South is not destitute of intelligence, nor devoid of that sentiment of resistance to tyranny which naturally inspires the oppressed to seek for freedom."[99] It was a common theme. Another person who self-identified as a "Resident in the South" wrote to the *New York Tribune* to ask whether enslaved people would destroy the Confederacy from within. The author suggested that, since millions of enslaved people would lack supervision as their masters fought in the war, they might take the opportunity to rise up and fight against their oppressors. Even before the war, planters confessed, "The only way in which they could discover that their negroes were spending their nights abroad, was as they fell asleep at their work on the following day. They even admit that half the negroes of a large settlement could hold nightly meetings in the swamps, and no white man would know anything of the matter."[100] The letter's author concluded that if the war made its way into the interior, enslaved people would inevitably free themselves and the South would fall because of it.

The enslaved people of Louisiana did not sit by passively as the state joined the Confederacy. Instead, they used the war as an avenue toward freedom through pragmatic forms of resistance to the status quo. In May 1861, in St. Mary Parish, dozens of enslaved people conspired to revolt against the government, but they were found out before they could execute their plan. Any white people deemed guilty of planning the insurrection were captured and killed, and a few white men were interrogated for having sex with Black women and helping them plan the revolt.[101] A few months after the planned insurrection, another began in the same parish, resulting in the deaths of thirteen Black people. Eventually, Twiggs was forced to send three infantry companies and an artillery battery to hold the region from total rebellion. While both insurrections were unsuccessful, they did yield one positive result for the parish's enslaved populace: military leaders expended a great deal of effort preventing further uprisings, which funneled resources away from the war effort. Military authorities were terrified that enslaved people in the parish would revolt again in 1862, and when the Confederate secretary of war urged Lovell to either keep the troops stationed there or send them to the front lines, Lovell responded that he needed them to hold "that densely slave-populated section."[102] Furthermore, Lovell and others were aware that enslaved New Orleanians were willing to fight for their freedom, as they had shown the French and Spanish decades prior. The *New Orleans True Delta* warned everyone in the city to search the quarters of enslaved people because "recent investigations have developed the fact that many of our negroes have fire-arms, bowie-knives and ammunition in their possession, and it is expedient that every slave owner should make a careful search of his negro quarters, and secure all such arms and ammunition." This language made it clear to readers that "the negroes in New Orleans also seem to be hatching mischief."[103] Thus, hundreds of potential defenders of the city were busy keeping the enslaved population in check instead of protecting the bastion of the Gulf when they were needed most.

It was also common for enslaved people to flee to U.S. lines when the opportunity presented itself. From the inception of the war, planters found it difficult to keep supposedly loyal enslaved people from escaping. Hundreds used the ships leaving New Orleans to smuggle themselves into Bermuda, Haiti, and Antigua for freedom. With so many white men being called into service, plantations were devoid of once numerous caretakers and taskmasters, and hundreds of enslaved people took that opportunity to free themselves in 1861. By the time U.S. soldiers arrived, this had already devastated plantations in the region. There were reports of some planters living in destitution because nearly all of the people they had enslaved had fled.[104] Enslaved people forced to march with Confederate soldiers from Louisiana regularly fled to Union lines during campaigns, and many risked their lives to gain their freedom. One formerly enslaved person noted, "When marsa watch the Yankee, nigger go; when marsa watch the nigger, Yankee come."[105]

As early as May 1861, federal government officials were aware that Moore had authorized the constitution of the Native Guards. The presence of a large portion of immigrants and African Americans volunteering in home guard units did not disturb government leaders initially, because many assumed the war would end well before a full invasion of the South was needed. Even after Simon Cameron, the U.S. secretary of war, received reports of immigrant merchants transporting weapons into the city, he still did not expect that there would ever be a full invasion of the Deep South.[106]

From the beginning, both sides recognized that European influence on their supposedly local war would dictate how the conflict would be fought and end. Already, European leaders had expressed interest in seeing popular sovereignty and American democracy come to an end, and the presence of thousands of immigrants gave them a reason to stay involved. Due to its history and location, New Orleans was key to how the international community viewed the war from a southern perspective. Prominent Unionist men from the city wrote to the president and his wife regarding diplomatic appointments in Europe because they knew the positions would play a strategic role in convincing French and British leaders that the Union was worth preserving.[107] Meanwhile, southerners hoped that the control of cotton and sugar would spur England and France to act on behalf of the South.[108] However, a writer for the *Daily Crescent* recognized that most of Europe did not respect the Confederacy because of its constitutional recognition of slavery.[109] A few prominent leaders in New Orleans knew that Europe would not side with them because of "their hatred and prejudices against slavery."[110] The black mantle of slavery continued to prevent France and England from acting. Nevertheless, Americans constantly worried that "the Confederacy will be recognized by the European powers"; such an act would end the war.[111] As a precautionary measure, Lincoln sent ministers to those European powers, and federal government officials waged the war with the threat of European intervention always hanging over their heads.[112]

The Native Guards' service in the South's most transnational city ensured that their parades and drills were known around the world. The Union, in turn, was forced to determine how to respond: Free and arm African Americans or remove them from the equation?

News of the Native Guards made its way into the North, and the question quickly arose: If the Confederacy is using African Americans to win the war, why is the federal government not doing the same? Soon after their constitution in the New Orleans home guards, exaggerated accounts emerged that over fifteen hundred Black men were drilling in New Orleans.[113] Some sought to "fight the devil with fire" by overstating the number of soldiers in the Native Guards, to give credence to the impression that the entire South was willing to employ free Blacks.[114] Another writer questioned the "arming of free negroes in the South," pointing to the Native Guards and writing, "What is sauce for the goose should be sauce for the gander," implying they should do the same as Louisiana.[115] There were exaggerated rumors of other southern states arming and using enslaved and free men for military service as well, and a writer for the *New York Times* argued that the government should offer "freedom on condition of surrender" instead of engaging in battle, should they meet Black soldiers in the field.[116] The *National Anti-Slavery Standard* called for Black soldiers because "it is a well ascertained fact, beyond dispute, that the Rebel Army numbers among its troops a large number of negro soldiers, forcibly impressed into its service, and compelled to fight against the North."[117] The author went on to advocate for the acceptance of free Blacks in the U.S. Army or other northern militias if they were willing to serve. Frederick Douglass knew of these reports, and he pushed for the Union to follow suit, questioning why Black men were seen as "good enough to fight by the side of Washington and Jackson, and were not good enough to fight beside McClellan and Halleck."[118]

Federal government leaders' rationale was that the mantle of slavery prevented the Union from using every available resource. Initially, President Lincoln was concerned that interfering with slavery in any form would cause the few loyal border states to join the Confederacy, and so he pushed members of

Frederick Douglass
(Library of Congress, Prints and Photographs Division)

his administration and the military to ignore the abolishment of slavery as a war aim.[119] In fact, in some cases he ordered his generals to enforce slavery, going as far as imposing the 1850 Fugitive Slave Law. The president's attorney general argued that "it is the President's constitutional duty" to follow the law, and "that means all the laws. He has no right to discriminate—no right to execute the laws he likes, and leave unexecuted those he dislikes."[120] However, as enslaved people fled to U.S. lines, this policy proved ephemeral.

The turning point was the First Battle of Bull Run. The Confederacy's defenses were built by enslaved people, and U.S. generals at the battle acknowledged these defenses as being the chief reason they lost. There were reports of thousands of enslaved people fortifying enemy positions near Manassas, though it turned out that these reports were largely inflated.[121] Congress finally took action by ending enforcement of the Fugitive Slave Law, informing military leaders that they no longer had to return enslaved people who were or could be used by the southern military in any capacity. The government adopted the policy of Major General Benjamin Butler, who argued that enslaved people were contrabands, and, as with any confiscated property, the military could hold and use them to their benefit.[122]

As the government acted against slavery, the question quickly became what to do with enslaved people. Many white northerners supported a policy of freeing them and then removing them from the nation. Florida was proposed as an ideal place for a colony of freed Blacks once the war was over because it was in the Gulf, supposedly had a climate suitable for Afro-descended peoples, and theoretically could be militarily separated from the rest of the seceded states.[123] However, it was argued in the *New York Times* that "there is no territory belonging to the United States adapted by soil or climate to the African"—a reflection of the longstanding racist view that Black people should live in warm environments. Additionally, if a colony were created too close to the South, its inhabitants would be at risk of re-enslavement. Liberia was too far away to transport millions of people, Haiti was under European influence, and anywhere near the United States was not an option. Some northerners advocated for the creation of a colony in Mexico or Central America, espousing the view that even enslavers in the border states would accept a settlement in Central America.[124] Lincoln became a proponent of colonization, with the initial idea in 1861 that, should the Union free the enslaved, freed people would relocate to present-day Nicaragua or Africa.

Federal officials considered whether enslaved people should not only be freed but also armed. Major General John C. Frémont was the first general to make freeing enslaved people a central mission of his command. Frémont had been the Republican candidate for president in 1856, and in 1861 he was the commander of the Department of the West. On 30 August 1861, in response to guerrillas who destroyed bridges and raided farms in Missouri, Frémont declared martial law in the state. This allowed his men to confiscate the property of any people they believed to be rebels—including enslaved people, since they were property per federal law at that time.[125] Frémont further directed the Department of the West to create a commission to manumit the slaves, thus making his the first major command in the U.S. Army to act against slavery. One writer hoped that his actions would "inspire others to look the real cause of war in the face and inspire the government with uncompromising earnestness to remove the festering cause."[126] A *New York Times* writer predicted that Frémont's proclamation "sounded the key-note of the campaign" and would lead the federal government to take away the South's greatest wartime asset, but Lincoln and officials in the War Department thought differently.[127] Lincoln eventually forced Frémont to retract the order because he wanted to separate the issues of war and slavery.

However, members of his cabinet continued to force the issue. The secretary of war in 1861, Simon Cameron, was among the first in the president's cabinet to push Lincoln to free and arm enslaved men. In a speech to Colonel John Cochrane's regiment in the fall, Cameron argued that freeing and arming African Americans was a war necessity, one that could aid the Union in victory while eradicating the institution that had caused the war. Cameron further advanced these views a few weeks later when, in his annual end of year report of the War Department, he "asserted the right and duty of the government to arm slaves and employ them against the rebels."[128] Cameron was following the lead of the secretary of the navy, Gideon Welles, who had authorized more Black men to serve in the U.S. Navy on 25 September 1861.[129] Cameron went on to release his report to the media and Congress before allowing the president to read it. When Lincoln read the report, he reportedly chastised Cameron for his premature statements. Like Frémont, Cameron was forced to retract his words.

Some northerners considered Cameron's position to be a "straightforward and common sense view of the subject," but Lincoln was not prepared to make freeing and arming enslaved people a war measure in 1861.[130] A few weeks after the report was published, Lincoln removed Cameron from the cabinet for his actions. Many cabinet members supported the president's decision, as Cameron was already proving inept in other functions as a secretary.[131] Caleb

Headquarters of the Department of the South
(Library of Congress, Prints and Photographs Division)

Smith, the secretary of the interior, responded to Cameron's proposition with the exclamation, "Putting arms in slaves' hands! If this be attempted to any extent, the whole world will cry out against our inhumanity, our savagery, and the sympathies of all mankind will be turned against us as they were against the blacks, that murdered and drove the French from Hayti."[132]

In March 1862, Major General David Hunter, the commander of the Department of the South, took things even further when he attempted to introduce African American regiments into northern ranks. Hunter's command comprised the states of South Carolina, Georgia, and Florida at that time, and he used his position in the Sea Islands to declare martial law, much like Frémont had. He then took the extraordinary step of passing out certificates of freedom to any enslaved people who asked for them.[133] Soon after that, he declared emancipation for enslaved people and organized a regiment of formerly enslaved men into the 1st Regiment of South Carolina Volunteers. When asked by members of Congress to explain his actions, Hunter replied in a letter that he had not organized a regiment of "fugitive slaves"; rather, he had assembled "a fine regiment of persons whose late masters are fugitive rebels."[134] Hunter's intent was to raise what he called a Negro Brigade of formerly enslaved men with the skills, temperament, and motivation to fight in the war. However, he had few allies who supported these measures.

President Lincoln was furious when he learned what Hunter had done, and, once again, he intervened in a general's command. It did not help that recruitment for the regiments under Hunter's command had been haphazard: white soldiers did not want to serve alongside formerly enslaved Black Americans, and it was claimed that many African Americans had not wanted to join the military.[135] Reportedly, Lincoln stated, "No commanding general shall do such a thing on my responsibility without consulting me."[136] He and the War Department offered no funds or equipment for Hunter's regiments, and after three months of no pay the units were disbanded. Hunter's failure was used to show that formerly enslaved men could not operate in the military. Only one company from the regiments remained in service before it fell apart from lack of pay as well. In a speech soon after its disbandment, Lincoln declared, "The difference between the black and white races in the United States is so broad, that it is impossible the inferior race" could stand equal to or exist peacefully with whites.[137] Lincoln's belief that Blacks and whites could not coexist accounts for why he refused for so long to implement a strategy of arming Black soldiers. He knew that such an action would compel the government to grant not only freedom but citizenship, and that his plan for colonization would therefore never work, as he could not force men who served to leave the country once their service was done. In 1862, the mantle of slavery was not only holding back the Confederacy. It was also holding the Union back from mobilizing hundreds of thousands of men who would have happily fought to put down the southern rebellion.

Some members of Lincoln's cabinet believed that removing all Blacks from the United States would fail to satisfy emancipationists because it failed to create equality for African Americans.[138] However, Lincoln found support in multiple religious leaders who proposed deporting African Americans to various nations in order to remove the institution of slavery from the nation without correcting it.[139] In the Caribbean, an appeal titled "The Free Blacks of America" argued that all "free people of color of the Slave States of America" should leave the South for Jamaica or somewhere else in the Caribbean that had laws protecting Black rights. The call to action was seen most by People of Color in New Orleans because of their location and trade.[140]

Abolitionist newspapers advocated for the emancipation of enslaved people not only on the grounds that it was right but because it could aid the nation. Frederick Douglass's *Douglass' Monthly*, along with many other northern publications, reprinted a pamphlet by the president of Haiti presenting lessons he had learned to make the war "short and the peace righteous." In it, he argued that freeing African Americans was not enough; formerly enslaved people also needed to be armed to fight against their oppressors to protect their freedom. Doing so would remind Americans of the values of "LIBERTY, INDEPENDENCE, OR DEATH!" and inspire them to fight.[141] Another argued that every example of enslaved people being set free—by decree of the Congress of Chili in 1811, the government of Buenos Ayres in 1812, the Congress of Colombia in 1821, the government of Mexico in the same year, and even the state of New York in 1827—demonstrated that "the motto of the negro, in the few instances where he has struck for his freedom, has always been Liberty, never Vengeance. In this regard, the mildest race in the world has been most infamously slandered, or absurdly misunderstood."[142] By this logic, if the federal government positioned itself as the ally of enslaved people, they would respond with loyalty and service.

African Americans were already demonstrating their loyalty to the federal government without serving in the military. In New Orleans, a few enslaved people set fire to eleven ships, valued between $100,000 and $250,000, that were vital to the defense of the state. The city was forced to use most of the home guards—including the Native Guards—to patrol the streets, and it was reported that up to seven hundred men spent their days and nights patrolling in the hopes of preventing further destruction. Many planters in New Orleans employed soldiers as guards for their plantations and houses, which took men away from the Louisiana war effort. Reportedly, some even feared leaving their houses without a guard, and some avoided staying away from their families overnight.[143] One correspondent estimated that, as a result, out of fifty thousand men capable of military service, only fifteen thousand had enrolled by May.[144] While this was a gross overestimation, there were indeed thousands of potential soldiers who did not join the military because they feared leaving their property at risk of destruction. Uprisings by enslaved New Orleanians thus aided the Union's war effort. These acts of rebellion showed whose side they were on.

New Orleans was not an outlier; enslaved men and women worked to aid the Union and seek emancipation throughout the South. Elsewhere in Louisiana, fourteen armed enslaved people escaped to the Comite River area, and all attempts to capture them proved fruitless.[145] Richard Fairchild reported that enslaved people in St. Mary Parish had been agitating for freedom long before a revolt led Lovell to withhold troops from protecting New Orleans.[146] Numerous reports emerged in Union camps of "contrabands" serving the military after seeking refuge in their lines.[147] One officer reported that nearly every day one or two enslaved people escaped to their lines to offer their services to the U.S. Army.[148] It was also common for enslaved people to escape to federal lines and report on Confederate positions and manpower, and sometimes even to act as spies for the military. For example, William Kinnegy escaped but then returned to Kinston, North Carolina, to report on Confederate encampments and free his wife and four children.[149] Another man, Samuel Williams, was given a certificate for his service as a guide and spy for the 3d New York Cavalry Regiment as they maneuvered through North Carolina. Even the famous Allan Pinkerton utilized formerly enslaved people as spies.[150] The most famous formerly enslaved man to aid the Union was Robert Smalls, who captured a ship, presented it to the U.S. Navy, and then gave its leaders information on Confederate batteries in the area to aid in victory.[151] One general wrote to the secretary of war that "the Negroes are our only friends, and in two instances I owe my own safety to their faithfulness. I shall soon have watchful guards among the slaves on the plantations."[152] It was clear which of the two sides enslaved Americans supported.

The Native Guards guaranteed that the questions of slavery and the Civil War could never be separated. The *Christian Recorder* quite aptly reported, "The Confederates, in fact, settled the fate of slavery, when they drilled and armed their negro regiments; and the Government merely corroborates that settlement, by authorizing the formation of a similar force on the other side. The difference is, that the southern leaders do not know what they are doing, while the Government is perfectly aware of the import of what it ordains, and thoroughly conscious that it cannot recede from its position." The author concluded that this "position is, however, manifestly and avowedly a provisional one; and the necessary conclusion is that the Federal cause is henceforth identified with the abolition of slavery."[153] The writer proved prophetic, as the constitution of the Native Guards set the stage for many actions the U.S. Army took later in the war.

Chapter 2

# *THE BACKBONE OF THE REBELLION*

## THE LIBERATION OF NEW ORLEANS

Years after the war, Admiral David Porter recalled that in 1861 President Lincoln had called the Mississippi River the "backbone of the Rebellion."[1] As the largest city in the South, New Orleans was an industrial and shipping powerhouse, exporting nearly half of all cotton and using its industry to prop up the southern military. Because of its strategic location, the city was a military asset vital to controlling the Mississippi River and disrupting southern supply lines.[2] President Lincoln and leaders in the War Department knew they had to capture and hold this militarily significant city if they hoped to win the war. Gideon Welles, the secretary of the navy, and Edwin Stanton, the secretary of war, worked in tandem to ensure control of the city, after which the U.S. Army would be in a position not only to defeat the South, but to do so with the contributions of African American men in the military. While the Louisiana Native Guards did not figure prominently in the defense of New Orleans, their presence in the home guards set the stage for the U.S. Army to mobilize them once the city was captured. In the spring of 1862, New Orleans was liberated from Confederate control, transforming daily life for both Black and white residents. When it took the city, the federal government also set the stage for African American men to serve in the U.S. Army. This chapter examines what it took to liberate the city from rebellious control and how the military was forced into the right conditions for the constitution of the Native Guards in the Department of the Gulf.

Because of New Orleans's location near the mouth of the Mississippi River—and its relationship with multiple trading partners in Cuba, Central and South America, and Europe—both sides recognized the importance of the

"Scott's Great Snake"—a plan to squeeze the Confederacy into submission (Library of Congress, Prints and Photographs Division)

city and the Gulf. The day after Fort Sumter surrendered, the *New York Times* reported that the federal government would make plans to cut off supplies and communication in the Gulf from Europe and South America.[3] Prominent men wrote directly to the president to suggest ways to take and hold the metropolis; one wrote that it was "the key to the strength of the Southern traitorous-combination."[4] New Orleans had a large population and a wealth of resources that the Confederacy needed and that the Union stood to gain from. New Orleans was the richest city in the South; according to some reports, the banks in New Orleans were the only ones in the entire region that remained solvent.[5] In 1861, General Winfield Scott devised the Anaconda Plan to cut off all supplies to and from the rebellious states with minimal loss of life. The government acted to end the war quickly. Soon after the bombardment at Fort Sumter began, ships were reported to be leaving the north to begin encircling the Gulf.[6] Rumors circulated that the ships were loaded with enough men and supplies to blockade the South for as long as necessary.[7] On 19 April 1861,

Lincoln confirmed these rumors when he ordered a general blockade of the Gulf of Mexico.[8]

Under command of Flag Officer William Mervine, the U.S. Navy sent ships to block the ports in the Gulf with the aptly named Gulf Blockading Squadron. Mervine was absent from command, so Welles directed the squadron to report to the most senior officer who was present, Captain William McKean.[9] The Confederate Congress ceased all trade with the United States and Europe in response to the blockade, in a bid to force Lincoln to reverse his order to avoid global economic impacts. Cotton planters in New Orleans took things further, passing an ordinance that banned the export of all cotton to foreign ports and ordering all planters to withhold their cotton from the city as well.[10] However, none of these actions stopped McKean from pressing forward with the blockade.

Within two months of the blockade, the Gulf Blockading Squadron moved to block smaller inlets to Louisiana in the Bayou Lafourche and Teche districts, further isolating New Orleans.[11] Shortly after the federal government positioned ships around New Orleans, a war correspondent reported that "a gentleman just arrived at Washington from New Orleans reports that the trade of the South is in a most deplorable condition. He states that Louisiana, Mississippi and Texas are suffering the most of any of the Southern States. In the latter provisions are becoming so scarce that the people will be in a starving condition when the blockade of New Orleans is complete."[12] Even those in Richmond admitted that "the only effective weapon of assault that the public enemy have yet wielded against us, is the weapon of blockade; and, so far, neither Southern ingenuity, statesmanship, nor pride has been able to provide a single measure for its counteraction."[13] David E. Twiggs's ineptitude allowed rampant corruption in New Orleans, and he did little to stop the blockade of the Gulf, leading the city's residents to distrust him.[14] Clara Solomon, one of the many prominent white citizens of New Orleans affected by the blockade, took note in her diary that even ships delivering mail were fired upon by the Union navy, noting that the suspension of mail not only cut off the city's social connection but its military capabilities as well. While the situation seemed dire in the city, she recorded, "We have not a sufficient force to oppose them. Oh! This state of affairs! Oh!"[15] Blacks and Creoles suffered even more than whites, as they were always the last to receive supplies during this time.

State government officials hoped that the blockade would spur Europe to join the war. Most European leaders accepted that the Civil War was a transnational war, and Spain, France, Britain, and even the multiple German states all attempted to use the blockade to further their individual goals. Agitations with European aristocracy had some northerners thinking of European countries as a secondary enemy of the United States in 1861.[16]

In December 1823, the Monroe Doctrine warned European powers that the United States would not tolerate colonization or the reconquering of nations that had declared their independence.[17] For decades, the doctrine prevented European nations from interfering in Haiti, Cuba, Mexico, and Canada. However, the outbreak of hostilities in the United States gave European leaders the opportunity they were looking for to violate the doctrine with little fear that the federal government would intervene.[18] Ministers in Europe reported that both France and Britain threatened to act on the South's behalf to get cotton, and some rightly feared that if the South won a major campaign, the European powers would side with the Confederacy and end the war before the summer was over.[19] The emperor of France planned to use the internal strife to broker a deal to invade the northern hemisphere with the backing of the new Confederacy to take Mexico or land in South America. However, the people of France opposed this action, which dissuaded the emperor from carrying it out.[20] Spain's ruler similarly hoped to reclaim territory in Mexico with the aid of the South.[21] Members of Britain's abolitionist proletariat opposed interference, and their voices deterred Prime Minister Palmerston from acting on behalf of the South. Almost as soon as the blockade was formed, Welles reported to McKean to expect shipments to New Orleans from Belgium to aid the southern war effort.[22]

Louisiana had a more international population than any other southern state, with a large immigrant community, People of Color with European heritage in the Native Guards, and European consuls stationed in New Orleans. From the beginning of the war, many New Orleans newspapers monitored "European Intelligence." Some southerners hoped Emperor Napoleon would act on the South's behalf. French officers and ministers visited New Orleans, and one French marine, Captain Nodler, promised to use his wealth and connections to secure a letter of marque—a privateering license for piracy in the Caribbean—in support of the Confederacy on behalf of the French people in New Orleans.[23] The French even threatened to supply frigates and other military aid to ensure the South was able to wage war on equal ground.[24]

Others believed that Queen Victoria would push the British Parliament to recognize the Confederacy, although it was actually cotton industrialists who were attempting to sway the government.[25] They speculated that if the US government withheld shipping out of New Orleans, London would be more likely to take action.[26] When additional European reports promised British aid, it was clear that the Civil War was more than a conflict between the northern and southern halves of the nation. The Union's saving grace was a British proclamation to keep their citizens out of the war that also prevented the military, British citizens, and any of their ports from assisting the South in any capacity during the conflict.[27] The proclamation was so severe that many took it to mean British citizens captured at sea supporting either side would be treated as pirates.[28] This did not stop William Russell from fighting against impressment as the British consul in New Orleans, because it was reported that on any given day dozens of British immigrants were dragged from the wharves "and forced by violence to serve in the 'volunteer' ranks!"[29] Some European immigrants genuinely supported Louisiana and joined the Irish, British, and French volunteer regiments in the city, which remained loyal to the Confederacy well into the war. However, conscripts made up a large part of the city's defenses in the spring of 1861, as the bulk of the volunteer forces were farther north in Virginia or other states supporting the southern military. Like the Native Guards, the immigrant conscripts eventually showed that their allegiance was not wholly to the Confederacy.

President Lincoln, like many northerners, believed that there was a strong pro-Union sentiment in New Orleans and that once the federal government liberated the city the true Americans would show themselves. There were even reports sent to the president claiming that a large part of the foreign population supported the Union. Lincoln received letters from New Orleanians praising his political beliefs; one informed him that he had "many warm friends" in the region.[30] Another person published an article that "a majority of the people were for the Union. Some said two-thirds were Union men, some three-fourths, but all said a majority."[31]

In response to the U.S. blockage, the *New Orleans Daily Crescent* published a list of everyone who had already joined a militia unit to defend the city should the U.S. Navy attack. The list included Creoles, Irish, Germans, Spaniards, Italians, Swiss, Scotsmen, English, French, old and young white men, and "The Free Colored Men of New Orleans."[32] However, many—on both sides of the conflict—understood the reality that the Native Guards, and most Black people, supported the Union. To a lesser degree, southerners feared that German and British immigrants would support the Union cause as well, if given the chance. Thus, Mayor John T. Monroe and Twiggs worried that a significant portion of the population might betray Louisiana if the U.S. military came to the city, and the two relied on loyal southerners organized into vigilance committees to surveil the populace.

Vigilance committees had operated in Louisiana for years prior to the Civil War, and they became even more violent when the war began because Monroe feared the Unionism that so many in the North were writing about.[33] These vigilante groups operated outside of the law and recruited loyal southerners.[34] Even before the war, there were public cases of vigilance committees using cannons to hunt down and kill those they deemed traitors to Louisiana, and they publicly clashed with the immigrant populace in the 1858 New Orleans mayoral election.[35] During the war, the committee in New Orleans worked with Monroe to aid the police and military officers whose job it was to resist the U.S. Army and curtail revolts by enslaved people. The vigilance committee was charged with rooting out any pro-Union men and women and arresting them, and the members took their charge seriously.[36] The *New Orleans Delta,* like other newspapers in the city, reported on the movements of the vigilance committee just as it reported on those of the police, treating the organization as a legal entity. Through the efforts of the committee, some men were charged for opposing the Confederacy, expressing sentiments for Lincoln and the Union, and, worst of all, advocating for the abolition of slavery.[37] However, the majority of those who bore the ire of the committee were either immigrants or People of Color who were seen as less than loyal when compared to their American or white counterparts.[38] The vigilance committee even targeted Black Europeans for entering New Orleans while conducting trade.[39] Members of the Native Guards—or any person of color—who were sympathetic to the Union risked not only the ire of pro-Confederate southerners but also retribution from members of the vigilance committee.

Some southerners took advantage of the vigilance committee to attack their enemies, sometimes without proof of wrongdoing. Catherine Rossvally's husband, Dr. Rossvally, was imprisoned by the committee just for having been born in the North. She was sick and lacked the income to support their three children, and so she was compelled to beg for his freedom.[40] Once an investigation confirmed that he was an assistant surgeon in the southern military, he was released.[41] Another man was reported to the committee for being "an Abolitionist and spy."[42] He was detained for some time as the committee verified that his son-in-law was in the southern military and that he had no northern paraphernalia. Others who could not prove their loyalty faced stiff penalties, from a beating to imprisonment.[43] A foreign correspondent in New Orleans characterized the new paradigm as follows: "The most cruel and atrocious acts are perpetrated by the rabble who style themselves citizens. The national failing of curiosity and prying into other people's affairs is now rampant and assumes the name and airs of patriotic vigilance." As the writer described, "Every stranger is watched, every word is noted, espionage commands every key-hole and every letter-box; love of country takes no eavesdropping, and freedom shaves men's heads, and packs men up in boxes for the utterance of 'Abolition sentiments.'" The author went on to observe that the richest city in the South had fallen and that now "there is a terrible substratum of crime and vice, violence, misery, and murder, over which the wheels of the Cotton King's chariot rumble gratingly, and on which rest in dangerous security the feet of his throne."[44]

As the Union blockade choked off supplies, many of the city's residents came to realize what their rebellion had wrought. Prior to the war, Louisiana was one of the richest states in the South. Cotton and sugar exports had been higher than in previous years, mortality rates had fallen, tobacco and rice production had gone up, and the value placed on enslaved people had risen as well.[45] New Orleans usually exported over 500,000 bales of cotton a year, but by the end of 1861 only 11,000 bales had left the port.[46] River commerce eclipsed $500 million in 1860, but barely passed $51 million in 1861.[47] The city's residents stopped using specie, and the banks were forced to accept southern paper money as currency, heightening inflation. Reportedly, some employers refused to pay their employees because of the lack of funds, and city officials considered shuttering the schools and releasing the police since they did not have the resources to run the municipal government.[48] Some teachers were not paid for their work during this time.[49] According to Solomon, supplies were dwindling quickly, and some of the city's wealthiest residents were forced to rely on "peasant faire" to survive.[50] She described seeing families going hungry in the city, and she was not the only one who witnessed the starvation the blockade brought. Soon enough, people found it difficult to procure items as basic as shoes due to scarcity and inflation.[51] Reports circulated throughout the Caribbean that the once proud city of New Orleans was now running low on tea, coffee, clothing, lead, sulfur, salt, quinine, beef, butter, and many necessities that could not be produced in or near the city.[52] Even Unionist cities that relied on trade with New Orleans suffered from the blockade; in 1861, dozens of merchants from St. Louis begged the president to allow them to sell their goods in the city, to no avail.[53]

After three hundred women stormed the mayor's office demanding food in August, Monroe was forced to feed the families of those serving in the military—but, of course, not everyone had a male relative serving in the military, and the government's resources were limited. The economic situation in the city became so dire that Mansfield Lovell issued an order barring "the ejection of families of soldiers now in the service of the [Confederate] government, either on land or water, for rent past due."[54] Because the economy of New Orleans (and, by extension, much of Louisiana) depended on external markets and trade, the U.S. blockade was very effective in disrupting the state's economy.

The city's Black residents, even the wealthiest among the Native Guards, suffered as the economy turned, though some were able to use Lovell's order to stave off eviction. Thus, serving in the home guards continued to benefit Creoles in the city. But, for many members of the lower classes, the situation grew dire. White immigrants no longer needed to be forced into the Confederate military; instead, they "rushed to arms with enthusiasm to support southern institutions" as "nothing remain[ed] for them but to enlist," according to one witness.[55] African Americans in New Orleans—already under threat because of the war—felt the economic downturn acutely. André Cailloux sold much of his property because he could not afford his interest payments anymore. He received a small profit from the sale, but his family was forced to move into a friend's home after the property was sold.[56] Many free Black families were in a similar situation, either forced to move in with other families or broken up because the heads of households could not afford to keep them all together.[57] The spiritualist Henry Louis Rey, who had multiple jobs, struggled to survive as the city ran dry.[58] Dr. Louis Charles Roudanez, one of the city's best doctors of color, could not get the necessary supplies to treat his patients. As one of the few Black doctors who treated everyone regardless of class or race, his skills were especially needed as yellow fever season neared in 1862.[59] Enslaved people in the city were expected to sell whatever goods their enslavers ordered them to sell and generate a profit daily, and failure to do so could result in being flogged or starved by their enslavers, who needed the money for themselves. In the city and on the plantations surrounding New Orleans, free and enslaved Black people were punished more and more brutally; it seemed as if whites were taking their frustration over the blockade and the economic downturn out on the one group of people who could not legally defend themselves.

The docks and shipyards that had once been lively were now empty. Merchants who depended on trade shuttered their businesses.[60] The best work available for much of the year was converting riverboats into gunboats for the Confederate navy. Eventually, the city's workers were tasked with creating two ironclad ships to control the Mississippi River, the *Louisiana* and the *Mississippi*. However, economic strain slowed their progress, and on 6 November 1861 the workers—in need of higher wages to keep up with inflation—started a general strike. Even after resolving the strike, the workers remained angry over their treatment and wages, and they sabotaged the launches of both ships. In a similar incident, a gunpowder mill was blown up and a group of men was captured attempting to burn one of the ironclads. In response, the *New Orleans True Delta* reported that there were "traitors in our midst."[61] The vigilance committee appeared to have failed to quell unrest in the city, and New Orleans was breaking apart from within.

When hundreds of Union prisoners were transported to New Orleans during the blockade, Twiggs and Monroe had a chance to demonstrate that they viewed the Native Guards as more than an opportunity for southern propaganda. In late September, they planned to march the prisoners through the city streets in a parade to demonstrate the South's might. The officers of the Native Guards offered the addition of their unit to the many others escorting the prisoners toward the parish prison, and initially Twiggs accepted their offer. A *Daily Crescent* editor expressed, "These men who came into a Southern State preaching freedom to the negro, are to be received and guarded by free negroes, natives of our city, who have taken up arms to defend it and its institutions." After pointing out that Captain Jordan Noble would be leading the march, the editor argued that the Union forces would soon "be taught that in the South alone is the free negro really respected, trusted, and appreciated."[62] However, at the last minute, Twiggs and Monroe balked at the idea of including the Native Guards because it would allow Black troops to show their power over white prisoners.[63] With thirty-six officers and eight hundred and seventy enlisted men, the Native Guards would have created an imposing figure of Black strength that the city's white leaders could not risk.[64] Furthermore, the vigilance committee already suspected the city's Black residents of being secret Unionists, and Twiggs and Monroe feared that the Native Guards would set the prisoners free or aid them in some other way. Their decision demonstrates awareness of how precarious control of African American society had become in New Orleans. More broadly, the presence of the Native Guards at such an event threatened to show the world that Blacks were equals and thus the war was moot, which in turn could inspire enslaved people to revolt. Monroe ended up calling upon only white militia men to march the prisoners through the city, where thousands of onlookers gathered to watch.[65]

While the blockade was effective in New Orleans, the Union's navy took additional steps to further weaken the rebellion. On 6 September 1861, Flag Officer Mervine was recalled from command after the secretary of the navy deemed him ineffective at stopping blockade runners and because he allowed southern forces to build up their defenses in the Gulf.[66] Flag Officer William McKean replaced him as commander of the Gulf Blockading Squadron. Welles and many in the War Department thought McKean would bring new vigor to the command and quell those in New Orleans who were resupplying from foreign ports and communicating with European officials. As the federal navy fortified its blockade of the city, officers turned their attention to securing the Union's control of the river. In August 1861, members of a naval board told War Department officials that bottlenecks in the ports of New Orleans were sufficient to hold the city and the Mississippi River.[67] Captain David Dixon Porter countered that direct action was still necessary, as the city remained vulnerable. Porter claimed after the war that he had appealed directly to President Lincoln with his plan to take New Orleans with naval action, and that Lincoln had been supportive of the plan, expressing an intention to present it to Major General George McClellan soon after their meeting.[68] But Porter's suggestion was ignored.[69] He believed for years after the war that if the War Department officials had listened to him and sent the navy early in 1861, the navy could have taken the city with "a dozen improvised gun-boats" with minimal loss of life and held the entire Mississippi River.[70] General McClellan, in his typical fashion, wanted to wait to take New Orleans until he had an overwhelming number of men. He wrote to Edwin Stanton that taking the city would be key in securing the Mississippi and capturing southern seaports to reestablish federal control in Louisiana, but McClellan wanted to continue training the army in preparation for such a movement.[71]

The U.S. blockade of the Gulf demonstrated that leaders in the federal government viewed New Orleans as a strategic location. As early as September, people in the city knew the Union was determined to take New Orleans.[72] Twiggs attempted to mount a defense against the blockade, creating a defensive network between the mouth of the Mississippi and New Orleans in the hope that Confederate troops could stop a ground assault if one began.[73] He even contemplated using Ship Island, a small barrier island less than seventy miles from the entrance of the Mississippi, near the entrance to the Gulf, as a defensive position from which to hold off a federal invasion, but Johnson K.

Duncan, an officer sent by Twiggs to survey the location, deemed it untenable because of the remote location.[74] Following Duncan's report, Twiggs withdrew his troops from Ship Island, aware that he did not have the manpower or the means to fortify the position.[75] Twiggs reported that as his men evacuated the island, they could see Union steamers approaching.[76] During this time, Twiggs and Monroe argued publicly over who controlled funds appropriated for the protection of the city, and, as a result, Twiggs resigned and Monroe and Moore sought his replacement.[77] Braxton Bragg and Pierre Gustave Toutant-Beauregard both petitioned for the appointment to return to their home city.[78] Instead, Mansfield Lovell—no one's first choice—was given the position.[79]

On 18 October 1861, Lovell was appointed commander of Department Number 1 and charged with defending the Gulf of Mexico.[80] Lovell headed to the city that month, aware that the federal military was already blockading the Gulf of Mexico.[81] Twiggs, who was in poor health and unable to prepare for an impending attack, reportedly told Lovell that the city was defenseless. However, Lovell later testified that numerous defenses were already under construction on the Mississippi and around the forts.[82] While Bragg was apprehensive about Lovell because he was from the North, he thought that Lovell was capable of putting up a defense should the Union come to the city.[83] Contrariwise, Bragg was simultaneously confident in Lovell because Lovell had been trained at West Point and served as the deputy street commissioner of New York City, one of the few cities in the nation larger than New Orleans.[84]

Lovell took over the city's defense at a difficult time; resources were scarce and soldiers were untrained. He tried in vain to correct the economic downturn the blockade had caused, even barring the practice of exchanging specie and Union money for goods in an attempt to save the southern dollar due to rising inflation.[85] Because Moore had channeled supplies to the Confederacy, the city was short on necessities, including ammunition and firearms. There was also confusion about leadership; between the mayor, the governor, multiple militias, and home guard units stationed in and around the city, no single person or entity was in command. Furthermore, as a nativist, Lovell disliked the city's large immigrant population. He had no misgivings about expressing that view, which heightened distrust among the city's residents.

However, the worst thing Lovell discovered—in his view—was that there were armed Black men in the city, and he took steps to change that.[86] He stepped up the work of the vigilance committee, and he began using its members, along with soldiers under his command, to arrest anyone they believed held Unionists sentiments. Dozens were arrested under his tenure, and some were even killed. In one of the more infamous cases, allegedly seven men were arrested and sent to the parish prison. From there, they were dragged out at night and hanged by a mob, purportedly out of fear that the men would escape and report the city's defenses to the U.S. Navy. There were smaller cases of elderly men being imprisoned for months for expressing approval of Lincoln and his policies, and of fishermen being arrested while conducting their trade under the mistaken belief that they were using their boats to flee toward the blockading fleet.[87]

While Lovell was taking these disciplinary steps, he was also making plans to defend the city. The Native Guards, along with the rest of the New Orleans militia, had been mobilized and ordered to train in preparation for an impending Union attack, but Moore knew the militia would not be enough.[88] Once Lovell became aware that the Native Guards were preparing for battle, he refused their assistance, determined to maintain the notion that they were unequal to and less capable than white soldiers. Lovell even requested more direct control of militia units so that he could disband or consolidate units he deemed ineffectual, but he was never given full control of the Native Guards or even the ability to remove their officers, since they were part of the home guards.[89] Ironically, nearly all of the city's leaders realized the Confederacy needed Black laborers—mainly enslaved people—to build the fortifications needed to protect the city.[90] However, Lovell did not want Blacks to serve in or directly support the military because of his racist beliefs. Lovell's position reflected the Confederacy's policy, as its leaders were afraid that the slightest elevation of status among free African Americans would lead enslaved people to agitate for their freedom. Louisiana law and tradition allowed the Native Guards to exist, but the southern War Department refused to allow free Blacks to serve in the military. One southern general thought that the South had "a superabundance of our own color" to fight and win the war, and therefore had no use for Black men in its ranks.[91]

Lovell continued to pursue Twiggs's policy of consolidating troops in the city, and he stopped the construction of new forts to focus, instead, on fortifying existing forts. He realized it was impossible to defend all of the city's access points, but the easiest route to victory was to prevent the U.S. Navy from entering the Mississippi, so he prioritized defense of the river's entrance. Sixty-five miles downriver of New Orleans, two large brick forts—Fort Jackson, the larger of the two, and Fort St. Philip, the smaller—faced one another, creating a vise to prevent Union ships from reaching the city.[92] Lovell assigned Brigadier General Johnson K. Duncan as the commander of the two forts, and Duncan began the laborious process of building up their defenses.[93]

Should the forts fail, Lovell predicted intense fighting on the shores, not unlike the fighting that had taken place in the Battle of New Orleans. In preparation for such a battle, all white men who were eligible to serve in a militia unit were compelled to enter service on the threat of arrest.[94] Dozens of immigrants were rounded up and forced to defend Forts Jackson and St. Philip. They were ordered to drill in their respective militia units, and any who failed to comply faced retribution from the vigilance committee that roamed the city seeking traitors. Free African Americans continued to drill in the Native Guards as well, all under the pretense of solidarity. However, both groups—to a large degree—felt forced to participate for fear of what could happen if they did not keep up appearances of loyalty.

In November, thousands of people who had been compelled into militia service participated in a parade through the city. The Native Guards were present, and most were unarmed, as usual. The event was a pass and review, a military term for an event where a commanding officer, in this case Governor Moore, inspects the men under his command as they march past him. With only a few weeks to organize, the pass and review was scheduled for 23 November 1861.[95] Monroe and Lovell organized the event in hopes of impressing Moore and the city's residents and demonstrating that the city was prepared for a Union attack. In these ways, the parade was a success. One correspondent thought the review "was the greatest and most imposing sight ever presented by the population of the Crescent City."[96] Captain Charles Sauvenet's company received special commendation for his military bearing and the skill of the men he led that day.[97] Moore praised the Black men on their well-timed drill and the uniforms of the Native Guards after the review, and this impression led him to utilize them in the future.[98] As a Black unit in French-influenced uniforms, the Native Guards stood out from the rest.[99]

The adjutant's report of the review demonstrated that Lovell and Monroe had succeeded in convincing their superiors of the might of New Orleans's forces.[100] Military officials estimated that over twenty-five thousand soldiers paraded through the streets. Solomon wrote that "although the Crescent City has contributed so largely to the Army, we *still* have enough to keep the invader from her soil."[101] The U.S. Navy would soon put her theory to the test.

Lovell was under the impression that soon the city would be impregnable, asserting that the armed forces would "defeat any force that shall attempt an invasion" on New Orleans once he had the powder and ships he needed.[102] He even orchestrated a chain defense between the forts at the mouth of the Mississippi to stop the U.S. Navy from sailing into the river. With nearly nine thousand soldiers, along with thousands more militia men and home guards, including the Native Guards, Department Number 1 seemed a force to be reckoned with.[103] Shipwrights in the city were even in the process of creating ironclad naval ships that theoretically would have been impenetrable to Union guns.[104] By December, Lovell reported that he could hold the city indefinitely if well supplied.[105]

In response to the South's construction of defenses on the river, federal government officials realized that it was a mistake to expect one command, the Gulf Blockading Squadron, to hold so much naval territory and capture New Orleans. The unit was split into two, and the secretary of the navy, following a suggestion from Captain Porter, sent down a man he knew had the skills necessary to counter the Confederacy's naval preparations: Captain David Farragut.

Captain Farragut was a lifelong sailor. Born in 1801, the Virginian was befriended and adopted by Commodore David Porter at a young age, and he later joined the U.S. Navy at the age of nine, where he served under Porter. Within three years of joining the navy, he had risen to the rank of prize master, a position that put him in charge of captured enemy ships during the

David Farragut
(Library of Congress, Prints and Photographs Division)

War of 1812. By the age of twenty, he commanded respect as a ship's officer with over a decade of experience in multiple smaller campaigns in the Caribbean against pirates. Because of these efforts, he received his first independent command in 1824.[106] When the Civil War began, Farragut was respected in naval circles for his knowledge and ability. He was the adoptive brother of David Dixon Porter, the son of the commodore and the man who pushed for his appointment to the Gulf Blockading Squadron. Farragut went on to prove through his leadership that Porter had chosen the right man.[107]

Prior to Farragut's arrival in the Gulf, the assistant secretary of war, Gustavus Fox, drafted a plan to take the city. It was an ambitious plan that came on the heels of the Blockading Squadron's capture of Port Royal, South Carolina. Now that navy leaders knew their ships could navigate the southern waterways easily, Fox believed that naval vessels could sail up the Mississippi River and reach New Orleans with minimal loss of ships or men.[108] It took some prodding, but Fox was able to convince both Welles and Farragut that his plan was worthy.[109]

On 23 December 1861, the Gulf Blockading Squadron was divided per the order of the secretary of the navy, and Farragut took command of the newly constituted West Gulf Blockading Squadron.[110] His squadron commanded everything from West Florida to the Rio Grande, and he was charged with blockading the Gulf of Mexico and the Mississippi River.[111] Privateers and pirates hired by wealthy merchants in the city had been able to abscond with an estimated $3 million worth of goods prior to his arrival.[112] Welles stressed that he wanted an end to blockade runners: "The importance of a vigorous blockade at every point to be under your command, can not be too strongly impressed or felt. By cutting off all communication we not only distress and cripple the States in insurrection, but by an effective blockade we destroy any excuse or pretext on the part of foreign governments to aid and relieve those who are waging war upon the Government."[113] In February 1862, while Farragut was still in the North awaiting his flagship, the *Hartford*, the West Gulf Blockading Squadron continued its preparations.

When a fleet of U.S. ships arrived at the mouth of the river, it could be seen by southerners with telescopes, and everyone knew there was only one destination for such a massive flotilla.[114] Once Farragut arrived, Welles instructed the new commander to "reduce the defenses which guard the approaches to New Orleans" in order to guarantee "the certain capture of the city of New Orleans."[115] Ground troops were sent to support Farragut and were stationed on Ship Island, but most of them did not know what their mission would be.[116]

Major General
Benjamin Butler
(Library of Congress, Prints and Photographs Division)

Soldiers on the ships commented on the "very rough passage" that made many men sick on their way to the Gulf.[117]

Meanwhile, Union ground troops were assigned to Major General Benjamin F. Butler, who was in the process of preparing to hold the Gulf. Butler was born on 5 November 1818 in New Hampshire, and he spent the majority of his life in the New England area, specifically Massachusetts. He was a socialite who held complicated views regarding African Americans. For example, he supported abolishing slavery earlier than did some other U.S. generals, but he was blatantly racist. His belief that Blacks were entirely inferior to whites indicates that his antislavery views were economically and politically motivated rather than morally informed prior to the war. In 1838, he graduated from Colby College in Maine and became a lawyer before marrying Sarah Hilldreth, an actress and socialite. He returned home and joined the Massachusetts militia in 1839, and by 1855 he was a brigadier general in the militia despite having received no formal military training. He was well respected among his men, who followed him into multiple engagements against Native Americans prior to the Civil War. Outside of the militia, he worked as a lawyer and politician, and prior to the outbreak of hostilities he cast fifty ballots for Jefferson Davis at the 1860 Democratic Convention.[118] He was among the first politicians to boast about his Irish heritage to gain political favor, and he used his understanding of immigrant relations to push for taxes meant to help the poor and sway the state to take care of Catholics and their churches.

Butler commanded the 8th Massachusetts Volunteer Infantry Regiment when the war began, and his troops were among the first to guard the nation's capital due to their training and proximity. On 16 May 1861, President Lincoln—impressed by Butler's military reputation and on the recommendation of his fellow generals—appointed the New Englander as a general in the Regular Army.[119] He had a reputation for being an unyielding commander and conqueror. For example, when he captured Fort Hatteras, the admiral who was commanding the fort requested that his men be allowed to leave the fort with their sidearms and retire from the battlefield if they surrendered the fort, all its armaments, and their primary arms. Butler replied that the terms for surrender were "full capitulation, *the officers and men to be treated as prisoners of war*—no other terms admissible."[120] Butler cited similar terms when he captured Fort Clark, and this was the reputation of the man leading the ground forces stationed at Ship Island.

On 5 October 1861, Butler created the Department of New England, which consisted of regiments from the six New England states, with Butler in command.[121] Butler publicly clashed with the governor of Massachusetts, John Andrew, over these regiments, and Lincoln wanted to remove Butler for the headache these disputes caused. Lincoln also knew that Butler, as a Democrat and former governor, could administer over New Orleans better than many of his contemporaries. For these reasons, Lincoln made sure that Butler was assigned to the expedition to liberate New Orleans.[122]

On 23 February 1862, the Department of the Gulf was constituted in the federal army, and Butler was appointed its commander.[123] The Department of New England was disbanded, and all members were assigned to the Department of the Gulf. The new department was charged with quelling the rebellion in the Gulf of Mexico and Pensacola Harbor, and, in August 1862, in West Florida as well.[124] Major General McClellan wrote to Butler that he should keep his "destination a profound secret," with the only exception being his chief of staff, Lieutenant Godfrey Weitzel, who was already planning the attack.[125] Even Captain John William De Forest, one of the most senior captains serving under Butler, was not aware of where the ships were landing until they arrived at their destination.[126]

Butler was given 14,000 infantry, 295 cavalry, and 580 artillery men, along with various other troops who would be loaned to the Department of the Gulf until they captured New Orleans, for a total of 18,000 men.[127] He split his men into three brigades under Brigadier Generals John Phelps (1st Brigade), Thomas Williams (2d Brigade), and George Shepley (3d Brigade). Meanwhile, Farragut had assumed command of the West Gulf Blockading Squadron a few days earlier and had been assigned all the naval forces. Farragut was given seventeen men-of-war and twenty mortar boats to ensure he could both transport and attack.[128] Butler felt so confident that they would succeed that he promised the president that he would not communicate with him again until they had taken possession of New Orleans.[129]

Plans to liberate the city were massive, involving the U.S. Navy, Marines, Army, and New England militia regiments all working together. Butler and Farragut worked in tandem to build up their ground and naval forces to ensure the Department of the Gulf would not only capture the city but would also be able to hold it. They were ordered to destroy the forts leading up to the city, leaving men within or nearby in case they were forced to retreat back to the Gulf. Should the navy fail to destroy the forts, Butler was ordered to lay siege until the forts capitulated. After taking both forts, Butler and Farragut were to attack defensive positions leading toward New Orleans, but to then stop outside of the city so as to not disrupt Union sentiment within.[130] By 25 February, Butler's wife, Sarah, was already writing to friends about the operation to take New Orleans, a sign of how closely Butler and Farragut planned to follow McClellan's secret orders as they prepared their attack.[131]

As the Federal military prepared to liberate the city, things were changing in New Orleans. Southern papers wrote extensively on the Native Guards, including the fact that they were willingly fighting for the world's first nation with Black enslavement as its cornerstone. A writer for the *New Orleans Daily Crescent* said, "This fine company of colored patriots was out yesterday afternoon on parade, and presented a truly brilliant appearance," continuing, "It will remain upon our memory as one of the pleasant reminiscences of the struggle in which we are now engaged."[132] At the beginning of the second year of war, Lovell ordered all troops in the city to organize for another parade. In short order, Lewis issued General Orders No. 1, which called up multiple units in the volunteer state troops, calling forth "The Regiments of Native Guards" as one of the units that should begin organizing for the upcoming festival.[133] On 27 January 1862, New Orleans held a large celebration to commemorate the one-year anniversary of leaving the Union.[134] Reportedly, twelve thousand men marched in the parade that day, including the Native Guards, who moved down Canal Street waving the Confederate and Louisiana state flags.[135]

Yet, despite being used for Confederate propaganda, the Native Guards did not receive respect in New Orleans or among soldiers in the home guards. By the beginning of the new year, there were thirteen companies in the Native Guards, made up of over a thousand men. The companies were designated, like many militia units, using the names of places, people, and mutual aid fraternal societies relevant to New Orleans: Beauregard, Crescent City, Economy, Labatut, Louisiana, Meschacebe, Order, Mississippi, Native Guards, Perseverance (also called Company of Native Guards), Savary, Turcos, and Young Creole.[136] The companies also had lettered designations for military efficiency; for example, Order Company was officially designated Company C. In January 1862, the Native Guards still lacked equipment and weapons; one company had only ten muskets.[137] Combined with their treatment by Lovell and many fellow New Orleanians, the men grew even more disenchanted. Absenteeism rose in the companies of the regiment as soldiers recognized that they would never achieve equitable treatment in the militia. For example, when state authorities wanted to use Black mechanics to assist in building ironclads to defend the city, the white mechanics said they would cease working, even if Black workers only worked at night and never interacted with them.[138] Despite their refusal to work in the same location as Black laborers, white shipwrights refused to work at night, to the detriment of the city's defenses.[139]

Members of the Louisiana State Legislature—planters and others who relied on slavery—passed a law on 23 January 1862 to disarm and disband Black units, which only affected the Native Guards. On 15 February 1862, the Native Guards were disbanded. Many of the men were disenchanted by this point, so no one in the regiment fought against this order. At the very least, they had demonstrated loyalty, and many of the Blacks in the city hoped that meant they could no longer be attacked for not supporting the South. The new law also forced all free white men into the militia "irrespective of nationality."[140] This meant that thousands of immigrants were conscripted into the Louisiana militia regardless of their allegiance or nationality. Those with political connections in Europe used those connections to force the governor to release them from militia service. The governor promised those who remained in the home guards that their units would never be allowed to leave the state and that their use would be limited to defense and police purposes only.[141] The newly formed Mayor General's Office in New Orleans mandated that all white men in the city between ages eighteen and forty-five defend the city in proper military formations should the Union attack.[142] Shortly thereafter, in March 1862, many white men were suddenly mustered into military service.[143] The removal and replacement of many men caused chaos in Lovell's lines at a moment when an attack was imminent.[144] Meanwhile, the Native Guards were released from service—temporarily, at least.

Once Farragut entered the Mississippi, Moore realized he needed additional men to defend New Orleans. After getting assurances from the southern secretary of war that he could accept any support he deemed necessary for local defense and special service, Moore began working to reconstitute the Native Guards.[145] On 24 March 1862, he issued General Orders No. 426, which reconstituted the Native Guards. In his order, he commanded, "relying implicitly upon the loyalty of the free colored population of the City and State, for the protection of their homes, their property, and for Southern rights, from the pollution of a ruthless invader, and believing that the military organization which existed prior to the 15th February, 1862, and elicit praise and respect for the patriotic motives which prompted it, should exist for and during the war."[146] Despite this flowery language, it was obvious that the regiment was reconstituted out of desperation and fear.

With this formal recognition, the Native Guards seemed more official than ever. Some of the Native Guards' white officers even made their way onto the register of officers of Louisiana State Troops, with their date of ranks backdated to the previous year.[147] However, the Native Guards were still not part of the Confederacy per Moore's assurances that home guard units would remain separate from the military. Once Moore reinstated them, nearly all of the men returned for drill, but Lovell and Lewis still refused to issue them proper weapons and equipment. Despite this lack of support, an informant who escaped to Union lines testified that the Louisiana Native Guards was "the best drilled as well as the best dressed regiment in New Orleans."[148] Jordan Noble was credited with keeping the men in line and ensuring that his regiment was always more disciplined than the white home guard units alongside whom they drilled.

Enslaved African Americans in New Orleans used this time of turmoil to their advantage. While white men scrambled to protect the city and abandoned their lands, some of the enslaved escaped and emancipated themselves. Some even made their way to Ship Island, where the officer in charge, General John Phelps, reported the arrival of two dozen enslaved people who were "intelligent and far more dignified and manly than many of their masters, whom they look upon with mingled feelings of pity and contempt as well as dread."[149]

One woman later attested that the federal army kept them all safe and free on the island.[150] Enslaved people began assisting the U.S. military on Ship Island, constructing barracks and building fortifications for pay and clothing. Most importantly, they shared information about what was occurring in the city with Union officers.

Ship Island was no paradise. Captain De Forest wrote to his wife that it was "the sandiest region this side of the Great Sahara."[151] Others complained that the water "had a laxative effect," and many noted that the white sand spread through the air easily; one soldier commented that there was "sand to eat, drink and wear." Alligators and anacondas in the Gulf made things both entertaining and dangerous when the soldiers made sport of killing them, but soldiers feared the sharks that sometimes appeared in the water.[152] Flies and mosquitos were numerous and spread disease easily and quickly.[153] Food supplies were lackluster, making dinner a depressing affair as well.[154] Reportedly, the quartermaster called it "a hell of a place to send 2,000 men." One soldier dubbed their training location an "accursed Sand bank."[155] An officer with the US Army Sanitary Commission described Ship Island as "a barren, desolate, sand-spit, left free for the most part to alligators and such reptiles as abound in the swamps and lagoons of the region," going on to detail "the painful and variable climate; the sufferings of the men from diarrhea, influenza, and rheumatism; the badness of the food, which was of salt meat . . . the badness of the water, and the wretched system of cooking," all of which made the island miserable to garrison troops.[156] One soldier estimated that there was a funeral every three days on Ship Island due to the nature of their encampment and disease.[157] Some officers noted that they were using a preparation spot similar to that of the British during the Battle of New Orleans in the War of 1812, but they were confident the results would be much different this time.[158]

The federal navy began to move on a normal, cold and rainy spring day; on 10 April 1862, the war would move to a new phase.[159] Unbeknownst to city residents, the Department of the Gulf was ready to wrest control of New Orleans from the Confederacy. Farragut was ordered to destroy the two forts guarding the Mississippi and then pass farther up the river toward New Orleans. Duncan had prepared Fort Jackson with over 630 men and seventy-five heavy cannons, and Fort St. Philip with nearly an equal number. Lovell's plan initially proved sound, as Farragut was hesitant to send his ships through the bombardment the two forts could create. For a few days, federal gunboats made demonstrations in front of the forts, and sharpshooters from both sides traded shots.[160] Lovell theorized that this exchange of fire would continue for

Artistic rendering of the Battle of New Orleans
(Library of Congress, Prints and Photographs Division)

a week or two before the U.S. Navy made a dash between the forts.[161] On 18 April—a little over a year after Beauregard's orders began the war—David Porter ordered his nineteen mortar schooners to begin shelling Fort Jackson in earnest, and with that order the Battle of New Orleans commenced.[162]

The navy bombarded the two forts that protected the entrance to the Mississippi River for days, typically starting at six in the morning and ending very late at night. An enslaved woman described how the cannons roared like thunder and produced smoke "thick and black as clouds."[163] One of the Union soldiers witnessing the shelling wrote, "The River seemed as if on fire for the firing was kept up night and day."[164] Another soldier thought the shells "looked like falling stars" as they hit the forts, and nearly all of the men in the flotilla believed they would quickly destroy the two forts.[165] They were in such high spirits that an officer with the Sanitary Commission expressed astonishment at "how much misery our soldiers will cheerfully endure," even as they occupied crowded transports that were under constant threat.[166]

Southerners in New Orleans had a different view of the bombardment. In a telegram that made it out of the city, one resident reported, "There has been a heavy continued bombardment of Fort Jackson all night. . . . The rebels in the fort represent themselves still cheerful, with an abiding faith in ultimate success." Lovell shared similar sentiments, expressing a belief that the forts and his men could hold out against the onslaught.[167] After a week, it seemed Lovell had a better summation of the situation: both forts were still standing, with Duncan reporting "little damage to us so far."[168] Confederate military leaders were putting all of their hopes in the forts because they knew that if the U.S. Navy made it to the city, there were not enough men or weapons to defend it.[169]

Farragut decided to go against the letter of his orders, and instead devised a plan to win the battle without destroying the forts protecting the river.[170] He determined that waiting until the forts were destroyed would not work because it could give the Confederate military enough time to further build defenses and give the shipwrights in New Orleans enough time to finish preparing the ironclad ships.[171] For these reasons, he decided to take the city as quickly as possible. While Porter and his mortars continued to rain down shells on the forts, Farragut ordered some of his men to cut the chain blocking his ships from going upriver.[172] The night of 24 April, Farragut's seventeen ships sailed through the crossfire of the two forts. Four did not make the trip due to damage, with one sinking to the bottom of the Mississippi, but the other thirteen successfully passed the forts. Farragut encountered the Confederate navy's vessels on the other side of the forts, but his superior warships easily dispatched them and even forced the Confederacy to scuttle its own ironclad in its first major battle. It was a victory for the flag officer as he sailed farther upriver.[173] News quickly reached New Orleans through the *Weekly Delta* that Farragut had maneuvered to "capture the city by avoiding the forts." However, residents of the city mistakenly believed there was "no serious cause for alarm," as the river batteries would stop him.[174]

As Farragut sailed past the forts, Butler was in the process of marching past them. Butler later criticized Farragut for leaving him behind while he sailed on to glory. Porter, likewise, was left to quell the forts that had originally been Farragut's charge.[175] The Department of the Gulf's ground forces were slowly moving across the swamps behind Fort St. Philip, wading through "mud and water up under our arms all the way," according to George Davis.[176] One of Butler's men reported to his parents that they passed by dozens of homes with no defense structures to block their paths. Some of Butler's forces reached Quarantine Station, a small defensive position located near the forts where many southern soldiers' wives and children stationed. It consisted only of two hospitals, a small cottage, and a brick warehouse, but to the men in

Forts St. Philip and Jackson, it was a vital location.[177] Positioned twelve miles behind the fort, Butler waited for Farragut and Porter's bombardment to cease so his men would not accidently be exposed to friendly fire. Butler assumed the commander did not think an attack over land was possible, because they faced no obstacles or defenses during their approach to the fort. Thus, he was easily able to cut off "all supplies, information, or succor" while his ground forces prepared their assault.[178]

While Butler and Porter maneuvered to take the forts, Farragut continued toward New Orleans. Many southerners thought that bypassing the forts meant little, since Lovell had months to prepare for an attack. The *Charleston Mercury* asserted that those months of preparation meant that Lovell "had ample time, and unstinted means, to complete the defences of the river, and he doubtless appreciates the importance of the stake involved in the security of the great Crescent City." Knowing this, the author wrote, "We presume, therefore, that the Forts which have been passed, and which are fully one hundred miles below New Orleans, form but the first of a chain of well-constructed defences, which must be encountered and reduced by the enemy, before he can reach the city."[179] However, the chain of defenses many hoped for did not exist. Two batteries attempted to fire upon Farragut's flotilla, but this display was more for show than an actual attempt to stop U.S. forces. A sailor who witnessed these events wrote, "None of those above Forts Jackson and St. Philip detained the fleet over 15 minutes. The rebels fled at first fire."[180] Lovell complained that it was a "want of discipline, system, and training" that resulted in inadequate defenses, failing to take responsibility for his own role in disciplining and training the men under his command. He later described the obstacles and chains he had attempted to fix along the river as having been swept away by high water, which allowed for ease of passage.[181] One war correspondent who saw what occurred characterized the situation differently, writing, "At the moment it was announced that the ships had passed the forts, it became evident to all reflecting persons that the city was defenseless."[182] By the afternoon of 25 April, Farragut was prepared to demand the submission of New Orleans, and Monroe was forced to admit that the city was "without means of defense and utterly destitute" before the Union forces.[183]

As Butler maneuvered by land and Porter by water, Farragut began the proceedings to liberate New Orleans from Confederate control. Newspapers in the city reported on the "Hostile Fleet" and waited for the communication from Farragut to reach the mayor.[184] But Farragut ran into an obstacle: his troop ships could not pass the forts, and until Butler arrived with his ground forces, he did not have the means to land and occupy a city as large as New Orleans. One of his lieutenants wrote, "We may be in a tight fix now, if the forts do not fall, and it is not safe for any one to leave our ships and go anywhere in a boat."[185] Lovell, sensing he could stall, met with Farragut's emissaries and declared that "he would not surrender the city, nor allow it to be surrendered . . . that he intended to fight them on land as long as he could muster a soldier." To discourage Farragut from shelling the city, Lovell warned that this would endanger women and children.[186] However, the bluff could only stand as long as Farragut did not have the means to fight on land.

The Union had a stroke of luck, because the Confederate soldiers defending the forts thought the battle was already lost. Conscripts in both forts, especially immigrants who were forced into service, were agitating to leave and protect their families in Quarantine Station and the city, but Duncan was determined to maintain his position, correctly believing that they could sustain defense of the forts. The defenders' remonstrations reached their apex on the evening of 27 April when dozens of soldiers in Fort Jackson "fell into line on the parade plein, under command of their Sergeants, with loaded muskets," according to a captain present. After being ordered to stand down, the leaders declared "they would fight no longer."[187] It seemed the majority of the men were on the side of the mutineers. The members of only one company sided with their officers, but the mutiny's leaders had apparently anticipated such an event, having already raised the drawbridge that would have allowed those outside the fort to assist their commanding officer. The events occurred so quickly that Duncan later reported, "The officers were helpless and powerless to act."[188] Realizing they were outnumbered and unprepared for such an event, the officers in Fort Jackson were compelled to let 250 to 300 of their men leave the fort. Others chose to stay, but only on the promise that they could leave when they wanted. These events had a demoralizing effect, and by the next morning Duncan realized none of the soldiers in either fort would continue fighting. By the afternoon of the 28th, he met with Porter to discuss the terms of his surrender.[189] Butler and Porter sent forces into Fort Jackson to accept Duncan's surrender, and shortly after occupying the forts, supply and troop ships under Porter's command met up with Farragut's forces stationed outside of the city. Butler was surprised to find both forts nearly undamaged despite the days' long attacks, and he believed with minor repairs his men could reinforce both forts and defend the river.[190]

With both forts pacified, New Orleans under threat of naval bombardment, and Butler's ground forces moving toward the city, Lovell and Monroe had a decision to make: fight or flee. Initially, they wanted to defend the city. They first attempted to form defensive lines with the intention that if Farragut attempted to invade, they could repel him. Lewis even found some obsolete muskets and a little ammunition and issued them to the Native Guards. Lewis finally gave Colonel Ogden a real order for the Native Guards: they were charged with guarding Esplanade on the east end of the French Quarter.[191] However, once news reached Monroe and Lovell that the rest of the Union's forces had passed by both forts, they realized their defenses were moot. Monroe ordered Lovell to evacuate the city, hoping they could save its inhabitants from a prolonged battle; however, Monroe also likely knew that his underequipped militia was filled with European immigrants who could mutiny like the men at the forts who were forced into service.[192] Lovell prioritized getting his men and weapons out of the city, evacuating them and their supplies to Camp Moore eighty miles north. He decided to abandon the militia units and civilians to the U.S. military. Residents of the city were informed through various papers, "In the presence of an overwhelming force of the enemy, it has become impossible to make anything like a practical or effective resistance," and they were warned against even small acts of violence that could lead to the destruction of the city by the U.S. Navy.[193] Butler later chose to leave the fleeing Confederates alone to a certain degree, believing that if he let "his men stay unmolested at Camp Moore . . . they are melting away faster than we could kill them," a statement Butler later regretted.[194] On 29 April, Union forces began moving in to take possession of the city, and the Battle of New Orleans concluded. As Lovell's men scurried away from the city, Butler's men moved in, effectively cutting the Confederacy into two.[195]

Shortly before editors at the *New York Times* received news of the Confederacy's capitulation, the paper reported, "With a hundred gun and mortarboats riding high above the city, ready to pour down upon it a torrent of fire and iron, it would be madness for the rebels to dream of any other terms than unconditional surrender." The war correspondent wrote, "Thus, by this splendid stroke of our river navy, we see not only the fall of the Southern Metropolis, but also a moral and territorial gain for the National cause," a victory that—once news reached the ears of Confederate soldiers—would "complete [their] demoralization." The writer proved prophetic in two regards: he was correct in surmising the terms of surrender the mayor would be forced to accept, and he also knew that "there can be no prospect to the rebels of recapturing the city," a statement that remained true for the remainder of the war.[196] The *New York Herald* reported that Union troops had retaken possession of the arsenal the rebels had taken in January 1861, but the arsenal was less valuable than it had been, as the Confederacy had distributed many of the arms.[197]

Meanwhile, the Native Guards experienced a combination of abandonment and exultation at finally being free of southern control. When members of the southern military and militia evacuated the city, the men of the Native Guards chose to stay behind with the mutineers and others who no longer wanted to show support for the South.[198] They refused to offer assistance when Lovell asked Lewis to supply men to carry goods for the military withdrawal.[199] The free Black men in the regiments made it clear that they did not support Monroe, Moore, or Confederate rule. Nearly a year later, Captain Rey invoked the American flag, exclaiming, "Beautiful starry banner, thy majestic folds finally extend over us!" As he recalled, "The regiment of Native Guards have seen the whole rebel army fleeing shamefully, leaving their women and children to the mercy of the victors." He went on, "When the gunboats came opposite the city, Gen. Lewis, pale and wasted, addressed our worthy ex-Colonel: 'Retire, immediately, young men; hide your arms and uniforms, otherwise you are lost.'"[200] Colonel Ogden ordered his men to lay down their arms and hide them until given further orders. The soldiers followed their colonel's final order and hid their muskets in Economy Hall, Claiborne Hall, and in the Marie C. Couvent School for Orphans.[201] Then, they waited to see what Union control would bring to New Orleans.

The Native Guards had not figured prominently in the city's defense because Louisiana was benighted by planters in the state government who wanted to maintain white control and black inferiority. It makes sense, then, that, when given the chance, the men in the regiments did nothing to support the Confederacy. After the war, congressional inquisitors were convinced that the only loyal inhabitants of the state were free Black and Creole people because of their actions in the aftermath of the Union arrival.[202] Those same actions set the stage for the establishment of the first Black regiments in the U.S. Army during the war.

Chapter 3

# *THEY WILL BE LOYAL*

## BUTLER, PHELPS, AND THE LOUISIANA NATIVE GUARDS IN THE U.S. ARMY

A question plagued the nation going into 1862: "What shall we do with the Negroe? However we may attempt to blind ourselves to his question, ignore it, pretend not to see it, suppress it, or put it away from us, like an evil to be shunned and avoided as long as possible, it is the most intrusive interrogatory that has met us since the war commenced."[1] As the two sides entered the new year, both had already come to a tentative answer to this question. The *Daily Green Mountain Freeman* applauded the federal government for employing formerly enslaved people as paid laborers in the U.S. Army in some areas. However, the paper—like many antislavery presses—pushed the government to do more. The Confederacy, too, found ways to use African Americans to aid in their war effort outside of military service. For both sides, the question of what to do with African Americans loomed large during the second year of the American Civil War, and the final answer, for the U.S. Army at least, came from an experiment in New Orleans.

The following chapter examines three distinct points during the summer of 1862: how the white and Black populace of New Orleans reacted to federal control, the complex motivations of Generals Benjamin Butler and John Phelps, and ultimately, how the combination of these factors, including military exigencies, created a scenario that demanded the constitution of the Louisiana Native Guards in the Volunteer Forces of the U.S. Army. This chapter demonstrates that there was no single impetus for the Native Guards; rather, multiple factors plagued Major General Butler and the U.S. Army in the Gulf, and the confluence of events set the stage for the federal government to allow Butler to enroll Black regiments on the U.S. Army rolls. The Black men of New Orleans latched onto the situation, and in doing so, they were able to prove their loyalty.

General Butler issued a proclamation on 1 May 1862 declaring New Orleans liberated from Confederate control. He depicted the Department of the Gulf as having rescued New Orleans from foreign control and occupation, and his men were the liberators—not conquerors. Butler issued his first general order that day, an order intended to set the tone of what it meant for the Union to control the city. In it, he declared martial law until the full restoration of municipal authority, granting himself and his men full authority over all public and private business in the city. All military arms were to be surrendered to the U.S. Army, and citizens were to renounce the Confederacy and swear allegiance to the U.S. government. Meanwhile, Butler suspended *habeas corpus*, censored telegraphs and newspapers to prevent intelligence from leaking to the rest of the South, made it clear that the economy was now under federal control, suspended all taxes except those that were used to support the federal government or were required to keep the city operating, and declared that federal law would be enforced at all times. The order also gave the army full authority to use military courts to punish anyone who interfered with their operations, a capability Butler used often during his term in the city.[2] He also attempted to placate residents of the city by letting them know that "all rights of property of whatever kind, will be held inviolate, subject only to the laws of the United States." This decision sustained slavery, since it was still legal per federal law.[3] While Butler allowed Monroe to operate the city government, General Order No. 1 made it clear that Butler and the military were in charge. Soon, Butler appointed the commander of his 3d Brigade, General George Shepley, as military commandant of the city.[4] With that, all military hostilities in the city ceased. However, that did not mean the region was quelled.

M. Honzeau, a Belgian citizen who fled New Orleans when it was discovered that he was an abolitionist, published two letters demonstrating the horrors that transpired as the Union approached the city. In a letter dated 13 May 1862, he wrote, "New Orleans is taken. Well, you who live far away cannot comprehend the delirium this has raised. Before surrendering it, the planters burned their cotton, their sugar, their steam cotton-presses and their refineries. They preferred this to confiscation and the thought that their goods would enrich their enemies." Honzeau continued, outlining atrocities: "But—shame and crime unparalleled—they also burned their slaves. Think of the degree of insane fury to which they were carried. They preferred to burn their slaves rather than to see them emancipated. Those who committed this atrocity—unparalleled in history particularly, because it did not hurt their enemies—those who did this deed called their inoffensive blacks together, and sent them into the work-shops and locked the doors; the fire was lighted and quickly did its work, while the masters waited outside to shoot with their rifles the child, the old man, the woman, or any who might leap from the window or roof to escape the dreadful flames." Honzeau took one solace from their suffering: "This revolution will in time be regarded as the great feature of modern history, not only because it hastens the freeing of American slaves, but because it furnishes the most wonderful example of social monomania—a furious monomania contracted under a long influence of the very spirit of despotism and pride."[5]

Honzeau's account demonstrated to everyone who read it that the true battle for New Orleans had just begun, as now the U.S. Army had to win over—or at least attempt to win over—the region's inhabitants while holding a large city with few men.

Many things changed in New Orleans once it was under Union control. First, all Confederate militias and home guards were ordered to disband, including the Native Guards. Second, food and clean water were in short supply, and sickness was already spreading through the city due to summer heat and

*General Butler Holding the Mob in Check at New Orleans* (1896), by Charles Stanley Reinhart (Library of Congress, Prints and Photographs Division)

sanitation issues, so the U.S. Army had to act to address these issues. Third, to the planters' dismay, thousands of enslaved people around the city abandoned their plantations. The situation resulted in a labor shortage that exacerbated the food shortage. Butler had to address all of these issues. This included taking steps to bridge the gap between two fractured societies, as Lincoln wanted to test the Reconstruction policies he was planning in New Orleans. Additionally, Butler had to navigate complicated relationships between Unionists and rebels in the city to truly bring it under his control. He was up to the task, but his methods left him with the moniker "the beast," a harsh label referring to his efforts to quell rowdiness. Soldiers who had been compelled to join the Native Guards laid down their arms on 1 May and prepared for life under Union control and the possibility that they, too, could be of use to Butler and the army.

The liberation of New Orleans transformed the city and exposed the true feelings of many of its residents. Some appreciated the military as a liberating force, while others jeered and even attacked soldiers on the streets. Members of Black society were ecstatic when the Union took the city in part because the federal government had recently freed all enslaved people in the District of Columbia, so many looked to the federal army as a liberation force. Henry Rey, like many Unionists of color, was hopeful that the return of the American flag would mean an improvement in circumstances for the city and its people. Madame Loreta Velasquez, a free woman of color, was among those who gained respect for the federal government once she no longer had to worry about the New Orleans vigilance committee arresting her.[6] Butler reported that all Confederate forces had fled the area within days of liberating the city, but that there were still a number of "various rebel secret associations" in the city plaguing the army with harassment and threats of murder.[7] Mansfield Lovell asked for authority to organize a guerrilla unit to attack the Union army, with the intention of causing turmoil.[8] Some men answered the call and even organized into companies while on parole in the city, and they were captured and sentenced to death for attempting to cause strife, though Butler commuted their sentences to imprisonment on Ship Island instead.[9] These events demonstrated that insubordination would be met with force.

Louis Charles Roudanez, a prominent African American doctor in New Orleans, took advantage of the arrival of the U.S. Army. Born to refugees of the Haitian Revolution in 1823, he received his medical training in France at the prestigious Faculté de Médecine before returning to the United States and earning a second medical degree from Dartmouth College in 1856. After graduating, he returned to Louisiana, where he established and operated a successful medical practice in New Orleans that treated both Blacks and whites. Dr. Roudanez was the embodiment of nearly everything that whites in New Orleans feared: he was highly educated and wealthy, and he had international connections that ensured his voice was heard. With the arrival of the military, Dr. Roudanez—like many African Americans—felt he could finally express his Unionist beliefs. He joined his brother, Jean-Baptiste, and a friend, Paul Trévigne, to establish the newspaper *L'Union* in New Orleans. They were backed by multiple supporters in the African American community, including Blanc F. Joubert, John Racquet Clay, Joseph Tinchant, and Francis Dumas, some of whom eventually went on to join the Native Guards.[10] Because its editors knew that many of their fellow African Americans were educated and had international connections, the paper was published almost exclusively in French. The first issue was published in September 1862, and from its inception, *L'Union* was a paper meant to bolster and publicize Black excellence in the city.[11] A war correspondent from the *New York Times* wrote about the groundbreaking newspaper, "There has recently been started a paper here called *L'Union.* It has a large circulation among certain of the creole population, and is liberally patronized by the people of mixed blood. My attention has been called to it by several persons. Some were *surprised* that such a sheet should be published in New Orleans; others again were *horrified.* I must confess I read some articles in its columns with astonishment."[12] This reported white horror reflected the broad realization that free People of Color could use their voices to uplift and inform one another.[13]

All of the officers from the Native Guards were ordered to lay down their arms, after which a few of the Black line officers approached the U.S. Army regarding service in the military. Captains Henry Rey, Edgar Davis, and Charles Sauvenet, along with Lieutenants Eugene Rapp and Octave Rey, asked to meet with Butler to surrender their arms, to discuss the terms of their surrender, and to inquire about the service of the Native Guards.[14] The officers asked Butler as early as May if they could join the U.S. Army, promising that if he agreed they would produce a ready regiment of men who were already drilled and knowledgeable in military affairs. There is no official account of this meeting, but it is apparent that Butler did not give an affirmative answer. Soon afterward, he wrote to Secretary of War Edwin Stanton that he was hesitant to use the Native Guards, writing that he hoped "that this war will be ended before any body of negroes could be organized, armed, and drilled so as to be effective."[15] Despite the rejection, soon after that first meeting, Charles

St. Manat—a former officer in the Native Guards—began working for the Union provost court as a translator of Spanish, French, and German, a position he held for many months.[16] Like St. Manat, many men who had served in the regiment went on to work in the Department of the Gulf.

Butler later testified to the American Freedmen's Inquiry Commission that during their meeting he asked Captain Sauvenet, "How came you, free colored men, fighting here for the Confederacy—fighting for slavery?" This is a question that many who learned about the Native Guards asked of the men who served. Sauvenet's reply echoed many soldiers' answer to that question: "We could not help it. If we had not volunteered they would have forced us into the ranks, and we would have been suspected. We have property and rights here, and there is every reason why we should take care of ourselves."[17] Charles Gibbons, one of the men who had served in the unit, testified after the war that they all feared that, if they did not join, their lives and property would be in jeopardy. He stated, "Without arms and ammunition, or any means of self-defense, the condition and position of *our* people were extremely perilous."[18] On a separate occasion, Gibbons said, "When summoned to volunteer in the defence of the State and city against Northern invasion, situated as we were, could we do otherwise than heed the warning, and volunteer in defence of New Orleans? Could we have adopted a better policy?"[19] However, many African American men would go on to regret that decision, even if they had little choice in the matter.

Governor Moore loved to boast about the Native Guards to show that the Civil War was not solely about slavery. But the men were not treated like real contributors to the war effort: they were not authorized any weapons, clothes, or rations for their service, and they had to use their own resources if they wished to furnish any of the expected trappings of a military unit. Sauvenet later informed Butler that, before the city's capture, the Native Guards had drilled but were not allowed muskets or bayonets, which Butler took to mean that "they would not let them have arms, whether because they were afraid to trust them, or because they did not have the arms to give them."[20] Both were true.

With the arrival of the U.S. Army, these fears abated, and many Black New Orleanians felt they had a real choice in which side they would support going forward. Union soldiers and officials who had been serving in the Department of the Gulf when the Union took the city recognized that many of the city's defenders—even the white ones—had been involuntarily forced into service, and the federal military's policy was to release them on their own recognizance. The majority of those released chose to align themselves with the liberating army.[21] Within days of Butler's arrival, Confederate general Johnson K. Duncan described how many of the men who had once defended the city had "enlisted with the enemy."[22]

During the U.S. Army's occupation of the city, Confederate forces in the region began to revolt against Lovell and Duncan, having realized that the entire area was now under federal control. U.S. soldiers stationed at the Quarantine Station were ordered to let any Confederate soldier who approached their lines enter if he gave the oath of allegiance to the Union. Former Confederate soldiers and allies who took the offer were given jobs rebuilding Fort Jackson and allowed to enter New Orleans.[23] Desertion rates skyrocketed among the South's forces, and Butler later mused that "more than half" of Lovell's men had returned to the city in civilian clothes acting as Unionists.[24] Many conscripted immigrants who had served in the forts volunteered to fight for the U.S. Army once given the chance.[25] Some of the city's inhabitants thought the only reason the U.S. Navy refrained from shelling the city was the presence of Unionist immigrants who would have died in the attack.[26] Within a month, Moore characterized the feelings of the city's residents to Jefferson Davis as follows: "Dormant disloyalty has awakened with the disaster that brings our enemy so near, and the murmers of the suffering mingle with the complaints of the mercenary, the taunts of the disorganizers, and the whispered tones of treason."[27] This sector of Unionists existed largely unseen in New Orleans.

Meanwhile, the outlook was bleak for non-Unionists. The War Department had received reports of a complete "reverse of the war," and now the fledging southern confederation was also threatened by a lack of supplies from its largest city.[28] Many southerners believed the federal military would start arresting everyone, and some feared a revolt of enslaved people was imminent. Clara Solomon summarized the feelings of many white citizens of the city: "Who can penetrate into the unknown future? Who can remove the veil in which a kind Providence had enfolded it? And would anyone have the desire to do so? Do we desire to prepare ourselves for coming events? I answer 'no.'"[29]

As Butler settled into his new command, the War Department began taking steps to bring all of Louisiana under federal control. To that end, on 2 June 1862, Brigadier General George Foster Shepley was appointed military governor of Louisiana. Shepley had a background in law and politics, having served as the U.S. attorney for Maine in 1848 and again in 1853 until the war began. While Shepley was the military governor of the state, he worked for the War Department, where he reported to Butler as a liaison between the depart-

General George Foster Shepley (National Archives and Records Administration)

ment and the people of Louisiana. He held that position until January 1864. With Shepley and Butler in command, Lincoln decided it was time to lift the blockade around New Orleans and South Carolina's Beaufort and Port Royal in "the interest of commerce."[30] Salmon P. Chase, the famed abolitionist and secretary of the treasury, added that even the consuls of New Orleans could resume trade once they proved they were not operating for the Confederacy.[31]

As military commander of New Orleans, Butler could have both a hard and soft touch when dealing with those in his charge. Many southerners viewed him as a despot, but Butler saw himself as a man who gave chances to everyone, allowing them to choose their own path. He believed the war was about slavery and aristocracy even while others insisted that it could be fought without acknowledging those facts. To his soldiers, he could be self-sacrificing, even giving money and supplies to the quartermaster to ensure his men were taken care of properly.[32] During his time in New Orleans, Butler wrote to Secretary Stanton, "In fact, this rebellion was at first inaugurated for the purpose of establishing a landed aristocracy as against the poor and middling whites, who had shown some disposition to assert their equality with the planter, and

*The Starving People of New Orleans Fed by the United States Military Authorities* (*Harper's Weekly*, June 14, 1862)

had begun to express themselves through organizations and on the basis of the Masonic Order into societies, of which the South is full."[33]

In that same letter, Butler took responsibility for protecting those whom he saw as victims in the war, writing, "The question of how to feed the people of this City and the surrounding country becomes of the utmost magnitude, and to it I have given the best exertions."[34] George Denison, the customs collector for the government, and Chase's cousin, wrote to his mother early in July that "thousands in this city are almost starving for food, and well dressed men and women beg for bread (frequently) from Uncle Sam's boys, to keep themselves and children from starving."[35] Butler went as far as to work with the governor of Louisiana to provide provisions for Confederate citizens, and after that proved inadequate, he issued Special Order No. 166 to relieve "the great distress now existing in New Orleans." The order allowed the military to purchase enough food to feed everyone in the city and to provide shelter for refugees, most of whom were enslaved people who had recently freed themselves.[36] By September, Butler reported that his commissary was distributing over $50,000 per month in food, supplies, and money to the white residents of the city, and that they were distributing double that amount to African Americans.[37] Pierre Beauregard theorized that any military force compelled to feed and care for the inhabitants of New Orleans would over-burden their supply lines.[38] The Department of the Gulf proved this theory wrong.[39]

Another issue for Butler was that the city's poor sanitation and warm climate allowed disease to spread widely. The Union's Sanitary Commission found it difficult to purchase food and water for the sick because of the city's economic circumstances, and many of the city's surgeons had already used what little medicine they had to treat soldiers who had gotten sick on Ship Island.[40] Doctors such as Charles Roudanez were still struggling to get supplies into the city even though the U.S. Army was there with new supply lines. Federal soldiers regularly became sick, and their convalescence took time and personnel away from the military. One soldier told his family he was "quite sick [with] very severe pains in the head, back and in fact all over" for over two weeks because of dirty quarters and sanitation. He blamed his illness—and that of others—on "vermin of all kinds" and the city's water and climate.[41] Another soldier complained that many of his fellow comrades were sick due to the constant rain, "very poor grub," and unclean fortifications.[42] Per usual, African Americans suffered even more, contending with white city residents and soldiers taking first dibs on the few supplies available during the first few months of liberation.

One of Butler's first actions was to ameliorate the sanitation issues and curtail yellow fever in the region. Within a month of his efforts, John Guild, a U.S. soldier who had served in the department since its constitution, exaggerated to his mother that they had nearly eliminated yellow fever in the city.[43] By July, Guild described his health as "excellent" thanks to the general's efforts.[44] Eventually, the arrival of additional supplies allowed for improvements in health among African Americans, too.

Overall, officers and soldiers serving in the Department of the Gulf treated the few truly pro-Union southerners well. Men who had once served in the Native Guards returned to the lives they'd led before the war, reopening many of the businesses that they had been forced to close because of the blockade. Prominent men, both Black and white, applied to Butler and Lincoln for appointments in the new regime, knowing they would be well received for their support.[45] Even some of the more recalcitrant citizens admitted that Butler's rule over the city was "very lenient." Butler's detractors and proponents both knew his goals were to reestablish business in the city, employ any who needed jobs, and even feed the starving people who had been affected by the Union blockade.[46] In a letter to a Confederate general about the guerrillas that the South used to target innocents in the war, Butler summarized his approach to the city: "That I punish the guilty marauders with promptness, the women and children of New Orleans, who sleep in calm, undisturbed quiet under our flag, will tell you; that I deal generously with my enemies a thousand and nineteen families of Confederate soldiers now being fed from my rations will testify." He ended the message with a directive toward his enemy: "That I will take care of, protect and avenge the wrongs and lives of my fellow-soldiers confided to my care you as a soldier can judge."[47]

In response to women in the city openly disrespecting him and his men, even spitting on officers in public, Butler issued his most infamous order, General Order No. 28,[48] which moved to ensure that women respected Union soldiers.[49] The order stated that "when any female shall, by word, gesture or movement, insult or show contempt for any officer or solder . . . she shall be regarded and held liable to be treated as a woman of the town plying her avocation."[50] In the parlance of the time, this meant Butler's men could treat women of high social standing as though they were sex workers if they insulted or abused the soldiers first. This did not give his men the right to physically or sexually abuse women; according to Butler, however, it did give them the opportunity to "pass her by unheeded" and if they became a nuisance afterward then they could be arrested and charged.[51] To southern women, Butler's order legalized the highest level of disrespect, but to Butler the rule was an appropriate solution to the behavior some women showed his men. One woman questioned, "Can a woman, a Southern woman, come in contact with one of them and allow her countenance to retain its wanted composure?"[52]

"The Ladies of New Orleans" before and after General Butler's famous proclamation (*Harper's Weekly*, July 12, 1862)

Many people disagreed with the order. Monroe attempted to take advantage of the situation to rile up men in the city and stage a coup, going as far as asking the French government to invade the city to help his people in response.[53] After Monroe's efforts failed, Butler removed Monroe from office and imprisoned him for a time. After his release, Monroe was not allowed back in office for the remainder of the war.[54] Even President Lincoln thought the order went too far, but Butler described to Lincoln multiple examples of women disrespecting Union soldiers.[55] Lincoln eventually saw the merits of the order upon seeing the results. As one naval officer wrote in his diary, there was a marked difference among the women after Butler issued the order.[56] Butler later wrote that "these she-adders of New Orleans themselves were at once shamed into propriety of conduct by the order, and from that day no woman has either insulted or annoyed my line soldiers or officers, and of a certainty no soldier has insulted any woman."[57]

Butler also focused his attention on ensuring that Blacks and Creoles in the city would support the U.S. Army. From the beginning of Union liberation, white New Orleanians had feared that the northern military would spur an insurrection among formerly enslaved people.[58] U.S. captain John William De Forest wrote to his wife, "As to the Negroes, they are all on our side."[59] Union officers regularly permitted enslaved people to run to federal lines for freedom, angering many white citizens in the city. One white woman recorded in her diary, "Should one of mine [run away], I would inflict severe punishment, & should discard them for ever." Despite the dangers, thousands fled to Union lines for freedom and employment alongside white volunteers, posing a challenge to the Union's military, which fed and clothed many of the refugees. For example, on 1 July, the provost marshal of the 12th Connecticut Volunteer Infantry Regiment reported over seven hundred "contrabands" in his camp drawing daily rations, and they still had to feed soldiers and their families in the follower's camp as well.[60] Families like that of Frances Doby followed the U.S. Army on their approach up the Mississippi to New Orleans, but unfortunately for Frances, her mother did not survive the journey after drinking contaminated water from a canteen.[61]

Butler wrote to the president, as he had done before, to ask for guidance about how to handle the fugitive African Americans so as not to violate presidential policy, and Stanton and the president agreed with Butler that "under the law of Congress, they cannot be sent back to their masters; that in common humanity they must not be permitted to suffer for want of food, shelter, or other necessaries of life." Stanton told Butler that he could employ people who fled to their lines after escaping slavery, but that he could not free enslaved in the region because the president had not yet made a decision about emancipation.[62] This was something Stanton did not need to worry about, as Butler still believed that only Blacks could labor in the climate of New Orleans, and he intended to use Black labor even if he had to induce them into the fields.

When Butler organized what he called "a force of several thousand Louisiana Volunteers," a regiment filled primarily with white immigrants, he made sure there were formerly enslaved laborers in their midst earning their pay, and that their families could utilize the commissary and quartermaster resources as needed.[63] Dozens of white-presenting enslaved people and freemen joined these early units.[64] For example, because of his light complexion, P. B. S. Pinchback was able to enlist in the 1st Louisiana Volunteer Infantry Regiment with other immigrants and Creoles of Color. Many Creole men in the Gulf did this without the knowledge of federal officials.[65] By September, the department reported nearly five thousand troops raised for service in the U.S. Army.[66] However, there were no Black regiments in the army yet. The closest to active service were men such as St. Manat, who was vital to Butler's administrative work in the transnational city, and men like Pinchback, who lied about their heritage to join.

P. B. S. Pinchback
(Library of Congress, Prints and Photographs Division)

Black women found work as well, working as nurses, hospital orderlies, seamstresses, maids, washerwomen, and cooks in and near Union camps. For example, the 12th Connecticut Volunteer Infantry Regiment employed over forty women within weeks of the army's arrival in the city.[67] Many U.S. soldiers bragged to their families about how easy their life was with formerly enslaved people to do the menial work soldiers often sought to avoid.[68] However, work in Union camps could be hazardous for Black women, as many white soldiers treated them with violence and disrespect based on generations of racism, sexism, and southern propaganda.[69] By August, the Department of the Gulf reported that over three thousand refugees, both white and Black, were working in their lines and repairing the city.[70]

Assisting the U.S. Army did not protect Black people from federal troops, who often mistreated People of Color in their own camps. A letter republished in the *National Anti-Slavery Standard* recounted how African Americans in Union lines were often treated. The author wrote, "The situation of the poor, unhappy blacks in this department, fed though they are by Union bounty. . . . are treated with great sternness and severity, amounting to positive cruelty, by many of our soldiers, who seem to regard them as hardly better than beasts."[71] The soldier who sent in the letter continued, "Not a few of our officers, I regret to write it, conduct themselves in the most unfeeling manner, toward these unfortunate creatures; and are, in fact, ostentatious in expressing their hatred and contempt of the 'damned nigger.' It is a sad truth that the Northern pro-slavery prejudice, where it exists, is much more harsh and intolerant than the traditional feeling . . . entertained by the native Southerner." The writer compared the enslaved to Native Americans and others who looked to men like Columbus and Ponce de Leon as saviors before being destroyed, expressing hope that Black soldiers in the Union would not find themselves in a similar position.

When the Department of the Gulf accepted African Americans into service, Butler had no policy regarding payment, and so pay was left up to unit commanders and those in charge of the refugees. While many were paid some small fee, or at least fed and clothed for their efforts, many worked for nothing. Some people in this position noted its resemblance to enslavement. Meanwhile, some white soldiers thought African Americans preferred this system so long as their families were fed and given a cot to sleep on.[72] Dozens of formerly enslaved people agitated for wages for months, and eventually Butler was forced to establish a policy regarding payment for labor. He even gave orders to clothe Black laborers, but due to shortages they were not always issued their clothing. Learning he had to pay enslaved laborers was a lesson Butler would not forget; during the rest of his tenure in New Orleans, he ensured that even enslaved people on plantations were paid wages for fear of what they may do if not treated well.[73] When the *New Orleans Daily Picayune* got word that the general had started paying African Americans wages for labor and wanted planters to do the same, the paper expressed the same sentiments that had led to the war: "The two great staples of the South—cotton and sugar—can only be profitably raised by the negro, and by him, *ex necessitate rei,* in a condition of servitude."[74] The belief that only Black people could profitably raise cotton and sugar was something Butler was not wholly against, as his actions showed during the summer of 1862; however, he demanded that they be paid or planters would have to forfeit their land to the military.

A curious consequence of the Department of the Gulf's taking in and paying refugees was the creation of a labor shortage in the region. Thousands of formerly enslaved men and women stopped working for their former masters, going on to work instead for the government or military. As a result, the economy of New Orleans came to depend on immigrant labor to a certain degree, as immigrants stepped in to fill roles once performed by enslaved men and women for wages. This shift led many men who had once looked to military service as a good source of income to seek other jobs that had not been available a few months prior. This situation was exacerbated, according to Butler, by "guerrillas [who] interfere with all white labor which would be peaceable and impress it into the rebel Army."[75] Eventually, the enemy soldiers in the region resorted to using cavalry units to scour the countryside and force able-bodied men into the southern military.[76] Thus, the Department of the Gulf experienced a shortage of white soldiers because so many were choosing to work for wages elsewhere instead of risking their lives for a cause they felt ambivalent about—and the relatively small number of men who were eligible and willing to join the Union were often compelled to fight for the Confederacy instead.

While the department employed thousands of African Americans, it did not have the resources to employ all who ran to the army, and Unionists worried about how to maintain the economy of the region should all enslaved people flee to Union lines. This situation led to a controversy that made even abolitionists question Butler and Union policy. After consulting with the president of the Jefferson Parish Police Jury, Butler ordered all enslaved people who were not employed as laborers to be removed from his lines, "leaving them subject to the ordinary laws of the community."[77] Butler's order intentionally left all enslaved people who were turned away from Union lines in a precarious position. It gave the police justification to arrest and return enslaved people to their enslavers in the region, leading hundreds to be recaptured and forced back into enslavement under the protection of the federal army.

Despite some of his controversial orders, Butler proved on a few occasions that the Department of the Gulf was there to elevate African Americans. In one case, the enslaved daughter of Mr. Landry, a supposedly respectable white merchant, fled to the U.S. Army after Landry beat her so severely she was near death. Butler was horrified to see her badly beaten body, and when Landry confirmed that the enslaved girl was also his own daughter, Butler was so incensed that he waited until the following day to punish Landry for fear he would go too far. Butler decided to free Landry's daughter and required her father and former master to pay her $1,000 with a promise never to interact with her again. The officers serving Butler followed his lead, treating enslaved people as equals and people, and in the middle of a court proceeding they inadvertently made Blacks legally equal to whites for a time: when a Black man was called to the stand during a trial, the opposing counsel told the major overseeing the court that "by the laws of Louisiana, a negro can not testify against a white man." However, the major asked, had Louisiana left the Union? The reply of "yes" gave the major the opportunity to declare, "Let the man be sworn!" thus making them equal before the law until Louisiana was governed by civil authorities again.[78]

White men in the region widely disapproved of Blacks being elevated to their level, and they often verbally and physically attacked the Union soldiers and enslaved people. One paper in nearby Shreveport touted that if New Orleans were attacked, aid for rebellion would be provided from within.[79] The paper further reported, "The Guerillas, with the exception of New Orleans and its immediate vicinity, now have the entire possession of the State of Louisiana." Their destruction, the paper reported, was rampant: "Its once fair fields are fast becoming a desolation, and its once happy people either utterly impoverished, or with this end, have not the melancholy privilege of occupying their desolated homes, but are refugees and know not where to lay their heads. New Orleans is full of people from Baton Rouge, from Donaldsonville, indeed, from all the towns on the river, people who two years ago were independent and happy, but are now penniless, and unable, by former education, to earn a living." The author went on that, in New Orleans, "The suffering among this class of persons no one can imagine, and many heart-broken and helplessly wretched are finding peace only in a pauper's grave." Commentators held that these circumstances arose because "robbers and cut-throats" had been "elevated into belligerents, and treated with consideration when they should be hung or shot like dogs."[80] Butler hoped that by limiting the weapons that were available, the Department of the Gulf could curtail efforts to arm guerrillas. Thus, on 14 August 1862, he told his officers they could confiscate the arms of any suspected rebel and free their enslaved people since they were traitors to the United States.[81] Two days later, he made it clear with General Order No. 60 that anyone found with a weapon was a rebel, and all property, including enslaved people, would be forfeited.[82]

Enslaved people aided the government in this endeavor, with one antislavery newspaper reporting, "Gen. Butler's order, that he would emancipate any slave who would expose any one who had concealed weapons, put a detective policeman in every house, and there cannot be a doubt but that some masters have suffered by their slaves finding weapons which they—the slaves—first hid away." In one instance, an enslaved man considered by his enslaver to be "a faithful servant, whom he trusted as he would his own wife or child," conspired with two additional servants and turned in their enslaver in a bid to free themselves and get their former master arrested.[83] Men who would later join the Native Guards turned in employers and enslavers for hoarding pistols, sabers, knives, and even specie for bounties.[84] Efforts to emancipate themselves through direct action or military presence led to complaints of insubordination on many plantations near New Orleans. The guerrillas even attempted to drive off the enslaved who refused to work. Within months of federal intervention, northern papers reported that "Planters' families [were] in a deplorable condition," as the people they enslaved were "almost in a state of revolt."[85] The public discourse in Louisiana suggested that Butler was essentially employing "every negro servant in the city" as a detective to root out Confederate sympathizers, according to a letter writer in the city.[86] Antislavery papers reported that the U.S. Army realized "everywhere the American General receives his most useful and reliable information from the Negro, who hails his coming as the harbinger of Freedom."[87] However, General Butler refused to take the drastic step of freeing every enslaved person under his command, still following the directive from Edwin Stanton.

Many of the troops in the Department of the Gulf disagreed with their general's order not to liberate all enslaved people, not purely because of their disdain for slavery but because they hated planters and Confederate soldiers who arrived at their encampments and made demands upon Union troops. Over time, soldiers in the federal army started to think like Private Jonathan

Allen, who "saw enough of the horrors of slavery to make me an Abolitionist forever."[88] Martin Williston informed his sister that serving in Louisiana and witnessing enslavement had given him the moral courage to become an abolitionist and ensure the Union ended the institution for all.[89] Another soldier wrote that Union soldiers gave "every reasonable aid to any colored brother" who escaped to their lines.[90] A chaplain of the 13th Connecticut Volunteer Regiment wrote to the editor of the *New York Times* that over two hundred enslaved people approached their lines begging for work despite the general's efforts to push them away. He recounted that one mother went from room to room telling them, "Take my children, if I must go back to suffer." Over a hundred of that group found work, but the rest were returned to a cruel fate with "dread, sorrow, and despair" written on their faces as they waited for their enslavers to pick them up at the customhouse or left the camp for the wilderness to live as maroons.[91]

In another instance, over a hundred people escaping slavery armed themselves with cane knives and went to the city. There, the police attempted to arrest them, and in the fight many were injured and killed on both sides—primarily the enslaved, as they lacked the experience, skill, and guns the police had. Only eleven members of the group escaped recapture, but when they made it to the army's camp, the troops hid them instead of turning them over, showing some solidarity.[92] There were many other instances of troops in the department issuing fraudulent work papers or hiding enslaved people whom they encountered. However, there were also instances where troops engaged against runaways, like the police, resulting in casualties to the military in an attempt to reinforce the same system of slavery that started the war. It was a time of conflict that the commanding general needed to resolve before the powder keg met a spark. One of Butler's top generals decided to light that match.

Brigadier General John Wolcott Phelps was described as a "tall, middle aged, stooping awkward looking man" by his soldiers, who thought he was quick-witted and swore like a man who had served in the military for nearly all of his adult life.[93] Born 13 November 1813 in Guilford Center, Vermont, he had all of the education and sophistication one would expect of a New England elite, and his graduation from West Point in 1836 meant he had the military training needed to become an officer. He served in the Seminole Wars and on the western frontier, rising to the rank of captain in the Regular Army. He resigned his commission in 1859 because he did not want to serve in the Mexican War, as he believed the war's only purpose was to increase slave territory for the South.[94] When the Civil War began, Phelps volunteered to serve

General John W. Phelps (Courtesy of the Guilford Historical Society)

once again. Described as one of Vermont's "earnest slavery-hating soldiers," he was appointed to a colonelcy in the Vermont volunteers before working his way up to brigadier general, a rank he obtained on Butler's recommendation.[95] In his correspondence recommending Phelps, Butler recognized his "deep religious enthusiasm upon the subject of slavery" as an ostracizing factor between Phelps and the rest of his men, but Butler also acknowledged that Phelps was a warrior who would "fight the battles of the North."[96] His leadership style was inspirational to many of his men; one lieutenant who served under him for a few months wrote, "There was not a man who would not have risked his own life to save that of Colonel Phelps."[97] General Butler personally wrote to the secretary of war to request that Phelps serve in his command because of his experience and skill.[98] Butler later trusted Phelps so much that he tasked Phelps with gathering and training many of the soldiers on Ship Island, and Phelps was the military commander on the ground who first took control of Forts St. Philip and Jackson.[99]

Phelps was an ardent abolitionist who believed that slavery was a moral ill, and he wanted to use his position to free enslaved people when possible. However, he did not support rights for African Americans completely, initially advocating—like Lincoln—for colonization and against suffrage for African Americans. But he was an advocate for women's education, believed that slavery needed to end, and sought the destruction of the Confederacy, and to that end, he acted independently of orders and sought to bring about his chief goal of ending slavery as quickly as possible. His men first witnessed this commitment when they arrived on Ship Island. On 4 December 1861, Phelps issued what many referred to as the "Phelps Emancipation Proclamation," which had no legal force but was meant to make it clear to his superiors, his men, and, most importantly, "the loyal citizens of the South-West" that he would fight to end slavery wherever he could. Stating "the motives and principles by which my command will be governed," Phelps argued that any slave state in the Union since the adoption of the Constitution was "in direct violation of that constitution."[100] He went on to trace the history of slavery and argued that it was antithetical to progress. Millions of enslaved people in the South would soon be free, he wrote, and poor whites would not want to replace them. Thus, a new form of labor needed to be introduced to save both Blacks and whites from planters. He made it clear that his command would push for free labor, the destruction of the Confederacy, the end of slavery, and equal working rights for any who engaged in noble labor. His simple motto was, "FREE LABOR AND WORKINGMEN'S RIGHTS."[101] The proclamation created the first schism between Butler and Phelps; Butler immediately distanced himself from the order, making it clear to their superiors that he had not suggested or authorized it.[102]

Phelps further proved his convictions as commander of Camp Parapet, a military camp about sixteen miles up the river from New Orleans, near Carrollton. There, he welcomed all enslaved people in his area of operation in a bid to end what he believed to be an exploitative labor system. He later wrote, "I found myself in the midst of slave region, where the institution existed in all its pride and gloom, and where its victims needed no inducement from me to seek the protection of our flag." After seeing "large numbers of enslaved" who were "loaded with chains and barbarous irons; some bleeding with bird-shot wounds; many . . . deeply scored with lashes," Phelps ordered his men to take direct action.[103] He went as far as ordering his soldiers to go to the plantations of planters who mistreated the people they enslaved, and if those soldiers happened to encourage enslaved individuals to seek freedom in his lines, he allowed them refuge without question. When planters sought redress for escapees, he offered no assistance and politely asked them to leave his camp.[104] He was so keen on welcoming African Americans to his outpost that his own officers complained, "They are coming into camp by the hundreds and are a costly curse. They should be kept out or set to work, or freed or colonized, or sunk or something." They further argued that the high number of Black people was a detriment to the army and their resources.[105] One of his men complained to Butler that Phelps was liberating any enslaved person who was punished even if they deserved it, and that he was using his position to welcome hundreds of undeserving refugees who should be working on a Louisiana plantation.[106] Nonetheless, Phelps continued to welcome people, seeing them as refugees rather than contraband, even after Butler ordered him to exclude all unemployed citizens, African Americans and whites alike, from the camp. He even wrote to Butler that they should raise fifty regiments of African Americans to prepare them for liberty and "prevent the necessity of retrenching our liberties, as we should do by a large army exclusively of whites."[107] Butler ignored the suggestion, but Phelps proved a hard man to ignore.

Phelps was among the first in Butler's command to push the general to make a decision about what to do with enslaved people. Early in the occupation, as enslaved individuals gathered around Camp Parapet, Phelps received a report that a large planter in the area, Mr. LaBlanche, was telling the people he enslaved to leave his plantation for Parapet or face his lash. Soon, over 150 enslaved people from his plantation had gathered around the camp, and Phelps ordered the plantation searched for weapons, contraband of war, and any signs the owner was aiding the rebellion.[108] Phelps wrote to Butler regarding the situation: "The whip, the chains, the stocks, and imprisonment are no mere fancies here; they are used to any extent to which the imagination of civilized man may reach." Phelps believed the situation demonstrated "the proper result of the conflict is the manumission of the slave." Further arguing to his commanding general, he wrote, "It is clear that the public good requires slavery to be abolished"; he continued, "it is evident that some plan, some policy, or some system is necessary on the part of the government" to aid the enslaved that flee to their lines.[109]

When Butler asked the neighbors about LaBlanche, they reported him to be "a humane man" who supported the Union. While LaBlanche claimed he did not approve "the 'exodus' of his negroes" to Butler, he did not seem as if he cared about recovering them. However, when Butler reported the situation to Stanton, he wrote what he thought was actually occurring: "Gen. Phelps, I believe, intends making this a test case for the policy of the government. I wish it might be so, for the difference of our action upon this subject is a source of trouble."[110] Indeed, their differences did create trouble, as Butler believed he should work in line with the government's policy and Phelps believed he should use his position to free the enslaved. One thing was now clear to Phelps: people escaping slavery to join Union lines would have to serve in the military to secure their freedom.[111]

Prior to orders from Shepley, Butler, or even Lincoln, Phelps began drilling and training the men from LaBlanche's plantation who were willing and able to serve in the military. Many other enslaved men near Camp Parapet joined as well, and in short order Phelps had nearly a full regiment of men forming lines. He personally drilled some of the men who had emancipated themselves and escaped to his lines, swearing while he instructed them on the finer points of military bearing and drill. Emile Detiége—a free man of color who had been educated on military drill by his uncle, a Belgian soldier who served under Napoleon—volunteered at the camp to help drill and train these forming units. Detiége also used his extensive knowledge to teach the men how to read and write, hoping they could be more than laborers after the war, making him the first teacher for many of the formerly enslaved soldiers.[112] Perhaps because of Detiége's connection to Phelps and the camp, the general's decision to emancipate and train the formerly enslaved was reportedly published extensively in Belgium.[113] By mid-June, Phelps had organized three hundred African Americans into five companies, and he petitioned Butler to allow him to enlist them in the army. While awaiting Butler's decision, Phelps sent over a hundred of them to Fort Jackson to train in the artillery arts with General Neal Dow. Even Dow was impressed with how quickly the men learned and with their eagerness to fight for the Union and their own freedom.[114]

General Dow played his own part in securing freedom for hundreds of enslaved men and women during his tenure in the Department of the Gulf. Like Phelps, Dow believed that slavery was morally wrong, and he petitioned Butler to act. Without orders to do so, Dow wrote freedom papers for enslaved people who asked for them, and his actions emboldened some to go back to their former enslavers and demand money and their personal property on the threat that Dow and his men would come to the plantation. One such white man complained to the military governor, Brigadier General George Shepley, who was more receptive to such complaints than Butler, but even that mattered little; Dow's actions were not against military policy since he did not make a blanket declaration like John Frémont had a year prior.[115] Some of the men whom Dow freed later made their way to Parapet to join the army.

Many of the men Phelps trained had successful careers in the military. A few of the men traveled to Vermont with members of Phelps's staff, and when the opportunity arose in 1863, they joined the 54th Massachusetts Volunteer Infantry Regiment, the first African American regiment raised in the North.[116]

Similar situations occurred for a few men who fled to Union lines. George Ellis was too young to serve in Phelps's unit when he fled to the camp, so he worked as a servant for one of the officers in the department. When that unit left the area, Ellis followed them back to Massachusetts, and once he was old enough, he joined the 55th Massachusetts in January 1865.[117] Octave Johnson took a more typical route toward Union military service. He escaped his enslaver in 1862 and hid in the woods for months as a maroon, hunting game and trading the meat for cornmeal with enslaved people on plantations. At one point, over twenty hounds were chasing him, and he and his group had to kill eight of them. They barely escaped the rest. Eventually he made it to Camp Parapet and found employment in the commissary's office before undergoing training to join the infantry in Louisiana.[118] Overall, Phelps was instrumental in training hundreds of men who eventually joined the U.S. Army when the time came.

On 17 July 1862, Congress passed Public Law No. 160—often referred to as the Second Confiscation Act—which stated, "The president of the United States is authorized to employ as many persons of African descent as he may deem necessary and proper for the suppression of this rebellion, and for this purpose he may organize and use them in such manner as he may judge best for public use."[119] Henry Wilson, one of the Republicans pushing the measure, pointed out that Black men had served in the American Revolution and that they had been significant in repelling the British during the Battle of New Orleans decades prior.[120] Abolitionists like Phelps took this new law to mean the president authorized African American troops immediately, especially since he was arming the same men from New Orleans about whom Wilson had spoken when he authored the bill. However, Phelps chose to ignore the president's clarification that Black men were to be used as laborers "for military and naval purposes."[121] On 30 July, Phelps wrote to Butler requesting "arms, accoutrements, clothing, camp and garrison equipage, etc., for three Regiments of Africans." Phelps informed Butler that he had already started to form units, telling his commanding general, "They are willing to submit to anything rather than slavery." Butler and even the president later echoed his argument for their use: "Society in the South seems to be on the points of dissolution, and the best way of preventing the African from becoming instruments in a general state of anarchy is to enlist him in the cause of the Republic." Phelps further stated, "It is for the interest of the South as well as for the North that the African should be permitted to offer his block for the Temple of Freedom."[122] With that, Phelps set the stage for testing the Union's policy on bringing Black men into the military.

The Confederacy took reports that Phelps was arming and training African American soldiers seriously, after having ignored the celebrated home guards of New Orleans a year prior. Southern generals reported that the U.S. Army, specifically Phelps, was arming Black soldiers for the infantry. Some of these reports grossly exaggerated the numbers of men serving, with one attesting that Phelps had over four thousand men.[123] One paper dubbed Phelps "one of the most ultra of abolitionists" for his actions, calling for his arrest.[124] Robert Lee wrote to Union major general Henry Halleck soon after he received the reports. Lee believed that Phelps, building upon the example set by Major General David Hunter, was arming and training enslaved men around New Orleans to "murder their masters" and initiate "a servile war, which is worse than that of the savage, inasmuch that it superadds other horrors to the indiscriminate slaughter of all ages, sexes, and conditions." Lee believed these "atrocities" were "punishable by all laws, human and divine," if true.[125] Thankfully for Phelps and for the Union, Lee's beliefs were not a deciding factor in the course of the war.

Northern readers soon became aware of Phelps's movements, and a writer for the *New York Journal of Commerce* summarized the views of many who disagreed with Phelps and with congressmen who allowed men like Phelps to employ African Americans for "any military service." The writer presented six key reasons against arming the formerly enslaved. First, the United States was more civilized than the British, who armed African Americans and Native Americans, and, according to the author, the nation should strive to be better than Europe. Second, "The American government is a white man's government," and thus only white men should defend the nation. Third, "the organization of blacks into regiments or any other military order, is a step and a long step toward negro equality." The writer acknowledged that this step had been taken during the Revolutionary War and argued that it was a mistake that had been corrected soon after the war. Fourth, the plan was too dangerous because African American soldiers could kill any white man they chose and white men were too prejudiced to work well with blacks in the military. Fifth, abolitionists were too liberal to fight, so the anti-abolitionists who filled the ranks would leave because they had nothing to fight for. And, finally, if the North armed the enslaved, the South could do the same at a rate of ten to one, expanding the Confederate army well beyond what the Union could field.[126]

The journal's statement concluded: "If we adopt this plan of arming slaves to fight their masters, history will record it as a step towards barbarism, precisely as it so records the English arming of North American Indians. It will be such a step. It will be a bid for murder, rapine, and horrors in the slave States. . . . It will debilitate our forces by introducing a weak and untrustworthy element into our armies." Most fearful of all, the paper summarized, "It is designed and will be hereafter used as an argument for, and a step toward the equality of the negro with the white race."[127] Conservative northerners went on to regurgitate these same arguments.

In contrast, the *National Anti-Slavery Standard* published editorials expounding on the capabilities of African American soldiers. In one, written from the testimony of a defeated French soldier who had fought in the French Republican Army to bring St. Domingue back under French control, he testified that "blacks fought well." He observed that the "mulattoes" were fierce due to their understanding of European battle tactics and their willingness to keep their army in the field, where they were most effective. Even formerly enslaved people, "half naked, with musket and sabre," proved to be disciplined soldiers willing to fight until the end. The writer believed that the *esprit de corps* and fighting spirit that these soldiers demonstrated proved "that blacks will go with enthusiasm wherever they are led, by whites or men of their own color, provided their steps never point again in the direction of slavery. Their stolid indifference vanishes when they have once got rid of the restraint of tyranny; they willingly incur the restraints of freedom to preserve their new position towards mankind."[128] Liberal northerners, especially African Americans with social standing, were wholly in support of testing whether Black men would fight as well as they had during the Haitian Revolution against the southern aristocracy.

The nation was divided over the question of whether these actions were prudent or not. Many northerners were happy to accept African Americans as labors and teamsters, but the idea of armed Black men serving in the military terrified many in the Union nearly as much as it did southerners.[129] Captain De Forest reported to his wife that he—and many of his fellow officers—had begun to accept the idea of Black soldiers after seeing how they drilled and trained for military life.[130] Conversely, Major General Lewis Wallace stated in a speech that an African American man "would be a poor soldier, in my opinion, who would fail to use every element of war which God Almighty gave him, if he could use it to his advantage." However, he was more than willing to use formerly enslaved laborers to make his soldiers comfortable, and he even called for every brigade to include a company of Black men who could act as personal servants and do menial tasks and build fortifications.[131]

Butler had already made it clear to Department of the Gulf officials that he believed a similar plan would work best for the army. Not all in the army were against the idea, as another major general held the belief that Black men "are acclimated to the South, and can endure the miasmas that would prove fatal to the soldiers of the North. They are strong, and many of them are intelligent. They may be more safely trusted with arms than the whiskey-drinking and quarrelsome rebel forces; and are eager to prove their gratitude for the benefits which freedom, brought to them under the shadow of our flag, has given them." Therefore, at best, Black soldiers were considered for garrison duty, and, at worst, they were considered for labor duty in order to relieve white soldiers.[132] Racist views like these followed the Black soldiers of New Orleans for many years.

Butler was aware of this strong sentiment in the North, cautioning Phelps against his actions and ordering him—and others in the Department of the Gulf—to employ formerly enslaved people only as laborers in the department's theater. Some applauded Butler for this order, with a war correspondent writing this was the right answer to "the negro question," as his order would "put aside the insanity on both sides of the contraband question and use negroes where they will be most useful."[133] However, upon receipt of those instructions, Phelps had a decision to make: follow orders or fight for what he believed to be right, even if many disagreed with him.[134]

General Phelps wrote that he refused "to become the mere slave driver" who only used the forming regiments to prepare the camps.[135] As hundreds continued toward Parapet for their "divine appointment" in the U.S. Army, Phelps had to decide how he would react.[136] He made it clear to his commanding officer that he was "willing to prepare African regiments for the defense of the government against its assailants," but he refused to use the men for labor and fatigue duty as ordered.[137] He even threatened to resign should Butler force the issue. Butler wrote to the secretary of war that Phelps's threat of resignation was a resignation letter, and that "his letter of resignation has left me no choice but insist that my order should be obeyed."[138] Butler wrote to Phelps, "I am somewhat surprised to receive your resignation." Then, demonstrating his legal mind, he steered the conversation away from their disagreement and toward military matters, writing, "Because of an order to do this necessary thing, to protect your front threatened by the enemy, you tender your resignation and ask for immediate leave of absence." Butler went on to point out that much of the fatigue work he requested was done by white soldiers, noting that "the soldiers of the Army of the Potomac did this very thing last summer in front of Arlington Heights. Are Negroes any better than they?"[139] Butler ordered Phelps to use his companies for labor duty to protect the camp from guerrilla attacks, and while Butler told the general that he did not accept his resignation, he was already preparing to remove Phelps from command.

Butler sent two friends, Christian Roselius and George Shepley, to the capitol to discuss the matter in person, and they conspired to accept Phelps's resignation so Butler could be free of the nuisance. There, Shepley petitioned both Stanton and Lincoln regarding more men, Phelps, and what they phrased "the negro question."[140] There were promises of sending over fifteen thousand additional troops to New Orleans, but they would take months to constitute and mobilize. Phelps's resignation was brought up again, and his refusal of orders did not bear well for his case; however, the War Department was not prepared to accept his resignation yet. African Americans could surmise that policymakers would side with Butler.

Salmon P. Chase wrote to Butler encouraging him to go further on the issue of slavery and side with Phelps, stating, "We must either abandon the attempt to retain the Gulf states in the Union or we must give freedom to every slave within their limits." Chase argued, "Military emancipation in the Gulf States will settle or largely contribute to settle the negro question in the free states." After the full abolition of slavery, Chase called for his friend to employ "colored soldiers to the defence of the Union," as Phelps had already begun to do. In time, Lincoln came to see the value in Phelps's actions and offered a solution: "They . . . know how to be cured of General Phelps. Remove the necessity of his presence." Lincoln repeated the overtures he'd made a year earlier to simply end the war, emphasizing that if the southern states surrendered, the Union would refrain from interfering with slavery; however, he also cautioned, "What I *cannot* do of course I *will* not do; but it may as well be understood, once for all, that I shall not surrender this game leaving any available card unplayed."[141] Lincoln's offer was once again dismissed, and in the coming weeks he made good on his threat to use every available means to bring the state back under control.

While Butler opposed the institution of slavery, he was not one to defy orders or suffer those who went against his. He wrote to Stanton, "Gen. Phelps, without orders and without my knowledge, has organized five companies of Negroes, and the first official information I had of his doings in that behalf was a requisition for arms and equipments."[142] He further wrote to the secretary that he believed African Americans would be poor soldiers, as they were "horrified of firearms."[143] Butler also wrote to Phelps, "By act of Congress, as I understand it, the President of the United States alone has the authority to employ Africans in arms as part of the Military forces of the United States," a reference to Public Law 160. Butler informed Phelps that, as of 2 August, "Every law up to this time, raising volunteer or militia forces, has been opposed to their employment. The President has not as yet indicated his purpose to employ the Africans in arms." After Stanton's response to his previous letter, he clarified that "the arms, clothing, and camp equipage which I have here for Louisiana Volunteers, is, by the letter of the Secretary of War, expressly limited to white soldiers, so that I have no authority to divert them however much I may desire so to do."[144] In private, Butler phrased the situation differently to his wife: "Phelps has gone crazy. He is organizing the negroes into regiments, and wants me to arm them."[145]

Butler's reaction ran counter to many of his decisions prior to the capture of New Orleans. As the man who created the contraband policy for the Union, he demonstrated for many months that he was willing to defy orders if he thought he was making the right decision. He demonstrated this in his approach to punishing women who showed disrespect to Union soldiers in New Orleans, and even in how he divulged plans for capturing the city to those from whom he needed counsel. Denison believed that the true cause of Butler's rift with Phelps was a product of the recognition that Phelps was receiving for standing by his principles; Denison wrote to Chase that Butler wanted the credit for himself, and he refused to agree with Phelps due to jealousy.[146]

Upon receipt of Butler's official correspondence, Phelps did not agree with his assessment of the situation, nor with the orders from Stanton, and he demanded to resign his commission. He wrote to his commanding officer, "It can be of little consequence to me as to what kind of slavery I am to be subjected, whether to African slavery or to that which you thus so offensively propose for me, giving me an order wholly opposed to my convictions of right, as well as of the higher scale of public necessities in the case, and insisting upon my complying with it faithfully and diligently, allowing me no room to escape with my convictions or my principles, at any sacrifice that I may make." Phelps went on, "I cannot submit to either kind of slavery, and cannot, therefore, for a double reason, comply with your order of the 31st of July, in complying with which I should submit to both kinds—both to African slavery and to that to which you resort in its defence."[147] It seemed Phelps had made up his mind that this action would define his career or end it.

Soon after this communication, Phelps sent his letter of resignation directly to the adjutant general of the U.S. Army, General Lorenzo Thomas, writing, "Finding it impossible to serve in this Department without doing violence to my convictions of right and public necessity, I respectfully tender you the resignation of my commission as an officer of the army of the United States, and request as early an acknowledgment of its acceptance as conveniently possible." Phelps also informed Thomas that he had "six hundred able-bodied men in camp," and that, by combining them with those "suffering uselessly in the prisons and jails of New Orleans and vicinity," he could easily raise "a good regiment of one thousand men, who might contribute as much to the preservation of law and good order as a regiment of Caucasians, and probably much more."[148] Thomas did not act on Phelps's suggestion, and the general's resignation was the only part of the letter to which he responded, effectively ending Phelps's career in the military through the process.[149]

Phelps's strong abolitionist convictions prohibited him from acting against what he believed was right.[150] His threats of resignation and public refusal to follow Butler's orders led President Lincoln to accept the resignation that Butler had pushed up the chain of command for Phelps. Lincoln had already made the decision to recall Phelps even if he did not resign, thanks to the efforts of Shepley and Roselius.[151] On 21 August, the War Department officially accepted Phelps's resignation—one day before Butler issued General Orders No. 63, the order that constituted the Native Guards.

There were civilians in New Orleans who wanted the federal government to abolish the barbaric business of slavery and follow Phelps's lead. One correspondent in the city wrote of the "abominations of the slave system" that remained well into Union occupation.[152] They had a solution, however: "Does the United States want recruits? It can have them by the thousand in this city at twenty-four hours' notice. Let the word go out that every able-bodied man of any color will be received as a soldier, and I verily believe a regiment of excellent recruits could be raised in three hours. Tough, strong, acclimated, accustomed to scanty clothing and fare, they would also possess a stimulus to exertion which the white soldier does not." That stimulus was simply "the hope of liberty, which in all ages has been the chief inspiration of the brave in their most heroic struggles. Add to this still another motive, which the white soldier has not, the knowledge that if defeated and captured horrible scourging and barbarities will be inflicted on them by their masters." The correspondent went on, "Under such impulses the black soldiers, half of whom have white blood in them, would fight desperately. Many of them are of gigantic size. Many years of oppression and wrong rankle in their memories and goad them on." He wrote, "The rebels had regiments of blacks partly drilled in this city. One regiment was armed, and pikes of three or four different kinds and rough 'negro swords' were being manufactured for the others. There need be no decree of emancipation of the slaves of rebels; but let the commanding General invite all able-bodied men, of whatever complexion, to enlist, with a promise of protection, pay, food, and clothing." If this were accomplished, the correspondent reflected, "Louisiana would furnish ten regiments of hardy recruits in as many weeks if Gen. Butler would call for them."[153]

A turning point for Butler arrived during a written exchange with his wife, Sarah. Butler, despondent over the developing situation with his general, wrote to her, "The Government have sustained Phelps about the Negroes, and we shall have a negro insurrection here I fancy."[154] Her reply was simple and prophetic: "Phelps's policy prevails instead of yours. The abolitionists will have this a war to free the slaves at once if possible, nothing else is thought of. The Administration will assent to it just as fast and as far as the country will sustain it."[155] Sarah was right, as many abolitionists publicly called for the employment of African Americans as soldiers, with a northern paper pointing out Black soldiers' use in multiple past wars and noting that "individual instances of negro bravery are abundant, and we can see no reason why a fair degree of pluck should not be found in the masses of them, especially when the inspiration is liberty for themselves and their race."[156] Eventually, Phelps publicly proposed "a military organization of the negroes," which should be used to destroy the "despotic government" that enslaved them. A *New York Times* writer observed—like Sarah had—that Phelps was pushing for the right course, writing, "Whether he [Phelps] has hit upon the most practicable means of solving the problem which he sees so clearly, may, perhaps, be doubted. But we heartily commend to every thoughtful citizen the substance of the General's creed, that 'to ignore Slavery in the present crisis is but little less disastrous than Slavery itself.'" The writer concluded, "This truth has been acquired by Gen. PHELPS at no small cost to himself. We can only hope that the country may not have to pay a proportional price before learning it as thoroughly as he has done."[157]

While Butler was still making up his mind, an attack at Baton Rouge in August demonstrated that the Confederacy was still a formidable opponent. For months, Governor Moore had complained to the southern secretary of war that Louisiana did not have the men and supplies needed to fight back against Butler and the Department of the Gulf. To Moore, the only thing keeping the Union at bay was his militia, which periodically disrupted Union lines.[158] In turn, Butler—believing the troops at Camp Moore were disorganized and their morale broken—did not put enough effort into holding Baton Rouge.[159] Butler did not fully comprehend that Confederate general John C. Breckinridge had left Vicksburg for Camp Moore, and that at Camp Moore Breckinridge had reinforced the demoralized troops.[160] Additionally, Moore authorized his adjutant for the militia to conscript all available white males soon after they lost control of New Orleans, which further bolstered their ranks.[161] The following month, the military in the region had enough personnel and weapons to retake Baton Rouge from Butler's forces stationed there.[162] The attack on Baton Rouge was significant enough that the U.S. Army had to abandon the city for fear of losing all their troops and Union supporters.[163]

This made General Butler fear that, in the future, the Confederate army would attack his headquarters in New Orleans. Butler petitioned Stanton for reinforcements to protect New Orleans from a similar attack, and he let Stanton know that the Confederacy might destroy New Orleans if he did not receive at least a few thousand more men. Confederate leaders knew that if they caused enough destruction, Europe would intervene to protect its own citizens.[164] As a result of these circumstances, Butler feared that, if the Confederates had their way, the destruction of New Orleans could bring about the end of the war altogether. Initially the secretary of war promised to send reinforcements, but following another failed campaign by General George McClellan in the North, those reinforcements never came.[165] After that, the secretary directed Butler to recruit in New Orleans.[166] Worsening the situation, soon after the attack on Baton Rouge, the War Department expanded the Department of the Gulf to include West Florida. While this meant gaining a few more men, it also resulted in the acquisition of a much larger area of operations.[167] Before the end of the month, Butler realized he had to act.

In the interim, men in the former Native Guards heard about the dispute between generals Butler and Phelps. A small contingent of officers made their way to Camp Parapet and spoke with Phelps about officering the regiment he was forming, but Phelps told them he had already submitted his resignation, meaning that he had no authority to answer such a question. However, Phelps took the extraordinary step of encouraging the men to speak with Butler in hopes that they could convince him to do what his resignation could not. Phelps wrote to Butler, "Several parties of the free colored men of New Orleans have recently come to consult me on the propriety of raising one or two regiments of Volunteers from their class of the population for the defence of the Government and good order, and . . . I have recommended them to propose the measure to you, having no power to act upon it myself."[168] The officers left Camp Parapet with a hope that soon they would join the fight.

The former Black officers of the disbanded Native Guards attempted to meet with Butler early in the year, and that meeting did not end well for them. However, Charles St. Manat and other visitors to the general were able to convince him to take another meeting, even though he had supposedly already made up his mind on the question of using Black men in the military. The commission endorsed by Phelps was able to convince Butler that they could solve his personnel crisis while also saving the army's position in the city.

Butler met with Sauvenet again, along with many wealthy and educated members of the regiments. They petitioned for the right to join the military and to pursue their own professional needs. In part by invoking the large number of refugees who needed jobs in the city, they convinced the general of the merits of their service. In combination with new questions about the Confederacy's ability to take New Orleans, Butler felt he needed to have another group meeting with them in August. At that meeting, the officers gathered to affirm their allegiance to the Union and promised that many of their fellow free African Americans in the region would follow their lead if they were officered in the U.S. Army.[169] One of the group's leaders asked the general for confirmation that Black men could serve as officers, as they had done before. Butler replied, "Yes, every one of you who is fit to be an officer shall be, and all line officers shall be colored men."[170]

After promising to form at least two regiments, he said, "My officers, most of them, believe that Negroes won't fight." According to Butler, their reply was almost unanimous: "*Oh, but we will.*"[171] Butler later testified, "In color, nay also in conduct, they had much more the appearance of white gentlemen than some of those who have favored me with their presence claiming to be the chivalry of the South."[172] Their light skin, intelligence, and willingness to serve appealed to Butler and convinced him to reinforce his command with thousands of additional troops.[173] His hope of ending the war before Black men could serve proved ironic, as he was ultimately the man who called on their service, beginning an experiment that changed the very foundation of Louisiana.

Within days of receiving his wife's advice and consulting with the men that Phelps sent, Butler wrote to Stanton, "Indeed we are threatened with an attack on the City of New Orleans. I am not specially disturbed at that. If it becomes at all imminent, I shall call on Africa to intervene, and I do not think I shall call in vain."[174] He later clarified in his autobiography that he planned to use "*all* the colored troops I could from the free negroes."[175] Butler drew from the logic that the freemen had invoked during their meeting, writing to Stanton, "I have determined to use the services of the free colored men who were organized by the rebels into the 'Colored Brigade,' of which we have heard so much. They are free, they have been used by our enemies, whose mouths are shut, and they will be loyal."[176] The question now became how to enlist African Americans in the military without breaking the labor-only order that the president had declared and that Butler had endorsed.

Weakening the Confederacy was a slow and arduous process. Once Farragut passed Forts St. Philip and Jackson, it took months for Butler to gain control of the city. Combating starvation, disease, a rebellious populace, labor shortages, and foreign agents who supported the Confederacy, Butler had to contend with a number of actors who wished the U.S. Army harm. Like many white men, Butler thought little of Black soldiers by August 1862, and if not for labor shortages, Phelps's actions, the fall of Baton Rouge, his wife's insights, and officers who had served in the Native Guards, Butler may not have "called on Africa." The combination of all of these factors opened the door for Black men to serve in the U.S. Army *en masse.*

Chapter 4

# *HASTEN ALL, OUR BLOOD ONLY IS DEMANDED*

## CONSTITUTION AND RECRUITMENT

In 1861, the notoriously conservative *New York Herald* published a proslavery argument for not arming African Americans in the Civil War. Arguing that the abolitionists' plan would result in anarchy, the author wrote that if formerly enslaved people were armed—"raised to the dignity of soldiers, and mingled together in the same ranks with the brave native American, Irish and German patriots"—it would have a debilitating effect on the military. Even worse, to the author, would be Black officers commanding them into combat. "The name of soldier has, hitherto, been considered as identical with that of gentleman," the author wrote, implying that if formerly enslaved men earned that title then they would prove themselves equal to whites.[1] This was the nightmare of many white people prior to 1862. By the fall of that year, it became their new reality.

That new reality did not come without its trials, however, as the constitution and recruitment for the Louisiana Native Guards was a difficult one. The following chapter explores that complex process, and how it affected both the white and Black populace of New Orleans. Formerly enslaved Black men were supposedly barred from entry, women and children of the men who joined were targets of white society, and Black men in the military were treated unfairly by their superiors. It was a tumultuous time, and still, the men who joined were willing to do so with only the promise of blood and death for their sacrifice. That is what it meant to join the Native Guards, and every single person who volunteered would have gladly paid that price.

On 22 August 1862, General Benjamin Butler issued the Department of the Gulf General Orders No. 63, calling for free African Americans "to defend the Flag of their native country, as their fathers did under Jackson at Chalmette."[2] He invoked Governor Thomas Moore's 1861 order to constitute the

Native Guards: "On the 23d day of April, in the year eighteen hundred and sixty-one, at a public meeting of the free colored population of the city of New Orleans, a military organization, known as the 'Native Guards' (colored), had its existence, which military organization was duly and legally enrolled as a part of the militia of the State, its officers being commissioned by Thomas O. Moore, Governor and Commander-in-chief of the militia of the State of Louisiana." By acknowledging the regiment's legal existence, Butler justified reconstituting the regiments in the Department of the Gulf. It was an ingenious move on Butler's part because President Abraham Lincoln could not disband the regiment, as he had after previous attempts to arm Black soldiers, without superseding the authority of a legally elected governor. In a private letter to Secretary of the Treasury Salmon P. Chase (a famed abolitionist), his treasury agent in New Orleans, George Denison, informed him, "By accepting a regiment which had already been in Confederate Service, he [Butler] left no room for complaint (by Rebels) that the Government were arming the negroes."[3] The order constituted the regiments "in the Volunteer Service of the United States" and made it clear they "shall be duly organized by the appointment of proper officers, and accepted, paid, equipped, armed, and rationed as are other Volunteer Troops of the United States."[4] Butler gave directions for mustering the men and officers into the army, and, within weeks, the first African American soldiers fighting for the U.S. Army joined the fray. The editors of *L'Union* made it clear the purpose of the Native Guards was for Black men to fight and "Die for Freedom!"[5]

Butler directed all former members of the Native Guards to report to the Judah Touro Charity Building on Front Levee Street so they could be mus-

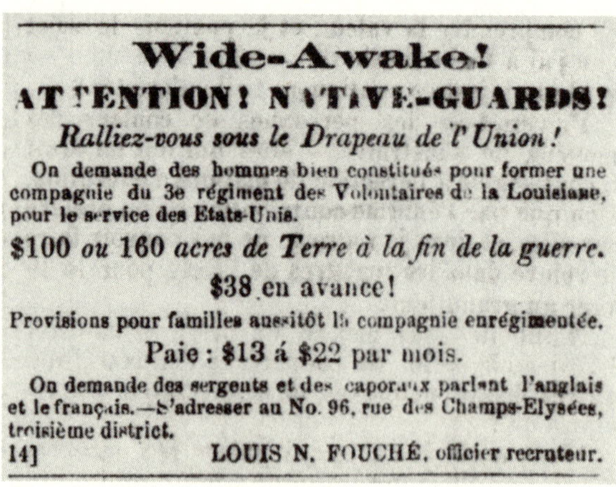


Native Guards' advertisement in *L'Union,* 18 October 1862 (Library of Congress, Prints and Photographs Division)

tered into federal service.[6] General Orders No. 63 promised the men they could expect treatment and pay equal to that received by white volunteers. To recently enslaved men, fighting for their freedom was a chance they could not wait for. The newly formed *L'Union* ran numerous advertisements for the Native Guards, informing readers that volunteers would receive a $38 advance for joining, and that enlisted men would be paid $13 a month, while officers would receive $22 a month. Arms and equipment would be provided for free, and upon the successful conclusion of the war, soldiers would receive $100 or 160 acres of land for their service.[7] According to the paper, within forty-eight hours of the order, over a hundred businesses and shops were shuttered in New Orleans as men rushed to join the U.S. Army.[8]

Within a week Butler reported to Secretary of War Edwin Stanton that he would have a full regiment over "1000 strong of Native Guards (Colored)."[9] The turnout was so great that the regiment was full within two weeks, and there were so many men that three additional infantry regiments of Native Guards were added as well. Butler kept his promise to use African Americans as line officers, captain and below; however, he selected white officers for the field grade ranks, major and above. All enlisted ranks—up to and including sergeant major—were Black men. These steps were groundbreaking because the federal government was still turning down other Black regiments at the time. Former senator Jim Lane attempted to constitute a similar regiment in Kansas, but because Kansas was a border state, Stanton turned down the offer and ordered Lane to demobilize the men.[10] Lane refused the order, but his unit was not accepted by the government or military until January 1863.[11] Because Louisiana was so far removed from the border states, there was little fear of losing additional states because of the Native Guards. Nevertheless, Major General Henry W. Halleck attempted to quell Butler's need to enlist so many men by informing him, "It is deemed of the greatest possible importance to hold New Orleans, and reinforcements will be sent as early as possible."[12] However, the Native Guards were already forming, and Butler asked Halleck for presidential permission to sustain the regiments he was prepared to field.[13] Halleck later told Butler, "The whole matter was left to the judgement and discretion of the department commander."[14] This meant that Butler could do what he pleased, and with that response nothing could stop the Native Guards from growing.

On paper, the regiments were only supposed to enlist Creole men who were free prior to the war. Butler even wrote to Halleck, "I have kept clear of the vexed question of arming the slaves."[15] Lincoln had made it clear that

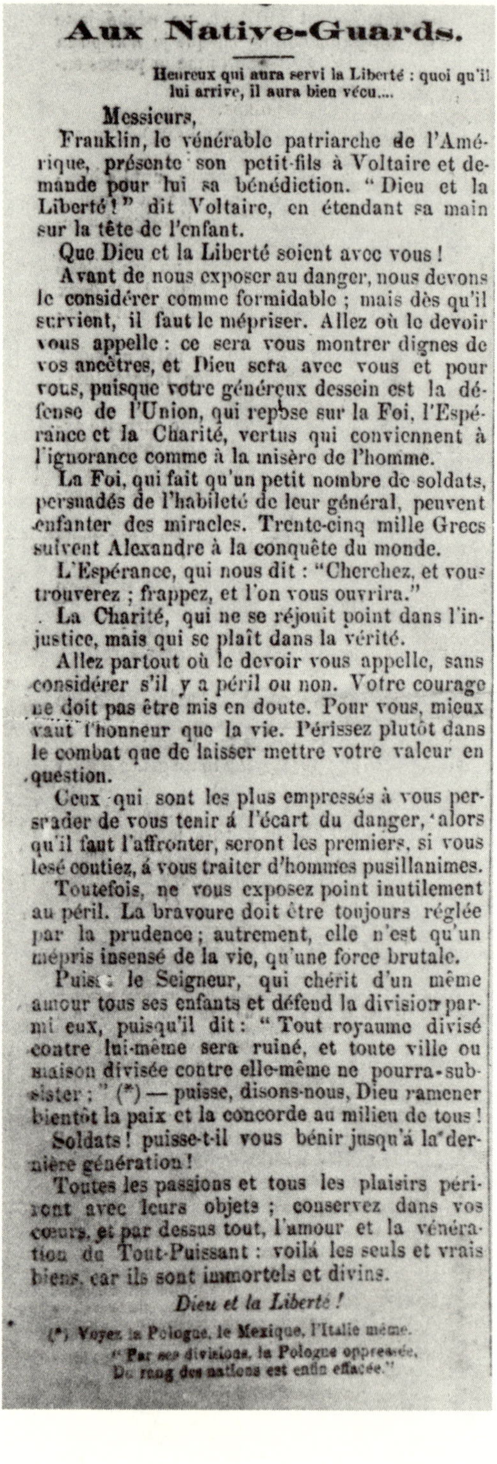

## Aux Native-Guards.

**Heureux qui aura servi la Liberté : quoi qu'il lui arrive, il aura bien vécu....**

**Messieurs,**

Franklin, le vénérable patriarche de l'Amérique, présente son petit-fils à Voltaire et demande pour lui sa bénédiction. "Dieu et la Liberté!" dit Voltaire, en étendant sa main sur la tête de l'enfant.

Que Dieu et la Liberté soient avec vous!

Avant de nous exposer au danger, nous devons le considérer comme formidable ; mais dès qu'il survient, il faut le mépriser. Allez où le devoir vous appelle : ce sera vous montrer dignes de vos ancêtres, et Dieu sera avec vous et pour vous, puisque votre généreux dessein est la défense de l'Union, qui repose sur la Foi, l'Espérance et la Charité, vertus qui conviennent à l'ignorance comme à la misère de l'homme.

La Foi, qui fait qu'un petit nombre de soldats, persuadés de l'habileté de leur général, peuvent enfanter des miracles. Trente-cinq mille Grecs suivent Alexandre à la conquête du monde.

L'Espérance, qui nous dit : "Cherchez, et vous trouverez ; frappez, et l'on vous ouvrira."

La Charité, qui ne se réjouit point dans l'injustice, mais qui se plaît dans la vérité.

Allez partout où le devoir vous appelle, sans considérer s'il y a péril ou non. Votre courage ne doit pas être mis en doute. Pour vous, mieux vaut l'honneur que la vie. Périssez plutôt dans le combat que de laisser mettre votre valeur en question.

Ceux qui sont les plus empressés à vous persuader de vous tenir á l'écart du danger, alors qu'il faut l'affronter, seront les premiers, si vous lesé coutiez, á vous traiter d'hommes pusillanimes.

Toutefois, ne vous exposez point inutilement au péril. La bravoure doit être toujours réglée par la prudence ; autrement, elle n'est qu'un mépris insensé de la vie, qu'une force brutale.

Puisse le Seigneur, qui chérit d'un même amour tous ses enfants et défend la division parmi eux, puisqu'il dit : "Tout royaume divisé contre lui-même sera ruiné, et toute ville ou maison divisée contre elle-même ne pourra subsister ; " (*) — puisse, disons-nous, Dieu ramener bientôt la paix et la concorde au milieu de tous! Soldats! puisse-t-il vous bénir jusqu'á la dernière génération!

Toutes les passions et tous les plaisirs périront avec leurs objets ; conservez dans vos cœurs, et par dessus tout, l'amour et la vénération du Tout-Puissant : voilá les seuls et vrais biens, car ils sont immortels et divins.

*Dieu et la Liberté!*

(*) Voyez la Pologne, le Mexique, l'Italie même.
"Par ses divisions, la Pologne oppressée,
Du rang des nations est enfin effacée."

Notice to the Native Guards, *L'Union*, 8 October 1862 (Library of Congress, Prints and Photographs Division) generals were not to purposely interfere with slavery at this point in the war, declaring, "No man must be enlisted who has failed to obtain his freedom through some recognized legal channel."[16] However, Butler and his officers enlisted many Black men—even those who had clearly escaped slavery—as laborers, farmers, and the like. A few months prior, Butler had also told his provost marshal that when he encountered recently enslaved individuals whose enslavers had told them to "go to the Yankees" to avoid feeding them, the provost marshal should treat those people as "manumitted and emancipated."[17] Additionally, some officers, such as General Neal Dow, were still issuing papers of emancipation to any who asked. Thus, multiple avenues toward legal freedom had emerged, and Butler could argue—if questioned—that the soldiers in the Native Guards had been legally emancipated. The situation allowed hundreds of formerly enslaved men to join the army a month before Lincoln issued the Emancipation Proclamation.

Per Butler's orders, enslaved men could claim their freedom and enlist in the military to perform labor duty. Over half who volunteered were formerly enslaved. Typically, their clothes, grammar, bearing, and trades made that status clear to the enlisting officers. Some white soldiers and officers in the Department of the Gulf disagreed with the general's policy of accepting any person who claimed to be free, petitioning him to stick to the letter of his orders. However, Butler's officers rarely verified if a recruit was free or formerly enslaved when enlisting them into the regiments. Soldier-turned-historian Joseph Wilson wrote, "Any negro who would swear that he was free, if physically good, was accepted, and of the many thousand slave fugitives in the city from distant plantations, hundreds found their way into Touro building."[18] Hillaire Zenon later testified that "he was a slave before the war and until I enlisted. Many men in our regiment were slaves but all were put down as free men."[19] Francis Dumas, a free man of color who owned enslaved people and a large plantation, gathered all of the eligible men on his plantation and asked them if they wanted to join him in breaking the bonds of slavery that affected all of them, and every man who said yes joined the Native Guards under him. Denison was both surprised and impressed that "nobody inquires whether the recruit is (or has been) a slave. As a consequence, the boldest and finest fugitives have enlisted." Denison summarized his feeling about the experiment, writing, "Without doubt it will be a success."[20]

The news that Butler intended to enlist and commission Black men into the U.S. Army hit the newspapers with force. Some newspapers, like the *Liberator,* simply reprinted the order.[21] In Butler's home region of New England, they thought "Gen. Butler has come to the very rational conclusion that men who are good enough to fight for rebellion may very properly be employed to fight against it."[22] The *Chicago Daily Tribune* noted Butler's phrasing: "The rebel governor of Louisiana having authorized the organization of regiments of free colored men, Gen. Butler *accepts* the regiments thus organized."[23] In the *National Anti-Slavery Standard,* a writer argued that these units were different from General Hunter's because the Native Guards had been created by the Louisiana governor, so if anyone was to blame it was the Confederacy and not the Union.[24] A writer in another paper mused, "If this is not returning the 'poisoned chalice' to the lips of those who prepared it, we don't know how it can be done."[25]

Criticism from southerners was to be expected. The *Daily Picayune*—published in New Orleans—summarized the Confederate position, articulating prevailing beliefs about African Americans among whites in the state: "The unfitness of the negro for military service is known to everybody. If he were not naturally a very inferior specimen of humanity, so far as the strong qualities needed in war are concerned, his life of slavery and subjection would render the adult slave a very unsafe person to be entrusted with a musket against the man whom he has all his life looked up to as his master and superior." This statement failed to acknowledge the realities of Louisiana's history, and the same paper had published praise of the Native Guards a year prior when the first regiments had formed. The writer continued, "But it is not the inferiority of the negro, his natural dullness and cowardice, his great indolence, and his awe of the white man, which so entirely disqualify the African for efficient military service, as that still more serious defect of any sort of sympathy in the contest in which he is required or invited to take part. The vast majority of negroes are contented with their situation in life."[26]

Of course, this assertion was incorrect, as African American newspapers made clear. These newspapers responded to the news with both elation and criticism. *L'Union* expressed appreciation for the presence of the formerly enslaved, and hope that both God and freedom would be with all those who served to uplift New Orleans's African American society.[27] One paper predicted that the Native Guards would help Butler "atone for his refusal to permit a negro insurrection in New Orleans, in the eyes of some of his northern friends." The paper also noted that "Gen. Butler turns the tables very handsomely upon" the Confederacy.[28] Another described Butler whittling the sharpest stick he could and thrusting the spear "into the sore body of Secessionism," a stick that was "cut from their own timber with customary Yankee ingenuity."[29] In Vermont, writers recognized that "by his quotation of the previous orders of Gov. Moore of Louisiana, [Butler] stopped the mouths of the rebels from protesting against the arming of negroes."[30] However, the paper also noted Butler's hypocrisy in preventing Phelps from arming African Americans and then going on to do it himself.[31] But the regiments were forming regardless of the circumstance that led to that reality.

Aspects of the original Native Guards' personnel and traditions carried over into the new units. Captain André Cailloux had served as a lieutenant in the home guards. He was familiar with many of the free Blacks of the city and helped to recruit hundreds of men, and he commanded Company E, also known as Halleck's Guards, in honor of General Henry Halleck. Cailloux was joined by fellow officers that included Charles Sauvenet, Edgar Davis, Octave Rey, Alcide Lewis, Hannibal Carter, and Charles St. Manat.[32] Lieutenant Morris W. Morris had the rare distinction of being the only Jewish African American officer to serve in both iterations of the Native Guards. The home guards had adopted a policy of using African American men as line officers; this was also the policy that Phelps had pushed forward before his resignation, as he believed Black soldiers would be more likely to follow and respect Black officers than white officers, who might mistreat them. The new version of the Native Guards took the same regimental formation that Louisiana had used for its militia before the war. In the beginning, the men wore brightly colored uniforms that were more festive than combat-oriented. Those who had their own weapons showed up with them, and it took some time before they were issued Union uniforms and muskets similar to the rest of the department. For a short time, the Native Guards stood out for more than their race.

Some New Orleanians did not like the new regiments' resemblance to the old Native Guards. The priest at the Institute Catholique, and others in the city who had assisted Jordan Noble when he organized the Native Guards, no longer blessed the men, their arms, or their flags like they used to do. The white priest was concerned that the regiment would set in motion a sequence of events similar to the Haitian Revolution.[33] Additionally, not all the men were original to the first regiment that had been constituted a year earlier; only about 108, or 19 percent, of the men from that regiment joined the newest unit initially.[34] To a degree, this was to be expected. Many of the men who had been forced to join the first iteration of the regiment held prominent positions of wealth in the city, and to join the military would have meant abandoning their families and positions. There was no external push from the citizens or government that would have forced men to join as well, which made this truly a volunteer organization when compared to the previous iteration of the Native Guards. Additionally, the Native Guards were no longer guaranteed to remain in the state or avoid combat, as soldiers in the original unit had been.

Over half of the 1st Regiment was filled with men who had been free prior to the war, mostly young men willing to fight.[35] More men joined additional units of the Native Guards as it became clear that the U.S. Army was not like the home guards; in the Native Guards, they would have a much better opportunity to earn a place of respect with their service.[36] Even those who did not join the Native Guards worked with the army in other ways, including recruiting for the Native Guards, supplying the regiment with resources, and giving formerly enslaved people whatever assistance they needed to serve. For example, the city's wealthy, free men later came together to form a Freedmen's Aid Association that paid premiums for crops, guaranteed fair wages for formerly enslaved people in the city, and helped find them homes and jobs if needed, all from the donations and assistance of men and women who had been free prior to the war.[37]

Just as Phelps's plans for African Americans in the U.S. Army came to fruition, his military career came to an end. For the remainder of August, Phelps watched as Butler made the same set of decisions that had led Phelps to become a pariah in the Department of the Gulf. Phelps took issue with Butler for only constituting the regiments "because it had been previously accepted by the rebels, not because it is right in itself."[38] Sarah Butler wrote to her husband, "A few who are disposed to find fault say you are doing the same thing for which Phelps was withdrawn."[39] Nevertheless, on 8 September 1862, Phelps received his official orders from the War Department informing him that his resignation had been accepted and his time in the military was over.

Sarah Butler's comparison of her husband to Phelps was apt, as Butler enlisted the Native Guards with no prior approval from the War Department.[40] After his initial letter to Stanton in mid-August, Butler constituted the regiments, enlisted soldiers, and made Black men officers, all without orders. He wrote to General Halleck regarding the "free brigade which was in the Confederacy and was willing to take service" in the U.S. Army, but Halleck never approved Butler's actions.[41] It took weeks for Butler to receive approval from the War Department for the Native Guards, but before that he used the same rational that Phelps had—that the Militia Act of 17 July 1862 gave him permission through presidential authority, and as the president's representative in the region, he could act until ordered to do otherwise.[42] Denison wrote to Chase that Butler was acting out of jealousy of Phelps, enlisting Black soldiers on his own terms so he could garner all the fame.[43] Jefferson Davis expressed anger that the federal government avoided approving or disproving the order, but few in the Union cared about his opinion.[44]

Phelps assisted in the initial constitution and training of the Native Guards until his departure from the Department of the Gulf. Writers for Bermuda newspapers acknowledged that Phelps would always be remembered as the man who endeavored to arm African Americans.[45] His men, both white and Black, loved Phelps and regretted that the War Department accepted his resignation while the regiments were forming. As he prepared to leave the camp, the general's officers gathered around him to praise him for all he had taught them. Even those who disapproved of his decisions loved the general as a gentle, firm, knowledgeable, and noble leader. Captain John De Forest referred to the gathering as a "farewell ovation to our fine old commander."[46] Many years after serving under Phelps, General Rush Hawkins said, to "that kind-hearted, quaint, honest old man, with his perfect sense of justice, the men and officers of my regiments owe a debt of gratitude, which can only be effaced from their memories when the last survivor of that command shall have passed away." Hawkins continued, "I have never known a man so free from the hypocrisies, sins, and vices which make humanity despicable as was John W. Phelps."[47] One captain in the Connecticut regiments stationed in New Orleans wrote that Phelps was "not crazy—no more than Paul was when he was accused of madness. He is a noble specimen of a true man."[48] Another reporter who met with Phelps after his resignation described his evident "love for justice and fidelity to principle," along with the "personal valor and military genius" that made the general a "true hero." He summarized, "If all our Generals had been like him, this rebellion would long ago have been crushed, and thousands, many thousands of precious lives would have been saved."[49] Notably, General Butler went on to cite only himself for constituting the Native Guards, usurping Phelps's legacy.

As Phelps rode out of the camp, his men gave him a rousing ovation, with some of the men reportedly crying. His final words to his officers were, "And now, with earnest wishes for your welfare, and aspirations for the success of the great cause for which you are here, I bid you good-bye."[50] When he made his way to his home in Vermont, the Confederate Congress declared that he and General Hunter were outlaws to the South, and for the crime of organizing Black regiments they were to be turned over to Jefferson Davis and put to death. The Vermont legislature asked Phelps to speak about his views to a joint session on 13 October 1862. There, Phelps stated, "There is one simple law of interpreting the Constitution—the sustaining of liberty; any other interpretation is wrong." He went on, "The sun never looked down upon a greater evil than American slavery. In ruling this great nation of slaves we have to a degree become enslaved ourselves."[51] Phelps understood that the moral implications of slavery extended beyond the South, and that it needed to be abolished across the nation.

Phelps was replaced by the newly promoted Brigadier General Thomas W. Sherman.[52] Sherman was born in Newport, Rhode Island, and as an 1836 West Point graduate and officer in various wars with Native Americans, he had the background to succeed Phelps as a leader and commander. However, Phelps did not know or trust Sherman since he was recently promoted and rarely interacted with him, and so, as Phelps was leaving Louisiana, he instead entrusted his legacy to another newly promoted general, Brigadier General Godfrey Weitzel. Phelps made a show of indicating his preference by meeting with Weitzel before leaving the Department of the Gulf. General Butler even informed Sarah Butler that Phelps had given "his horse, epaulettes, sash, and spurs to Weitzel."[53] Weitzel was a favorite of both Butler and Phelps, and had been promoted by the War Department on Butler's word. As the engineering officer for the department, Weitzel had been instrumental in capturing New

General Godfrey Weitzel
(Library of Congress, Prints and Photographs Division)

Orleans after careful study of the city, and he was already serving as the city's military mayor between 14 July and 30 September, as Shepley was directed back to Washington.[54]

During this time, Butler's prejudice against African American soldiers made the future of the Native Guards seem bleak. John William De Forest, captain of the 12th Connecticut Volunteer Infantry Regiment, sought a colonelcy in the Native Guards after meeting with Captain Francis Dumas. Dumas—a Creole of color—impressed De Forest with his suavity, intelligence, and culture at a dinner party they both happened to attend. However, Butler informed De Forest that he intended to use the Guards for garrison and fatigue duty around New Orleans because African American troops could not and should not fight. De Forest believed he would never get a promotion to general if he only commanded troops in labor duty, so he withdrew his application for the colonelcy. He told his wife that the regiments were destined "for fatigue duty, such as making roads, building bridges and draining marshes; they will seldom put into battle."[55] Many New Englanders agreed with Butler that African Americans would not make good soldiers. When the governor of Connecticut was asked if New England would follow Butler's lead, he replied, "It seems to me that the time may yet come when a regiment of colored men may be profitably employed. But now, if a company of that class should be introduced into a regiment, or a regiment into a brigade (the regiment or brigade being composed of whites), it would create so much unpleasant feeling and irritation that more evil than good would result."[56] Demonstrating how pervasive prejudice against Black soldiers was in New England, Colonel Charles Paine, who was recruiting for another regiment of Louisiana Unionists, wrote to his father in Massachusetts that "Genl Butler is organizing a free nigger regt, but don't let people think that mine is nigger."[57]

By September, the Native Guards began to take shape in the U.S. Army, and many initial reactions were positive. Denison mailed an update on the situation to Chase: "A free colored Regt., formerly in Rebel service, is being organized," he wrote, and went on, "The free negroes of Louisiana, are certainly superior, as a class, to the [white] Creoles (descendants of French and Spanish settlers). They are intelligent, energetic, and industrious, as is evident from the fact (as stated to me) that they own one-seventh of the real estate in this city."[58] One correspondent visited the city to see "those novel volunteers in Uncle Sam's costume" and concluded that they would excel at the task of defending southern forts.[59] Additionally, Butler had been correct in surmising that Confederate leaders planned to attack New Orleans and force out the U.S.

Army, but the addition of more troops helped to bolster his defenses and deter an attack.[60] Thus, the Native Guards were seen as successful from the date of constitution.

A correspondent from the North visited the Touro Building when he was in New Orleans early in September so that he could witness the "free colored citizens, who daily go through company drills, and on each evening have a dress parade, at which twelve hundred stout men perform the duties of a soldier with an aptitude and precision that would do credit to men of whiter faces though not necessarily of braver hearts." He took notice of a sign next to the entrance that said "Phelps Guards," which listed over a hundred men in one of the companies who remembered their time under Phelps so favorably that they had decided to name themselves after the general. However, members of the regiment preferred to be called the "Chasseurs d'Afrique," a nod to both their European and African ancestries. The writer sampled the food that the soldiers prepared, noting that it was of excellent quality because so many were cooks, and he watched them practice their drill; they took "great pride in the business," he wrote. By the end of his tour he believed that the soldiers were excellently suited to guard southern forts.[61]

As Butler had promised, he commissioned Black officers for the 1st Louisiana Native Guards Regiment.[62] However, Black officers were a familiar sight in New Orleans, as some had served in the Battle of New Orleans in 1814.[63] Officers in the Native Guards demonstrated that African American society in New Orleans was educated and cultured. For example, First Lieutenant Paul Porée and Second Lieutenant Hippolyte St. Louis had backgrounds and economic statuses similar to those of André Cailloux and went on to serve alongside him in both iterations of the Native Guards.[64] Many had Creole ancestry, which, according to one correspondent, gave them the appearance of white men; and their upbringing in the city afforded them good educations, which compelled another correspondent to note, "I found on one or two occasions, that I was conversing with men of no ordinary knowledge and mental capacity."[65]

The racist connotations that Black men needed to look or sound white was not lost on anyone during the war, but not all of the officers in the 1st Regiment needed European connections or blood to earn the respect of the community and the military. John H. Crowder was born in Louisville, Kentucky, to free African American parents in 1846. He taught himself to read and write, worked his way up to become steward of a steamboat—the highest position an African American man could hold—and earned the respect of those around him. When the U.S. Army liberated New Orleans, he was among the first to volunteer for service in the Native Guards. Because he was only sixteen, he had to lie about his age to recruiting officers.[66] His skills and respect among the community helped him to merit a lieutenancy in the regiment, earning him distinction as one of the youngest officers in the U.S. Army, and the youngest Black officer.

Butler knew that the highly intelligent Black men who held high places in New Orleans society would make their way into the officer corps if they chose to, and, of course, many had already served in the regiment, so they had experience in those positions. He also knew that the region's formerly enslaved and less prominent men would feel more comfortable serving under officers with whom they felt a sense of commonality. The captains were directed to recruit their own companies in many cases, and this fostered a strong *esprit de corps* between the officers and their men.[67] The plan worked well. For example, Cailloux recruited for Company E of the 1st Regiment. Like most in his position, he recruited from among people he knew; even those in the Friends of Order were encouraged to join his company. Because of his stellar reputation as a leader prior to the war and the fact that he recruited men who respected him, Cailloux was easily elected as the lieutenant for Company E.[68] Jordan Noble, too old to serve himself, also recruited for the Native Guards, assuring people that the federal government was on the side of the enslaved.[69] Charles Hughes, a man too disabled to fight, left his job as a baker to recruit for the regiments as well. Together, these examples demonstrate that recruitment was a group effort in the Black and Creole society of New Orleans.[70] With the additional support of publications like *L'Union*, the Native Guards had a number of ways to recruit men. Serving under Black officers was a point of pride for many soldiers in the Native Guards, and Black New Orleanians were likewise proud to watch their men don the Union uniform and march through the city streets.

The rest of the officers assumed their roles haphazardly. Some were promoted from the enlisted ranks of volunteers. For example, Emile Detiége—the Black Belgian man who assisted Phelps—volunteered as a private in the regiment. However, his experience as a trainer and teacher led to his election as lieutenant.[71] In addition, because the War Department was sending reinforcements slowly, Butler met with white men in the area who expressed a willingness to command soldiers in an African American unit. He also shifted personnel in the Department of the Gulf, resulting in promotions to higher ranks for some white Native Guard officers. Finally, Butler took advice from his colonels and from prominent people in the city who suggested that staff officers and people in other administrative roles fill the regiment. Robert Gould, a U.S. soldier with the Department of the Gulf, once characterized his officers as "a pack of jackasses and thieves" in a letter to his mother. Unfortunately, the Native Guards had to endure a number of incompetent white officers who ended up in the regiment because they'd had little hope for promotion in their regular units.[72]

Recruitment efforts led to an eclectic 1st Regiment. For example, in Company C, Pierre Silvester and Eduard St. Cryr were both sixteen, and, together, they made up the youngest group of enlisted men in the regiment. The eldest man among them, Brazile Brown Jr., was a fifty-three-year-old carpenter. Nearly twenty other men were in their forties, and more than half were in their thirties. Over a third of the men claimed to have European blood; many of them were the regiment's Creole officers. On the regiment's roster rolls, a number of men were described as mulatto, yellow, fair, or bright skinned. The most common trade among the men was laborer, which was also the most common profession among the formerly enslaved, but the regiment also included skilled professionals, such as bricklayers, shoemakers, and carpenters.[73] The majority of the men were considered "French Catholics" by their commanding officers, a fact that alienated the Protestant chaplain assigned to the Native Guards.[74] Despite the regiment's heterogeneity, the men shared a common cause that united them against slavery and the South.

Drawing of the line officers of the 1st Louisiana Native Guards
(*Harper's Weekly*, February 1863)

The process of officer selection later caused problems for the Native Guards due to deep-seated racism in the North. Even men who thought of slavery as wrong—either on moral or economic grounds—did not see Black men as their equals. Most had never interacted with a free African American, and most of the People of Color they had met before coming to New Orleans were most likely enslaved. This situation gave rise to profound prejudice, as many white northerners associated the state of enslavement with all Blacks. Additionally, the southern propaganda campaign during antebellum slavery helped to form this narrative. Whites believed Blacks were lazy, shiftless, childlike, and cowardly, while also, paradoxically, representing them as savages and barbarians who might resort to violence against those who had formerly enslaved them.[75] Like Butler, many who chose to officer the Native Guards did so under the belief that Black soldiers were inferior and likely to flee once battle began.

However, the white commander of the 1st Regiment, Colonel Spencer H. Stafford, was not one of these men. Before accepting a commission in the federal military, Stafford was a lawyer in New York. He served as the assistant provost marshal for New York as a captain in the New York State Militia. He was also a lieutenant colonel of the original Ellsworth Fire Zouaves, an office he had to resign to accept his position leading the 1st Louisiana Native Guards. Colonel Stafford had a stellar reputation in the North. One northern paper declared, "He is a man of unquestionable courage, perfect independence of the opinions of others when he thinks he is right, and of excellent military ability and energy."[76] Stafford's initial mission after accepting the position was to facilitate recruitment for the Native Guards and bivouac his forming unit. On 30 August, Stafford began the recruitment program in earnest, following Butler's direction. He also worked with the Department of the Gulf and the men in his regiment to repair the Judah Touro Building and prepare it to house all the volunteers.[77]

As the 1st Louisiana Native Guards Regiment mustered into service, another groundbreaking event occurred in September: President Lincoln issued the preliminary Emancipation Proclamation. In it, he declared that "all persons held as slaves within any State, or any designated part of a State, the people whereof shall then be in rebellion against the United States, shall be then, thenceforward and forever free."[78] Lincoln issued the proclamation on 22 September 1862, and he gave the rebels until the new year to lay down their arms or face the consequences of losing their enslaved populace. However, Confederate leaders chose to ignore his words. Five days after the proc-

*The First Reading of the Emancipation Proclamation before the Cabinet* (1866), engraving by Francis Carpenter
(Library of Congress, Prints and Photographs Division)

lamation was issued, the government made the Native Guards the first official Black regiment in the U.S. Army during the Civil War.[79] The governor of Vermont, Frederick Holbrook, attempted to persuade Lincoln to return Phelps to the military; however, Phelps did not accept the position because it was not backdated to the date of his resignation, meaning his period of absence from the military was preserved in the record.[80] While the Native Guards did not get Phelps back, the federal government was finally ready to take steps to abolish slavery.

Legally, not much changed in New Orleans for the enslaved population, as the preliminary emancipation excluded slavery there because the region was not in open rebellion. However, some enslavers freed enslaved people who had not already emancipated themselves. One report from New Orleans stated, "The emancipation proclamation makes much more of a row in New York and Boston than here. Indeed, emancipation had been effectually accomplished when the proclamation came," concluding that the Department of the Gulf was already freeing enslaved people through various means.[81] Some of the Catholic clergy in the city expressed, "It is the last card thrown on the table but it is also the total destruction of the South and the signal for a cataclysm"—that being "a new San Domingo," a reference to the Haitian Revolution.[82] Privately, Benjamin and Sarah Butler felt the proclamation had been made to appease the ardent abolitionists, and they also knew this meant Chase had the president's ear in Washington.[83] Eventually, the Department of the Gulf issued General Orders No. 88, which freed all enslaved people unless enslavers could prove themselves loyal prior to the Union involvement in the region.[84] With the introduction of the Native Guards, it was obvious that even though slavery was technically legal, it was nearing its end in New Orleans.

Because of the proclamation, many northerners began to see the need for a unit like the Native Guards. The author of one editorial asked, "What is to be done with the liberated slaves? is a huge question." However, the more pressing question was, "How shall we break down the army of the rebels?" The answer to both, the author suggested, could be found in the case of the Native Guards. Participation in the militia for the newly freed African American man would "thus be put at once upon his manhood. The strongest stimulus will be given him to make the best use of his powers in supporting himself and his family, and the government that is helping him."[85] Sarah Butler, who had pushed the general to use Black troops, took some credit for his employment of the Native Guards and pushed him to field the men in the artillery and cavalry once the president issued the proclamation.[86]

While arming and training African American men in New Orleans, Butler also had to feed and clothe their families. He wrote to his superiors, "We have with us a great many Negro women and children, barefoot and half naked." He reported that his commissaries were distributing over $50,000 per month in food to whites in the region, including to planters who claimed to be starving, and "issuing rations to the amount of nearly double the amount required by the troops" to African Americans in the city.[87] The following day, after his report to Halleck, Butler ordered his officers to house "negro women and children who have sought protection within your lines," directing them "to take possession of such houses in your neighborhood as belonged to well-known and ascertained rebels, as will be sufficient to cover those you have and provide for those coming in."[88] He later expanded the use of rebel homes and wealth to directly support the families of soldiers in the Native Guards.[89] Butler was also able to use his position to force planters in the region to hire Black laborers on militarily seized plantations for wages instead of white laborers or enslaved people. This maneuver helped to ease the burden on the Department of the Gulf, and it was among the first steps toward contract labor in Louisiana, a hallmark of Reconstruction in Louisiana that many African Americans later regretted.

Many whites in New Orleans were alarmed to see Black soldiers marching through the city again, as they were now marching for the federal government and the men had weapons. Earlier during the Union's occupation, Butler had ordered all New Orleans residents' arms to be confiscated to protect his men and to keep the law.[90] This order had been issued just weeks before the first African American regiment was formed, so it now looked like a deliberate effort to disarm whites and then arm Blacks for a planned race war. In September, the Department of the Gulf issued General Orders No. 71, which aided the military in distinguishing "the disloyal from the loyal citizens and honest neutral foreigners residing in this Department."[91] It required registration of country of birth, location, naturalization papers, and time in the United States. Most worrisome to immigrants, the order made it clear that anyone who gave false testimony would be severely punished. Foreign nationals even felt targeted by white soldiers in the U.S. Army. The French consulate informed the department that American soldiers had pillaged the homes of two French citizens, a common complaint by both Americans and immigrants in the region.[92] The complaints took on racial overtones when the Native Guards were fielded, as foreign consuls reported multiple acts of violence and pillaging by "negroes in the service of the United States."[93] The situation was exacerbated because some of the formerly enslaved soldiers had once been in the service of those same immigrants.[94]

Immigrants were now completely under the direction of the Department of the Gulf, another loophole that Butler exploited. To him, all foreigners were, in a sense, citizens of the United States if they lived in the country. This legal status meant they were subject to American laws and his own federal jurisdiction. He argued as much to multiple foreign consuls, who took issue with their subjects being forced to take oaths to another nation and follow their military orders.[95] Butler's reasoning violated a missive that General Halleck had sent him a few weeks earlier that said, "Oaths are not to be prescribed by us to aliens, nor to be required of our own citizens as conditions of rights or privileges."[96] However, Butler believed that "there can be no such thing as neutrality by a citizen of the United States in this contest for the life of the Government. . . . Every citizen must find himself on the one side or the other of that line, and can claim no other position than that of friend or enemy of the United States."[97] Thus, under Butler's rule, immigrants and all citizens in the region had to choose a side or he would choose for them.

Immigrants sought to circumvent this edict by petitioning European nations for certificates of citizenship in their home country in a bid to retain their property and act independently of Butler.[98] Even French Catholic priests in the city secured these certificates in hopes that they could keep themselves and the church out of reach of the military.[99] Further demonstrating their loyalty, Black Creoles with similar European ties chose not to pursue citizenship certificates outside of the United States, instead opting to side with the Union.[100] The petitions were a double-edged sword for those who received them, however. When Butler required the city's inhabitants to register their allegiance to the United States or another nation, he declared that people enslaved by immigrants from France and Great Britain were free, since their enslavers' countries had already outlawed slavery.[101] It was a shrewd maneuver that allowed him to free hundreds of enslaved people and gave them the option to join the Native Guards as free African Americans.[102] Other European nations later repeated this argument, making it difficult for Europeans to continue enslaving people.

As the regiment took shape, many southerners took note. A war correspondent from New York wrote, "At Camp Parapet I saw what I had often heard of, but never expected to see—an entire regiment of slaves, regularly organized, and drilling to the best of their ability." The correspondent was surprised to see the forming soldiers marching in what he called "English style," and while he admitted he was proslavery, he became convinced from watching them that they would make good soldiers and that abolition was "a military necessity."[103] A correspondent for *L'Union* wrote a similar report, noting that the men exhibited good discipline and that their camp was well maintained.[104] One of the captains, Henry Louis Rey, was so proud of his men and their training that he wrote to the paper that its readers should "come visit our camp." He continued, "In parade, you will see a thousand white bayonets gleaming in the sun, held by black, yellow, and white hands." Rey went on to assure visitors that the racial acrimony that existed in the rest of the South was not an issue, writing, "Be informed that we have no prejudice, that we receive everyone into the camp."[105] However, that was not wholly true.

While white and Black soldiers trained alongside one another, the two groups were by no means treated as equals by military authorities. In addition, northern white soldiers held generations of contempt and prejudice toward African American soldiers. One white soldier noted, "Toward the black man we feel none of these delicate sentiments of equality."[106] Their prejudice, according to Butler, resulted from the belief that "from childhood up, the word of command had been implicitly and abjectly obeyed by the negro. His master's voice was his perfect guide."[107] Men whose behavior did not reflect this idea of the good Black man could be severely punished. One correspondent described how a Black soldier could be "mercilessly flogged, shot, hung, or burned alive according to the enormity of his offense."[108] For example, one Black man in Thibodeaux was accused of attempted rape, and with no evidence he was found guilty and sentenced to death.[109] Punishment for even minor crimes was rampant.

The 1st Louisiana Native Guards Volunteer Infantry Regiment quickly reached its recruitment goal. The regiment was officially mustered into federal service on 27 September 1862 and was in the field by October.[110] Denison reported to Chase that the men were properly drilled and trained, and the 2d Regiment was well on its way to joining them.[111] Butler reported the constitution of the regiments to his superiors with high hopes that they would perform well in service to the U.S. Army.[112] On 1 October, the men marched down Canal Street, as they had under the Confederacy, but this time they marched "to the old native air of Yankee Doodle," according to their chaplain.[113] Denison thought they looked stalwart, hardy, well proportioned, and neatly uniformed, and that they exhibited great endurance. Unlike Moore, however, Butler intended to call on the men to serve as more than mere propaganda. The general had begun to realize he could use them to hold forts or other large areas of operations, and he went as far as requisitioning arms for three full regiments.[114] Their officers, both white and Black, predicted that "they will fight with a suitable motive before them to induce them to action and inspire them to courage."[115] Indeed, if they did not fight, treatment after capture on the battlefield would be most severe; it was a struggle for their lives.[116]

The Native Guards continued to encounter obstacles, including hostility from European immigrants. Multiple French citizens publicly insulted and mocked members of the 1st Regiment, to the degree the soldiers felt they had to treat immigrants as any other group of rebels. The acting French consul attempted to report their responses as unwarranted assaults on his countrymen, but Colonel Stafford stood by his men and their actions, leading Butler to caution the French consul that his people should watch their own prejudices "against my colored soldiers" if they wanted to avoid a similar situation.[117] European immigrants were regularly caught transporting letters and resources to Confederate lines, which cast suspicion on many immigrants. Furthermore, many foreign merchants were actively raising funds for the rebel military, some even directly arming Confederate forces in the region.[118] Butler wrote to Stanton, "Without the aid furnished by foreign mercantile houses in New Orleans . . . I am convinced by the most irrefragable evidence, this rebellion would have wholly failed to arm and supply itself."[119] Even worse, there was still a hope in the South that Paris would come to their aid and intervene on their behalf, and French immigrants in the region perpetuated this fear.[120] Count Eugène Méjan, a pro-southern consul from France, heavily supported European intervention, and he consistently clashed with Butler over the issue.[121] The two sparred publicly and diplomatically, to the degree that the secretary of state was concerned France would invade New Orleans on Méjan's behest.

White southerners, incongruously, could not fathom why African Americans were volunteering to fight in the war on the side of the North. One paper declared, "WE DOUBT IF THERE COULD BE FOUND IN THE ENTIRE UNIVERSE A MORE DEGRADED SPECTACLE THAN THAT OF A REGIMENT OF NEGRO SOLDIERS FIGHTING IN SUPPORT OF THE FEDERAL GOVERNMENT." The writer went on to argue that "The slaves of the South might justly enough take their masters' interest to heart" and choose to fight for the Confederacy if given the chance, and continued, "At all events, if the South enlisted slaves in its armies, they will at least fight for something in which their personal interests were engaged." The writer concluded, "No motive can possibly actuate the negro soldier in the North save the bounty or the pay which he receives from a Government which loathes and despises him."[122] A soldier in the Native Guards disagreed with this sentiment, however, writing to *L'Union*, "They find it strange that men whom they held curbed under their tyrannic laws for so long a time should attempt to raise their head to inhale with full breast the, though still feeble, breeze of liberty and justice which at present fills the air for them."[123]

While southerners expressed anger and disbelief that African Americans were enlisting in the U.S. Army, Butler demonstrated confidence in both the Native Guards and Colonel Stafford.[124] He directed Stafford to continue recruiting another regiment due to the number of volunteers, and he started to think of ways he could use the Native Guards for more than fatigue duty. Like the line officers in the 1st Regiment, those in the 2d Regiment were educated Blacks and Creoles.[125] The regiment was mustered into service on 12 October 1862. The success of the first two spurred the creation of a third, and plans were underway to create three additional regiments.

The regiments' growth necessitated additional officers of Stafford's caliber. Colonel Nathan W. Daniels was chosen to lead the 2d Louisiana Native Guards Volunteer Infantry Regiment, and for his first mission he was to train his men and rendezvous with the 1st Regiment to hold the Opelousas Railroad.[126] Daniels was the only commanding officer of one of the initial three infantry regiments who was familiar with the region. Born in New York, he had spent most of his childhood in Ohio before coming to Louisiana. When the war began, he went back to Ohio to serve in the Army of the Ohio, and he was serving in the provost marshal's office in New Orleans when Butler selected him for command.[127] Daniels commanded the 2d Regiment until he resigned in 1863, and, like Stafford, he was proud to officer the Native Guards.

Daniels was directed to select his own staff, and in that duty he inadvertently made history. While working with the 1st Regiment, he encountered Captain Francis Dumas. Like Captain De Forest, Daniels was tremendously impressed by Dumas. Daniels noted his ability to speak three languages, the fact that he had enlisted into the Guards nearly a hundred men whom he had previously enslaved, and his wealth and intelligence.[128] He wrote to Butler on 29 September 1862 requesting the promotion of "Francis Ernest Dumas, Captain Co. B 1st Reg't La Native Guard, free col'd" to the rank of major and placement on his own staff.[129] Butler, who was similarly awestruck by Dumas, agreed with Daniels's summation and endorsed his promotion and transfer. Major Francis E. Dumas became the first of only three Black men to hold the rank of major in the Union army, and he was the only major of color who commanded troops in combat.[130]

Captain P. B. S. Pinchback was another African American officer of note who served in the regiment. Pinchback was the son of a planter, Major William Pinchback, and a mother of mixed race, Eliza Stewart. Stewart had been freed by Major Pinchback after he impregnated her. It was often said that Captain Pinchback could pass for a white man, but he chose to identify as African American. He attended school in Ohio and then worked as a cabin boy before being promoted to ship's steward. After the U.S. Army liberated New Orleans, Pinchback snuck through rebel lines so he could serve in the military. Described as irreverent, intemperate, combative, and confident, he was among the first to join the Native Guards when Butler put out the call.[131] He raised his own company to serve in the 2d Regiment, and his men loved him. After the war, he recalled his time in the Native Guards as "the only time in my life I have felt anything like Patriotism."[132]

Like the 1st Native Guard Regiment, the 2d contained an eclectic mix of New Orleanians. Many of the men were described as more dark skinned than those in the 1st, and, indeed, more formerly enslaved people had started to join the Union's ranks.[133] Most of the enlisted soldiers were laborers from the sugar-growing Teche district of Louisiana, meaning they had likely been enslaved men who had freed themselves upon news of Lincoln's preliminary Proclamation. One lieutenant described the men of Company F as "mostly contrabands."[134] It was an accurate assessment. When André Cailloux left the

1st Regiment for the 2d, he personally enrolled dozens of formerly enslaved men into the new unit. However, there were still skilled workers among the 2d Regiment's ranks, especially among the officers. The average height in the regiment was five feet and six inches, and many were thought to be strong and sturdy. Together, the regiments' notoriety grew along with their size.

The Native Guards had garnered fame in the North by this time, and Black men traveled to New Orleans specifically to join the regiments. For example, Hannibal and Edward Carter were brothers from New Albany, Indianapolis. Their father, George Carter, had moved the family to Vicksburg prior to the war to pursue his business affairs, and that is where they were living when the war began. After the U.S. Army liberated New Orleans, the brothers took a steamer down to New Orleans when they heard inklings that the military would commission educated Black men.[135] Because of their father's business dealings and their own training in the trades, the brothers spoke well and passed the tests of commissioning into the military. Hannibal, in particular, was an eloquent speaker, and even after the war it was noted he was "shrewd, sharp, and wise."[136] Edward Eugene Carter was commissioned as a captain in the 1st Regiment, and Hannibal was commissioned in the 2d. Captain William Barrett, originally from Cincinnati, was selected to command Company B, a position he held until medically retired a year later.[137]

One of the 2d Regiment's many famed soldiers traveled farther than most. Joseph T. Wilson was born in Norfolk, Virginia, in January 1837. His mother, Louisa Wilson, was more than likely mixed-race, of British and Native American descent, and his father, Bristol, was an enslaved man. Accounts emphasize Wilson's fair skin. At a young age, he fled to Massachusetts after revealing the identity of a fugitive from justice. After receiving a limited education, he eventually found work on a whaling ship in the South Pacific, and then worked on a railroad in Chile. Wilson was in Chile when he heard about the war, and he used his own funds to travel to New York to fight on the side of the Union. He attempted to join the military as a white man, but it was discovered that he was Black and he was barred from entry. Dejected, Wilson traveled to New Orleans for two reasons: to look for his father, who had been sold through the city's slave pens, and to join the Native Guards. Wilson arrived in time to join the 2d Regiment as a private. He was not the only man of color to travel to New Orleans to serve in the army, but he arguably traveled farther than any other in the Native Guards.[138]

At least two of the men who joined the 2d Louisiana Native Guards Volunteer Infantry Regiment were from Africa. Wimba Congo and August Congo, each named for the region in Africa where they were born, had been enslaved

Joseph T. Wilson
(reproduced from his book
*The Black Phalanx*, 1888)

and illegally transported on the slave ship *Wanderer* to the state three years prior. When they heard that the U.S. Army was recruiting and freeing enslaved men for military service, they "threw down their hoes in the field, and marched boldly to the Touro building, and in broken language declared that they wanted to fight for the United States," according to *Douglass' Monthly*. When they attempted to join Captain Pinchback's company, they initially were turned away because of their poor English, but, at the urging of one of Pinchback's officers, the captain relented and allowed the men to join. As their English improved, they regaled their fellow soldiers with tales of Africa, including stories about their customs, tribes, and kings. The men appreciated hearing a description of Africa that was more nuanced than the accounts of the "dark continent" they had grown accustomed to from white narrators. Frederick Douglass's paper called for ten thousand more men like them to serve in the Native Guards.[139]

By contrast, some members of the Native Guards felt the regiments were not recruiting enough from the city's wealthy African American populace. *L'Union* published a letter to the editor containing the transcript of a toast by Captain Henry Louis Rey of the 1st Regiment to his "tardy compatriots." The letter said, "The chains of our brothers are breaking. The whips of the planters, reeking with blood, are going to dry. Immense happiness!" Captain Rey passionately continued, "The affectionate son will no more see men without heart and without shame, who order him to raise the clothes of his mother, and to tear her palpitating flesh, and make him there, immovable, swallowing his powerless rage, contemplating with a sorrowful eye this grievous spectacle of a humanity without mercy." He spoke directly to Black men about the benefits of joining: "Men of my race, when will you comprehend that in living in the same errors as your oppressors, you retard the march of progress, which would bring with it a social and political amelioration for you?" Then he chastened them: "Break, then, the chains of your slaves who are burning to enroll themselves for the defense of the Union and for the right of man. How many of you stay behind, governed by puerile fears and greed of fain, retarding our march, obstructing the brilliant path which we ought to go over? Come then, to join us; come to aid us to undermine the old errors, to let the entire world know that our poor race is denigrated, calumniated." Rey continued to disparage wealthy African Americans in New Orleans: "What a shame for you to permit that your slaves seek a place in our ranks, when you, yourselves, ought to be there!" His words were powerful and direct, making it clear the war was about slavery and that the Native Guards was both a route to freedom and a liberating force for Louisiana.

Finally, Rey described the honor of serving in the U.S. Army: "We can proudly proclaim that we have a country to defend, a flag to make respected, for it protects and shelters us. Famine tortured our women and children; the Nationals have relieved their hunger. We were treated with contempt; we are now respected as men." He called for the free class of the city to join the Union's ranks: "Hasten all; our blood only is demanded; who will hesitate? Men with the heart of the pelican. Let us be worthy sons of the heroes of the plains of Chalmette of 1814 and 1815, and not the slaves of the 'fugitives' of Chalmette of 1862."[140] It was an impassioned toast—one that was reprinted in numerous newspapers in Louisiana and the North—and it may have aided the regiments in recruiting additional African American officers.

African American women were not excluded from this recruitment effort. A woman could demonstrate patriotism to the Union and its cause by serving as a nurse, knitting socks and mittens, working on men's uniforms, and knitting cold-weather clothing in the winter months. Many Black and Creole women in New Orleans volunteered to serve as nurses, seamstresses, washerwomen, and in many other roles, for both Black and white regiments.[141] Through their efforts, these women tethered themselves to the Native Guards and showed that it was not only the men who were transforming New Orleans during the war.

The growing regiments needed more space to drill and train. They moved from the Touro Building to Camp Strong, which was near the Louisiana Racetrack and right outside of the city. Stafford complained that supply officers failed to give them adequate wagons and resources to move, and they were even issued discarded equipment that other soldiers no longer wanted. To him, "It was the most indifferently supplied regiment that ever went into service."[142] But their new location gave them the opportunity to drill and train without interference from the city's residents. A correspondent for the *New York Times* visited Camp Strong in a surprise inspection, and he was impressed by the conduct and military bearing of the Native Guards, who formed lines and columns within moments of learning that there was an inspection. The correspondent attested, "I have seen older white regiments, with more regimental drills, that are not their equal." He noted that while many soldiers in the companies he saw had a "superficial appearance [of] white men," one captain was very dark; and, overall, he observed "the diversity of color among the men and officers."[143] Within weeks of relocating, it was common knowledge for those who visited the region that "the first object of curiosity that greets your ear is from the mouth of a negro soldier the guard—'Who goes there?'" Should you give an improper response, "the probability is that you will immediately thereafter require the services of a surgeon to extract the ball, or that of an undertaker to plant you in a becoming manner."[144] The letter writer made it clear that the Native Guards controlled everything around the camp.

While training at Camp Strong, the Native Guards experienced the typical accidents that occur when men who have not handled weapons before are given arms and expected to act as soldiers. The first man to die in the Native Guards was Sergeant Eugene Francis. While a corporal in the regiment was practicing firing his weapon, he mistakenly discharged it in Francis's direction. The ball struck and killed Sergeant Francis.[145] Private Limerick Davis died while training at Camp Strong on 6 October after enlisting on 10 September.[146] The most common cause of death was sickness, usually from the typical illnesses that ailed all military camps during the war. Because the Native Guards were given inadequate medical care in comparison to their white counterparts, ill soldiers tended to languish longer, which resulted in a perception that they were lazy as they slept in bed succumbing to sickness. Claude Maistre, a Catholic priest, was one of the few white citizens in the city who worked to aid the men who were stricken with disease. He raised funds, ministered to them, and sometimes simply consoled them until they recovered.[147]

As Daniels trained the 2d Louisiana Native Guards, there were additional changes in the rest of the Native Guards as well. Colonel Stafford was given command of Camp Strong, as he was at that time the most experienced of any army officer training and commanding African American troops. Major Chauncey Basset, a former captain in the 6th Michigan Volunteer Infantry Regiment and a staunch abolitionist, was given command of the 1st Louisiana Native Guards Regiment in his place. Janson Payne, a twenty-eight-year-old white assistant surgeon for the 21st Massachusetts Volunteer Infantry Regiment, was assigned as the chief surgeon for the 1st Regiment. Asa Barnes, a white Episcopal minister and former first sergeant for the 31st Massachusetts Volunteer Infantry Regiment, was assigned as chaplain. As the two regiments trained in Camp Strong, new orders came down that the 1st Regiment was to prepare to move out and that the 2d would soon join them in a campaign in Lafourche Parish.[148]

Within two months, the 1st and 2d Regiments had formed and were ready to defend New Orleans with officers and soldiers of color from the city's Creole society and African American men from the North and from Africa. Together, they answered the call to sacrifice their blood for the Union cause, and within weeks they were tested.

Chapter 5

# *WOE TO ANY MAN WHO FLINCHES*

## THE RESULTS OF THE LOUISIANA NATIVE GUARDS' EXPERIMENT

The Louisiana Native Guards received their first taste of combat and learned what it meant to be soldiers within weeks of their constitution in the U.S. Army. If they failed, faltered, or even flinched, it would reflect upon all Black men in the army, and racists in both the North and South would point to their weakness as proof that Black men did not belong in the military. Both white and Black officers in the Native Guards were aware of this fact, and all were prepared to demonstrate that Black men performed well in the field and in combat. This chapter examines that first test and demonstrates that when given the chance, not a single man flinched when it mattered.

In October 1862, General Godfrey Weitzel was directed to form an expedition to Donaldsonville, Louisiana. There, Weitzel was to hold the entire Lafourche Parish for the Department of the Gulf. Donaldsonville, along with all of Bayou Lafourche, was described as "the richest in the State, and cultivated like a garden, producing great quantities of sugar" for the southern economy, and the Department of the Gulf's leaders wanted to control this region.[1] When Butler was forming the units for the expedition, he assigned the 1st Louisiana Native Guard Regiment to accompany Weitzel.[2] Butler hoped that by removing the Native Guards from New Orleans, he could resolve the issue of Black soldiers patrolling the city streets, which consistently caused issues for his command when they interacted with the white populace.[3] According to Butler's missive to General Henry Halleck, the mission in Donaldsonville was to "cut off supplies of cattle for the Rebel Army."[4] It was a crucial step in Butler's larger plan to open Union railroad communications and sugar supply routes throughout all of western Louisiana once Weitzel captured the parish.[5] Weitzel marched toward Donaldsonville with a brigade consisting of "five

Regiments Infantry, four companies cavalry, and two [artillery] batteries," according to George Denison, and they arrived at the city on 25 October 1862.[6] Their fellow white soldiers, for their part, believed they could accomplish the mission without the Native Guards.[7]

In total, Weitzel had nearly three thousand men, while his opposition, led by Brigadier General Alfred Mouton, had about half as many Confederate soldiers. To assist Weitzel, Butler assigned two draught-class steamers, steamships capable of maneuvering through the shallow parts of the bay, to attack Mouton's batteries at Berwick Bay. The ships quickly gained naval superiority on the waterways, and they successfully cut off Mouton's supply lines from Texas.[8] Along with the 8th Vermont Volunteer Infantry Regiment, the 1st Louisiana Native Guard Regiment was charged with protecting the force's lines, maintaining supplies between military stores and Weitzel, and securing the Opelousas Railroad for military use.[9] The units were assigned under the 8th Vermont's commanding officer, Colonel Stephen Thomas.[10] Captain James H. Ingraham of the 1st Louisiana Native Guards wrote to the papers, "We are still anxious, as we have ever been, to show the world that the latent courage of the African is aroused," as they awaited their first chance to confront Confederate forces. He continued, "While fighting under the American flag, we can and will be a wall of fire and death to the enemies of this country, our birthplace." Finally, he wrote, "If any cowardice has been exhibited since we left Camp Strong . . . it has been exhibited by the rebels."[11]

However, the soldiers' first test of courage was quite different than expected. Trains could not move down the railroad tracks because of an overgrowth of grass and weeds, as well as obstacles that had been placed there by Confederate soldiers. The two regiments were ordered to clear the grass and obstacles and rebuild the unused railroad lines. However, they were not issued scythes or large enough knives, so they were forced to get on their hands and knees and pull the grass by hand. Progress was slow, as they also had to fell trees to rebuild tracks. It took them two days to progress twenty-three miles to reach Boutte Station.[12]

As the 1st Louisiana Native Guards and the 8th Vermont completed their tedious task, the rest of Weitzel's men were maneuvering to engage with Mouton's troops. The same day that the Native Guards reached Boutte Station, the two armies met at Labadieville. Weitzel's men engaged with Confederate troops nine miles outside of the city of Thibodaux in what was categorized as a "sharp engagement" by Butler.[13] The Battle of Labadieville was a rousing success. At the cost of eighteen killed and sixty-eight wounded, the U.S.

Army killed an enemy colonel, along with dozens of his men, and captured nearly three hundred prisoners, their weapons, and an artillery piece.[14] As U.S. soldiers pushed onward, they "captured two 32-pounders, two 12-pounder howitzers, and considerable rolling stock," a large haul of artillery pieces that Weitzel later put to use.[15]

The surviving rebel soldiers retreated from the battlefield across Berwick Bay, and as they did so their lines crossed where the 1st Louisiana Native Guards and 8th Vermont Regiments were clearing the railroad. Colonel Stephen Thomas received a report on 28 October telling him that the Confederacy was amassing forces at Des Allemands Station and placing a platform car as an obstacle with two artillery pieces acting as offensive measures to the Union approach toward the station. Thomas ordered both regiments under his command to form lines and prepare for battle; it was the first time the Native Guards' soldiers heard these words in earnest. The 8th Vermont Volunteer Infantry Regiment was positioned to attack the right of the Confederate troops' position, and the 1st Louisiana Native Guards was positioned to attack the left. Artillery was positioned toward the middle of the two regiments on a Union flatcar, and all of the men were to approach forward as one. Thomas, aware that this was the first time the men of the Guard were seeing battle, told them, "If one of you hesitates, I shall shoot him on the spot!" He impressed on the men that capture or retreat meant death, declaring, "Woe to any man who flinches."[16] He ended by saying that they were fighting for the glory of God and that they should avenge "the blood that has flowed from the lacerated backs of yourselves, your mothers, wives, and sweethearts."

After Colonel Thomas's rousing but threatening speech, the men moved forward prepared to lay their lives down to secure the Des Allemands railway station. However, all they found was a deserted station, the bridge across the bayou burned by Confederate soldiers, and four artillery pieces the Confederates had left behind in their haste to flee from a potential battle. Mouton later reported that his men were "so worn out by the labor required to destroy the Des Allemands Bridge" and by the run of the Confederate forces that they could barely march and it took them hours to reach his lines.[17] After assessing the damage dealt by the Confederacy, the members of the 1st Louisiana Native Guards and 8th Vermont worked together for two days rebuilding the bridge and railroad tracks so the army could be resupplied by their main force in New Orleans.[18] They eventually completed their tasks and met with the main body of Weitzel's forces at Lafourche crossing. There, they were ordered to continue rebuilding and repairing railways as far as Brashear City. Weitzel was so successful that Governor Moore disbanded the militia in Lafourche Parish in a bid to conscript some of the loyal men into the Confederate army after realizing they could offer no further defense in the region.[19] By the end of the campaign, the Native Guards soldiers had cleared over fifty-two miles of railroad tracks, restored nine culverts, rebuilt two bridges, and faced the threat of imminent death by both the Confederacy and their commanding officer. They did it all with the military bearing expected of any soldier in the U.S. Army.[20] Weitzel reported that the men had performed their tasks adequately. When Chase heard of their efforts, he noted to Butler that accounts of the unit to the administration were promising, writing, "The only error is that the experiment is begun too late."[21]

*Pickets of the 1st Louisiana "Native Guard"...*
(*Frank Leslie's Illustrated Newspaper,* March 7, 1863)

The presence of the 1st Louisiana Native Guards in Lafourche spurred the change that many abolitionists had hoped would occur in the region, as great numbers of enslaved people began to self-emancipate. The fact that some of the Black soldiers were once enslaved in the same region played a key factor in their movements. According to a formerly enslaved woman from the parish, it was common for enslaved men and women to work in the sugar fields "bare-feeted and half naked" for nothing but a shack to sleep in, "something to eat and a few rags to wear" prior to the arrival of the U.S. Army.[22] Many enslaved people used the presence of the military to change their circumstances. For example, it was reported by the Adjutant Colonel Charles Paine that three men escaped their plantation; one had a shotgun and another a knife, and the shotgun had evidently been used within days based on its condition when found and the one missing round.[23] Alexander Pugh, a planter in the parish, reported that dozens of the people he had enslaved escaped to Union lines early in the occupation. Eventually he wrote in his diary that they "are still leaving, some every night. The plantation will probably be completely cleaned out in a week."[24] By November, Pugh wrote of an outright rebellion and the effective end of slavery on his plantation. Other plantation owners could only watch as soldiers stormed their land, took their food, and emancipated the people who were enslaved, as the owners were too scared to attempt to stop the U.S. military. One woman later recalled her mistress biting her finger in anger the day she realized the military was there to free the people she'd enslaved.[25] According to an officer who witnessed it, twenty-eight men training for the Native Guards attempted to leave Weitzel's camp "armed with guns and knives, clubs, etc.," with plans to raid a nearby plantation.[26] Men who had emancipated themselves and continued to help emancipating others made up the bulk of the Native Guards. There were three types of formerly enslaved people in the units: those who had been voluntarily freed by their former masters, those who had been freed by military order, and those who had escaped to the federal lines.[27] One planter wrote to a friend, "I have feared for a long while that the negro would prove unreliable whenever an opportunity presented itself of their obtaining their freedom," and the presence of African American troops became an opportunity for many enslaved people.[28]

Weitzel feared the possible reprisals by men in the Native Guards upon those who had enslaved them. Butler, on the other hand, accepted the situation as a "necessary evil following this system of labor, and the rebellion, as far as I can see."[29] Black soldiers walked onto plantations and both directly and indirectly galvanized many enslaved people with their freedom and with military protection. Eventually, Weitzel had a miles-long followers' trail behind his lines. He wrote to Butler that he had more formerly enslaved people following his trains than men under his command, and that he had no way to feed or clothe all those who now depended on him.[30] Growing frustrated with the situation, Weitzel asked for the removal of the Native Guards from his ranks, but Butler did not heed his request. Instead, he informed Weitzel that he still planned to send the 2d Louisiana Native Guard Infantry Regiment to join him, and that he was to hold all the roads and approaches in the region.[31] Ultimately, that is what Weitzel did, and as an indicator for the majority of their tour of duty in the U.S. Army, "both regiments of Native Guards" were assigned guard and fatigue duty.[32]

Weitzel requested to return the formerly enslaved people—now well into the hundreds—back to their enslavers.[33] He did not want to force the formerly enslaved back onto plantations, but Butler thought their labor was crucial to the region because of the need for food and to restart Louisiana's economy.[34] With Butler's guidance, Weitzel created a contract labor system that paid the men $10 a month and offered military protection and food for them. Within weeks, it was reported by one of the white soldiers that "we are too remote from the loyal section of our land for the North to fully appreciate the importance and magnitude of General Weitzel's achievements." His men subjugated the district of Attakapas and became involved in nearly every facet of military operations in the region. Their contributions were so vital to opening trade that one correspondent credited them with securing "the commerce of the country" because of the amount of sugar, hide, cotton, and other goods that were now being transported through New Orleans.[35]

The formerly enslaved men and women of Lafourche were not too far removed to know what was actually occurring in the parish. One man, who was a boy when the U.S. Army arrived, later recalled that his father served as a cook for the military. After being set free, his father and mother earned 30 and 15 cents, respectively; it was so little that he and his family nearly "starved to death."[36] It was a sign that Weitzel's contract system did not benefit African Americans, though it did help the white planters who owned the land.

Sadly, the Native Guards received their first mass field casualties while holding the railroad in Lafourche. A large explosion occurred, killing a few members of the 8th Vermont and injuring over a dozen soldiers, including four men in the 1st Louisiana Native Guards. Two theories emerged regarding the incident. The first was that one of the soldiers had been smoking while on duty next to an ammunition car. The second was that sparks from a locomotive moving through their lines reacted with the ammunition car, which was too close to the tracks. The explosion was significant enough that "a number of human limbs were afterwards found in the vicinity," according to a nearby war correspondent.[37] These were not the last field casualties for the Native Guards as the men continued to hold the region for the military against guerrillas and disease.

Men in the Native Guards used their position in the military to help free, feed, and even house those in need. Young John Crowder wrote to his mother after arriving in Lafourche that he had met a mother and young daughter who were starving to death, and he begged his mother to take them in, even to give them his own room. He reminded his mother that she was old and frail and could use the help. The reason he had joined the military at such a young age and was seeking help for her, he wrote, was so she could "live like a white lady."[38] Crowder's wish to help those he encountered as a soldier while also supporting loved ones he had left behind was shared by many in the Native Guards.

The families of the men experienced reprisals as a result of their service. The few resources that were assigned to the families of the Native Guards were often stolen, and those that were delivered were of the lowest quality.

Louisa D'Aunoy, wife of Manuel D'Aunoy (National Archives and Records Administration)

Prior to the war, it had been common for free men to marry enslaved women in New Orleans. A man paid for accommodations and furnishings on or near the land where his wife lived, and he could see her whenever she was not engaged in work. However, the men of the Native Guards were often verbally or physically prevented from seeing their wives and other family members by the white people who employed them.[39] Frequently, soldiers' wives and mothers were assaulted both physically and sexually. In response, parish police sometimes arrested these women, supposedly to protect them.[40] The police also arrested some women simply for not carrying papers proving their residency, even though Butler did not require it. They used these arrests as a means to harass members of the Native Guards.[41] The parish police essentially were acting as slave catchers.

The men in the Native Guards felt these effects acutely. For example, Private Auguste Perrauld's mother was an enslaved woman who had married a freeman, but she was still enslaved by Oscar Perrauld per the law. For years, she hired out her time and visited her husband, but once Oscar found out that Auguste had joined the Native Guards, he had Auguste's mother jailed by the city police. Auguste informed Stafford, who subsequently requested that Butler order her release. Butler endorsed the letter and sent it forward to the provost marshal. If the marshal could prove that she was innocent, she was to be released.[42] Frustrated, Butler disbanded and reformed the city's police to address issues like this and protect soldiers' families.

Black soldiers in the Native Guards were not paid due to a combination of factors. The promised advance pay and bounty from the War Department failed to materialize, and the paymaster for the regiment refused to issue the regular pay the men were owed.[43] Even if they had been receiving pay, it would have been less than promised; soon after Congress passed Public Law No. 160, it passed Public Law No. 166—often referred to as Militia Act of 1862—which removed the word white from the 1792 militia law and fixed Black soldiers' pay at a lower rate than whites' because Congress thought no Black men would see combat and to ensure that there was no semblance of equality in the ranks.[44] Their low pay was further reduced because they were charged for their uniforms, unlike white soldiers. Black New Orleans residents who were not in the military suffered similar treatment.[45] Even as Black men went into combat roles, their pay was reduced to cover the cost of their clothing.[46]

The chief cause of these inequities was the paymaster, Lieutenant Colonel Richard Irwin, who refused to disburse the soldiers' monthly pay. Stafford attempted to convince Irwin and the War Department to pay the men, but to no avail.[47] The pay issue led to destitution for the men and their families. Landlords used their poverty as an opportunity to remove troublesome tenants, evicting many of the families of those who were serving in the U.S. Army.[48] Men who attempted to find new lodging for their families—and, in doing so, removed their wives from enslavers who were mistreating them—were unable to find suitable locations.[49] A combination of racism and rebellious sentiment led to these forms of punishment, and unfortunately this occurred in more than just Louisiana during the war.[50]

Colonel Stafford brought the situation to the attention of his commanding general. In a letter, he described the government's failure to pay the troops and explained that it put the men in financial straits. Stafford requested that Butler forbid landlords from evicting the soldiers until they were paid. On 6 November 1862, Butler did just that: he ordered the suspension of all evictions for families of Union soldiers on the basis of past-due rent. In his now famous fashion, Butler quoted the order from Lovell that barred evictions of Confederate soldiers on a similar basis.[51] Thus, his order merely adapted a law already in use in Louisiana for Union soldiers. As the Native Guards made up the majority of soldiers who hadn't been paid and who had dwellings in the city, they were the chief beneficiaries of the edict.[52]

As the first full month of the experiment came to an end, public sentiment started to shift strongly in favor of the Native Guards. Frank Barclay, one of the writers for *L'Union,* visited Camp Strong and reported on the men's discipline and skill with firearms and their camp's neatness.[53] One letter from New Orleans published in the North stated, "In regard to arming the negro, I am in favor of it. They will make good, hardy soldiers." Many Republicans argued that African American men would become more disciplined, law-abiding, and masculine in the Native Guards. The end result would be "an unprecedented flow of good, honest, industrious citizens. You will have all the trades and all the arts, the laborer, the farmer, the mechanic, and your society will be utterly changed."[54] *L'Union* spurred a recruitment effort that continued to advertise a $100 bounty, 160 acres of land, and $13 a month for any African American who enlisted, despite the fact that the men in the first two regiments were still not being paid.[55]

Butler was so impressed with the Native Guards that he planned to include them in his most ambitious campaign, an effort to take Port Hudson. He intended to send the first two regiments to Port Hudson, one of the strongest Confederate positions on the river.[56] Butler and Weitzel believed that about eight thousand Confederate troops were divided among three positions at Port

Hudson, Ponchatoula, and Camp Moore.[57] They planned to wait to begin the battle in the spring, to ensure warm weather for the campaign. However, Confederate generals correctly surmised that taking Lafourche was "the first step against Port Hudson."[58] Thus, they took preemptive measures to fortify Port Hudson against such an attack.[59] One of those soldiers wrote to his sister that the U.S. Army would "meet with a warm reception."[60]

As Weitzel settled into the Lafourche district for the winter with the Native Guards, federal leaders strove to account for those they freed while respecting Union men and their property. Weitzel's orders from Butler were rather simple: He would allow planters who pledged their loyalty to keep their land. They would be required to pay their laborers $10 a month, with $3 expended for clothes and food. Weitzel was to disarm everyone to prevent guerrilla attacks and violence, he was to meet with African American leaders to assure them that all acts of Congress would be enforced, and he was to leave behind a force of men to ensure federal rule of law. Weitzel was then ordered to create a military district west of the Mississippi River designated the District of Lafourche, with multiple forts to hold the district from Confederate hands.[61]

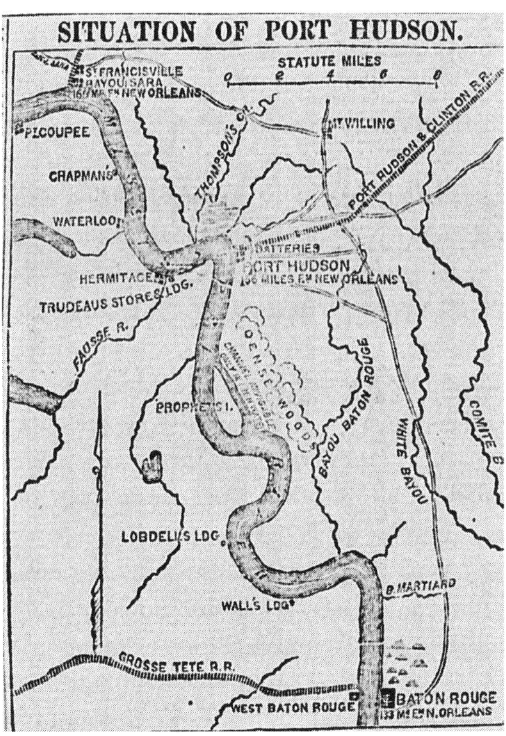


Port Hudson's position in February 1863
(Library of Congress, Prints and Photographs Division)

Weitzel still had his doubts about African American soldiers' willingness to sacrifice their lives for the Union. On 5 November, he wrote to Butler that he could not command the Native Guards anymore, as there were more Blacks than whites in his area of operations and the Native Guards were too troublesome. He wrote, "Since the arrival of the negro regiments symptoms of servile insurrection are becoming apparent . . . [white] Women and children, and even men are in terror. It is heart-rending, and I cannot make myself responsible for it." He went on to say that he had no confidence in their fighting ability, and he expressed a belief that the Native Guards were guilty of many of the crimes that white planters were reporting to him. Specifically, he described a few enslaved men who were not in the Native Guards who "assaulted the overseer" as proof that "the entire community thereabout are in hourly expectation and terror of a general rising."[62] Butler, however, retorted that not a single man in either unit had given him evidence of disloyalty. The general wrote, "You do not complain in your report that they either failed in [their] duty in that respect, or that they have acted otherwise than correctly and obediently to the commands of their Officers, or that they have committed any outrage or pillage upon the inhabitants." When Weitzel was tempted to turn down command of the District of Lafourche to avoid commanding the Native Guards, he was informed by Butler "these colored regiments of free men . . . must be commanded by the Officers of the Army of the United States," and until Weitzel's retirement or transfer, that officer was him.[63]

The men in the 1st Regiment did not enjoy patrolling the District of Lafourche. Their most common task was fatigue duty, hard physical labor reminiscent of the labor that enslaved people were often made to do. As many of the men had been free prior to the war, one of the Black officers believed "This was the worst time we had been exposed to such fatigue," a statement that was possibly true for many in the regiment. Their second-most-regular task was guard duty, which typically entailed guarding plantations on which some of the men had once been enslaved. Their bivouac sites were of the lowest quality, even by military standards. One officer later swore that their encampment resembled the "low wet holes inhabited by crocodiles, frogs, mosquitoes and rats."[64] Furthermore, Stafford was forced to break the regiment into separate companies to hold the large district, meaning that the men could not train and drill together and that they could not assist one another should their fellow soldiers or citizens of the district verbally or physically attack them.

By December, the 1st and 2d Louisiana Native Guards Regiments had been fielded, and according to a war correspondent, they were thought to be "doing excellent service in the division under Brig. Gen. Weitzel."[65] Weitzel, for his part, said that he had "undisputed possession of this country now, and this part of the campaign is a perfect success."[66] Butler wrote that he planned to recruit additional companies of "heavy artillerists, in which branch of service they excel." Additionally, "a company of light artillery, and a squadron of cavalry."[67] Butler wrote to Republican senator Henry Wilson that he had "two regiments of Native Guards (colored) in good condition and doing good service in the field, [and] another of the same sort has recently completed its organization."[68] Butler had finally received an official response from the War Department authorizing the enlistment of the Native Guards a few weeks prior. Finally, the men were given some assurances regarding pay and bounties for their service.

On 29 November 1862, Butler followed the plan that Phelps had laid out earlier that year, enlisting African Americans into artillery units. They formed the 1st Regiment Heavy Artillery (African Descent), and their mission was to garrison the batteries in New Orleans while they trained under their white officers. Around this time, the 3d Louisiana Native Guards Infantry Regiment also took shape.[69]

The racial makeup of the 3d Louisiana Native Guard Infantry Regiment was similar to that of the 2d Regiment. Butler was able to free and enlist men who had previously been enslaved by immigrants, and he used the Confiscation Act to take from those he deemed disloyal. Many in the 2d and 3d Regiments who had been enslaved before enlisting were considered to be of darker skin than most men in the 1st Regiment. The Teche district garrisoned by the Native Guards supplied additional enlisted men who joined the regiment. Butler struggled to find educated African Americans to serve as officers, and Colonel John Nelson enlisted Barclay's aid to call for additional volunteers. *L'Union* ran multiple editorials calling for educated French- and English-speaking free men of color to serve as either commissioned or noncommissioned officers in the Native Guards.[70] However, because there were so many laborers on the rolls of the 3d Regiment, some of its officer and noncommissioned officer positions remained unfilled. Even those who didn't directly serve in the military still assisted the U.S. Army by offering supplies and aid.

Similar to its sister regiments, the 3d Louisiana Native Guards Volunteer Infantry Regiment was organized and mustered into service quickly; however, despite the success of the previous two regiments, racist white officers used the men for the most trivial of tasks. According to a soldier in the department, the men in the 3d were "detailed for picket duty on sugar plantations to protect the operatives in sugar making." They were sent there so "that the white troops may be left unshackled to operate in the field."[71] Butler phrased it to the president that they were needed to preserve sugar production in the region held by Weitzel. Furthermore, their picket duty appeased racist soldiers in the other units because "there need be no fear of ill consequences from white men feeling a repugnance to fight by the side of blacks."[72] Most infuriating for white planters in the region, the Native Guards were patrolling the Teche district in the Lafourche Parish, the same area where many of the formerly enslaved in the 2d and 3d Regiments had once toiled.

The 3d Regiment differed from the prior two, as its line officers' positions were not exclusively filled by Black officers. To fill the gaps, Butler recruited elites from the New England regiments in the department whom he knew would lead the men with care and tact. Also, while all of the noncommissioned officers were still Black, the ranks were filled with more formerly enslaved people than had been the case in the previous two regiments. This was the first time the men of the Native Guards would learn what it was like to serve under a majority of white line officers, and for many it was a bad experience.[73] In the end, they wished that they, too, served under African American line officers. Unfortunately, this did not come to pass. The makeup of the 3d Regiment's officers became the standard a few months later.

As the unit prepared to move toward Weitzel's command, the men paraded through the city, "presenting a truly brilliant appearance." A writer for the *New Orleans Daily Crescent* said, "It will remain upon our memory as one of the pleasantest reminiscences of the struggle in which we are now engaged."[74] However, not everyone in New Orleans was proud of the three infantry regiments and one artillery battery the Department of the Gulf had raised from the African American and Creole class of the city. Priests in the archdiocese refused the sacrament to soldiers who joined the U.S. Army, and some went as far as offering "some indecent and shameful" words to Black children in the city.[75] One soldier reported that the men were often "hooted at in the streets of New Orleans as rabble of armed plebeians and cowards."[76] According to Stafford, the taunts were intended to cause the men to retaliate in kind; if they did, they would provide evidence that they did not belong in the Union uniform.[77] On some occasions, the men did respond with their own derisive comments or even violence, but for the most part the Native Guards attempted to uphold a certain level of decorum. Eventually Butler interceded, saying, "My colored soldiers . . . are to be protected from the insults of all persons," and he promised to use a military commission to punish "the party found . . . to be in the wrong."[78]

Upon arrival in Lafourche, the 3d Louisiana Native Guard Regiment was assigned to sugarcane duty, a difficult and unpleasant mission. Soon after preparing the land for the next year's crop, the 3d and 1st spent the next few weeks foraging around the parish and capturing rebel weapons, which terrified Weitzel and whites in the region, who feared the men would kill enslavers. Black soldiers confiscated fifty-one muskets, salt, sugar, and a sloop ship used to run the Union blockade.[79] In response, whites hurled numerous insults and curses at the men, and a few even attempted to attack them. However, they soon learned that men of the Native Guards were not submissive, as the soldiers fought back and defended themselves when needed.

Black soldiers in the regiment may have taken clandestine steps to rid themselves of Confederate soldiers. A corporal from the 8th Vermont informed his family, "Yesterday, our boys, with the 1st La., (colored) took several prisoners. Some they let go, others they keep, and some the negroes shot."[80] He claimed that after Colonel Thomas questioned the prisoners, "The negroes heard the examination, followed them beyond the pickets and shot them." There is some evidence that this happened, as the Black soldiers were searched and Confederate money was found. Events like these were, unfortunately, quite common during the war from both sides.

Want of discipline was a common concern in the city. White residents regularly complained about "impudence to white people" by the soldiers in the regiments.[81] Many of the men in the Native Guards were accused of stealing oranges, chickens, and other small items to feed themselves or their families. However, their need to steal to survive was an understandable consequence of the fact that they were still not being paid and some of their families were now homeless as a result of racism. Nevertheless, to prove their discipline, some of the officers in the Native Guards overcorrected when chastising their men. Captain Emile Detiége provides an example of such action. On 9 December, while in camp, the captain approached a new recruit named Joseph DeGruy and gave him an order to fall in for morning drill. DeGruy moved too slowly for Detiége's liking, and, in response, the captain grasped him around his collar, shook him, and yelled, "Did I not tell you to come immediately?" DeGruy yelled back, "Don't shake me that way." The situation escalated to the point that DeGruy thrust his hand into Detiége's face to push him away and stop the assault, but this only angered Detiége more. He pulled his officer's revolver and then fired twice at his new recruit. Detiége later claimed he shot DeGruy for disobeying orders. The second shot killed him, and the captain was indicted—but not convicted—for murder. After the incident, Detiége continued in his role as a commander in the Native Guards, but he grew more hesitant to discipline, and DeGruy's death later became a factor in ending his military career.[82] Overall, soldiers in the Native Guards were disciplined compared with those in other units in the Department of the Gulf. An overview of all the general courts-martial conducted between September and December 1862 notably does not include any members of the Native Guards; conversely, many of the white soldiers from New England faced multiple charges, ranging from drinking on duty to violence against women.[83]

The greatest accomplishment of the Native Guards was the liberation and elevation of enslaved people in their area of operations. The regiments were filled with those who had been enslaved prior to the war; the 1860 census only counted 2,578 free African American men between the ages of fifteen and fifty-nine.[84] With over three thousand men serving in the regiments by the winter, not only did the population of freed people in the region increase, but their military service solidified their place in the nation. When a white soldier encountered an older enslaved man who was near tears with joy, the soldier said, "Uncle, freedom will do you no good; you are just on the edge of the grave." The man replied, "I knows dat well enough, but I've got my boy; and I bless you all, kase you give im free."[85]

As the year came to an end, Butler summarized his efforts with the Native Guards. In taking Lafourche, he said, they held "the richest portion of Louisiana."[86] He complained that the War Department still failed to reinforce his command, and the Native Guards were the only troops to help him hold his expansive department. Nevertheless, he was proud of the two regiments guarding the Opelousas Railroad, writing, "I could not have moved as I have were it not for my negro units."[87] While none of the regiments had seen combat against Confederate soldiers yet, one officer in the 1st Louisiana Native Guards believed "that there is not a regiment in the service more willing to share the hardships of marching and bivouacking, and more desirous of meeting the enemy than this regiment."[88] The president was proud of the accomplishments of the Native Guards and glad that planters were making arrangements to pay formerly enslaved individuals without congressional edicts.[89] Indeed, by the end of the year even John Durnin, the brother of James who was then encamped with the southern Army in Baton Rouge, wrote to his sister that they could only listen to reports of the U.S. Army change Louisiana and capture their sugar. Although they had "guns stacked and ready," the department's position in New Orleans was too secure to risk an attack.[90] Since the Native Guards were secure in their holdings, Butler shipped "the first sugar ever made by free black labor in Louisiana" to the president, noting that the taste should be all the more pleasing without the "flavor of the degrading whip."[91]

Butler's shipment of sugar from Louisiana was only one of many examples of societal shifts taking place by the end of 1862. Butler himself took note of the "great change in [the] social and political system" of Louisiana, one he realized would and could only occur as a great shock to the government and populace. Officers who had once doubted the department's actions now realized that slavery was doomed and free labor would be the standard for the region under Union control, inadvertently fulfilling the proclamation that Phelps had issued one year earlier. Butler said that he learned three lessons in his tenure that he passed on to Lincoln: free white labor could be more economical than labor by enslaved people, paid African Americans could be profitable to plantation owners, and military control was needed to ensure that free labor was sustained. Butler expressed that he did not want to carry the latter duty over the long term.[92]

The Native Guards appreciated the efforts of their commanding officers to let them serve their nation. One man wrote to *L'Union*, "They know the good intentions of the Government of the United States and those of Gen. Butler in regard to them . . . there is not a single man of color who is not ready to shed his last drop of blood in aiding to maintain here the Federal authority, and who does not pray daily to God that the energetic Commanding-General, who knew how to transform a city of iniquities into a habitation of justice, be never removed from this Department."[93] In another letter, a soldier wrote that nothing could break his trust in Colonel Stafford.[94] Butler, in turn, demonstrated full confidence in African American soldiers. With three regiments totaling over 2,700 men already in the field, he ordered the enlistment of an additional infantry regiment and two artillery batteries that were training at Camp Strong. He later assessed the men he recruited into these units: "They were intelligent, obedient, highly appreciative of their position, and fully maintained its dignity." In his summation, "Better soldiers never shouldered a musket."[95]

On 19 December, the officers of the Native Guards reported to General Weitzel that the men in the regiments had performed every duty assigned them. Finally presented with an opportunity to rid himself of the regiments for a while, Weitzel ordered them to garrisons at Forts Jackson, St. Philip, and Macomb. As the men slowly left Lafourche, they continued to hold the roads and railways until properly relieved by incoming units.[96] Desertions under Weitzel were remarkably low considering the harsh treatment from members of the white populace and a commanding officer who did not support the men.

1st Regiment of the Native Guards at Fort Macomb
(*Harper's Weekly*, 1863)

There were twenty-nine desertions in the 1st Regiment, twelve in the 2d, and ten in the 3d.[97] The three forts to which the Native Guards were assigned were relatively close to New Orleans, and they constantly exposed the men to racism, but these new locations also afforded them the opportunity to see their families and enjoy their time in the city. According to a war correspondent, Colonel Stafford's men loved him; he inspired "signs of joy and animation at his presence among them." Stafford showed off his men and "the alacrity of their movements" when a correspondent from the *New York Times* came to visit their new locations a few weeks later. In the correspondent's write-up, Stafford spoke fondly of them: "'You see my men can work, Sir, though people say they can't fight,' said the Colonel, triumphantly. 'We don't trouble our heads much about waiting for transportation. Put me down in a forest with those same fellows and I'll build you a city, for I have every useful trade represented among them.'"[98] Within a few months, the men proved to their commander that African Americans could and did make good soldiers for the U.S. Army.

The success of the Native Guards became the definitive answer to the question that plagued the nation as the president's 1 January deadline for the

Emancipation Proclamation loomed: "What is to be done with the liberated slaves?" An editorial in New Orleans answered, "The results of Gen. Butler's negro regiments are looked to with much interest, as tending to settle this, one of the great problems of the war."[99] Writers for northern newspapers argued, "If they can be enlisted into volunteer regiments do this," and that those who could not fight should be protected by those who could. The quartermaster general, Montgomery C. Meigs, wrote in his end of year report that African American men were the key to the South's ability to last as long as it did in the war, and that if the U.S. Army would just adopt the same stance on Black soldiers, it could win the fight. Meigs ended, "In this work the loyal inhabitants of the country, white or black, must be compelled to assist, and it is impossible to cast aside the millions of recruits who will offer themselves for the work . . . animated by the strong desire not merely for political but for personal liberty."[100] Although there were some whites in the country who hoped colonization could still address the question, the Native Guards had proved that Black men were staying and fighting for their country.[101] Through military service, African American men proved their courage and supported themselves and their families.

All of the regiments of the Native Guards were a success.[102] A year prior, the Native Guards had been ordered by Governor Moore to escort and march Union prisoners through New Orleans. His order had been countermanded at the last minute out of fear of African Americans publicly controlling white men. In an ironic turn of events, dozens of those same men in the Native Guards marched about twenty Confederate guerrillas through the city to the cheers of Unionists in the winter of 1862. According to Denison, "It seemed a just retribution."[103]

Chapter 6

# *PROVE THEMSELVES WORTHY OF YOU*

## GENERAL BANKS AND THE PURGE

"One bright day in December, some excitement was created on the levee by the appearance of several large steamers coming up the river, loaded with soldiers, their bands playing and the men cheering as they passed the city," wrote Admiral David G. Farragut. He soon realized that "It was the army of the new commander of the Department, Gen. N. P. Banks, now sent to supersede General Butler. The change was a surprise to many." Farragut was among those who were surprised.[1] That was the day many officers and soldiers in the Department of the Gulf learned that General Benjamin F. Butler had been replaced by General Nathaniel P. Banks, beginning a new phase of the war.[2]

In many respects, the Louisiana Native Guards had already proven themselves to the Department of the Gulf and the federal government; however, 1863 began with a new commanding general and a new set of problems for the regiments. Racism was always a problem for the first Black regiments in the U.S. Army during the Civil War, but a change in leader also meant a change in the command climate for everyone. These changes affected people in and out of the military, and the following chapter examines those changes and the effects they had on the Louisiana Native Guards. In doing so, it proves that the men in the regiments continued to substantiate themselves in new ways while fighting new enemies.

The success of the Louisiana Native Guards and the Department of the Gulf led a writer at the *Freemont Journal* to muse, "Who can beat Ben. Butler?"[3] However, Butler proved to be his own worst enemy. As George Denison reported, "I know of but one fault to be found with Gen. Butler. He has (in my opinion) been altogether too willing to permit his friends to make fortunes."[4] Notoriously, Butler and his brother, Andrew, pursued a number of illegal business ventures together. Andrew had joined Benjamin in the city early in the campaign. He was often called Colonel Butler as a courtesy, but he held no rank in the U.S. Army.[5] The brothers allegedly worked together to enrich themselves through multiple business ventures, confiscating liquor, cotton, cattle, and medicine, and possibly receiving kickbacks from northern merchants for certain actions beneficial to their business transactions. In a letter to Salmon P. Chase, Denison stated, "Col. Butler is a brother of Gen'l. Butler and come out with the army and immediately commenced doing business. He is not in government employ. He is here for the sole purpose of making money." By September 1862, according to Denison, Andrew Butler amassed over "half a million dollars." While Denison believed Benjamin Butler to be innocent in his brother's graft, his acquiescence made him culpable. Denison further theorized that the conflict between Butler and General John Phelps had worsened the situation, as "Gen. Phelps is beloved by his soldiers, and no man has suspected his integrity and disinterestedness. This is not strictly true of Gen. Butler, for . . . many soldiers and citizens—Union and Secessionists—think he is interested in the speculation of his brother (Col. Butler) and others." Denson thought the public suspected that Colonel Butler was not only corrupt but that he worked with the Confederacy to enrich himself and his brother to the tune of nearly $2 million toward the end of the year.[6] General Butler later argued that all his transactions totaled a little over $800,000, with his brother's profits being near $200,000—far less than the $2 million suspected by his detractors in the city.[7] Nevertheless, within a month of the rumor mill circulating these stories, even Butler's friends suspected that the brothers were working together and using the military to protect their illegal business practices.[8]

White southerners were already looking for a reason to remove Butler, and between his treatment of southern women and foreign citizens, whom William Seward and Abraham Lincoln did not want to anger, federal government officials were compelled to act. By August, Butler heard rumors that he would be replaced. He wrote to Sarah Butler, "They have an absurd story here that Banks is to be sent down to take my place. I wish to heaven he would come!"[9]

Nathaniel P. Banks completed his basic education at a young age, then worked in a mill for years before teaching himself law and moving into politics. His upbringing and workman's life gave him a military build; unlike Butler, Banks was considered tall and handsome. Banks was a stout Republican and politician from Massachusetts who served in the House of Representatives between 1853 and 1857 before becoming governor of Massachusetts in

General Nathaniel P. Banks
(Library of Congress, Prints and Photographs Division)

1858. When the war began, he was president of the Illinois Central Railroad. As a fervent Unionist, he decided to offer his services to the military. Similar to Butler, he had more political connections than military experience, and it showed in his lack of military ability. He was commissioned directly to the rank of major general in the volunteer forces on the same date as Butler, 16 May 1861. Banks commanded the Department of Annapolis and the Department of the Shenandoah before he was given command of the Military District of Washington.

In these roles, he gained experience administering a large command and overseeing a military district prior to coming to New Orleans. Banks was considered more predictable than Butler—a stable choice to appease Republicans ahead of an election year. Because of Banks's political interests, many southerners knew he would not ruffle any feathers in the South for fear of jeopardizing his aspirations.[10] While not a defender of slavery, Banks was not an abolitionist, and he did not endorse Black rights of any kind. As governor of Massachusetts, he vetoed a bill that would have allowed free Blacks to serve in the state's militia in 1859. His political stance on the issue of enslavement—

and his penchant for fence-sitting on important issues—had a significant effect on the futures of the Department of the Gulf and the Louisiana Native Guards.[11]

General Banks gained popularity during the Civil War. In the lead-up to the 1864 presidential election, he seemed like a natural choice for the Republican nomination if Lincoln decided not to run again.[12] However, he proved to be an inadequate battlefield commander, losing horribly against Thomas Jackson in Virginia before arriving in New Orleans.[13] Like many others, Butler thought the War Department's orders would leave him in charge and that Banks would serve under him. Major General Henry W. Halleck even told him, "The rumor in regard to your removal from command is a mere newspaper story, without foundation."[14] However, on 14 December, Chase told him that the newspaper accounts were true—he was going to be replaced. Chase thought Banks's skills in administration were on par with Butler's and that he was among the Union's greatest talents, and while Chase believed that Butler had done more work for the Union and African Americans than any other general commissioned by the president, he was under pressure to remove Butler from command. Butler preferred to resign than serve under someone else's command, but Chase convinced him not to resign and helped him to get reassigned instead of ending his military career.[15]

Butler issued one final order during the change of command ceremony: "Relieved from further duties in this department . . . I take leave of you by this final order, it being impossible to visit your scattered outposts, covering hundreds of miles of frontier of a larger territory than some of the kingdoms in Europe. I greet you, my brave comrades, and say farewell." He thanked his soldiers for their service, their construction of multiple encampments that they had held against the Confederacy, their tenacity in the face of numerous hardships, both military and civil, and their enforcement of federal law and order during his tenure in command. Perhaps alluding to the reasons for his removal, he noted that the department had landed with a military chest of only $75 but returned over a half million dollars to the federal government while supplying themselves from the Gulf region. He finally turned his attention to the Native Guards and People of Color who could help the army: "By your practical philanthropy you have won the confidence of the race and the slave. Hailing you as deliverers, they are ready to aid you as willing servants, faithful laborers, or, using the tactics taught them by your enemies, to fight with you in the field."[16] Colonel Stafford responded to Butler's praise of the Native Guards as follows: "They look upon you as their Creator and their Father.

. . . They will, when opportunity offers, seek to prove themselves worthy of you, who made them what they are."[17] Starting at noon on 16 December, the Department of the Gulf was officially under the command of General Banks.

Butler and his wife, Sarah, left New Orleans on 24 December. At the time, he did not know if his military career was over or if he would serve in another area of operation. *L'Union* published letters from Black soldiers who were praising the general on his day of departure, with some of the Native Guards making it clear they would miss him as a Unionist and leader.[18] Hundreds crowded the wharves to see him off, some in tears. Farragut was there to see the man he had grown to respect as a fellow liberator of New Orleans. While Banks did not attend the parting ceremony, many from the Department of the Gulf were there to send off their former commander. As Butler's ship slowly left, Farragut's flagship fired off a saluting salvo, and the shore battery did the same. As his ship disappeared over the horizon and the crowd dispersed, reportedly the last to wave goodbye was an elderly African American woman who said, "Good-bye, honey, you never stole nothing from me."[19]

Numerous changes took place under Banks's command. The Department of the Gulf was co-designated the XIX Army Corps, which was appropriate given the size of the command and its mission.[20] General George Shepley remained the military governor of the state, but Banks, whom he was supposed to assist, curtailed his power.[21] Halleck even authorized Banks to interfere with General Grant's mission if Banks saw fit, because the president still saw New Orleans and the lower Mississippi as vital to Union success in the war.[22]

White southerners—most notably foreigners and planters in the region—were happy that Banks was in New Orleans. The secretary of state, William Seward, took the extraordinary step of saying that Butler's removal was intended to placate them. Seward sent out a circular stating, "Banks would be in command at New Orleans, and would take measures that there should be no interference with foreigners."[23] Count Eugène Méjan was also recalled for his public tiffs with Butler, and the French hoped that without Méjan and Butler clashing there would be no further troubles between the two sides in the city.[24] By February, Banks reported to Edwin Stanton that he had met with all foreign government officials and had given them "all the consideration they could possibly claim." Foreign agents were on friendly terms with the new commander.[25]

Many white Americans in the city were ecstatic that the "Beast Butler was superseded by General N.P. Banks," for Banks promised "protection of private rights, and amends for wrongs committed by the troops under his command."[26] Jefferson Davis issued an order, similar to the order he issued against General John Phelps, declaring Butler a felon, and Davis ordered everyone in the South to treat Butler as an outlaw who should be hanged if captured.[27] White citizens came together and wrote a letter to Lincoln—which Banks endorsed—thanking him for removing Butler and calling his time in command "tyrannical & oppressive & to the last degree offensive."[28] Some Union generals recognized that rebels and foreign sympathizers were thrilled specifically because they could act more freely without a leader like Butler who would punish them for stepping out of line.[29] The chief wish among white southerners, however, was that Banks "would disband the negro regiments."[30] Several planters met with Banks on 22 December 1862, begging him to withdraw the Native Guards, as the presence of Black troops was detrimental to their system of labor and they feared that the impending Emancipation Proclamation deadline would incite a revolt.[31] One planter wrote a letter begging Banks "to disarm the negroes at least for the present and place white men" nearby instead.[32] Banks took such requests seriously, but Captain Henry Louis Rey described the planters as hostile to liberty and the Black race when dismissing the proposition in *L'Union*.[33]

As General Banks prepared to take the Department of the Gulf into the new year, African Americans were preparing for the president's 1 January deadline, as it meant the emancipation of all enslaved people in the South, even if only politically. One abolitionist paper called it "the birthday of liberty," as slavery would no longer be protected by federal law.[34] The General Convention of the Methodist Protestant Church resolved "that we heartily endorse the Emancipation proclamation of President Lincoln, because it strikes at that baleful cause of all our civil and ecclesiastical difficulties, American slavery—the sum of all villainies, the darling idol of villains, the central power of villainous secessionism, but now by the wisdom of the President about to be made the agent of retributive justice in punishing the culmination of villainous enterprises, the attempt to overthrow the most glorious civil government that God's providence ever established upon earth."[35] When the Department of the Gulf directed all "places of public worship" under their control to read and pray over Lincoln's proclamation, many white churches rebuffed the call.[36] However, Claude Maistre—one of the few Catholic priests who supported the Native Guards—read Lincoln's Emancipation Proclamation to his congregation and called for the abolition of slavery in New Orleans. *L'Union* recognized him as "a sincere and devoted friend of the Union," but his fellow white citizens abandoned his church, and he received multiple lynching threats.[37]

Frederick Douglass, at the Cooper Institute in New York and with the backing of the Emancipation Proclamation, asked again when Black men would fight alongside Union generals like they had with Washington and Jackson.[38] A correspondent in the Department of the Gulf wrote, "So important, indeed, do I deem this proclamation of Mr. Lincoln, that I consider it surpassed in magnitude of its humanity only by the inspiration of the Sermon on the Mount."[39]

However, the region in and around New Orleans was deemed not to be in a state of rebellion, per Lincoln's directive, and this loophole allowed some enslavers to retain the people they were enslaving. Others found it difficult to forcibly keep African Americans in a state of servitude, as seen in Lafourche. Some planters emancipated their enslaved to free themselves of the burden, and in other cases the people they had enslaved freed themselves because of the presence of the military and the Native Guards, who actively assisted emancipation efforts of enslaved people. In the rare cases that enslavers fought to retain the people they'd enslaved, they found that many white and Black soldiers in the Department of the Gulf were willing to enforce emancipation no matter what.[40] The Emancipation Proclamation was also a transnational maneuver that helped to prevent Europe from entering into American affairs.[41]

However, the biggest factor regarding the New Year deadline was that the federal government began accepting Black soldiers into the U.S. Army in larger numbers.[42] Some northerners questioned the merits of enlisting Black men into the U.S. Army. The *New York Times* summarized four key points that defenders of slavery used to answer the government's Black question. First, the *Times* writer outlined, "The negroes will not fight." However, the men in the Native Guards had already demonstrated in small skirmishes that they were willing and capable of fighting. Second, "Whites will not fight with them—that prejudice against them is so strong that our own citizens will not enlist, or will quit the service, if compelled to fight by their side." However, white officers in the Native Guards, the 8th Vermont, and the Department of the Gulf had already demonstrated that this was not universally true. Although prejudice existed in the ranks, it did not compel a large number of men to resign their service in the military. Third, "It is said we shall get no negroes—or not enough to prove of any service." Once again, the Native Guards proved this argument moot, as four infantry regiments and an artillery battery had been raised in a single city—with more to come—demonstrating that Black men would enlist when given the chance to serve. The final argument was that "the use of negroes will exasperate the South."[43] There was some truth to this point. Many of the ardent rebels in New Orleans grew angrier upon the sight of armed Black men, especially those they had previously enslaved. Of course, failing to make a strategic maneuver that could help win a war out of fear of the enemy's response is partially illogical. Furthermore, the Native Guards—and the entire Department of the Gulf—proved that the military could address potential problems with the right leadership. The Louisiana Native Guards thus stood as a rejoinder to any objections against Black soldiers serving in the military.

Indeed, the Native Guards had already changed the U.S. Army. Within weeks of the 1st Louisiana Native Guards Regiment being constituted in New Orleans, the War Department informed Hunter's successor in the Department of the South that he could "receive into the services of the United States such number of volunteers of African descent as you may deem expedient, not exceeding five thousand."[44] Hunter's forces, which had been disbanded earlier that year, were reconstituted under General Rufus Saxton and their new colonel, Thomas Wentworth Higginson, on 7 November 1862. The War Department continued to allow generals to enlist formerly enslaved men in the military, and on 13 January 1863 the 1st Kansas Colored Regiment was mustered into federal service.[45] The success of the Native Guards in Lafourche proved to many northerners that it made sense to allow free and formerly enslaved Blacks to serve as soldiers. Going into 1863 and onward, their numbers continued to grow in the U.S. Army. However, they were still an experiment, and General Henry Halleck, the army's general-in-chief and chief strategist of the Union war effort, informed General Ulysses S. Grant that if the Native Guards with "Banks near New Orleans should be satisfactory, a much larger force will be organized during the coming summer."[46] The Native Guards were widely recognized for spurring change in the U.S. Army going into 1863. It was up to Banks to continue that experiment for the military.

Despite this recognition, racist rhetoric continued to proliferate. One white soldier wrote, "The niggers had as good a right to be shot as anybody."[47] Another soldier bemoaned to his family, "What's the use to have men from Maine, Vermont, and Massachusetts dying down here in these swamps"; to him, "You can't replace these men, but if a nigger dies, all you have to do is to send out and get another one."[48] One soldier swore that if he had the choice between shooting a rebel or a Black man, he would "shoot the nigger first for I still think a white man is a little better than a nigger."[49] Claims about undisciplined troops continued to circulate as well. One officer reported to a New Hampshire newspaper: "There are endless complains of burning, stealings, ravishings, and lesser crimes" by the Native Guards, and he theorized that

"Gen. Banks will have to disband them or put them under iron rule," and if that was not enough, then Banks would have "to garrison the black troops at some fort away from civilization."[50] A *L'Union* writer argued that many of these claims were unfounded, based solely on the accounts of white residents who wanted to slander the Native Guards.[51] It is possible that some formerly enslaved men roamed the countryside in need of money and food after escaping enslavement, but those men would have had no connection to the Native Guards or the military if and when they did commit any crimes.

Within days of taking command, Banks wrote to Halleck that he had garrisoned the Native Guards and that they were already on labor and guard duty.[52] A war correspondent from the *New York Times* visited the regiments under their new regime, and his words demonstrated the racial hierarchy that existed during the war. He was shocked to meet "Capt. [Edgar] Davis, of Company A . . . with light blue eyes, ruddy complexion, soft silky hair, and a splendid moustache of a sandy color nearly approaching red." He went on to write, "I would have defied the most consummate expert in niggerology, by the aid of the most powerful microscope, to discover the one drop of African blood in that man's veins; still, there it was upon the record against him." When the men moved toward the railroad for their next movement, he saw the "Women . . . , of all colors, taking leave of their husbands and brothers—and some of the feebler sex with an amount of fairness and refined physical beauty that many a white woman might covet." Like many who met the men of the Native Guards, he was impressed that "all of them conversed fluently in two languages—French and English—were well posted up in history and general literature, and during the long range of subjects—civil, literary, political or moral—which I brought expressly on the tapis, I found on one or two occasions, that I was conversing with men of no ordinary knowledge and mental capacity." The correspondent ended by quoting one of the officers of color present for duty: "If you doubt us, why not give us the chances of proof which we have so long and vainly been imploring?"[53]

Jefferson Davis did not wish to give the Native Guards the opportunity to prove their worth, and he issued an order directed at the regiments the day before Butler left New Orleans. The order contained four declarations. First, it said that officers—white and black—were "not entitled to be considered as soldiers engaged in honorable warfare, but as robbers and criminals." As such, they were all sentenced to death if captured. Second, all the enlisted soldiers of the Native Guards were "instruments used for the commissions of crimes, perpetrated by his [Butler's] orders, and not as free agents." Thus, they were not to be paroled if captured. Third, all formerly enslaved Blacks who were captured would be reenslaved if they were not executed. Fourth, any officers found serving alongside similar units would be treated the same as those serving in the Native Guards, a blanket attack on the units expected to take shape after the Emancipation Proclamation was issued.[54] Davis soon convinced the Confederate Congress to make his order a law, and the entire southern military had orders to treat Black soldiers as instruments of criminals and their officers as criminals already sentenced to death.[55] Davis's order demonstrates that even he recognized—and possibly feared—what the Native Guards meant for the U.S. Army and the new phase of the Civil War.

Some soldiers complained that Banks was not as strong an administrator as his predecessor, and he was also found wanting as a military strategist. Lincoln, it seems, even considered recalling Butler to New Orleans when Banks showed that he was remissive in his approach to enslavers.[56] Similar to when Reverdy Johnson arrived in the city a year prior, Banks reversed many of Butler's policies, to the delight of the white New Orleanians. Banks also failed to maintain the quality of sanitation that Butler had achieved just a year prior. Within months of taking control, some of the troops renamed one of Banks's encampments "Camp Diarea" because every soldier stationed there was affected with diarrhea. Some also got fevers and other symptoms, resulting in hospitalization.[57] One soldier told his wife they rarely received soap, and nearly every man was infested with fleas.[58] However, reports from Banks and his officers show he spent just as much time as Butler, if not more, administering and fixing New Orleans and the large expanse under the charge of the XIX Corps.[59] Many of the officers in the Department of the Gulf were corrupt, possibly having thrived under Butler's command. A few were court-martialed for accepting bribes, and in one instance a rebel named Robert Gould paid a lieutenant from Connecticut for fake passes to leave the city.[60] To Banks, Butler's neglect of small matters and minor corruption by Butler's brother had been tantamount to treason.[61]

While many of these changes did not directly affect the Native Guards, Banks made one major change to how enslaved people were treated. Unlike Butler, Banks entertained planters who planned to preserve slavery in some form. Planters from Lafourche and other rich parishes met with Banks at the St. Charles Hotel in February and persuaded him to allow them to continue to use enslaved labor for the good of the southern economy. Banks, in turn, promised his men would induce enslaved people to return to plantations. Forced Black labor remained in Louisiana thanks to Banks.[62] The compensation that Butler had promised would be granted, but the planters could wait until the end of the year to pay. Naturally, they could debit the accounts of enslaved laborers for clothes, food, and any other necessities, and enslaved people would be forced to labor until the end of their contracts or risk not being paid at all. If caught not working, they could be forced to work for the government without any form of compensation before being returned to a plantation for contract labor.[63] Additionally, Banks offered all planters west of the Mississippi, "without reference to past political opinions or relations," the opportunity to sell their goods in the New Orleans markets.[64] While the order was meant to aid the government and the economy, in actuality it aided planters and strengthened their position in the region. All told, it was a disastrous compromise that Black laborers grew to hate over the course of Banks's tenure in command. Some residents of New Orleans feared that Banks's regime would be similar to the system enacted by *le Code Noir* years earlier.[65] George Hepworth, an officer in the 4th Native Guards, wholly disagreed with Banks's plan, believing it was the antithesis of their mission.[66] Another of Banks's white soldiers noted that he simply "patted rebels upon the back and told them what good fellows they were."[67] Complicating the problem even further, the Emancipation Proclamation excluded the sovereign territory of Native Americans, so the hundreds who were enslaved on their territory were still legally enslaved even though tribes such as the Choctaw openly supported the Confederacy.[68] With so many groups working to keep People of Color enslaved, the stage was set for numerous clashes between African Americans and those who wanted to subjugate them.

African Americans, however, saw themselves not as enslaved laborers but as free People of Color who could choose who they worked for and when they worked. This schism caused numerous issues in the department's area of operation during the year. Men who wanted to freely leave their plantations and join the Union army faced overseers who would openly punish them with the military watching. For example, a Black laborer left his plantation and attempted to join the Native Guards. As one of few formerly enslaved men who was literate, he could have been a noncommissioned officer. However, he was instead captured by the department's provost marshal, beaten until he was bleeding from the head, and then returned to a plantation to labor in St. Bernard Parish by white Union soldiers. There, he was ordered to spend eighteen hours in the stocks, with an additional six hours with his hands tied together in front of him while his elbows were bound behind him so mosquitoes could cover his back, followed by an additional six hours in the stocks before finally getting twenty-five lashes. The provost later wrote that the man only wanted to join the Native Guards so he would have nothing to do and plenty of food to eat from the government.[69] Denison expressed that, under Banks, slavery was nearly reestablished due to the general's conciliatory policies, but thankfully many officials in the department did not fully acquiesce to this change.[70]

The regions west of New Orleans continued to cause trouble for the Department of the Gulf, and Banks continued to send troops into Lafourche and Bayou Teche. Despite Banks's efforts to the contrary, Blacks continued to be emancipated under his tenure.[71] The provost who had captured and returned laborers to their plantations was later removed, and charges were filed against him once his commanding officer found out what he had done.[72] U.S. cavalry officers freed dozens of enslaved people, although even these acts of liberation revealed the officers' racism: they reported enslaved people, along with mules and horses, as beasts of burden captured for military use.[73] Another cavalry soldier reported purposely going into prisons and jails to liberate enslaved people whose only crime was attempting to escape enslavement. The following month, the same soldier told his wife that his regiment had raided a Confederate encampment to take supplies and free enslaved people, showing that, under Banks's command, some Union soldiers in the XIX Corps were still following the examples of Generals Phelps and Butler.[74]

Naturally, the men serving in the Native Guards regularly worked to free enslaved people when they had the chance. On the Raceland Plantation in Lafourche Parish, an overseer complained to Banks that Black officers in the regiment had arrested and threatened to shoot him for his treatment of the people he enslaved and his treatment toward the wife of one of the soldiers. The officers informed all of the enslaved people on the Raceland Plantation that they were free and did not need to work an enslaver anymore, and that the government would feed and care for all of them if they followed the men back to camp.[75] Captain John De Forest wrote to his wife that often when they helped enslaved people secure their freedom, they were gifted food by enslaved people in return, and he was able to subsist almost exclusively on these gifts for a while.[76] George Hepworth, the labor superintendent for the department, recognized after witnessing these events on a few plantations that "it is very seldom that you hear a good laugh from [an enslaved] black man." Instead, wrote Hepworth, they only appeared happy when asked, "Uncle, would you like to be free?"—a question that many of the men in the Native Guards loved to ask their brethren of color.[77] As one officer noted, the question often brought tears to the eyes of the freed person, who responded in the affirmative.

The 4th Louisiana Native Guards Regiment was activated on 10 February 1863, the first under Banks's command. While the unit had begun organizing under Butler, the men continued to train and recruit even as they feared that Banks would hamper their progress. Banks chose Colonel Charles W. Drew to lead the new regiment. Unlike the previous colonels, who had all been chosen by Butler, Drew exhibited prejudice against African American soldiers. Despite his selection of new officers like Drew, Banks made few changes to existing white leadership in his first few months. Colonel Nathan Daniels was still in command of the 2d, Colonel John Nelson commanded the 3d, and Colonel Spencer Stafford commanded the 1st and maintained overall command of all the regiments, which were still considered unattached to the divisions.[78] With the activation of a 4th Regiment, the men in the Native Guards were growing frustrated that they continued to be assigned garrison and fatigue duty, with no combat missions. Fortunately, their commanding officer—Colonel Stafford—worked to rectify that issue.

As Butler and Weitzel had done a year prior, Banks withheld the Native Guards from combat campaigns because he believed that African Americans would not fight. Some of his officers questioned this belief; one colonel wrote to a friend after an expedition alongside the Native Guards in Baton Rouge,

Colonel Nathan Daniels and Major Francis Dumas
(Library of Congress, Prints and Photographs Division)

"If white men had endured for our country's sake what the whole of this party has for the last twenty-four hours, this war would have ended long since." He ended his missive, "Don't tell me these men will not fight."[79] Allegedly, Butler had questioned the officers of the Native Guards on this matter before commissioning them in the U.S. Army. When Butler asked a Black officer why he thought his men would fight, the officer responded, "General, we come of a fighting race. Our fathers were brought here slaves because they were captured in war, and in hand to hand fights too. We are willing to fight. Pardon me, General, but the only cowardly blood we have got in our veins is the white blood."[80] The Native Guards were determined to prove to Banks and to northerners that they were true soldiers.

Colonel Stafford thought that the low desertion rate in his regiments was proof that the Native Guards resisted the demoralizing effects of segregation and racism in order to prove themselves. Recognizing that many of his Black officers were not Protestant, he asked for a Catholic chaplain.[81] However, that was highly unlikely since Pope Pius IX had called for the United States to allow the Confederacy to exist in peace.[82] Stafford also moved to get his men into combat. On 3 January 1863, he wrote to Banks regarding his men's performance, and he told his new commanding general that his men should be allowed to fight or, if they were deemed unfit for military service, they should be released from their duty of guarding New Orleans and the railroads. It was a bluff, as Stafford had no intention of disbanding his regiments, but he hoped that he could use the fact that Banks needed their manpower to leverage actionable missions for the Native Guards. Finally, Stafford appealed directly to the War Department with an endorsement to General William T. Sherman that the harassment the members of the Native Guards experienced in New Orleans was too much. The men were given inadequate materials and no combat missions, their families were being attacked, and they were not being paid.[83] Stafford hoped that by going above Banks, his commanding general would be forced to finally use the Native Guards properly.

Whether in retaliation to Stafford's gambit or because Banks was responding to the planters' request regarding moving Black troops out of the city, Banks issued the 2d Native Guards Regiment orders on 9 January to Ship Island, the same place that had been dubbed the sand pit of the region by white soldiers before liberating New Orleans. The chief quartermaster of the department made the suggestion to Banks because he believed that "negroes do not suffer, are very strong and would fight should it be ever be necessary," while the white soldiers who were stationed there were getting sick.[84] The racist belief that Black men were immune to the climate was prevalent in the XIX Corps. The 2d Regiment's mission was to guard military convicts and prisoners of war to the island. Ship Island also served as a refueling stop for steamers navigating the Gulf, which meant the island received consistent traffic from federal vessels. Only seven companies were sent to Ship Island, and the remaining three were sent to Fort Pike to guard the nine-mile Pass Rigolets, which connected Lake Pontchartrain with Lake Borgne and the Gulf of Mexico.[85] Banks and his staff officers thought that Black soldiers could easily hold the forts since they were not likely to be attacked.[86] However, living inside of fortifications that no one seemed to care about proved to be perilous for the Native Guards. An unnamed officer near Vicksburg wrote that the desolation of war destroyed the morale of both soldiers and civilians, and the white men the Native Guards met on Ship Island proved his summation correct.[87]

Once the 2d Regiment arrived on Ship Island, its men discovered that the fortifications were essentially nonexistent for a location the Union held for over a year. Daniels was able to find a "good Headquarters" for himself and his senior staff to operate out of, but he could find "no barracks for my soldiers" adequate for the weather or the number of men.[88] Thus, the first mission of the regiment was to fell trees, build shelters, and fortify the island. Captain Hannibal Carter helped Daniels by ordering his company to work tirelessly for their colonel. After a month, Daniels reported that his regiment had fortified their new location by building "rifle pits, barricades, and two large magazines."[89] Soon, the members of the Native Guards realized there was little chance that the Confederate navy would ever be able to invade Ship Island. One small upside to garrison duty was that the soldiers had easy access to New Orleans. For example, Captain Charles Sauvenet was able to regularly see his wife and children thanks to the position.

Though their mission seemed boring, it presented the Native Guards with their first taste of real combat. While garrisoning Ship Island, the men were assigned a reconnaissance mission outside of the fort in April 1863.[90] They marched toward Pascagoula to record Confederate troop movements along the way. After completing their mission, they turned around to return to Ship Island. On their return, Daniels had the idea to destroy a nearby railroad so enemy forces could no longer use it. However, as they marched back to Ship Island, they encountered Confederate soldiers in superior numbers, and the two sides had a brief engagement.[91] During the battle, Major Francis Dumas's men were heavily outnumbered, and a cavalry charge was baring down on them. By himself, Dumas charged his horse toward the attacking force. Seeing their

Officers of Battery No. 6, 2d Louisiana Native Guards, 1863
(Library of Congress, Prints and Photographs Division)

major rush toward organized enemy troops alone, his men followed suit, and, together, they repulsed the cavalry. Dumas personally captured the standard bearer during the melee, and Colonel Daniels reported that Dumas, along with Lieutenants Jones and Martin, displaying "unflinching bravery, and admirable handling of their commands, contributed to the success of the attack, and reflected great honor upon the flag under and for which they so nobly struggled." Daniels concluded his report, "Repeated instances of individual bravery among the troops might be mentioned; but it would be invidious where all fought so manfully and so well."[92] The 2d Regiment successfully repelled Confederate forces at the cost of two killed and seven wounded.[93] It was both the first and last major battle for the 2d Regiment, as their position at Ship Island meant they were too far inside Union lines to engage with rebel forces.[94]

The true battle at Ship Island was not between the Union and the Confederacy, but rather between Black and white Union officers stationed on the small barrier island. Before soldiers arrived on Ship Island, they were loading transports at Algiers, close to Nim's famous artillery battery. A few soldiers in the Native Guards were guarding the ammunition shed when a white artillery officer attempted to enter with a lighted pipe. When one of the Native Guard soldiers confronted and stopped the man, the white officer grabbed his weapon; in response, several Black soldiers took up their weapons to support their comrade. The soldiers in Nim's battery grabbed their weapons, and the two units faced each other as if they were on the field of battle. With the full support of the Native Guards, Lieutenant Colonel Alfred Hall of the 2d Regiment stepped in to mediate the situation and ordered both sides to lower their arms.

On Ship Island, the 2d Native Guards faced additional troubles from fellow members of the Department of the Gulf. Colonel Henry Rust, the commander of Ship Island, balked at the idea of Black troops; he expressed in his diary: "The feeling of certainty that I have got to leave my two good companies here to come into collision with these niggers has made me feel homesick, and I have serious thoughts of resigning."[95] Rust only agreed to leave after Daniels promised not to mix Rust's white units with Daniels's Black ones. Rust's soldiers followed their outgoing commander's lead, expressing hatred toward the men in the 2d Regiment. When Daniels attempted to group the units together for better cohesion to protect Ship Island, the white soldiers nearly rebelled against him and his Creole officers. White officers outright refused the orders of superior Black officers, and their white soldiers soon did the same. Daniels arrested a number of them, and he wanted them court-martialed for violating the 9th Article of War.[96] Racial tensions on both sides escalated to an insurmountable point. Given that reaching a resolution was impossible, the white soldiers were transferred from Ship Island by Banks. While this was the first instance of near racial violence within the Department of the Gulf, it was, unfortunately, not the last. These events showed that Black officers were still not treated like officers in the U.S. military. A writer to the *Liberator* expressed concern about what this meant for military cooperation among the officers,[97] and a war correspondent argued that it was a sign of an epidemic of racism in the Department of the Gulf.[98]

An anonymous white lieutenant stationed in Baton Rouge wrote in the *New York Herald*, "Suppose I am detailed for picket duty in company with a detachment from this black regiment under command of a negro captain. Why, of course, the negro being a captain, and I only a lieutenant, he is my superior officer. I must not only obey him, but I must politely touch my cap when I approach him. I must stand while he sits, unless his captainship should condescendingly ask me to be seated." This situation, in his view, was unbearable. He continued, "Negro soldiers are all very well; but let us have white officers, whom we can receive and treat as equals everywhere, and whom we may treat as superiors without humiliation." A war correspondent who spoke to the unnamed officer reported that this "was the prevailing opinion among officers. Among the private soldiers, however, there was a feeling of stronger hostility, and some went so far as to threaten to rebel against lawful authority

Company C, 2d Louisiana Native Guards, 1863
(Library of Congress, Prints and Photographs Division)

if the negroes were to be regarded as their equals and treated as such."[99] While the *Herald* tended to exaggerate its reports to appease Democratic readers, it seems Banks believed reports such as this to be true, and acted on them.

To Banks, the problem was not white officers who refused to respect fellow officers; rather, it was the existence of Black officers that created the predicament. Already frustrated with officers of color—who he felt were interfering with plantation labor systems—Banks followed the suggestion of Lieutenant Colonel Alfred G. Hall and convened competency boards to evaluate the fitness and ability of the Black officers assigned to the Native Guards. From their inception, the boards were never meant to allow Black officers to pass. But wanting to project an appearance of fairness, he also ordered the evaluated of white officers.[100] Only a small number of Black officers survived their examination boards; Captain P. B. S. Pinchback was among those few.[101] While Banks distrusted African American officers, the same could not be said of all of his soldiers. For example, a war correspondent witnessed Captain André Cailloux "at General Banks' headquarters in company with at least fifteen prominent military officers: and he was a marked personage among them all."[102] Cailloux was admired by his men, but white officers on principle often did not respect those who officered Black men, especially Black officers. When Captain S. Rygard, commander of Company B, 1st Artillery Native Guards, ordered Second Lieutenant John Langdon, a white man, to stand guard, Langdon purposely ignored the captain and was still found not guilty at his court-martial.[103]

Like Banks, the men serving in the Native Guards read newspaper reports about their activities. *L'Union* was one of the most popular, but it was by no means the only source of information in the regiments. J. T. Paine, the surgeon for the 1st Native Guards Regiment, sent money and a letter to William Lloyd Garrison, the owner of the *Liberator*, requesting back issues of the widely read abolitionist newspaper to give to the soldiers and officers.[104] Thanks to their avid reading, the men serving in the Native Guards gained a broad understanding of what General Banks and the federal government were doing with their experiment in Louisiana.

In short order, the officers of the Native Guards realized that Banks intended to use the competency boards to dismiss Black officers, and they began to protest the discriminatory effort. Captain Samuel W. Ringgold wrote directly to Banks protesting that "a Board of Examination has been formed to investigate the Military Capacity of the Colored Officers of this Regiment and . . . the officers detailed to compose said board are in the majority of inferior rank . . . whose promotion would be effected by our dismissal."[105] In a group letter signed by officers of multiple regiments in the Native Guards, they wrote to Banks, "From the many rumors that have reached us . . . we are led to believe that it is the intention of the General to relieve us."[106] Captain Arnold Bertonneau and Lieutenants Ernest Morphy, Octave Rey, and Robert Isabelle passed their reviews, but they were so demoralized from the process that they willingly resigned in March rather than serve under Banks.[107]

Banks's efforts led to a widespread loss of motivation among the members of the Native Guards. His lack of respect for Black officers led white officers to disrespect them as well. New white officers were commissioned to lead the soldiers, and many of them proved to be incompetent. For example, Edgar A. Peek, lieutenant of Company A, 3d Louisiana Native Guards, was court-martialed for being habitually drunk on duty, and Banks had to remove him from service because of it.[108]

Furthermore, Banks expressed no intention of using the Native Guards for combat, another demoralizing factor for the men in the regiments. Despite Banks's personal feelings regarding African American service, federal government officials realized that units like theirs were needed to win the war. Lincoln wrote to Governor Andrew Johnson in March: "The colored population is the great available and yet unavailed of, force for restoring the Union. The bare sight of fifty thousand armed, and drilled black soldiers on the banks of the Mississippi, would end the rebellion at once."[109] Thus, while Banks was taking away men, the federal government was in the process of expanding the Native Guards.

Officials in the War Department agreed with Lincoln that the Louisiana Native Guards were a force multiplier for the Department of the Gulf, and they dispatched General Daniel Ullman to New Orleans to recruit additional units. In a speech a few years after the war, he claimed he had told Lincoln that he believed "the most direct way to crush the rebellion" was to use Black soldiers, and that this was "the surest path to the extinction of slavery." Slavery, Ullman argued, was "a millstone about the necks of our society, to sink us deep into the sea of Vice," and he hoped the abolishment of slavery would free the nation of a "putrid carcass" that corrupted everyone.[110] He had begun preparing to raise a brigade of African American troops a year before he received the opportunity to do so.[111] While he was not directed to recruit regiments for the Native Guards, he did raise his brigade from the same population in New Orleans and Baton Rouge.[112]

Major General Daniel Ullman
(Library of Congress, Prints and Photographs Division)

The largest issue for Ullman was not a lack of soldiers of color who wanted to serve, but the question of which Union officers would command them. Ullman expected the planters in New Orleans to cause the most problems for him, but by the time he arrived in May 1863, Butler had already pacified them to a certain degree in 1862. However, Ullman soon found out that "the whole mass of the officers, not only of the regular army, but where we did not expect it, of the volunteers, had an implacable prejudice, which led them to say and do many foolish things."[113] He believed these acts were perpetuated by "a large majority of the white officers of every grade in Louisiana."[114] He informed the adjutant general of his assessment within days of arriving in Louisiana, noting that he experienced opposition to Black recruitment from all sides in his post because of General Banks and his white officers.[115] A provost marshal in a Wisconsin regiment described the existence of a large cabal of "Negro hating officers" who sent racist men to regiments intended to enlist Black men.[116] Hepworth, a New England officer who asked to commission into the 4th Regiment, described the Black men as unintelligent, the women forgetful of their sex, and both as claiming sophistication they did not have.[117] Sentiments like his were rampant in the XIX Corps.

Even amid this prevailing culture of racism, some white troops recognized that they stood to gain from the enlistment of Black soldiers. The War Department advertised numerous positions for officers to command African American troops, and even privates and noncommissioned officers were eligible for these roles.[118] Once a private proved that he had received the minimum required military instruction, he could apply for examination to the officer corps. If at that point he still needed additional schooling, he could receive further instruction for free until he passed the exam. The War Department endorsed this plan further by granting thirty-day furloughs to enlisted men who applied to the schools and received endorsements from their superior officers.[119] During his command, Banks promoted privates up to the rank of captain.[120] It was a system that allowed the lowest ranked man to become an officer if he was willing to command Black soldiers, but the schools and examinations did little to prepare the new officers. Men who had undergone only a limited course of study were fitted for command, from lieutenant up to lieutenant colonel.[121] Additionally, commissioned officers thought it natural to apply for command of Black regiments purely for one or two additional ranks.[122] For example, Lansing Porter used his position training soldiers in the Native Guards as proof that he deserved a promotion.[123] According to Ullman, there was only one thing that calmed the "highly wrought feelings" of white soldiers:

"when they thought they discovered an opportunity for promotion."[124] He described how men became enthusiastic about Black troops when they learned that they could become officers or gain promotions.[125]

The fact that many of the Black officers Banks was removing were more highly educated than some of the white officers recruited by the War Department was not lost on the Native Guards. Joseph Wilson attested that Black officers' "dash and manly courage, no less than their military aptitude, was equal, and in many cases superior, to those found in the regiments of Maine and New York."[126] Nevertheless, the policy of recruiting barely competent white officers became standard, and their erstwhile prejudice followed them into their new positions and affected the soldiers who served under them.

In Ullman's words, Banks and many of his staff officers "heaped indignities upon Nigger Officers."[127] Weeks before Ullman had stepped foot in New Orleans, Stanton authorized Ullman to remove any commissioned officer from command for any reason.[128] The drastic step was needed. Wilson wrote that Banks's racist policies "checkmated recruiting" in New Orleans.[129] Banks was not alone; some white officers said publicly that they hated the expansion of the Native Guards. Second Lieutenant George D. Wiseburne of the 133d New York Volunteer Infantry Regiment resigned his commission and declared he would not serve in an army alongside Black men because it would make them equal to him and other white men.[130] Wiseburne was subsequently court-martialed for attacking Lincoln as well, and leaders in the Department of the Gulf publicized his removal and threatened similar action to anyone who repeated similar treasonous actions. After that, others used more subversive means to indicate that they did not want to serve alongside the Native Guards.[131]

Because Banks was using the competency boards to justify removing the few Black officers in the Native Guards, and Ullman was constituting new units of both infantry and artillery, there were numerous open positions for officers and enlisted men who could leverage their military careers from a corporal to lieutenant or captain if they were willing to serve in a Black unit. To avoid some of the incompetent and racist officers Banks was appointing, Ullman sought out his own officers from other commands to serve in his regiments.[132] While still in New York, he met with white officers he thought would serve well in the new brigade. Ullman realized that, at best, he would end up with a mix of officers—some who hated African Americans and some with abolitionist leanings.

Not all of the officers who volunteered to serve in the Native Guards held contempt for African American soldiers. Some—especially the German immigrants—were repulsed by the thought of slavery, and they commanded in the regiments to prove the dedication of both Black and immigrant men to the U.S. Army. There were a few line officers who, like Colonel Stafford, realized that the heart of the war was the fight for abolition, and they wanted to elevate Black soldiers.[133] For example, in George Hepworth's autobiography about his time with the Department of the Gulf, he recalled an incident involving his body servant, Tom Taylor, whose enslaver came to reclaim him. According to Hepworth's account—written with the racist undertones and tropes of a white writer capturing a Black voice—Taylor said that "if a white man acts gallantly on de field, and gives ebery ting he got for his country, de people all praise him; but, if a black man does the same ting, nobody cares a cent." As Hepworth wrote, Taylor then demanded, "Now, I did all I could at Baton Rouge; and what I ought to have is my freedom." Hepworth promised to shoot Taylor's enslaver if he attempted to reclaim Taylor, and he was later sent to join the regiments after proving his bravery in combat.[134] Like Hepworth, many white officers aligned themselves with People of Color inside and outside of the military. Some even did so to the detriment of their own careers. Ullman acknowledged that for some white officers, accepting an appointment in a Black regiment could result in a loss of relationships with friends and family.[135]

Aware of Ullman's growing prominence, Banks began to reverse some of his own policies and worked to recruit more men for the Native Guards. He called for thousands of additional recruits, and he wanted to put them all under his own control.[136] Banks even decreed a fight-or-work policy, which dictated that if free Black men were not fighting for the Department of the Gulf then they would have to work on the plantations that were under military protection under a one-year contract.[137] It was a coercive policy that forced Black men to choose how they wanted to serve Louisiana, either in the military or in the fields. The result was the constitution of dozens of additional infantry, cavalry, and engineer units full of Black men who would rather fight.

Among the soldiers that Banks recruited for the Native Guards was a man who became a national symbol of enslaved people's suffering and perseverance. Peter, who also identified as Gordon, had been enslaved on the large estate of John Lyons. He escaped in March 1863 and made his way to the Native Guards regiments stationed at Baton Rouge.[138] When medical officers examined Peter's back, they were astonished to see the amount of scarring that covered his body. The medical examiner wrote that he had never examined someone with so many lacerations before.[139] Photos and drawings of his back were circulated across the North to demonstrate the horrors of Louisiana slavery. Initially called "Whipped Peter" or "Poor Peter," the photo then came to be known as the "Scourged Back." According to an abolitionist in Pennsylvania, Peter's plight "excited both the sympathy and indignation of every humanitarian" who saw it, and his bruises were seen as proof of the reality of enslavement in Louisiana. Covered in nothing but rags when he arrived in Baton Rouge, Peter explained in French that his overseer had whipped him so severely he had been bedridden for over two months; his enslaver had fired the overseer for disrupting the labor on his plantation. When Peter was able, he fled his enslaver's plantation, chased by dogs for days, and covered himself with the smell of onions to hide his scent. Eventually, he made his way toward U.S. lines.[140] After passing the medical protocols that Banks had put in place, Peter was able to join the U.S. Army as a guide and, in his own way, fight back against those who tortured him and his brethren so severely.

As the regiments expanded, Second Lieutenant Robert Isabelle in the 2d Regiment updated *Douglass' Monthly* about the Native Guards, writing, "The 1st Regiment Louisiana Volunteers, Native Guards, are at the English turn, a few miles below the city, where they are building a fort. Seven companies

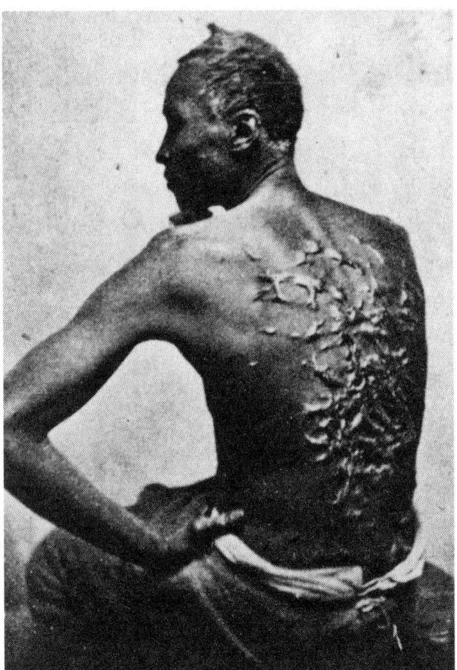

Whipped Peter, also identified as Gordon
(Library of Congress, Prints and Photographs Division)

of the 2d are at Ship Island, fortifying the place. The 3d regiment is at Baton Rouge, the Capital of the State, fortifying that town."[141] Men in each of these regiments were frustrated that they were not being used properly. The XIX Army Corps was expanding into new territories, and the Native Guards were holding already pacified areas. For military men, sitting around and conducting fatigue duty was no way of life, and their frustration eventually made its way to the ear of the commanding general.

Stafford continued to push for Banks to use the Native Guards for more than garrison duty. He wrote to the general that the number of Black soldiers joining the army was unprecedented but that they could not be "fairly tried in the present service in which they are engaged, and while scattered in detached companies." Stafford hoped he could convince Banks to bring the companies of the 2d back together and use the infantry regiments for combat; he promised his superior officer, "When tried, they will not be found wanting."[142]

While he was not able to convince Banks to reorganize the 2d Regiment, orders came down for two of the other regiments. On 17 March 1863, the 1st and 3d Regiments were ordered to march to the harbor, board the transport ship *General Banks,* and proceed to Baton Rouge. The regiments arrived on 19 March, and they worked with the 4th Native Guards to rebuild Fort Williams.[143] However, small acts of service were not enough to change the perception of the Native Guards. As Colonel Stafford marched his soldiers through the streets, the white citizens exhibited their disrespect. Julia LeGrand wrote in her diary that the soldiers were nothing but impudent thieves who stole food from whites when they were sent outside of the city. She referred to Stafford as a "creature" in command of Black soldiers who were besmirching the once proud "Stars and Stripes." Her sentiments were shared by many city residents, who continued to harass and attack members of the Native Guards.[144] The men quickly learned they were not wanted in Baton Rouge.

While stationed in Baton Rouge, the few Black officers in the 3d Native Guard Regiment grew weary of dealing with the "scorn and contempt" they received from white officers, white enlisted men, and the city's inhabitants. When Black officers of the Native Guards asked white officers simple questions, white officers gave "abrupt and ungentlemanly" answers. Many whites in the military were insulted even to be spoken to by an African American officer.[145]

Banks called all the Black officers of the regiment to his office to discuss the matter, and after listening to them, he asked them to return the following day. Banks told all of them that the government's policy was not to commission Black men, and so they were better off resigning than being fired and humiliated. They believed this was true, and together the officers resigned in protest while mentioning the racism and prejudice they experienced from their fellow officers to their commanding general.[146] Captain Leon Forstall penned a letter, signed by himself and all sixteen Black officers of the 3d Regiment, admonishing Banks and Nelson for their treatment of the Native Guards.[147] The Black officers hoped that their resignations would force Banks to treat the remaining soldiers of the Native Guards better.[148]

However, they soon realized it was all a trick orchestrated by Banks to remove competent Black officers from service. They attempted to regain their positions in the military, but it was too late, as their replacements were waiting for them when they returned to camp to collect their things. One of the officers wrote to Stanton explaining how Banks had convinced them to resign when in actuality he planned to coerce them and already had their replacements waiting.[149] The entire debacle only made Banks look worse to his Black soldiers, and the schism between them widened.

On 7 April, all of the officers who had resigned from the 3d Native Guards came together once again, and they signed a petition expressing their desire "to assist in putting down this wicked rebellion. And in restoring peace to our once peaceful country. And wishing to share with you the dangers of the battle field and serve our country under you as our forefathers did under Jackson." The officers offered to help recruit for the Native Guards and constitute new companies as they had under Butler the year prior. They only asked for one change: "give us a commander who will appreciate us as *men* and *soldiers,* and we will be willing to surmount all outer difficulties." They were sure that they could prove their worth to the U.S. Army, but Union authorities ignored their plea.[150]

*Douglass' Monthly* reported, "There are rumors of some trouble at New Orleans, growing out of the feeling of the white soldiers towards the black regiments." By spring of 1863, the paper noted, it was "quite common . . . for certain soldiers of these new regiments to insult and even beat these loyal Africans." The *Douglass' Monthly* writer continued sarcastically, "These gentlemen cannot bear to have the United States uniform so degraded as when worn by 'niggers,' so they show their bravery by attacking in numbers a single African, thus showing their superior courage and bravery." Lieutenant Isabelle informed the free press, "Seventeen of the colored commissioned officers of the 3d have resigned, owing to some disagreement between them and Col. Nelson." He also offered a theory as to why so many whites in the military hated the officers in the Native Guards, writing, "One mistake is made by the northern soldiers and officers, they think that all the colored population in New Orleans are contrabands. They have not been made aware that several thousands of this class, are free-born, well-educated property-holders, who have always enjoyed all the respect and privileges, with the exception of voting, of other citizens." Isabelle further elaborated, "Hundreds of them have graduated in Europe, are licensed to practice all kinds of professions, are doctors, dentists, &c. Silversmiths, portraits-painters, architects, bricky-ers, plasterers, carpenters, tailors, cigar-makers, &c.—all responded to the call, of Gen. Butler, closed up their establishments, and enlisted us privates in the regiments of Native Guards to fight for the Union."[151] Perhaps Lieutenant Isabelle was right that the department's white officers did not know the backgrounds of the soldiers of color, or perhaps the officers did know and they were simply jealous to encounter men whom they deemed inferior with class, education, and wealth. There was even an additional third option, that white officers simply did not care about class, education, and wealth because the men were Black. Either way, under Banks's command the men felt unwelcome in the U.S. Army. However, many refused to be deterred, as an officer named John Crowder showed when he wrote to his mother, "I do not intend to resign, nor will I resign unless I am the only black officer in the Service, as long as there is a button to hold to I will hold to it."[152]

While the soldiers in the Native Guards endured constant insult from their superiors, they continued to create change in Louisiana. Their work freeing enslaved people was a testament to their willingness to give back to the African American society of the state. By 1863, an officer in the 4th Regiment noted that nearly every plantation near Baton Rouge was affected by the presence of the U.S. Army, and tens of thousands of acres of sugarcane went unharvested due to the exodus.[153] Some of those who had been freed or abandoned worked independently of the government or enslavers to grow and sell their own food.[154] Men in the regiments continued to legitimize their relationships through legal marriage even while white southerners attempted to separate them. In one instance, two soldiers were married by one of the regiments' Black ministers, with all of the men in attendance dressed in "white pants and vest with white gloves," and the women in splendid white dresses to match, according to a Black soldier who stood as witness to the ceremony.[155]

As these changes unfolded in New Orleans, the War Department made significant changes to the U.S. Army. In May 1863, the War Department issued General Orders No. 143, which constituted the Bureau of Colored Troops.[156] The newly formed bureau had one mission: organize and supervise the creation and use of African American units in the federal army.[157] Officials in the new bureau planned to assign officers to supervise the selection of commanders, and the order indicated that noncommissioned officers would be selected from among the Black men serving in the units. The orders gave the adjutant general of the army the power to recruit in the Mississippi Valley and took recruiting duties away from Banks and his cadre of officers. All of the new units would be designated "__ Regiment of U.S. Colored Troops" in the order in which they were activated in the USCT. Major Charles W. Foster was chosen to lead this new organization. Adjutant General Lorenzo Thomas toured much of the Mississippi Valley to speak with and recruit African Americans for the U.S. Army, and Black Louisianans respected him for his zeal.[158] These events stood in stark contrast to Thomas's plan a year earlier to raise what he called the African Descent regiments. Banks responded that he already had five such units in New Orleans in an attempt to keep Thomas out of the city.[159]

Not wanting to lose control of the growing Black regiments, Banks attempted to keep the Native Guards out of the USCT, and it took another year before the regiments joined. Until then, Ullman continued to follow his presidential directive. The units he raised were not part of the Native Guards or the USCT even though they worked closely with those regiments in Louisiana. The regiments that Thomas raised were designated to follow Ullman's in number, and both men continued to recruit more Black soldiers for the U.S. Army.

Once Ullman was able to recruit more Black soldiers, he issued General Order No. 7 on 10 June 1863. He later attested that the order was "an appeal to the freedmen to enlist. The effect was very great, and we were proceeding very rapidly when we were brought to a standstill by an order from Gen. Banks, to forward all my enlisted men, armed and unarmed to Port Hudson, where they were employed on the trenches."[160] Ullman's efforts allowed multiple regiments and batteries to be raised in Louisiana from free and formerly enslaved African Americans. One soldier wrote to his family that the nearly five hundred Black men he saw drilling for service under Ullman would make a "first rate regiment" once completed.[161] Before that could happen, however, Banks took away some of those men for a large campaign in Port Hudson. Raw recruits were quickly equipped and shipped to aid the XIX Corps in their efforts. One of the units mustered under Ullman had little time to prepare before being forced into the field, and while their discipline and military appearance were considered good despite the situation, their military arms and accoutrements were worn.[162] With their little training and old equipment, the first troops raised by Ullman were joining the Native Guards in one of the largest campaigns on the Mississippi. The African Americans serving in both of their units prepared to fight on behalf of all Black men in the nation.

During his tenure, Banks had worked to purge the most visible affront to white southerners: African American officers. Even as new generals contributed toward their individual recruiting, Banks worked to remove Black officers and used the Native Guards for as little combat duty as possible. It was an unjust action and a betrayal of everything the regiments had done for the Department of the Gulf and lower Louisiana. Within a few months, the command environment among the Native Guards shifted from a culture of growing equality to one of abhorrence and racism. By the summer of 1863, the men were determined to find a way to prove themselves to General Banks—and the nation—and continue the experiment of African American military service in the Deep South.

Chapter 7

# *WE PROVE OURSELVES MEN!*

## THE SUMMER OF 1863 AND THE SIEGE OF PORT HUDSON

"Is the negro not a man? Is he not capable of bearing arms? Has he not talent? Has he not courage?"[1] George Williams asked these rhetorical questions about African American men serving in the U.S. Army during the summer of 1863. Williams, like many in the United States, understood that service in the military was much more than an opportunity to fight for one's nation; it was the best chance to prove one's manhood during the nineteenth century. Manhood was a badge of honor, integrity, and fortitude that meant you were deserving of rights, as only men held many of the privileges of citizenship in the country. A denial of manhood was akin to a denial of all rights, and Black soldiers knew they needed recognition as men to gain the rights they all deserved. Through bearing arms—proving talent and courage on the battlefield—soldiers of color demonstrated their bravery, countering generations of southern rhetoric that had framed all People of Color as infantile. Enslaved people in their fifties were still referred to as boy or girl because of their social status. Even those who were free, like members of the large Creole society of New Orleans, were often seen as less than the city's white inhabitants, who were often less educated. Recruitment posters invoked these inequities; one stated, "For generations we have suffered under the horrors of slavery, outrage and wrong; our manhood has been denied, our citizenship blotted out, our souls seared and burned, our spirits cowed and crushed, and the hopes of the future of our race involved in doubt and darkness."[2] The events of 1863 set the stage for the soldiers serving in the Native Guards to show that all African American men were indeed men.

According to *L'Union,* the day African American soldiers were given muskets to fight for the government, they became citizens and men worthy of equal treatment.[3] However, the soldiers in the Native Guards still endured discrimination from white fellow soldiers and white southerners, so they began to think of ways to capitalize on their military service to demand equitable treatment from the government. They developed a campaign intended to prove their worth to the nation. That campaign was bolstered by events that transpired during the summer of 1863, and the following chapter explores these occurrences and how they forever changed the way Americans viewed Black soldiers in combat. This chapter proves that the battles that occurred during that fateful summer helped to solidify Black manhood—and later Black citizenship—in the United States.

Since October 1862, officials in the Department of the Gulf had planned to take Port Hudson. Major General Benjamin Butler had intended for the Native Guards to join the expedition from the beginning. George Denison told Salmon P. Chase that the Native Guards were going to get "a chance to show themselves" at a strongly fortified position versus an open field of battle. Denison was worried that Port Hudson was too strong a position, believing it the true point of battle for the Mississippi River versus Vicksburg.[4] However, these plans died quickly after Butler left. During the spring of 1863, Major General Ulysses S. Grant was maneuvering toward Vicksburg, upriver of New Orleans. The War Department ordered Banks to take control of the lower Mississippi, starting with the blueprint Butler had created a few months prior. Butler later complained that if Banks had acted on the plans as soon as he arrived, he could have taken Port Hudson months before it was fortified.[5] However, he did not, and the Department of the Gulf had to make up for his mistake. Banks realized as early as February that Confederate forces were reinforcing Port Hudson and that the fight would be an uphill battle.[6]

Taking Port Hudson was critical to President Abraham Lincoln's strategy to split the Confederacy. It was widely understood on both sides that this campaign would decide the war.[7] General Henry Halleck told Banks that the Union needed to capture both Vicksburg and Port Hudson in order to secure all of the Mississippi and enable the army to capture Richmond.[8] Halleck wanted Grant's and Banks's commands to work together to take the Mississippi; he feared splitting them up because, if one failed, the Confederate army could attack the other from the rear. Grant promised to send twenty thousand men to help take Port Hudson, but Banks did not get the message in time to plan for reinforcements. Thus, the two generals began moving independently of one another early in the campaign, though Halleck continued to hope they would work together to secure the Mississippi for the U.S. Army.[9]

Despite early plans to include the Native Guards in these maneuvers, both Butler and Banks expressed some trepidation about using the regiments in such a large assault. Their reasoning boiled down to the familiar refrain that they would not fight. When Butler testified about using Black soldiers, he said they would fight as well as they could, but if pushed to the point of retreat, they would group together because that is what they did on plantations. From this point, he said, they would stand together in a frightened mass and wait for death instead of fleeing the field as white soldiers would do.[10] Banks expressed similar opinions. Despite the actions of the 2d Native Guards a few weeks prior, he believed they would falter in a larger fight. George Hepworth correctly surmised that decades of southern propaganda had led northern men to believe Black men would "throw away their arms, and flee in terror like so many monkeys" at the moment combat commenced. This belief was enshrined into northern officers' approach to utilizing the Native Guards.[11]

Stafford sent a deluge of letters to Banks and the War Department regarding the use of his men solely for garrison and fatigue duty, pointing out that it was not a good public relations decision on Banks's part, given that Banks wanted to outshine Butler and his constitution of the Native Guards. Likewise, George Denison continued to report to Chase that African Americans in New Orleans made good soldiers but were underutilized.[12] Despite these appeals, Banks continued to hesitate to use Black men to fight, preferring to assign them work that resembled the labor many of them had done when they were enslaved. Further demonstrating Banks's racism, when the army captured Berwick Bay on its way to Port Hudson, he ordered his men to transport "the fruits of the campaign," meaning "wagons, mules, cattle, horses, and negroes."[13] While the Union's General William Dwight was advancing toward Port Hudson, he told Banks that, after the Native Guards rounded up all the cattle and found hidden horses, they were to be brought back to the city instead of used for anything else.[14] Within days, they had captured hundreds of cattle to supply the army with beef in their upcoming operations.[15]

As the XIX Corps was undermanned and Port Hudson was purportedly heavily garrisoned, Banks could not justify refusing to use troops who were doing nothing more than patrolling an already secured region or sitting in camp. He assigned the 1st, 3d, and 4th Native Guards to his 1st Division, leaving them unattached to a brigade. He also left a detachment from the 2d Regiment at Ship Island and assigned the artillery battery to the defenses of New Orleans, both in the 2d Division. The rest of the 2d Regiment was assigned to the 4th Division.[16] Banks's chief motivator may have been the white residents of New Orleans, who were wary of armed African Americans garrisoned so close to the city and patrolling the streets. Because Banks's aims were disingenuous, he had done little to prepare the regiments for battle. He thought claiming Port Hudson would only take a few days, and he did not plan on using the Native Guards extensively in such a short battle.[17] A writer for the *New York Tribune* theorized that many northerners "have generally become willing that [Blacks] should fight but the great majority have no faith that they will really do so. Many hope that they will prove cowards and sneaks—others greatly fear it."[18] The operation on which Banks was sending the Native Guards would test that theory.

In January 1863, Banks had Weitzel drive all the Confederate soldiers out of the Teche district, resulting in a major battle with Confederate general Alfred Mouton's forces at the juncture of the Atchafalaya and Bayou Teche.[19] Shortly after, he had offshore batteries destroy the Confederate ironclad ship *Cotton* and return to New Orleans. The combination of these two acts meant the Department of the Gulf could send more men to Port Hudson without encountering additional Confederate troops. This was the first step toward attacking the stronghold at Port Hudson, thirty miles up the river from Baton Rouge.[20] The next step was to launch a naval campaign to attack Port Hudson. Admiral Farragut had naval superiority of the lower Mississippi River. As early as December, Farragut had been planning how he would attack both Vicksburg and Port Hudson, and now he was ready to act.[21] On 14 March, he began bombarding Port Hudson.[22] The USS *Mississippi* was sunk on the first day, but the U.S. Navy kept up the assault while Banks organized the ground campaign. During that time, the Union cavalry assisted in drawing the attention of the rebel forces.[23] By March, Banks had thousands of ground troops positioned at Port Hudson to assist the cavalry and navy in harassing the citadel, but they failed to lure the Confederate soldiers inside the fortress into a full fight, and the U.S. Army left having done little damage.[24]

The famed self-emancipationist Peter was captured in one of the expeditions to open the Mississippi for the U.S. Army. His southern captors knew who he was and wanted to make a point to the African American man who had notoriously dared to free himself and assist the military in liberating the region from enslavement. His captors tied him up and beat him until they were sure he was dead. They left his limp body near the river, assuming he would decay there. However, Peter displayed the same tenacity he had shown when he escaped from enslavement. He survived the beating and returned

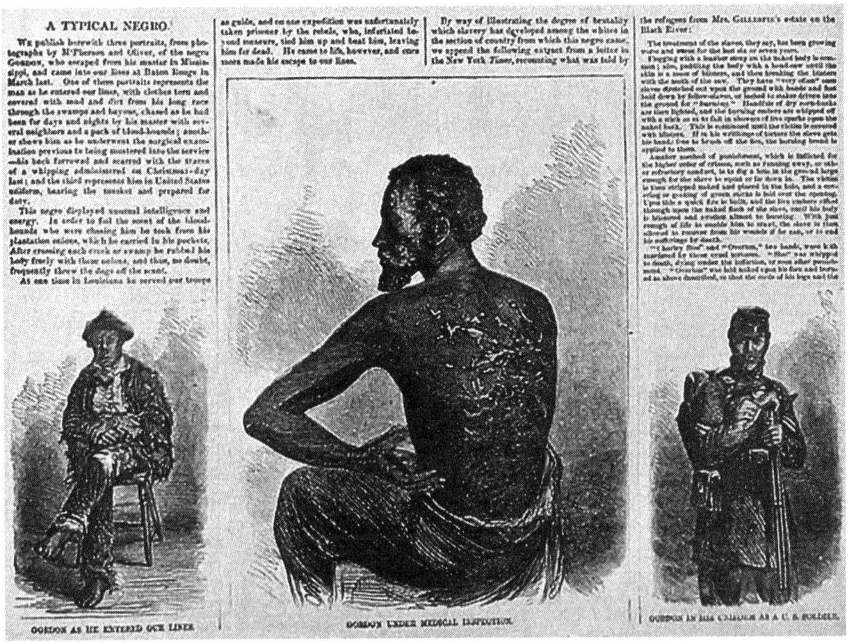

A TYPICAL NEGRO.

We publish herewith three portraits, from photographs by M'Pherson and Oliver, of the negro Gordon, who escaped from his master in Mississippi, and came into our lines at Baton Rouge in March last. One of these portraits represents the man as he entered our lines, with clothes torn and covered with mud and dirt from his long race through the swamps and bayous, chased as he had been for days and nights by his master with several neighbors and a pack of blood-hounds; another shows him as he underwent the surgical examination previous to being mustered into the service—his back furrowed and scarred with the traces of a whipping administered on Christmas-day last; and the third represents him in United States uniform, bearing the musket and prepared for duty.

This negro displayed unusual intelligence and energy. In order to foil the scent of the blood-hounds who were chasing him he took from his plantation onions, which he carried in his pockets. After crossing each creek or swamp he rubbed his body freely with these onions, and thus, no doubt, frequently threw the dogs off the scent.

At one time in Louisiana he served our troops as guide, and on one expedition was unfortunately taken prisoner by the rebels, who, infuriated beyond measure, tied him up and beat him, leaving him for dead. He came to life, however, and once more made his escape to our lines.

By way of illustrating the degree of brutality which slavery has developed among the whites in the section of country from which this negro came, we append the following extract from a letter in the New York *Times*, recounting what was told by the refugees from Mrs. Gillespie's estate on the Black River:

The treatment of the slaves, they say, has been growing worse and worse for the last six or seven years.

[illegible]

GORDON AS HE ENTERED OUR LINES.

GORDON UNDER MEDICAL INSPECTION.

GORDON IN HIS UNIFORM AS A U. S. SOLDIER.

Column entitled "A Typical Negro," including before and after images of an enslaved soldier named Gordon
(*Harper's Weekly*, July 4, 1863)

to the 3d Regiment, where he was made a sergeant and prepared to assist in capturing Port Hudson.[25]

As the XIX Corps prepared to attack Port Hudson again, Banks maneuvered to ensure the army had a fair chance at success. He asked Admiral Farragut to move his ships and men upriver, between Port Hudson and Vicksburg. This created supply and communication lines between Grant and Banks. It also cut off Confederate supplies and communication on the Red River. Farragut was credited for securing naval supremacy in the region.[26] The campaign succeeded, however, due to the combined efforts of Generals Banks, Weitzel, Grant, Dwight, Halleck, and Admiral David Porter, in addition to dozens of unnamed officers who helped to coordinate the large navy-ground attack on two strategic locations simultaneously. While preparing to take Port Hudson, the XIX Corps engaged with Confederate forces in small skirmishes in Louisiana throughout April, and eventually the Union was able to force the Confederate forces into Texas for long enough to advance into position.[27] Banks held a large dinner with all of his officers, at which Farragut led a toast reminding everyone that any of them, including him and Banks, could die in the upcoming attack. However, he said, "There will be others to continue the battle. There will always be a *last* man, and he will carry the flag on to victory and glory, and will save the country! Gentlemen, here's to the health of that last man!"[28]

As the Native Guards moved toward Port Hudson, they did so without Colonel Stafford. Stafford had ordered a few of his men to gather wood for the impending attack, and as they crossed the Union lines to gather the materials, they were questioned and harassed by Captain J. P. Garland and his troops from the 31st Maine Volunteer Infantry Regiment, who were standing guard. After Stafford rode over to his men several times to get passes for them to leave and reenter Union lines, he had enough and confronted Captain Garland himself. Stafford allowed his anger to get the best of him—a flaw that had plagued him throughout his military career. According to Stafford's official record, he reportedly called Garland a "pusillanimous white livered coward" and referred to President Lincoln using "disrespectful or contemptuous language."[29] He nearly rode his horse over Garland and a few of Garland's soldiers during his tirade. The colonel went on to accuse everyone in the Maine regiment of being thieves who constantly verbally attacked and harassed the Native Guards, and he threatened to harm a few of them if they did not get out of his way.[30] Stafford was jailed and subsequently court-martialed for the crime of conduct prejudicial to good military order and discipline and contemptuous language toward the president of the United States. However, his punishment was likely related to his defense of the Native Guards. Indeed, he attested that he only acted as he did because the captain in question had called one of Stafford's officers a "black son of a bitch."[31] Rumors of a conspiracy among the senior officers of the Native Guards were further exacerbated after Colonel Daniels was arrested weeks later for misusing resources on Ship Island and imprisoned for a few months in the city away from his command. It started to seem, to many, that Banks was purposely removing supportive colonels from the Black regiments.[32] Stafford was found guilty of the charges and dismissed from federal service in September. For the Native Guards, Stafford's dismissal represented another event in a series of losses after the departures of Generals Phelps and Butler. They lost yet another leader who had fought for their rights in the U.S. Army and New Orleans.

Stafford's removal resulted in numerous changes for the Native Guards. Lieutenant Colonel Chauncey Basset took command of the 1st Regiment, and Lieutenant Colonel Henry Finnegass was given command of the 3d after Colonel John Nelson was assigned overall command.[33] The 1st and 3d Native

*Bombardment of Port Hudson by Admiral Farragut's Fleet*
(*Frank Leslie's Illustrated Newspaper*, June 27, 1863)

Guards served as the rear guard for the Department of the Gulf as the attack against Port Hudson began. Basset was a staunch abolitionist, and he joined the Native Guards because he believed service in the military would secure citizenship and equality for African Americans. The men respected him and knew their new commander would lead them into battle honorably. Basset's only hesitation was that his regiments were assigned to General William Dwight, another leader who had expressed a lack of faith in Black troops.[34] Denison reported to Chase that the Native Guards did not want to wait in Dwight's rear, and officers in the regiments protested against "the stigma of alleged cowardice from their race" and sought to "vindicate their rights and abilities as soldiers."[35]

Banks intended for the XIX Corps to move toward Port Hudson by way of the Teche district that the Native Guards had liberated the year prior. Banks split his forces into four divisions, and the Native Guards were assigned unattached to General Christopher Augur's division.[36] They were positioned at a staging ground in Alexandria, Louisiana, and then headed toward Port Hudson on 14 May 1863. On 19 May, the XIX Army Corps' ground forces surrounded Port Hudson and assisted Farragut in capturing the fort. Banks reportedly began the envelopment with about thirteen thousand effective troops.[37] The 1st and 3d Native Guards Infantry Regiments were ordered to help secure the Mississippi River for the U.S. Army. General Banks had inadvertently set the stage for the first major campaign for African American soldiers in the Civil War.

Banks sacrificed men to determine the best place to attack, sending out pickets in the hopes that enemy troops would expose their defenses, positions, and manpower.[38] After nearly a week of this, he began making plans for a massive assault scheduled for the morning of 27 May.[39] Like many of Banks's plans, it was rather simplistic. His artillery would fire for hours while the infantry lined up, forcing Confederate soldiers to keep their heads down from the artillery fire while his infantry approached. Farragut would provide naval support from the water and cease all fire at the same time as Banks to ensure the infantry were not injured through friendly fire.[40] With over twenty thousand men under his command on land and water, Banks assumed that even with heavy losses he could take Port Hudson with this tactic. With everyone in place, the battle commenced at 6:15 in the morning on 27 May as Farragut's warships began to shell Port Hudson.[41]

The Native Guards were among the first to attack Port Hudson from the Union line's extreme front right, and they would be among the last to leave the battlefield that day.[42] Initially, the regiments were supposed to protect the rear on the extreme left, but General Banks, evidently wanting to test the combat ability of Black soldiers, acquiesced to their request to fight on the front lines. General Dwight wrote to his mother prior to the attack that he intended to use the Native Guards as a test for the fate of all Black troops in the U.S. Army.[43] John Ogee, one of the many men who had emancipated themselves and joined the 3d Regiment, looked at the defenses of Port Hudson and wondered to himself whether it would have been better to stay in the woods than face such an enemy.[44] Young officers such as Captain Edward Carter, the commander of Company I, 1st Native Guards, were facing true battle for the first time, and they knew that if they faltered it would mean the end of Black officers in the military. Once given the order, around one thousand men from the two regiments left the trees and slowly made their way toward the citadel. Approximately four hundred yards from the defenses, the Confederate defenders unleashed hell. Anselmas Planciancois, the color sergeant for the 1st Regiment, was the first to die when a shell took off half of his head in front of the entire regiment.[45] It quickly became evident that the XIX Corps was not prepared for the assault.

Banks had underestimated the defenses at Port Hudson and did not commit all of his forces to the attack. He also did not properly coordinate his attack on the left or right, leaving troops exposed on both sides.[46] According to one soldier, the only thing that was done right was the artillery assault early in the morning.[47] Weitzel assaulted the left of Port Hudson with his forces and was repulsed by heavy fire before being forced to stop to hold his position. His own men later lamented that he was slow to act because of his engineer

*Assault of the Second Louisiana Regiment . . . at Port Hudson*
(*Frank Leslie's Illustrated Newspaper*, May 27, 1863)

training, preferring to consider his next step even with bullets flying over his head.[48] Thus, the right and center parts of the battlefield became the most significant areas of battle. The fire on the right was withering, and the white forces who were with the Native Guards fled the field because they could not withstand the onslaught. The terrain was perilous due to natural and man-made obstacles that blocked their path.[49] The Native Guards, however, continued to press on as their officers repeatedly called for open charges. One of the men attested that, with artillery and musket fire "louder than the thunder of Heaven" surrounding them, the Native Guards marched over dead white soldiers as men continued to fall.[50] They marched across the battlefield and reached the Confederate entrenchments, resulting in hand-to-hand combat. Two companies of Native Guards were able to hold a defensive position in close proximity to the enemy for a time until Confederate artillery fire was too great and they, too, were forced to retreat. Because the Native Guards were the last to retreat from the right that day, they were the most visible of the Union regiments. Union soldiers who had retreated to safety watched the African American soldiers continue marching, fighting, and dying.

Because the Native Guards were the only Union element on the field, all fire from the right of Port Hudson was focused on them, and yet they continued to attack. Soldiers jumped in the moat surrounding the fort in an attempt to circumvent enemy fire, others fired back at Confederate soldiers, and some even attempted to climb the walls. Repelled again, the men reformed and attacked numerous times. Dozens of men died; six were killed defending the 1st Regiment's flag alone.[51] However, they continued to form lines and press forward. Captain Carter led one of the charges toward the defenses and was repulsed as well. A white soldier said that they "fought with the desperation of tigers," taking out their bayonets and fighting hand to hand when needed.[52] The young Lieutenant John Crowder was killed in the melee.[53]

Captain André Cailloux embodies much of what happened on the day of the Native Guards' most famous attack. Cailloux led his men against six thousand Confederate soldiers. When a musket ball shattered his arm, he continued to press on. Raising his good arm, he told his troops, "Steady men, steady," as they continued their approach. Suddenly, a shell hit Cailloux, killing him instantly. His soldiers continued their charge until they were being fired upon at near point-blank range. It was finally enough to push them back, but only slightly. Following Cailloux's example, the men continued to press forward, not knowing that no other units were continuing their attack. According to the *Liberator*, the Black soldiers' combat proficiency incentivized the Confederate forces to continue firing out of fear that the Native Guards would take the fort.[54] While Cailloux lay dead and his men continued to fight on, some hoped to pull his body back from the entrenchments. Reportedly, one man limped toward the front lines after being shot in the leg, desperate to charge Port Hudson's defenses one more time.[55] A war correspondent reported that one man held a Confederate soldier and ripped the skin from his face with his teeth because all his other weapons had failed him in the melee.[56] However, the Native Guards were eventually forced to retreat, and Confederate soldiers continued to fire on the Black troops as they withdrew from the field. One Confederate artillerist expressed pride at having forced the Native Guards to leave their dead.[57]

Realizing that the Native Guards had no intention of stopping unless they were ordered to, Basset told the men to conduct a full retreat.[58] The men formed lines as if they were on the parade grounds and marched coolly from the battlefield even as Confederate soldiers continued to fire at them. It was a spectacular display of military bearing that proved Black soldiers' courage. Ullman wrote to Edwin Stanton, "The brilliant conduct of the colored regiments at Port Hudson, on the 27th has silenced cavaliers and changed sneerers into eulogizers. There is no question but that they behaved with dauntless courage."[59]

Possibly in a drunken stupor, Dwight called for another charge later in the day. Thankfully for the Native Guards, Finnegass refused to follow the order, which he knew was a bad idea.[60] Nelson realized that Finnegass would not lead another charge and decided it was best to follow suit. However, they had to appease Dwight to prevent him from forcing the issue, so Nelson ordered the regiments to fire on Port Hudson from the safety of a grove of willow trees approximately six hundred yards from the defenses.[61] While Nelson knew the regiments would not hit anyone, he hoped the noise would satisfy Dwight and save them from sacrificing any more men in uncoordinated attacks. Other companies on the far left continued to assault Port Hudson, but most officers adopted Nelson's stance by the afternoon. However, the position of the Native Guards kept them in range of the citadel's artillery, and members of the regiments continued to receive wounds from shell and shot being fired into their lines. Eventually, Banks called for everyone to pull back once he, too, realized the XIX Corps would not take Port Hudson on 27 May.[62]

Multiple accounts described how close the Native Guards came to taking Port Hudson. Reports show that they were very close to seizing the citadel, as some of the men made it past the moat before being killed. Wilson recalled that the regiments were "up to the brink and base of the fortified elevation" before Confederate troops "emptied their rifles, cannon, and mortars upon the very heads of the brave assaulters, making of them a human hecatomb."[63] One reporter thought that if the Native Guards had been properly supported with artillery and reserve forces, the regiments could have opened a path and taken Port Hudson that day.[64] John Dixon, a Confederate soldier, recalled nearly a year later that he "was in a terrible hand-to-hand engagement with those black wretches."[65] His brother wrote in his diary that the Native Guards nearly overtook their position during that battle, demonstrating that even the defenders were aware the Native Guards nearly took Port Hudson.[66]

Nevertheless, the Native Guards did not take the fort, and Banks resorted to a prolonged siege while his ground forces and pride recovered.[67] Thankfully, the siege was successful, and it was only a matter of time before the Union won control of the Mississippi.[68] Due to an information embargo that Banks attempted to enact, many inaccurate reports circulated during this time. For example, some early accounts described the 2d Regiment as leading the charge and even credited Colonel Nelson with leading them into battle; however, the 2d Regiment was not present on 27 May.[69] Lincoln also received a telegram claiming that the "rebels were thoroughly whipped, and left a large number of killed and wounded on the field."[70] This was untrue as well.

The battle was devastating to the Native Guards. Jefferson Davis called it a disaster for the U.S. Army.[71] One of the Native Guards' white officers later attested that they fought from six in the morning until sunset.[72] The result was that every single company that was engaged at Port Hudson suffered casualties, and some would have been considered combat ineffective by today's standards.[73] The Native Guards were in a state of disarray after losing dozens of men and at least three of their officers.[74] One soldier from New York wrote to his wife that there were only 125 men left in his whole regiment by the battle's end.[75] Some reports exaggerated the number of men who had died, leading to inaccurate claims that the entire army had been lost.[76] In truth, the XIX Corps suffered about two thousand casualties among all of its attacking troops, but this number was significant enough that it took weeks to prepare to attack again. The Native Guards lost dozens of men because they attacked en masse and did not receive support from additional units. Twenty-six men died in the 1st Regiment alone, including a number of its officers.[77] Algernon Badger, a U.S. officer who fought in the initial battle, recognized that they had "lost a great many men taking Port Hudson. Our men had to cross an open plain to reach the Rebel entrenchments, and in doing so, the fire from the enemy mowed them down like grass."[78] One soldier serving in the Department of the Gulf acknowledged the value of this sacrifice in a letter to his family, writing that the Native Guards had ensured that Banks would eventually take Port Hudson.[79]

Andre Cailloux's sacrifice went on to exemplify the efforts of all the Black soldiers who died. Wilson noted that Cailloux's body remained in front of Port Hudson's breastworks after the battle. The citadel's commander sent a missive to Banks, informing him that he could collect the Union bodies located there; however, Banks responded that he had no troops in that area. The combination of Cailloux's proximity and Banks's response meant that it took over a month before the Native Guards were able to recover Cailloux's body. Nearly everyone who had been present at the battle attended the funeral after he was recovered. Wilson attested that Black and white New Orleanians came to honor an American hero—and, symbolically, all of the men who had fought that day.[80] Cailloux's funeral, which was so large that people lined all of Esplanade Street, also included the bodies of other officers who were recovered weeks after the 27 May attack. Numerous soldiers in the Native Guards were present, both as guards and as witnesses as their fallen heroes were laid to rest. Hundreds mourned the men's passing and honored them for proving Black excellence in battle.[81] Henry Rey had resigned his commission prior to the battle, and he was disheartened to hear that Cailloux, a man he'd known for many years, had fallen in combat. Ever the spiritualist, Rey stated that he contacted Cailloux's spirit in a séance shortly after his death; according to Rey, even in death Captain Cailloux called for the men to continue fighting for the U.S. Army. Rey reported that Cailloux said to him, "You will need victims to serve as stepping stones to liberty: we have been the first steps, we will need more."[82]

Not all of the men who fought at Port Hudson received the same funeral rites as Cailloux; most were given much smaller funerals with little fanfare. Banks left many of the men to die and rot: dozens of bodies were left out in the heat and sun, and a few men who were still alive were captured by the Confederacy. There are accounts of soldiers being carried from the battlefield, killed, and buried in mass graves near Port Hudson. Many soldiers and even officers whose bodies were returned to their families were honored by few. Lieutenant John Crowder died in the battle; his mother, Martha Ann Stars, whose financial situation he had hoped to improve, could afford only a pauper's funeral for her heroic son.[83] The military did little to honor Crowder, and many of the enlisted soldiers were buried in similarly unceremonious ways once their bodies were recovered.

Banks realized he needed additional troops if he planned to take Port Hudson, so he called on his forces stationed throughout Lafourche and other areas. Thousands of white troops marched to help take the citadel, and most of the remaining Black troops in the area were pushed into garrison duty. General William H. Emory was tasked with protecting New Orleans and the surrounding region, and among the dozens of units that served under him was a small detachment from the 1st and 2d Louisiana Native Guards. The 4th Regiment was also considered part of the attacking force, but in reality it was stationed at Baton Rouge, while the bulk of the 2d Regiment was still on Ship Island.[84] Some of the new regiments that Ullman had raised were used to garrison around the region. Thousands of Black troops were being trained in Brashear City, which became the staging hub for the new regiments raised by Ullman and Thomas before they moved out to aid the Department of the Gulf in whatever ways were needed.

After the attack on 27 May, Confederate forces attempted to force the XIX Corps to abandon Port Hudson by attacking New Orleans. It was a bold plan: gather as many rebellious guerrillas and regular soldiers as possible who were not trapped in Vicksburg or Port Hudson and attack the city. Confederate troops who had been forced into Texas were recalled to help enact the plan. There was hope among the Confederate leadership that the majority of the city's white populace would welcome the attacking force and join the fight. If the attack proved successful, Banks would have to pull back from Port Hudson, and the troops trapped inside could attack Grant's rear and save Vicksburg.

On the evening of 13 June, Confederate cavalry invaded the Atchafalaya and Pointe Coupée Parish region. They purposely moved to stop the U.S. Army from recruiting more men for the military. They raided horses, mules, and men, and threatened anyone who supported the Union war effort. The few remaining white Union regiments relied heavily on the Black regiments, who were still undergoing training, to hold the region. Those Black troops made up the bulk of the forces available to repulse the raid. Two days later, Confederate cavalry continued to raid the parishes, and the XIX Corps was still recovering from another failed assault that Banks had not properly planned.[85]

The Native Guards remained at Port Hudson despite losses on 27 May and the invasion in Lafourche. Banks sent a missive to Emory to send "all the colored troops which [Ullman] has raised, whether armed or unarmed."[86] The fourteen hundred untrained men who had been raised by Ullman were sent to Port Hudson to assist in the siege, and they were primarily used for fatigue and picket duty.[87] All of the soldiers of color were assigned to Augur's 1st Division, which made his the largest of all besieging the citadel.[88] Sergeant Peter was among those who were hard at work supporting the military to ensure the XIX Corps took the fort; an article in the *Liberator* speculated that he must have recalled the former overseer who had heavily scarred his back as he fought during the siege.[89] In June and early July, companies from multiple

Weitzel's command post in front of Port Hudson (Library of Congress, Prints and Photographs Division)

Native Guards regiments either aided in siege operations or attacked the entrenchments directly. While these efforts never reached the same intensity as the attack in May, dozens of men died during the siege.[90]

During the siege, the men of the 1st Louisiana Native Guards Engineer Regiment displayed particular courage. Tasked with building the siege positions for the military, the men marched double quick to build redoubts and breastworks dozens of times while under enemy fire. One correspondent wrote that they looked like cattle "going to a slaughterhouse." However, they were committed to serving their country and proving they belonged on the battlefield. Without even a revolver to defend themselves, the regiment served the Department of the Gulf for the duration of the siege.[91] African American soldiers were constantly digging trenches and moving to guard positions, and some even acted as sharpshooters in outposts; they were instrumental in every facet of the siege.[92] According to Ullman, sometimes they worked twenty-hour days.[93]

On 14 June, the XIX Corps made another push to take the citadel at Port Hudson. Banks hoped he had finally amassed enough men and artillery to break the enemy's defenses.[94] From 11:00 p.m. on 13 June until 2:00 a.m. the next day, Farragut shelled Port Hudson with mortar.[95] Starting at 3:00 a.m., they launched a combined assault of infantry and artillery, and the navy attacked from the water.[96] However, it was another uncoordinated and failed assault, and the XIX Corps suffered an additional eighteen hundred casualties because of poor leadership and planning. An officer who suffered grave injuries that resulted in the end of his career wrote to his family after the assault to describe the dozens of men he had lost leading his Michigan company that day.[97]

The Native Guards were held in reserve, so they did not lose any additional men to Banks's poor planning.[98] Soon after the failed attack, Banks called for one thousand men to storm Port Hudson in a massive assault. Knowing that the attackers would suffer the same fate as those who had attacked on 27 May and 14 June, Banks called for soldiers to volunteer to fight. When Basset asked for volunteers, every single soldier in the Native Guards stepped forward to cross the field again, despite the losses they had taken just a few weeks prior and the knowledge that this was an all-or-nothing assault.[99]

Banks turned down their service, however. He intended this to be a final charge that would confer honor on all those who fought and died. Instead, he only accepted a little over fifty men from each infantry regiment.[100] Only those selected from the 1st and 3d Native Guards marched with the 13th Connecticut in a planned assault on the fort.[101] Thankfully for all who volunteered,

Banks realized the folly of his plan prior to the attack.[102] Instead of attacking Port Hudson *en masse* again, Banks viewed this as a protracted siege; as long as the U.S. Army contained the Confederate troops in Port Hudson, eventually those troops would be starved out of their battlements. Inside Port Hudson, the Confederate soldiers had decided to give no quarter to any Black soldier. Many of the Union soldiers besieging the fort believed it would soon fall; a soldier wrote to his family, "Port Hudson is doomed and all there is in it."[103]

There were many casualties during combat over the course of the siege. However, most deaths were caused by malaria, diarrhea, typhoid, and other diseases. Like the rest of lowland Louisiana, the areas around Port Hudson attracted mosquitoes, and the combination of heat, trench life, and poor hygiene meant that sickness spread easily during the summer months. Long after the war, a soldier named Andrew Sherman recalled the "malarial atmosphere" and the "unwholesome water and its disease-imparting mosquitoes" that he encountered during his time there.[104] A captain in the 53d Massachusetts Volunteer Infantry Regiment thought like many northern officers: Black soldiers "can be put into unhealthy localities in the department and not suffer like white men."[105] Many northern officers held similar beliefs regarding Black soldiers. The result was that the Native Guards were used almost exclusively for trench duty, and they were positioned near the front lines of the siege longer than white soldiers, who supposedly needed longer to recover. Black soldiers, like Manuel J. D'Aunoy in the 1st Regiment, suffered for weeks from disease before they died through white neglect.[106] Their vulnerability was compounded by the fact that the best surgeons and doctors declined to work in Black regiments due to racism and fear of being ostracized. Thus, the Native Guards were left with barely competent doctors to treat them while they were exposed to illnesses endemic to the Deep South.

However, disease was not Black soldiers' only enemy, as the Native Guards' counterparts in Ullman's Brigade were under attack. In the raid in Pointe Coupée, two companies of the 1st Native Guards Engineers and thirty men from the 12th Maine were almost captured unarmed because the transport ships carrying their weapons and equipment were either burned or ransacked while they marched toward Port Hudson.[107] Though most of these men escaped, a large number of troops were caught. One of the white captains telegraphed that dozens of men had either been captured or killed, and that Confederate leaders wanted the XIX Corps to break from Port Hudson.[108] Banks sent a small group of reinforcements to help, but he wanted to keep the bulk of his forces on the siege.[109] Admiral David Farragut left Port Hudson to see

Theater of command during the Port Hudson campaign
(Library of Congress, Prints and Photographs Division)

the disaster for himself, and he became convinced that it was a distraction, not a real attack.[110]

But the Confederates were not done. First, they attacked Lafourche, then, on 23 June, they targeted Brashear City. The untrained African American men in the city who were readying themselves for a future in the military assisted in defending Brashear alongside white combat veterans. Raw recruits fought and died defending the city from a surprise attack with weapons they had not been trained to use. A white soldier who bore witness to these events attested that "a colored company of the [7th Regiment] made a good stand, but were to cut to pieces." He thought nearly all of them were killed, and the few who survived ran to the trees where white troops were running to avoid capture.[111] Despite their efforts to defend Brashear, it was captured by the Confederates, and it became clear that Farragut's assumption that this was only a small distraction had been false.[112] Banks hoped that it was still possible to capture Port Hudson before the Confederates compelled U.S. forces to abandon the siege.[113]

Hundreds were captured during the fall of Brashear City. The Native Guards lost many men, as well as families who were there.[114] One of the Union lieutenant colonels who was captured thought the Confederates killed any

Black soldier they found, because he saw none in the prisoner camps. However, he also acknowledged that many of his own men had stripped off their uniforms to avoid being captured as soldiers, aware that Black men in uniform were in particular danger.[115] Thousands of Black men were reenslaved, and Black women were raped and reenslaved.[116] Some reports listed as many as seven thousand returned to enslavement in one fashion or another. The raids strengthened Port Hudson's defenders, who hoped they would soon be relieved from the siege.[117] At the same time, it demoralized the citadel's besiegers, who had supplies and family members in Brashear.[118] General Emory wrote to Banks after the fall of Brashear, "It is a choice between Port Hudson and New Orleans."[119] Banks had already pondered this subject weeks prior; as he explained to General Halleck, if he left his position then all of the troops in Port Hudson could move against either New Orleans or Vicksburg. Thus, he would either defend New Orleans and abandon Grant or siege Port Hudson and abandon his forces in New Orleans. To Banks, the best choice was to maintain the siege at all costs.[120] Banks wrote back to Emory that he chose Port Hudson, and that Emory's forces would have to be enough.[121]

The Confederate advance into the Department of the Gulf's area of operations did not end at Brashear City, and soon Fort Butler was under attack. Hundreds of men died defending the fort. Their defenses were not enough, but the navy helped turn the tide of battle for the federal defenders by attacking from the water.[122] The Confederacy's failure to capture Fort Butler was a turning point in its assault, and slowly the Union was able to push the Confederate soldiers out of the region. General Weitzel wrote to his old commander that he must have been pleased to hear that the Confederacy's advance had halted at the fort named after him.[123] By the end of June, it was evident that Banks would not withdraw his troops from Port Hudson, and that Grant would not dislodge his forces from Vicksburg.[124] In New Orleans, a couple of African Descent regiments were raised for sixty days to aid in defending the Department of the Gulf in the absence of so many troops at Port Hudson. In one of the Confederacy's last-ditch raids, one of the companies raised by General Ullman helped to defend a depot that the attackers at Port Hudson needed. Soon enough, the *New York Times* recognized that all of those who hated Black soldiers would "acknowledge the value to the nation of our black friends down here."[125]

While the Native Guards suffered great losses during the attacks on Port Hudson, their actions set the stage for African Americans to serve in large numbers in the war. Banks wrote to his wife that the Native Guards "fought splendidly! Splendidly!," and he even told her he thought their actions on 27 May were the bravest he'd ever witnessed in combat.[126] In his official report, Banks credited the Native Guards for their bravery on the field multiple times.[127] General George Andrews was impressed, too, and wrote to his wife about the siege.[128] A war correspondent expressed that General Dwight "had the idea not only they were men, but something *more than men,* from the terrific test to which he put their valor."[129] In the nation's capital, a brigade of Black troops was raised because of the 1st Louisiana Native Guard's valor at Port Hudson. A similar wave of recruiting followed in many U.S. states.[130] André Cailloux became a martyr who represented the sacrifices that even a wealthy African American was willing to make to secure equality for his people.[131] George H. Boker wrote a poem titled "The Second Louisiana: May 27th, 1863," encapsulating this new phase of the war. The poem evokes the men standing "arm to arm, knee to knee" prior to their charge at Port Hudson, and recounts their struggle against insurmountable odds. "'Freedom!' their battle-cry—'Freedom! or leave to die!'" These, the poem's speaker says, are the only words from their mouths. Boker suggests that white and Black soldiers should stand together as comrades in arms, worthy of mutual respect.[132] Wilson, while reflecting on his time at Port Hudson, wrote many decades after the battle that "nature seems to have selected the place and appointed the time for the negro to prove his manhood and to disarm the prejudice that at one time prompted the white troops to insult and assault the negro soldiers in New Orleans."[133]

Many Americans privately and publicly reflected on what Port Hudson meant for African American soldiers. In a letter to his brother, John Gould wrote, "You have heard doubtless a great deal about negro Soldiers. I am inclined to believe that they will make good soldiers, better in fact, in drill and discipline than whites, but as to whether they will fight as well remains yet a mooted question, certain it is that they fought well at Port Hudson." Gould went on to write, "I saw negro servants pick up guns that white soldiers had thrown away and after getting ammunition go forward into the fight."[134] After the war, General Ullman wrote that he had witnessed the regiments make multiple charges: "[They] were exposed to a terrible fire, and were dreadfully slaughtered. While it may be doubted whether it was wise to so expose them, all who witness these charges agree that their conduct was such as would do honor to any soldiers."[135] A correspondent present at the battle wrote about the 1st and 2d Louisiana Native Guards, although he meant the 1st and 3d Regiments, as the 2d was not present during the siege: "Six times did they charge upon the fortifications, clambering over a huge abattis and marching unitedly forwards, while at each stop the concentrated fire of the adjacent batteries lessened their ranks with a fearful rapidity. Fully fifty per cent. of their number were left dead upon the brush-heaps to denote their bravery. The remainder received at the hands of the commanding General and his battle stained comrades, that generous appreciation which their deeds had earned." Recognizing the true significance of their actions, he concluded, "A revolution in sentiment toward colored troops took place upon that field of carnage which in itself was a glorious victory."[136] The *New York Times* declared that "their conduct was heroic. No troops could be more determined or more daring. . . . The highest commendation is bestowed upon them by all the officers in command on the right." The author concluded: "The severe test to which they were subjected, and the determined manner in which they encountered the enemy, leaves upon my mind no doubt of their ultimate success."[137] The editors of *L'Union* celebrated the Native Guards' excellence in battle in two articles, titled "The Rebels and the Negro Question" and "Will the Negro Fight?"[138]

Port Hudson was a watershed moment for the Native Guards, and by extension for the U.S. Army's USCT. Hepworth speculated months after the battle that the Native Guards may have been too effective, which could lead the Copperheads to limit their use for fear "that the end of the war was close at hand."[139] Ullman similarly reflected that the Native Guards had fought so well that white soldiers and officers were realizing, "They fight too well, 'We must not discipline them,' for if we do, we will have to fight them some day ourselves."[140] According to Wilson, "The whites were only too glad to take a drink from a negro soldier's canteen, for in that trying hour they found a brave and determined ally, ready to sacrifice all for liberty and country."[141]

One paper noted, "When the colored regiments were first formed, many applications were made by white men for commissions in those regiments possible, under the impression that they were merely to do ordinary garrison duty in comparative safety."[142] After the battle at Port Hudson, expectations shifted significantly. An unnamed Black man in the nation's capital wrote to the *Christian Recorder*, "There never was, nor there never will be, a better opportunity for colored men to get what they want than now."[143] His words proved prophetic, as the federal government moved to expand Black recruitment.

Soon after the Native Guards' actions at Port Hudson became public, another regiment raised from Louisiana citizenry by General Lorenzo Thomas became famous for its role at Milliken's Bend near Vicksburg eleven days later.[144] The 9th Louisiana Infantry Regiment (African Descent) was commanded by the newly promoted Colonel Hermann Lieb. The regiment was made up of formerly enslaved men from Louisiana and Mississippi bold enough to volunteer. They were stationed at Milliken's Bend, a small town with a hospital where soldiers wounded in Vicksburg were sent. The regiment was supported by the 11th Louisiana (African Descent) and the 1st Mississippi (African Descent).[145] The men had not yet been well trained, but the forming regiment was called into action anyway for a small reconnaissance mission. Around 3:00 a.m. on 6 June, southern cavalry attacked the regiment while soldiers were returning to their post in Milliken's Bend, but the infantry quickly formed lines and dispersed the attack. Lieb correctly surmised that his position would soon be under fire by troops attempting to help Confederates in Vicksburg, and he called for reinforcement to hold his position. Soon, he had the 8th, 9th, 11th, and 13th Louisiana Infantry Regiments (African Descent) at his disposal, along with the 1st Mississippi Infantry Regiment (African Descent). Sure enough, around 3:00 a.m. the following day, twenty-five hundred Confederate troops from Texas arrived via a night march to try to catch the U.S. forces off guard. The southern soldiers attacked, screaming, "No quarter! No quarter to negroes or their officers!"[146]

The six hundred U.S. soldiers were well prepared and instantly formed defensive lines to repel Confederate forces, while gunboats nearby rained down artillery fire as well. The fighting was intense and lasted for hours; at numerous times, soldiers fought hand-to-hand using their bayonets.[147] The fighting grew so intense that men broke their bayonets killing one another in the melee. Five hundred Black soldiers with little prior training showed themselves to be capable fighters, killing dozens of Confederate soldiers while waiting for additional reinforcements. It was reported that four officers and twenty-four enlisted men were killed, sixty-six men total were injured, and over one hundred were missing, presumed captured by Confederate soldiers.[148] Upon finding out the number of prisoners who were subsequently killed, the raw recruits of color helped to capture over two hundred Confederate soldiers in later battles.[149] Captain Miller, the commander of I Company of the 9th Louisiana Infantry Regiment (African Descent), wrote after the battle, "I never more wish to hear the expression, 'The niggers won't fight.' Come with me, a hundred yards from where I sit, and I can show you the wounds that cover the bodies of sixteen as brave, loyal, and patriotic soldiers as ever drew bead on a rebel."[150] The Battle of Milliken's Bend, the Siege of Port Hudson, and the 27 May attack buoyed Black soldiers in Louisiana and across the nation.

After the casualties at Port Hudson and Milliken's Bend, some conservative voices expressed a belief that this would finally teach Black men that they did not belong in the military. A war correspondent for the *New York Herald* wrote, "The experience of the negroes at Port Hudson has not been of a character to induce enlistments, on the contrary, they know as well as the whites now, what war is, and they will not be over anxious to place themselves in a position to render their present idle life uncertain." The author concluded, "I very much doubt if the recruiting of negroes hereafter will be anything like as brisk as it has been heretofore."[151] This writer proved wrong, as African Americans expanded recruitment to unforeseen levels.

Frederick Douglass—and many other free African Americans in the North—moved to capitalize on the actions of the Native Guards and other Black soldiers in Louisiana to increase recruitment and sway public opinion. After holding a convention in Philadelphia to promote enlistment, Douglass and fifty-three local leaders signed a document meant to encourage African American enlistment in the USCT. A new broadside was printed from their document and distributed across the nation; in bold and large letters, it declared, "MEN OF COLOR TO ARMS! TO ARMS! NOW OR NEVER."[152]

Despite the significance of Port Hudson and the increase in African American soldiers in the U.S. Army, racist sentiment continued to flourish in the Union. A paper in New York titled the *World* referred to Cailloux's sacrifice at Port Hudson as the canonization of a "defunct darkey," and Cailloux himself as a "well-known 'bull-nigger' of New Orleans."[153] A letter writer to a New England journal wrote that the events of Port Hudson proved the inferiority of Black troops because so many were killed.[154] The *London Times* published a scathing article regarding the Native Guards and what occurred at Port Hudson that took a very different view of the events of 27 May. First, the writer attacked President Lincoln's decision to emancipate enslaved people, which "was intended to frighten the Southern whites into submission" but instead made them more aggressive, according to the author. Next, the author believed the war was now a servile war, but the African Americans of the South were too passive to participate. Finally, the author argued that the results of Port Hudson demonstrated that Black troops would fight as hard as the Black soldiers who fought in the Haitian Revolution had. Ignoring the contradiction of their own words, the author believed if the U.S. Army continued to train Black soldiers to fight and kill, then the war would become more violent. African American soldiers, according to this author, were both inferior and prone to viciousness. Thus, they argued for the military to stop using "these unhappy

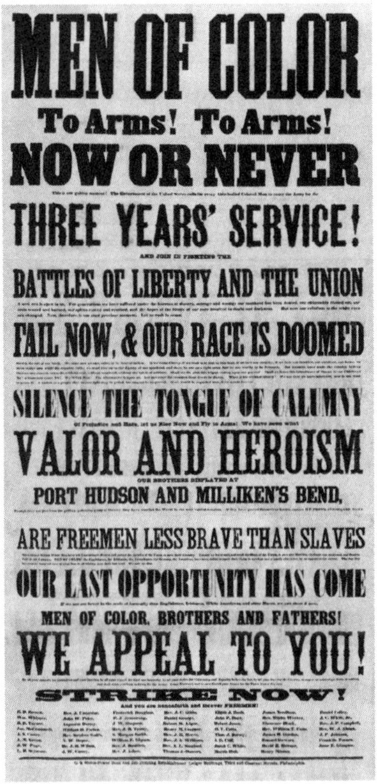


"Men of Color" broadside
(Smithsonian National Museum of African American History and Culture)

Africans, whose clumsy frames are no match for the sinewy and agile white Americans." The article concluded that if Blacks remained in the military, "Reprisal will provoke reprisal, until all men's natures are hardened, and the land flows with blood."[155]

There were also many northerners who acknowledged that Black troops provided a public good—though often even these accounts contained racist ideas as well.[156] In contrast to the *London Times* author, a writer for the *Morning Post,* also in London, thought the bravery exhibited by the men in the Native Guards "was never excelled, and but seldom equaled."[157] Even Confederate soldiers who survived the battle attested that the Native Guards "fought like tigers," and admitted that they learned to respect Black soldiers on the battlefield.[158] Furthermore, *L'Union* noted that the events of 27 May redefined African American participation in the war.[159] As an interesting aspect of this new phase, the editors of *L'Union* began publishing in English in addition to French. As it became apparent that the two African American societies of New Orleans were operating as one, the paper was published in English to reach those who could not read French.[160] While not consistent, the publication of English-language versions helped to broaden the paper's audience.

Even the enslaved African Americans around Port Hudson attempted to aid the U.S. Army in capturing the rebel stronghold. David Porter, now an admiral in the navy, reported that, while laying siege to Vicksburg, he accepted around five hundred formerly enslaved men on his ships. Porter employed hundreds of formerly enslaved men on his gunboats, transports, powder vessels, and store vessels. He believed that the formerly enslaved were "better than the white people here whom I look upon as brutes and half savages."[161]

While still reeling from the events of 27 May at Port Hudson, the Native Guards experienced a change in designation on 6 June. On 1 May 1863, General Banks issued General Orders No. 40, which was both flattering to and dismissive of Blacks serving in the army. It was also a shrewd maneuver intended to supersede units organized by General Daniel Ullman. The order proposed eighteen five hundred-man regiments of infantry, engineers, artillery, and cavalry, organized into three divisions across three brigades called the Corps d'Afrique. Banks wrote that "every corps depends upon the influence of its officers upon the troops engaged"—and, to him, Black officers were not up to the tasks. He publicly blamed them for lax discipline in the Native Guards and called their service unsatisfactory without substantiating his claim. General Orders No. 40 stated, "The Commanding General desires to detail for temporary or permanent duty the best officers of the army, for the organization."[162] The order set the stage for later changes in the Native Guards.

General Orders No. 47 redesignated the four infantry regiments of the Native Guards the 1st, 2d, 3d, and 4th Infantry of the Corps d'Afrique on 6 June 1863, and all of the troops General Ullman had raised were redesignated the 6th, 7th, 8th, 9th, and 10th Infantry of the Corps d'Afrique. The 5th Regiment was organized from a unit in Pensacola, so that they could easily garrison that area. Ullman was directed to send his troops to Port Hudson to join the new unit, and each company was ordered to reorganize to the new formation. All of the engineering and artillery units in Louisiana were subsumed within Banks's new formation for Black troops.[163]

The units were initially split into two divisions: the 1st Division, led by General Ullman; and the 2d Division, led by Colonel Holcomb. The two divisions contained a total of 3,612 men.[164] Inadvertently, Banks authorized African American cavalry regiments in the Department of the Gulf. While General Benjamin Butler had organized the 1st United States Colored Cavalry in Virginia after leaving Louisiana, Banks organized the second, designated the 1st

Cavalry Corps d'Afrique, in his zeal to control the regiments. Colonel James Grant Wilson, a seasoned cavalry officer, was assigned command of the cavalry regiment in September.[165] Thus, the new designation and reorganization also brought about new units and new ways for Black and Creole men to serve the U.S. Army.[166]

General Benjamin Butler wrote many years after the war that the designation change from Native Guards to Corps d'Afrique showed a loss of equality in the eyes of military leaders.[167] Meanwhile, Hepworth noted the similarity between the new designation and the European Corps d'Armée, which may have appealed to many of the French-speaking Creoles in the regiments.[168]

Despite disagreeing with Banks's orders, Black New Orleanians still supported the Union army. *L'Union* published an editorial declaring, "To Arms! It is our duty. The nation counts on the devotion and courage of its sons. We will not remain deaf to its call; we will not remain indifferent spectators, like strangers who attach no value to the land. We are sons of Louisiana, and when Louisiana calls us we march." The piece ended with a reminder that this fight was for much more than victory on the battlefield: "To Arms! Who would think to save himself by neutrality? Would the enemies of the country and of our race have more respect for those who hold themselves timidly apart than for the brave who look them in the face? In what century and in what land has man made himself respected in wartime by cowardice? The scorn of the conqueror is the recompense of weakness."[169]

General Ullman used *L'Union* and the events of Port Hudson to increase recruiting in Louisiana, issuing General Orders No. 7 on 10 June to appeal to both white officers and possible recruits. First, he told his officers that they were commanding both free and formerly enslaved people, and that they needed to be cognizant of both in their command. After encouraging more men to join, Ullman addressed People of Color in Louisiana: "Your brethren at Port Hudson have shown to the world that they can and will fight, and have displayed as dauntless courage as ever illuminated a battle field. Emulate their noble example, and fight under the glorious banner of the Republic."[170] The timing of Ullman's expanded recruitment was fortuitous, because many of the nine-month regiments that Banks had brought with him would soon muster out of the military, and the general hoped to use the regiments to fill the gaps in the army in Louisiana.[171]

After a few additional weeks of fighting at Port Hudson, the campaign for the Mississippi reached its end. First, Vicksburg famously surrendered on July 4 due to the combined efforts of General Grant and Admiral Farragut. The well-timed victory made both men heroes to Lincoln and to Americans across the nation.[172] The outcome had been expected; Confederate Joseph Johnston wrote to a fellow rebel leader during the campaign that their only hope for success against Grant was if he committed "some extravagant blunder."[173] Port Hudson could have surrendered in June if Banks had been willing to give concessions to the defenders, but he had orders to disarm the soldiers, so he could not accept their surrender.[174] However, with the fall of Vicksburg, the troops in Port Hudson realized they were fighting a battle that was already lost, and they surrendered to Banks's forces on 8 July 1863 under the terms Banks presented.[175] The following morning, the U.S. Army officially took control of the citadel and the defenders stacked their arms outside. By Banks's tally, the Union offensive had included forty-five days of siege warfare, with twenty-one days of fighting.[176] Purportedly, the defenders had been beaten long before they surrendered: they had no provisions, and many had resorted to eating rats to survive.[177] Governor Moore later said, "The reduction of the stronghold of Vicksburg and Port Hudson necessarily changed military movements in the Southwest. Their loss was serious to the whole country, and especially to Louisiana."[178] With the capture of both Vicksburg and Port Hudson, General Banks reported that, finally, "The Mississippi is opened."[179]

In July, General Banks praised the Corps d'Afrique, by which time their service had become legendary. Banks issued a special commendation to the regiments for their actions at Port Hudson and their defense of Louisiana during numerous raids.[180] Their commanding general even told his superiors, "No troops could be more determined or daring" than the Corps d'Afrique.[181] Privately, however, Banks wrote to General Halleck that he believed they were better suited for fatigue duty, but because of their numbers and his manpower needs, he would keep them in the field.[182] Totaling over ten thousand men among all the regiments by August, the Corps d'Afrique was more important to the Department of the Gulf than any other one group.[183] When the Corps d'Afrique was reviewed after the siege, the units were deemed still fit for duty, the soldiers' military bearing good and proper, and all of their weapons ready for use.[184] Given that the Corps d'Afrique had been key to gaining access to the Mississippi, positive sentiment about their service increased further.[185] The prominence of the entire Department of the Gulf grew when Congress passed a resolution thanking Banks and all of the men who took part in the siege.[186] Amid growing praise for African American soldiers, the War Department asked Douglass to recruit farther South in the areas of Vicksburg and

Port Hudson, and Banks could only watch as the once small regiments under his command began to grow.[187]

General Lorenzo Thomas did not forget his regiments that fought at Milliken's Bend. Upon receiving reports of the battle, he wrote to Colonel Isaac F. Shepard, "I knew they would fight bravely after proper instruction, but little thought they would do so well on being so recently raised."[188] In a letter to Stanton, Thomas praised his men for both their bravery and tenacity in the face of an organized enemy. When Colonel Shepard was up for promotion, Thomas requested that his commission to general be backdated to 7 June for his leadership.[189]

Banks, for his part, continued his overtures to southern planters and Confederate soldiers. He ordered all the sidearms returned to Confederate officers "in consideration of their gallant defense," and while they were not supposed to wear them, many of them did anyway. He further ordered Emory to find "some comfortable house or houses" for them so they could be relaxed during their stay in the city that hundreds died to protect from a Confederate invasion.[190] Finally, he ordered Andrews to start the process of paroling hundreds of privates and noncommissioned officers being held at Port Hudson so they could take up residence in New Orleans.[191] According to Andrews, the parolees did not even have to fake an oath to the federal government per Banks's verbal orders, indicating that Banks was indifferent to the sacrifices of U.S. soldiers.[192] Within a week of capturing Port Hudson, all of the enlisted Confederate men who had been holding the citadel were reported as paroled.[193] While some parolees took oaths not to rejoin the war, many of them did so anyway. According to Ullman, the label of oath breaker was unsurprisingly common among the southern ranks.[194] It was only when some captured white Union officers died by Confederate hands after surrendering that Banks finally sent some of the prisoners still on parole North instead of allowing them to roam freely.[195]

The Corps d'Afrique's success forced some in the Confederacy to reconsider their policy regarding African American Creoles in southern ranks. There were calls in the South to use free Black men in Confederate regiments because they had already proved their ability to fight in Union regiments.[196] Confederate soldiers at Port Hudson were impressed by Black soldiers' abilities in battle.[197] Governor Moore later called for enslaved people to perform military labor, but stopped short of calling for the enlistment of Blacks as soldiers in the military.[198] Confederate Dabney H. Maury wrote to Confederate Samuel Cooper, the adjutant and inspector general for the South, "I again call your attention to my request into the Confederate service the company of creoles of Mobile." Recognizing that "when Spain ceded this territory to the United States in 1803, the creoles were guaranteed all the immunities and privileges of the citizens of the United States, and have continued to enjoy them up to this time," the general proposed "to make heavy artillerists of them, for which they will be admirably qualified."[199] The adjutant's office endorsed the request, and it was subsequently submitted to the southern War Department on 20 November.[200] The Confederate secretary of war, James Seddon, responded, "Our position with the North and before the world will not allow the employment as armed soldiers of negroes. If these creoles can be naturally and properly discriminated from negroes, the authority may be considered as conferred."[201]

Many southern generals recognized how dangerous the enslaved were to their war aims. Confederate soldiers patrolled their quarters and broke up any assemblies among them for fear they were conspiring to aid the U.S. Army.[202] One officer wrote directly to Seddon that they could never allow any Black men to serve because doing so would prove that their entire reason for starting the war was wrong.[203] Later, another southern general petitioned directly to Jefferson Davis, arguing that slavery was no longer a boon to the Confederacy. He argued for arming the most loyal enslaved men, noting that they would only fight if they and their families were guaranteed freedom afterward. The general also argued that slavery was the reason why Europe would never recognize the Confederacy, and only by turning away from slavery could the Confederacy become a country. By his logic, through arming and freeing enslaved men, they could solve their personnel shortages, earn recognition from Europe, free themselves from an impediment that slowed their army, and use Black men as the Union had done.[204] But these arguments and the success of units like the Corps d'Afrique did not convince Davis of the merits of freeing enslaved people. To do so would have negated the entire purpose of the war.

In August 1863, the Department of the Gulf held a general military review to celebrate capturing Port Hudson. It was a grand spectacle. Generals Thomas, Andrews, and Ullman led regiments of the Corps d'Afrique in the review. Like the parade that Governor Moore had held two years prior, it was a show of the city's military might. One soldier marveled at the number of "infantry, artillery, and cavalry marching in review and saluting the general," and he told his wife that all of the "gentry from the city were out to witness the review in their splendid carriages, and the city Brass Band discoursed excellent music on the occasion."[205]

The Corps d'Afrique's presence was both familiar and conspicuous.[206] When the Native Guards had marched in 1861, they had done so with limited weapons and equipage. When the Native Guards had marched under Butler in 1862, the regiments had been comprised of raw recruits who had only shot at a few guerrillas in Lafourche. The men of the Corps d'Afrique marching in the fall of 1863 were quite different. They were well equipped and battle hardened, and they had already proven themselves at Port Hudson and Brashear City as courageous soldiers willing to sacrifice for the Union. The XIX Corps had successfully repulsed all regular military forces from New Orleans, and now they only had to contend with small guerrilla raids near the major cities in the Department of the Gulf's area of operations.[207] Like Baton Rouge, Port Hudson now served as a key location for the military, second only to New Orleans, which was still considered the prize of the Mississippi.[208] Many expected the XIX Corps to focus more on Texas, and a *New Orleans Times* writer wrote, after watching the regiments, "The President never struck so vital a blow at this rebellion as when he authorized the organization of these colored soldiers."[209]

The actions of the Corps d'Afrique changed the Union army. The quartermaster general's official report to the secretary of state, William Seward, read, "The newly raised negro regiments showed great valor and devotion, and forever in this country dispelled all doubts as to the capacity of this oppressed race for the defense of their newly acquired liberty."[210] In a letter to the president, Stanton commented on what the African American soldiers in Louisiana meant to the nation and the war effort in 1863: "Many persons believed, or pretended to believe, and confidently asserted that freed slaves would not make good soldiers; they would lack courage, and could not be subjected to military discipline. Facts have shown how groundless were these apprehensions. The slave has proved his manhood, and his capacity as an infantry soldier, at Milliken's Bend, at the assault upon Port Hudson, and the storming of Fort Wagner."[211] Stanton's views about arming enslaved men from New Orleans had thus shifted. Invoking manhood, Stanton mirrored the language Frederick Douglass had used in his broadside. General Lorenzo Thomas echoed this sentiment, writing to Senator Henry Wilson that Port Hudson and Milliken's Bend "demonstrate the value of the colored troops" to the U.S. Army.[212] President Abraham Lincoln expressed a similar sentiment: in a letter to James Conkling, he wrote that many of the military's victories in the summer of 1863 had only been possible thanks to soldiers of color, and that, when the war was over, it would be apparent that regiments like the

Corps d'Afrique had saved the nation. The president wrote, "You say you will not fight to free negroes. Some of them seem willing to fight for you; but no matter. Fight you, then exclusively save the Union."[213] Indeed, officials at every level of government recognized the success and value of the regiments.

During the summer of 1863, French soldiers successfully took over Mexico City, and in July, Mexico was declared a monarchy subject to French rule. These events were the culmination of the invasion France had initiated a year prior.[214] Seward wrote to Stanton, "Our colored troops have proved themselves brave and gallant soldiers and are just the men we shall require in our service, if engaged in a war with England or France."[215] As the largest force in the Gulf, the XIX Corps would be the first to respond to any incursions into the United States, ready to face France if called upon.

This heroism of the members of the Corps d'Afrique dramatically shifted attitudes about Black soldiers. The corps' men combated racism in the ranks and from the general public, an unsupportive commanding general, and the loss of African American officers. Despite these challenges, they proved themselves men. Now widely acknowledged as heroes, the dead at Port Hudson were described in one newspaper as "a better Proclamation of Freedom than even President Lincoln's."[216] George Williams summarized it best in 1887 with a poem that closed his history of African American service in the Civil War, titled "The Negro Volunteer":

> They struggled and fought, with courage fraught,
> With love for the cause of the Nation;
> They knew in the strife for the Union's life
> They must buy Emancipation.[217]

Chapter 8

# *DISSATISFACTION AND DISCONTENT*

## RECRUITMENT AND SERVICE IN THE CORPS D'AFRIQUE

Despite the Corps d'Afrique's strong performance in numerous engagements, treatment of its troops worsened under General Banks. By September 1863, Captain P. B. S. Pinchback was the only Black officer stationed at Fort Pike, and he could no longer take the invective nature of Banks and his fellow white officers. Pinchback tendered his resignation, citing "inimical" white officers who responded to officers of color with nothing but "dissatisfaction and discontent."[1] Numerous Black officers and soldiers in the Corps d'Afrique shared Pinchback's experience, culminating, in one instance, in a revolt against white officers who abused soldiers and raped Black women in Fort Jackson. Service in the Corps d'Afrique turned many potential Black soldiers away from the federal government and the military as they realized that, with Banks in charge, these institutions did not serve the best interests of African Americans in New Orleans. By the waning months of the war, those who had once proudly served in the Native Guards agitated for social and political reform to receive dignity, respect, and opportunity for their community. Thus, the following chapter is a somber one, as it entails rampant sexual and physical abuse by white officers who took advantage of the command climate created by their commanding general. Even with this appalling treatment, the men continued to serve with honor, and new regiments were formed to join the fight for freedom.

Pinchback's resignation was part of a longer struggle in the ranks. His resignation letter was the last in a series of complaints he wrote on behalf of all the Black officers in the regiments. In a letter dated March 1863, Pinchback pointed out a number of inequities: the fact that white officers were excused from examining boards, the constant fatigue that prevented him and others from having enough time to prepare for the boards, General Banks's threats of not paying Black officers, and the treatment of his men by white officers.[2] Lieutenant Robert Isabelle resigned his commission after only a few months under the new regime because he could not stomach the rampant racism in the XIX Corps.[3] Joseph Follin wrote in his resignation letter that he was leaving because "prejudices are so strong against Colored Officers, that no matter what be their patriotism and their anxiety to fight for the flag of their native Land, they cannot do it with honor to themselves."[4] G. T. Ruby wrote to the *Liberator* that he was disheartened that "Northern prejudice" had spurred a wave of resignations, given that many of the resigning officers had proven themselves worthy of respect and equal treatment.[5] General Butler echoed these views, writing to the Freedmen's Inquiry Commission, "I can hardly conceive of a greater injustice than has been done in compelling the resignation of these colored officers."[6] By the end of 1863, African Americans in New Orleans knew they were fighting two wars: one to ensure their *freedom* and another to ensure their *rights*.

General Banks's treatment of Black soldiers affected his tactical decisions. As early as February 1863, Butler received reports that Black soldiers had started pretending to shoot at Banks with air guns out of frustration.[7] Even after Port Hudson, the clerk for the 3d Louisiana Native Guards Infantry Regiment mused in the regimental diary, "Now, why were the colored troops left unsupported? Why were they sent on such hopeless missions?" The clerk wondered if it was Colonel John Nelson or Banks who was to blame. Of course, there was no definitive answer.[8] The regimental diary demonstrates that, even at the height of their success, the men were seriously questioning who they were following into battle. An unnamed African American Unionist wrote directly to President Abraham Lincoln begging him to "give us something to fight for, Black Soldiers [and] Black officers."[9] Soldiers in the regiments sought a leader whom they were willing to follow into combat, and who respected their worth in turn. With Colonel Spencer Stafford's removal, General George Andrews was the one many of the men came to look toward for support.

General Andrews was considered by some to be intelligent and less racist than many of the other options to lead the Corps d'Afrique. He was born in the New England area in 1828 and received a good education. While not a full abolitionist, he had opposed the enslavement of People of Color long before his tenure in the military. He graduated from West Point in 1851 at the head of his class, a rare distinction. He left the military for a number of years, then rejoined in 1861 as a lieutenant colonel in the 2d Massachusetts Infantry Regiment when the Civil War began. He fought in multiple campaigns, most notably the Battle of Antietam, before joining the XIX Corps.[10] While he was not as fervent about Black soldiers as General John Wolcott Phelps, Stafford, or even Butler by the end of 1862, Andrews did indicate that he thought Black men could make good soldiers. While he commanded from Port Hudson, he issued General Orders No. 12. In it, he declared to his troops that he would not tolerate abuses of African American soldiers or officers and that disobeying Black officers meant disobeying his own orders. He promised to punish any offender with "unrelenting severity" and said that he did not want to hear anyone question the use of Black soldiers since the president had already settled the matter.[11]

A war correspondent who visited the now-Union citadel while Andrews was in charge marveled at the sight of Black sharpshooters patrolling the parapets at every available point of attack.[12] George Denison wrote to Salmon P. Chase that Andrews could make a better leader for the Corps d'Afrique than Ullman.[13]

In a letter to his wife, Andrews wrote that he was looking forward to using the Corps d'Afrique to control Port Hudson.[14] Colonel Stafford begged to be reinstated as the commander of the regiments, but Andrews recommended he be removed from service.[15] Tired of Stafford's pleas for the War Department to use Black troops, General Banks sided with Andrews and removed Stafford from his department. Soon after, General Ulysses S. Grant sent two divisions

Infantry under review at Port Hudson
(Library of Congress, Prints and Photographs Division)

from the XIII Corps to support Port Hudson, and Banks reorganized the reinforcements in the XIX Corps.[16] Finally, it seemed, the Department of the Gulf had enough men to hold their large area of operations while campaigning in the field.[17]

Andrews demonstrated commitments to recruiting, improving the Corps d'Afrique, and using Black soldiers. On 20 October 1863, he appointed Lieutenant Colonel Samuel Quincy as the acting assistant inspector of the regiments, hoping Quincy's experience leading multiple engagements and his part at the Battle of Chancellorsville would be beneficial to the Corps d'Afrique.[18] Quincy and Andrews created a school for white officers to learn from Quincy's experience, and they hoped to create better leaders out of the men Banks had assigned to the regiments.[19] Additionally, Quincy and Andrews believed that education was key for enlisted men of color, so they established schools for them as well.[20] Quincy took training so seriously that he wrote the "Camp and Garrison Manual" for the Corps d'Afrique; it was later published for the entire U.S. Army in 1865 as *A Camp and Garrison Manual for Volunteers and Militia*.[21] Quincy expressed the hope that he and Andrews would make the Corps d'Afrique "one of the best corps in the Army."[22] Andrews slowly stepped into a role that required him to mediate between the Corps d'Afrique, General Banks, and white soldiers stationed at Port Hudson. He was uncomfortable in this position, given Banks's scrutiny of his Black troops.

Andrews's timing was apt: the U.S. government fully committed to using African American soldiers after the summer of 1863, thanks in large part to the efforts of the Native Guards at Port Hudson. Through the efforts of Ullman and his bureau, recruitment exploded in Louisiana for the remainder of the year. Multiple new infantry, cavalry, and engineering regiments were formed in the Corps d'Afrique. Most were formed from men recruited in and around New Orleans, but Ullman also allowed his recruiters to bring in men from outside the city who were of the right age and build. In a letter to Edwin Stanton, General Lorenzo Thomas described his plans to raise twenty thousand men along the Mississippi River. It was one of his regiments that fought at Milliken's Bend before they could finish their training.[23] Additionally, the federal government expanded conscription to include African Americans on 3 March 1863, which opened the door for Ullman, Thomas, Andrews, and Banks to forcibly recruit more men for new regiments. Many of the infantry regiments were moved to Port Hudson for a combination of fatigue and guard duty; this was also a way for Banks to move Black soldiers out of New Orleans to quell the public's ire.[24]

Thus, by the fall of 1863 multiple recruiting efforts were underway in Louisiana. They were led by four generals, all of whom sought the fame that came with raising the most able-bodied regiments in the state. Due to their combined efforts, over twenty-seven thousand African American troops were raised in the Mississippi Valley alone by the end of the year. Andrews proposed to Thomas that they combine their forces into two divisions to increase their fighting capacity, but the growing Black regiments still encountered challenges that prevented their unity—namely racism.[25] A writer for one paper countered the racist view that Black men shouldn't fight for the Union with, "Each negro soldier enlisted and sent into the field diminishes by one the number of white men to be drafted. Any squeamish fellow who objects to having his fighting done by a 'nigger,' should at once report himself to the nearest recruiting officer and volunteer."[26]

As early as June 1863, Ullman impressed upon his recruiting officers that they needed to entice men to join. However, he sought such high numbers of recruits that the officers turned to violence to force men into the ranks. Ullman had ordered his officers to be kind to formerly enslaved people in the region, all while reinforcing the racist southern rhetoric that Black people were docile and would make easy subordinates. While he endorsed the "law of kindness," his officers did not follow suit.[27] For example, a white merchant complained that recruiting officers had forced his Black servant into the military by simply letting the man touch a pen as proof he volunteered for service. In another instance, policemen beat an old man and forced his son to join the military.[28] The recruiters blamed the police for being overzealous in their charge to help, but the damage was done and many People of Color began to fear recruiting officers and police in the city.[29] Soldiers in the Corps d'Afrique joined the recruiting effort under Ullman's direction. In one instance, four soldiers carrying a pass signed by the general forced their way onto a plantation and threatened to shoot any white person who interfered as they enticed men to join and women and children to leave for New Orleans and freedom.[30]

Ullman was clear that any man who served was guaranteed freedom under the Constitution and the right to be treated as a human and a man in the military. To Ullman, "the first gun that was fired at Fort Sumter sounded the death-knell of slavery," and he fully intended to see that cause through.[31] However, his regiments also targeted free people. Thirty-six individuals in Baton Rouge claiming they were already free were arrested and housed with enslaved people, then threatened with service in the military.[32] They signed a petition attesting that they had already been freed. Soon, Ullman was directed to work under General Andrews to ensure he was following directives and to unify the Corps a bit more, but that was not a position he wanted to endure.[33] General Lorenzo Thomas revoked all of Ullman's special powers in September through his own authority to ensure Ullman fell in line.[34] In response, Ullman temporarily left his division for an independent command at Morganza in the newly constituted Southern Division of Louisiana.[35]

General Andrews wanted to recruit additional Black soldiers for the Corps d'Afrique. Like Ullman, he recognized that both his white officers and the white inhabitants of New Orleans opposed the military's use of African American soldiers. Andrews noted that rebellious white sympathizers openly attacked Black men on plantations to coerce them by threat not to join the military.[36] Despite these circumstances, Andrews was determined to recruit more men for the regiments now that he was in control. Like General Phelps a year prior, Andrews ordered his men to visit plantations and bring back enslaved people for employment in the military. General Charles Stone complained directly to General Banks about the number and quality of people Andrews was bringing to Port Hudson.[37] In one such example, on 3 August 1863, Andrews sent a contingent from the 1st Corps d'Afrique Infantry Regiment, along with a few men from other companies, to Jackson. There, they recruited fifty men for the 12th Corps d'Afrique Infantry Regiment. However, that evening, Confederate forces found them in camp and attacked them. Over a hundred men from the Corps d'Afrique—both white and Black—were captured in the ensuing battle before they were able to retreat back toward Port Hudson for safety.[38] While that battle was a loss, it showed that Andrews was willing to risk the lives of his men to free and recruit men into the army.

He was not alone in these endeavors. General Thomas appointed Brigadier General John P. Hawkins as the commander of the African Descent regiments he had raised. He intended for the units to work in tandem with Ullman's Brigade. However, the vast distance between Ullman's and Hawkins's units meant they rarely interacted with one another during the war. Nevertheless, Thomas wanted his brigade's number designation to follow closely behind Ullman's to reflect a link between them.[39] Within a year, Thomas reported that he had raised over fifty-six thousand troops in the Deep South, and that he created six infantry regiments, three light artillery companies, and one cavalry regiment filled with Black troops in Louisiana.[40]

Because the Department of the Gulf encompassed a large area of operation, Ullman and Andrews had a sizable population of men to recruit from. The expansion of the Corps d'Afrique had enormous consequences for Black

Sergeant Manuel J. D'Aunoy, Company G, 73d United States Colored Infantry
(National Archives and Records Administration)

New Orleanians. One example is Charles Franklin Crosby, commonly called Charley. Crosby was born in Kentucky, but because of the interstate slave trade, he lived in Alabama and Florida before emancipating himself and volunteering to join one of Ullman's engineer regiments.[41] Crosby attested that he joined around the age of twelve or thirteen, and that he drilled and fought with his regiment until the end of the war. The details of his situation do not conform to the military's rules, as Ullman had ordered that no men under five feet, four inches, could join.[42] Lewis Reed, who served in the 9th Corps d'Afrique, had little choice but to serve, and his son, Henry Reed, attested after the war that he never saw his father again after military recruiters forced him into the army. According to Lewis Reed's service record, he served for the entirety of the war and achieved the rank of sergeant before dying from pneumonia one year after the conflict. He never knew where his family was due to his forced separation.[43]

Unsurprisingly, Banks was a critic of the growing regiments' officers of color. In a letter to his wife, he admitted that "they fought splendidly" at Port Hudson; however, they "require only good officers to make the best troops the government will have."[44] Even in his glowing report, republished throughout the North, the general commented, "They require only good officers, commands of limited numbers, and careful discipline to make them excellent soldiers."[45] However, there were some who thought of Black officers as good leaders.

In an 1863 letter to Edwin Stanton, Massachusetts governor John Andrew argued that the army should include "line officers, assistant Surgeons & Chaplains" who were Black.[46] Stanton first informed Andrew it was up to the president before letting him know it was at the discretion of the generals in the field.[47] Stanton went as far as authorizing additional Black officers. For example, he telegrammed William Adair that if he raised a full regiment of Black men in Pittsburgh, Pennsylvania, they could have Black officers.[48] This was a marked change from a telegram Stanton sent to Rufus Sibb Jones, who had asked a year earlier to constitute a Black regiment from the same city.[49]

Eventually, the War Department ruled against the widespread use of Black officers in the U.S. Army—excepting chaplains and recruiting officers, as men in these roles never commanded white soldiers in battle.[50] Long before any of these decisions, General Banks had already decided he did not want Black men commissioned in the XIX Corps, and General Andrews also did not support Black officers in the regiments.

Banks worked for months to remove Black men from the officer corps. In his first official report of the regiments, he detailed their numbers and his plans to replace them because, in his words, they were "detrimental to the service," and their presence "demoralizes both the white troops and the negroes."[51] In a letter to the president, Banks described Black officers as "demoralized from various causes." Chief among them were persistent tiffs between Black officers and white officers and soldiers. Banks never found fault with the whites who typically started these quarrels through insults and disrespect; instead, he accused officers of color of "discreditable character."[52] When African American officers resigned, were injured, or died, Banks always replaced the departing officers with white officers, a policy at odds with the Native Guards' tradition of allowing the men to elect their own officers.

Banks even worked to remove white officers who supported Black soldiers. For example, Colonel Nathan Daniels was still under arrest by the fall of 1863, and he was angry with Banks for holding him on such frivolous charges when in reality he was being punished for supporting his men against racist white officers. Daniels eventually realized that his only option was to resign his commission; otherwise, Banks could hold him until the end of the war.[53] Colonel Nelson was soon accused of cotton speculation, and he too faced a choice of either resigning his commission or enduring a prolonged court-martial that

Native Guards at Port Hudson
(National Archives and Records Administration)

would embarrass him and the 3d Regiment.[54] With the removal of Stafford, Nelson, and Daniels, Banks demonstrated that even white officers from the Corps d'Afrique were at risk of being fired if they supported the Black soldiers. The only colonel left in place from the original Native Guards was Colonel Drew. Like Banks, he expressed open resentment toward Black officers.

While the Native Guards had fought admirably at Port Hudson, they did retreat from the field of battle to the tree line when ordered. Banks used their withdrawal from the field as a reason to dismiss a few Black officers in the 1st Regiment for cowardice, ignoring the fact that they had acted upon orders and that white officers in the 3d Regiment had done the same.[55] Banks also removed a number of officers from command for disobedience and minor offenses. Lieutenant Colonel Henry Finnegass was dismissed for his refusal to lead a charge after being ordered by General Dwight and Colonel Nelson.[56] Captain Alcide Lewis was removed from command the day after the 27 May attack for being a "coward" and acting "ungentlemanly."[57] Second Lieutenant Hippolyte St. Louis was removed from command for similar reasons on 4 June.[58] Before the month was out, Second Lieutenant Louis A. Thibaut was removed from command as well.[59] Banks seemed to have forgotten that just a year prior he also had retreated from battle when his forces were outnumbered and outgunned.[60]

Additional officers resigned in protest of Banks's decisions. Captain Samuel Ringgold, still stationed at Ship Island, passed his competency board in

July 1863 but resigned shortly afterward.[61] A few months prior, Captain Arnold Bertonneau had resigned as well. He wrote that he had joined the regiment in hopes that "the success of my country would suffice to alter a prejudice which had long existed" against African Americans, but thanks to his time in the Department of the Gulf, his "five months experiences proved the contrary."[62] In a letter to the adjutant general's office regarding his resignation, Captain Joseph Follin wrote, "Daily events demonstrate that prejudices are so strong against Colored Officers, that no matter what would be their patriotism and their anxiety to fight for the flag of their native Land, they cannot do it with honor to themselves."[63] Perhaps the greatest loss for the men was Major Francis Dumas's resignation. He held a rare distinction as the only Black major in the Union army who had experienced combat, which garnered a degree of respect that even Banks could not wholly ignore. However, Dumas realized he could better serve the Creole society of New Orleans as a civilian than under the command environment that Banks had fostered.[64] Within a year, Banks had successfully removed most of the Black officers who commanded in the Corps d'Afrique, and those he could not remove resigned due to prejudice and racism from Banks and his white officers. These events set the stage for a new phase of war for Black soldiers in Louisiana.

Banks was left with a new problem: Who would officer the Corps d'Afrique? He had little intention of using the regiments in another large battle unless he had to, and, like John De Forest a year prior, this dissuaded the most capable officers from joining the corps. Men who could secure promotions in their own units had no reason to leave their units for the Corps d'Afrique. According to soldiers who witnessed the situation, this left "men disqualified by want of character and capacity for the discharge of the humblest duties in the regiments to which they belonged."[65] Banks replaced the educated free men of color with uneducated, often incompetent white officers. He ran advertisements in newspapers offering transportation to New Orleans and a commission to any white person who volunteered to command in the Corps d'Afrique.[66] One former officer noted that some of them could not even read or write, and some Black privates were more educated than their white leaders.[67]

According to a Black officer who resigned, some Union commanders took the openings in the Corps d'Afrique as an opportunity to unload their "very imperfect examinations" on the Louisiana regiments without having to go through the trouble of removing them from service.[68] Lieutenant Charles Kennedy, for example, sent his "very poor clerk" to join the regiments.[69] John Kelly was promoted from second lieutenant to major upon accepting a position in the 2d Regiment.[70] William M. Grosvenor, a captain who was injured at Port Hudson, accepted a colonelcy in the Corps d'Afrique when he made the move.[71] George Harding, a man who was captured while fighting at Donaldsonville near the Native Guards in September 1862, returned to Port Hudson and was astonished at both the size of the Corps d'Afrique and the number of white officers who now volunteered to serve and gain promotions. He recalled that, previously, a culture of reluctance to officer one of the Black New Orleans regiments had prevailed, and now he noticed that even men from his home state of Indiana were jumping at the chance to officer the regiments in order to jump a few ranks.[72]

The commissioning boards that Banks had set up for the Department of the Gulf gained a reputation for being difficult, as Banks wanted to prevent educated officers of color from passing. However, officials in the War Department also recognized that white officers who passed the exams were less capable than those in other regions, so they restricted all the white officers who passed in the XIX Corps to that corps only, fearing they would not succeed elsewhere in the army.[73] Commissioners in the Department of the Gulf proposed transferring the examinations for the Corps d'Afrique to Albany, New York, due to the disparity in testing, with the hope that new officers selected for Louisiana would seem equal to the rest of the federal army.[74] Even when educated Black men passed the commissioning board, Andrews—under pressure from Banks—turned down the option of commissioning additional officers. He wrote to the president of the commissioning board, "I cannot at present under any circumstances approve the application of a colored person for a commission in the Corps d'Afrique. The time for this may come, but it is not now."[75] It was clear that, from the top down, Black officers were not wanted in the Department of the Gulf.

The new officers negatively affected recruitment drives because of their incompetence, but they were not the only problem. The military's treatment of Black men was the chief impediment to recruiting. Many of the Black officers in the 2d Regiment signed a petition calling out the military for not paying soldiers in the Corps d'Afrique what they had been promised. In retribution, Banks issued Special Orders No. 126, removing Captains Hannibal Carter and Edward Chase and Lieutenants Louis De Gray, John Latting, Jasper Thompson, Calvin Glover, Joseph Wellington, and George Watson for publicly calling out Banks and the military.[76] However, African Americans in New Orleans knew their real crime was being Black men who called for equality to whites under Banks's regime.

Shortly afterward, officials in the Department of the Gulf attempted to constitute the 6th Louisiana Volunteer Infantry Regiment (Colored) on 4 July from men in and around New Orleans. On the heels of Port Hudson, military leaders expected a wave of volunteers. However, according to the colonel in charge of recruiting for the new regiment, "the 1st and 2nd Regiments Corps d'Afrique . . . spread reports highly prejudicial to recruiting" that they had still not been paid their "bounty and pay as other United States Volunteers."[77] Banks learned that the pay situation was widely known in the city, and it had turned many away. The muster rolls of the Corps d'Afrique support claims of pay disparity.[78] Officers who were removed because of Banks's purge reported that their accounts were not properly closed and that they never received the back pay they were due.[79] Part of the pay discrepancy was caused by Congress's requirement that Black soldiers cover their own clothing by taking it out of their pay. Clothing was expensive and extensive for a soldier, including a trimmed hat, forage cap, uniform coat, two blue flannel sack coats, two pairs of trousers, three flannel shirts, three flannel drawers, four bootees and stockings, leather stock, great coat, stable frock, fatigue overall, and blanket.[80] The system was similar to that of the Native Guards under the New Orleans home guards, which had required Black men to purchase their own equipment and accoutrements.

Rumors about how white officers treated Black soldiers and the fact that Banks was no longer allowing Black officers a commission proved detrimental to recruitment efforts. By 13 August 1863, the still forming 6th Regiment was mustered out of service due to lack of interest and support. Many free Black men in the city came together to demand rations and clothing for Black troops, and free rent for the troops' wives. The former commander of the 6th Regiment indicated that if these demands were met, he could likely raise "a fine Regiment" quickly.[81] But, instead of addressing these issues, officials in the Department of the Gulf took steps to quell distrust among recruits by punishing any enlisted man who spoke out against how the military was treating Black soldiers around the recruiting depot with "a ball and chain for twenty days, or any other punishment as the commanding officer . . . may see fit to inflict," through Special Order No. 6.[82]

Another issue was the substandard and sometimes even rotten rations that the men and their families received.[83] One man sent a letter to Lincoln, reporting to him that some of the Black officers and soldiers refused to purchase the low-quality food from the regiment, preferring to live off the land or from "potatoes and other vegetables . . . coming down the river."[84] To curtail these efforts, the inspector general's office suggested enforcing existing rules that required any contraband and food acquired by soldiers to be turned over to the commissary or quartermaster.[85] Soldiers' families, too, were often ignored by the military, furthering Black soldiers' sense of disrespect and alienation in the army. In a rare case, Norreddin Cowen, a white officer in the 3d Illinois Cavalry, wrote to President Lincoln that he had witnessed men, women, and children of color suffering from neglect and starvation because of the low-quality food available and lack of assistance in farming to feed themselves.[86]

The men serving in the Corps d'Afrique continued to experience many of the same illnesses they had since 1862. Sanitary Commission officers noted that men serving in cavalry units seemed to get sick more often than infantrymen because of the long marches and exposure along their journeys.[87] Scurvy and dysentery were the most common ailments. The men depended on visits from Sanitary Commission agents, who tended to arrive with desperately needed resources, including rations, blankets, and even medicine for the hospitals.[88] Compounding matters were the rampant disease-spreading mosquitoes, which one soldier described as the size of bees.[89] Moses Webb, a private in Company D of the 2d Corps d'Afrique, suffered from multiple diseases, and, according to statements from his fellow soldiers, he lingered for months as the illnesses ate away at his body. He died in December 1863, not in combat but from disease and poor medical care.[90] Exacerbating the effects of a lack of resources for the Corps d'Afrique was the racist belief that African Americans were naturally resistant to the heat and diseases of the Deep South, so they were constantly pushed into the field with little protection and water, unlike their white counterparts. Hundreds of men died like Webb, not in battle but because their white officers thought Black men did not need basic necessities or rest.

Compounding the issue were subpar hospitals and medical officers serving the regiments. An anonymous soldier wrote to the War Department that the doctors serving his regiment were students who barely knew what they were doing and who openly ignored men with swollen legs. He wrote that some were possibly murderers, alleging that when one man angered his white captain, the captain spoke to the doctors, who gave the private medicine that killed him. He described another instance in which he witnessed a private in Company D get kicked out of the medical tent by the doctor and left to suffer and die outside. He ended his letter by noting that he could not sign his name because, if the letter fell into the wrong hands, he feared he too would receive some medicine from the doctors for describing their practices.[91] While there is no evidence to confirm these accusations, enough similar statements circulated in the USCT that it seems possible the doctors serving the regiments tampered with medicine to quiet soldiers who angered them. Even General Banks wrote to the adjutant general's office that competent doctors turned down the offer to serve in the regiments, leaving them with students and individuals who had little or no choice but to take the position.[92]

In addition to poor health and sanitation, crossing waterways in the Department of the Gulf's area of operations was dangerous, and rising water levels in the spring amplified that danger. On an April day in 1864, eight members of the 2d Engineers Corps d'Afrique drowned alongside twelve white soldiers and two officers from other units.[93] Unfortunately, accidents like these were a constant for soldiers conducting labor duty.

Racist white New Orleanians posed a threat to soldiers in the regiments as well. Despite their success at Port Hudson, Black soldiers were still publicly attacked on the streets, and in one instance a Black sergeant pulled his revolver and threatened to shoot a man during an attack in New Orleans.[94] Incidents like this occurred throughout the war, but the biggest fight centered around the streetcars. General Butler had ordered the desegregation of streetcars in New Orleans in 1862, but the judge in a local court ruled that the order violated Louisiana law.[95] To avoid standing for long periods of time in the heat, members of the Native Guards often forced their way onto whites-only streetcars. Eventually, the situation resulted in multiple assaults on streetcar drivers and passengers, and in one incident a soldier even pulled his weapon and threatened to shoot the driver if he were not let on.[96] Stafford wrote to Butler on behalf of his men, and Butler pushed the operators to relent or risk the military taking over the entire operation. The companies were compelled to let Black officers—but not soldiers—ride on streetcars reserved for whites, a palatable compromise for the city's white residents, who viewed the often lighter-skinned officers of color as more sophisticated. But this gesture was insufficient for the remaining men, who were still expected to endure discrimination.[97] To whites, this was another sign of Black impudence, spurred by military service, that needed to be stamped out.[98] Unsurprisingly, Banks sided with the streetcar operators when violence erupted between his soldiers and the white drivers. Because Banks had removed most of the Black officers by the fall of 1863, even the original compromise became moot since it affected so few of the men. Banks went on to rescind Butler's original orders, and the streetcar operators were allowed to segregate their vehicles once again. It was not until 1865 that they were forced to reintegrate, and even then only soldiers in uniform were allowed to ride any car they chose. Disputes among the streetcar operators, Black soldiers, and other New Orleans residents continued to arise into the Reconstruction period.[99] Furthermore, there was a racist practice of requiring free People of Color to register with Louisiana or risk imprisonment that preceded the war, and the registry continued for far too long, even under federal control.[100]

Even the churches in New Orleans turned against the Corps d'Afrique, a heartbreaking experience for many of the men in the regiments. In 1861, the Catholic Church in New Orleans overwhelmingly supported the Native Guards, even anointing the home guards and allowing them to train and organize at the Institute Catholique, which Captain Henry Rey's father had helped to create. By 1863, the Catholic Church in New Orleans had disavowed Black soldiers. Priests reported to the archbishop that they feared another Haitian Revolution would take place if Black soldiers continued to train in the city and grew more emboldened. Reportedly, many of the priests took oaths to Rome and other foreign nations to avoid any semblance of loyalty to the United States, and they used their supposed dissociation from the war to justify withholding sacraments from soldiers. Banks did nothing to compel the Catholic Church in New Orleans to reverse these practices even though a majority of the members of the Corps d'Afrique were Catholic and the Protestant chaplain for the regiments rarely visited them. This ambivalence spurred priests and nuns to attack the families of members in the regiments. Women and children were publicly admonished for their relationships to Black soldiers, and children of color in Catholic schools were taught that it was wrong for Black men to push for equality through military service. Churchgoers verbally and physically attacked the families of the soldiers in the Corps d'Afrique, and some churches even refused to bury members of the regiments when they died, even those who had been lifelong members.[101] A writer for the *Richmond Enquirer* wrote, "For a Negro to enlist in the United States service constitutes an offense in the eyes of the priest which should cut him off from the consolations and hopes of religion."[102] Few priests disobeyed the Church's edict.

Racism remained endemic across the nation. One of the sergeants from the 1st Corps d'Afrique was sent to New York after losing his leg from a gunshot wound he had received in combat. By all accounts, this man should have been treated as a war hero who made a physical sacrifice for his country. However, on his way to the hospital to receive a prosthetic, he was accosted by a city railroad conductor who refused to let him board because he was under orders "not to allow negroes to ride in the cars." According to the *New York*

*Tribune,* scenes like this were normal in New York because officials at all the city railroad cars refused to transport Black men, even soldiers who were in uniform or visibly injured from combat.[103] It was a sign to men in the regiments that, in the North as well as the South, they were not wholly welcome even if they made sacrifices for their country and served honorably.[104]

A final determining factor for many men faced with the choice of joining the Corps d'Afrique was the knowledge of how they would be treated if they were captured by the Confederate army. After the events at Port Hudson, it was clear to all African Americans that Jefferson Davis's threats to give them no quarter were serious. Officers and soldiers in the Confederate military expressed contempt and anger toward Black soldiers, and especially toward Black officers and the white officers who led them. When Black men were forced to surrender, they were often killed, and some were tortured after being injured in the field. There were also many cases of men being enslaved, similar to those who were captured after the fall of Brashear City. Southerners boasted that these events would curtail efforts to deploy more USCT regiments. It was not uncommon for a southern cavalry member to start marching captured Black soldiers and then for another to shout, "These niggers are tryin' to git away" before an entire company opened fire on them.[105] Even white officers were not immune to this treatment; Lieutenant George Coleman was reportedly hanged alongside twenty Black privates from the Corps d'Afrique when they were captured.[106]

General Ullman wrote to Secretary Stanton, "They understand their position full as well as we do. They know the deep stake they have in the issue—that, if we are unsuccessful, they will be remanded to worse a slavery than before. They also have a settled conviction that if they are taken, they will be tortured and hung."[107] One Union surgeon who witnessed atrocities against captured Black soldiers attested that he had witnessed numerous instances of Black troops being assaulted and even killed for their choice to join the military.

The death of Lieutenant Oscar Orillion, along with dozens of his men, demonstrates how real these threats were. Orillion was among the few African American officers who remained in the Corps d'Afrique after passing numerous tests. He was leading Company B of the 1st Infantry Regiment when Andrews sent his men into Jackson for recruitment purposes, and he was among one hundred men captured on the evening of 3 August.[108] As they were marched toward Confederate lines, four of the captured soldiers decided that it would be better to escape than march to their own deaths or enslavement. Frank Powers, who led the Confederate contingent, ordered his men to kill the escapees. As his men lined up to fire at the escaping men, the others who had been captured saw their own opportunity to escape during the commotion. In retaliation, Powers ordered all prisoners shot. In the ensuing massacre, dozens of men, both white and Black, were killed. One southern officer boasted about killing thirteen Black men with his own pistol. Others were lynched; their mutilated bodies were found hanging from trees afterward. Of the one hundred men captured, very few escaped, and only one made it back to U.S. lines to continue his service in the military. Lieutenant Orillion died in the massacre along with his men, and Confederate soldiers treated his body with contempt.[109] Stories like this deterred potential volunteers from joining the Union.

Despite all of these impediments to recruitment, the Corps d'Afrique grew under General Andrews. The promise of equality and citizenship evidently outweighed sporadic pay, mistreatment, discrimination, and risk of torturous death. By August 1863, the Corps d'Afrique reported over ten thousand men ready for service, with additional regiments still in preparation for constitution.[110]

The Corps d'Afrique was headquartered at Port Hudson under Andrews, and Banks sent as many Black soldiers there as possible. He ordered Ullman to send any and all African American recruits to Port Hudson to join the newly organized regiments. There, they were assigned to the next regiment to be filled by Andrews.[111] Port Hudson was possibly a worse location than Ship Island for the men who were stationed there. Colonel Richard Irwin summarized what their life was like: "The heat, especially in the trenches, became almost insupportable, the stenches quite so, the brooks dried up, the creek lost itself in the pestilential swamp, the springs gave out, and the river fell, exposing to the tropical sun a wide margin of festering ooze."[112] Because of the racist belief that African Americans were naturally protected from the summer heat and disease, Black soldiers were expected to drill and labor in the "ooze" on a daily basis. The Corps d'Afrique was charged with undoing the defenses that the Union army had spent months building during the siege, and they were directed to clear all the trees and swamps surrounding the area in case Confederate troops invaded again, as they had in June.[113] Many white soldiers and officers expressed the belief that soldiers of color were better suited for this backbreaking labor.

Multiple companies were assigned to Port Hudson soon after the Department of the Gulf took over the citadel, and their primary mission was labor duty. Banks's adjutant learned that there were hundreds of men from the corps prepared for "day work" and various fatigue duties.[114] At Port Hudson,

Black soldiers were detailed for fatigue duty on twelve-hour shifts. A group would begin at 6:00 a.m. and wouldn't be relieved by members of another Corps d'Afrique unit until 6:00 in the evening.[115] Even while resting, they always had to be ready to fight as they worked to rebuild the fortifications around their position. The newly constituted 7th Corps d'Afrique Infantry Regiment was positioned along with the 1st Corps d'Afrique Engineer Regiment on canal duty.[116] The 2d Corps d'Afrique Regiment was positioned at Ship Island to guard the prisoners and sugar plantations in the area.[117] The long hours and difficult work were reminiscent of the labor that many of the men had done when they were enslaved.

On 15 September, Lieutenant Colonel Basset complained that his regiments were required to supply fifty men every other day for fatigue duty. Whether through spite or some other militaristic need, the following week his regiments were detailed for daily labor and fatigue duty, for which he was made to supply one officer, three noncommissioned officers, and forty-eight privates. By October, they were expected to supply additional men to build fortifications for the Department of the Gulf's large area of operations.[118] The work schedule for members of the Corps d'Afrique was so intense that some regiments did not even assign noncommissioned officers; the 9th Regiment, for example, reported that they had no need for them. Because the soldiers never drilled or left camp, they only needed privates.[119] Lieutenant Colonel David Branson, who commanded one of the regiments raised by Thomas and now attached to the Department of the Gulf, complained that, since their arrival, they had been given excess labor duties while the white troops in Morganza did nothing but watch.[120]

In December 1863, Ullman told Senator Henry Wilson, the chair of the Military Affairs Committee, that his regiments were used too often for fatigue duty. Ullman believed if they were given more chances to see battle, they could prove themselves again, but if they continued to labor and dig trenches, then they would not be effective in combat because they never had time to train.[121] However, this was all by design. General Lorenzo Thomas indicated that every Black regiment he raised freed one white regiment from fatigue and garrison duty, something Banks fully supported.[122] Demonstrating how reliant the Department of the Gulf was on Black labor, the entire engineer brigade in the fall of 1863 was made up of the three Corps d'Afrique engineer regiments.[123]

To make matters worse, those on fatigue duty were rarely supplied with fresh food or allowed to express any form of comradery on duty. The labor wore out their clothes as much as their bodies. A white major who temporarily supervised the Corps d'Afrique noted that nearly all of the men needed additional clothing, for which they would have had to pay out of pocket.[124] Captain Edward Carter's medical discharge attested that he could not serve as an officer because of a list of ailments, but his health quickly improved after he left the military. He thrived as a politician and became active in his community thanks to his renewed vigor.[125] Joseph T. Wilson was hospitalized and honorably discharged in the fall, after which he traveled back to Massachusetts and joined the famed 54th Massachusetts Infantry Regiment. Wilson served in the regiment until February the following year, when he was injured in the back and abdomen at the Battle of Olustee in Florida.[126] His decision to rejoin the army after leaving Louisiana indicated that, with better treatment, Black men wanted to serve in the federal army.

The most meaningful task the men undertook was ensuring that other African Americans secured their freedom. While many planters had already abandoned their plantations, they typically took some of the people they enslaved with them when they fled. On one such plantation, just eighty-two miles north of New Orleans, many formerly enslaved people were left to die because their enslavers thought them too weak to survive or be useful; however, they thrived and started farming the land without government or planter intervention. Eventually, members of the Department of the Gulf assisted them by supplying them with a wagon and a couple of mules.[127]

Men serving in the Corps d'Afrique took more direct action to ensure that everyone in their area of operations was granted freedom. On one expedition, members of the 1st Regiment patrolling St. Bernard Parish allegedly went onto plantations, put white men under armed guard, then took wagons to help enslaved men, women, and children leave the plantations under their protection. They offered the men the opportunity to join the regiments, and reportedly some did.[128] Members of the Corps d'Afrique took on the responsibility of removing thousands from generations of enslavement.

Enslaved men and women assisted the Department of the Gulf from outside of the military as well, because they knew *their* soldiers needed the help. Other regions in the South often reported having to force workers to contribute to public projects, but New Orleans remained an outlier because Butler had adopted a policy of paying workers for their efforts.[129] Banks went on to make laborious service, mainly on plantations, compulsory in the region. Nevertheless, the military and the economy depended on formerly enslaved

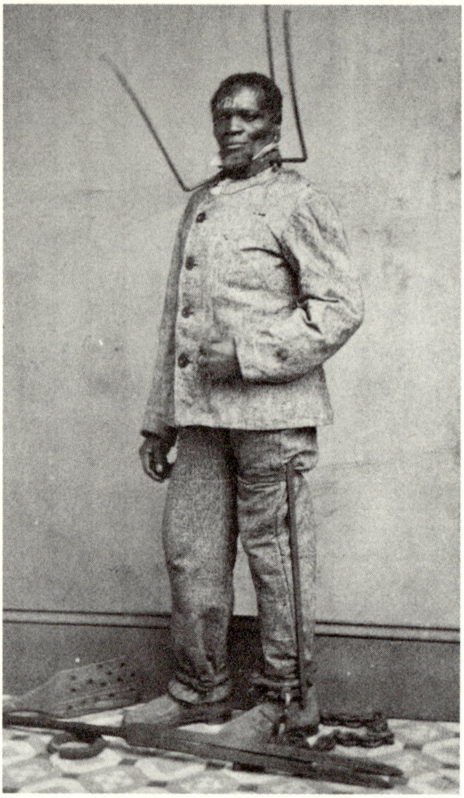

Wilson Chinn, a formerly enslaved man of Louisiana
(Library of Congress, Prints and Photographs Division)

people who were not in the military. Even the hospitals and nurses' camps relied heavily on Black men and women who worked as cooks, nurses' aides, laborers, plumbers, grounds men, commissary aides, bakers, horse caretakers, scavengers, and protectors. Without formerly enslaved African Americans, the army could not have functioned.[130]

The members of the Corps d'Afrique gave back to the community that supported them in numerous ways. One of the most visible ways was the creation of the Comité Central des Natifs, more commonly referred to as the Freedmen's Aid Association. Free African Americans in New Orleans founded the Comité in December 1862, but it took some time for it to grow in popularity and usefulness. By 1863, its members were able to purchase crops and set up employment for hundreds of formerly enslaved people in the city.[131] Soldiers offered protection, work, and money to support the Comité, and together the two groups demonstrated a strong sense of unity among the formerly enslaved and free Black inhabitants of New Orleans during the war.

In addition to all of the military changes occurring in the Department of the Gulf, a number of political shifts became necessary as Reconstruction began early in Louisiana in comparison to most of the South. The secretary of war informed the military governor of Louisiana, George Shepley, that New Orleanians wanted a new state constitution and a real governor. In a plan coordinated between Lincoln and Stanton, Shepley was directed to begin voter registration in the parts of Louisiana under federal control, hold elections, and use the military as needed to secure the elections for citizens who took oaths of loyalty to the U.S. government.[132] A few months later, on 8 December 1863, Lincoln issued the Amnesty Proclamation, which allowed the state to reenter the Union if 10 percent of eligible voters took the oath of allegiance and if new constitutions guaranteeing freedom for enslaved people were created.[133] Per Lincoln, this paved the way for the election of a new governor "with a loyal State Government and loyal representatives in both branches of Congress." Louisiana was the first state positioned to reenter the Union.[134]

Lincoln's plan prompted a resurgence of conservative dogma in Louisiana. The state constitution stipulated that free Blacks who had served in the military could possibly vote in the future, and it gave no opportunity for enfranchisement to those who were still legally enslaved. The African Americans who had fought in nearly every major battle felt the injustice of these decisions. Banks, on the other hand, thought the president too radical, and said that he would not help Lincoln get renominated.[135] Despite Lincoln's plans for Louisiana, the federal government did not have full control of the state just yet.

The South still controlled a large swath of Louisiana, and on 2 November 1863, Governor Thomas Moore was succeeded by Henry Allen as the state's southern governor. It was a strange election, since the federal government had a military governor controlling the state and the Department of the Gulf was headquartered in Louisiana's largest city. Allen was a Democrat and former Know Nothing. He was also a Civil War veteran, with injuries and disabilities that affected him during his tenure as governor. In his first speech after becoming governor, he called for state guard units that would be separate from the Confederacy, like the home guards had been. Their role would be to protect Louisiana's borders. However, Allen's control over the state guards was short-lived, as the Confederacy conscripted those men out of desperation.[136] Allen worked to make sure that the southern Trans-Mississippi Department—the primary antagonist for the Department of the Gulf—succeeded in Louisiana, even drafting policies to go around the blockaded parts of the Gulf, but the Union army was already too entrenched in the region to be defeated.

Artistic rendering of Lorenzo Thomas addressing the Corps d'Afrique
(Library of Congress, Prints and Photographs Division)

Nevertheless, the U.S. Army continued to encounter its own challenges. By the end of the summer of 1863, Banks seemed to trust his men even less than they trusted him. He issued General Orders No. 64, which stated, among other things, that "soldiers of the Corps d'Afrique will not be allowed to leave their camps, or to wander through the parishes, except upon written permission, or in the company of their officers." This marked a reversal of Butler's treatment of soldiers of color, as white soldiers were still permitted to leave their camps without a chaperone or a note. General Orders No. 64 also stated, "Arrests of persons, and seizures of property, will not be made by colored soldiers, nor will they be charged with the custody of persons or property, except when under the command, and accompanied by duly authorized officers."[137] Banks's order recalled the treatment of New Orleans's home guards in 1861, as soldiers of color were afforded less power and status than the police who patrolled the streets. The order indicated to planters that he would side with them should disputes arise between whites and Blacks.[138]

It was clear Banks had chosen white unity over the protection of African American rights. His orders forced men and women back onto plantations under the threat of arrest or imprisonment. For some, this was akin to slavery. Frederick Douglass declared that the command environment created by Banks "is our chief danger at the present moment; it practically enslaved the negro, and makes the Proclamation of 1863 a mockery and delusion."[139]

Banks's treatment of the members of the Corps d'Afrique set the command climate for Louisiana and all African Americans under the control of the Department of the Gulf. In his chef d'oeuvre, *The Black Phalanx,* Joseph Wilson attested that, while walking in New Orleans in his military uniform, white soldiers from the 24th Connecticut Infantry Regiment halted him and ordered him to take off his jacket. When he resisted, they began to tear off his clothes with force. The only thing that stopped the assault was another white officer recognizing him and ordering them to cease and give him back his clothes. Wilson wrote that he saw other men serving in New Orleans treated similarly.

Events like these led to clashes between Black and white troops across the South.[140] In one such instance in Carrollton, a Black soldier was attacked while defending an innocent woman on the street. He stabbed his white attacker and was later found guilty of murder despite the evidence showing he had been attacked.[141] An English visitor to the city recalled seeing similar scenes.[142] White officers who commanded Black regiments also experienced violence. In one case, a white lieutenant was killed by white citizens of Louisiana for the crime of being "a damned Nigger officer," according to a witness.[143] Officers of USCT regiments later attested that these dynamics continued to affect their lives in Louisiana even after the war.[144] A study conducted by James G. Hollandsworth Jr. over a century after the war concluded that many of the white officers of Louisiana regiments became targets of massacres simply because they commanded Black soldiers in combat.[145] George A. Halster wrote soon after the war that he was proud to have served alongside men like Major Francis Dumas and Captain André Cailloux. He claimed to hate the prejudice he had witnessed under Banks toward those he and others called "nigger officers," and he believed that many of the Black officers were more gentlemanly and humane than the white officers.[146]

The shifting tide spurred some of the last few officers of color to leave the military. Captain Emile Detiége resigned his commission; he was perhaps the only remaining officer who could say he had trained some of the men alongside General John Phelps at Camp Parapet.[147] Captain Charles Sentmanat, whose actions supporting the Department of the Gulf had helped to convince

Butler of the merits of New Orleans's Black men and was the only Black captain to remain in the unit, resigned in the fall.[148] Isadore Kinney, a Black soldier serving in the regiments, wrote to his mother in September that all of his Black officers planned to resign before the end of the year.[149] However, eight Black officers remained in the 1st Corps d'Afrique going into the next year. Still, the large number of resignations demonstrates the lack of respect they experienced from their commanding general and other government officials.

With the resignation of so many of their original officers, the loss of Colonel Stafford, and an indifferent superior in Banks, the members of the Corps d'Afrique were left to cruel and abusive officers. General Ullman described his assessment of the situation to Senator Wilson: "I well know that those prophets who declare that negroes never will make soldiers are striving to force their prophecies to work out their own fulfillment by appointing ignoramuses and boors to be officers" in the Corps d'Afrique.[150] The situation slowed recruiting; to compensate, in General Orders No. 77 Banks ordered the provost marshals to "forward to the nearest recruiting depot all able bodied males for service in the Corps d'Afrique" on 27 October 1863.[151]

In the midst of the multitude of recruitment and service challenges the regiments were facing, Lieutenant Colonel Augustus W. Benedict, a white officer assigned to the 4th Corps d'Afrique Infantry Regiment, catalyzed an all-out revolt that nearly derailed all the progress the Corps d'Afrique made in the Gulf. Benedict's fellow officers described him as "rough," "very strict," and "a little hasty at times," and said that he "formed a habit of going around at inspection and if a man's dress did not please him, he would knock him about and hit him."[152] He reportedly used brass knuckles or a sergeant's sword to punch his subordinates.[153] According to one of his subordinates, "It was a common thing" for Benedict to hit his men "without any cause whatever." In two separate instances, Benedict "spread a man on his back, [drove] stakes down, and spread his hands and feet, [took] off his shoes, and [took] molasses and spread it on his face, hands, and feet." He left one man outside in the sun all day spread eagle then put him out again the next morning in the same position covered in molasses while staked to the ground. When punishing two of his soldiers, he reportedly told one of his lieutenants that "he did not care" if they died from his punitive measures.[154]

It was not lost on the soldiers that Benedict's actions were reminiscent of enslavers in Lafourche Parish, from a time in their life the soldiers thought they moved past when they joined the Union army. For example, at one point, Benedict had soldiers hung by their thumbs. A white soldier of the XIX Corps was shocked to find two Black people near Homesville "tied up by the thumbs, with a piece of meat hung just near enough to them so that they could not reach it."[155] Soldiers in the 4th Corps d'Afrique attempted to address Benedict's behavior through formal military channels, reporting him to their company commanders, his superiors, and then to Banks. However, Colonel Charles W. Drew, Benedict's superior, was often accused of committing the same crimes, or at least allowing them, and Banks was ambivalent at best when it came to white officers abusing Black soldiers. After a deluge of complaints, the adjutant general, Lorenzo Thomas, informed the XIX Corps that dismissal awaited any officer who mistreated their soldiers, but Thomas's promise of punishment did not yield meaningful change. By December, the 4th Corps d'Afrique was stationed at both Forts St. Philip and Jackson. On the 8th, Benedict and his men were ordered to report to Fort Jackson to consolidate the regiment in one location. Many of the soldiers asked to remain at Fort St. Philip so they could escape Benedict, but their officers cared little about their wants and ordered them to join the rest at Fort Jackson.

Upon arrival in their new location, Benedict wanted to reestablish the punitive rule he had created at St. Philip.[156] Two of the regiment's drummer boys, Harry Williams and Munroe Miller, left the guard lines at Fort Jackson without permission, and Benedict happened to catch them when they attempted to return. He asked if they had received permission to leave, and they lied to Benedict that they had. As punishment for this deception, Benedict whipped them with a teamster's whip in front of the regiment and the fort's commander, Colonel Drew.[157] According to the official report after the incident, the soldiers were already "aggravated by his previous conduct toward the men of the regiment, and the severe punishments to which he had been in the habit of resorting." Following Benedict's actions, "About an hour after the whipping of the music boys referred to, by about half of the regiment rushing upon the parade with their arms, shouting, and discharging their pieces into the air. The shouting and threatening language used was directed against Lieutenant-Colonel Benedict." Demonstrating their anger, one soldier reportedly threatened to "kill all the damned Yankees!" Some of the men decided to release the Confederate prisoners the regiment was holding, and others used the schism as an opportunity to leave the fort unhindered.

Most of the soldiers focused their anger directly toward Benedict. Reportedly, men shouted, "We will not stop firing until we have him. . . . Give us Colonel Benedict; we did not come here to be whipped by him. Kill Colonel Benedict; shoot him." Drew, seeing the situation develop, sent Benedict to his quarters for his own safety, and when Benedict felt he was no longer secure, he begged one of his fellow officers to hide him on a ship that was sitting in the river. The report noted that the men soon realized he "was on board the *Suffolk,* lying at the levee." They rushed over and began firing their weapons toward the ship and the air to demonstrate their frustration. No one was injured or killed, and eventually the rest of the officers calmed the men through "assurances that justice should be done them." By 7:30 that evening, the last shots had been fired into the air and the men of the 4th Corps d'Afrique willingly "retired to their quarters."[158] While no one was hurt, reports out of Fort Jackson led many to believe an open insurrection had begun. The chief culprit was the commander of the *Suffolk,* who sent out messages that mutineers had captured Fort Jackson and fired on ships in the river, that white officers were dead, and that the battle was lost.[159]

Benedict initially escaped to New Orleans after his men began firing on the *Suffolk.* Eventually, General John P. Hawkins heard what had occurred and called for an investigation and charges against the mutineers.[160] By that point, the soldiers had already stacked arms, apologized, and made it clear to Drew and the other officers that their anger had been directed toward Benedict because of his cruel abuses over the last few months.[161] Both Colonel Drew and Major William E. Nye attested that, after Benedict had left Fort Jackson, order had been restored.[162]

However, within days, the story that the 4th Corps d'Afrique had attempted to kill a lieutenant colonel in the army circulated across the world. Most of the accounts were simply retellings of a report by a *New York Times* correspondent who had been sent to investigate. He commented extensively on the "moral courage" of the white officers and wrote that "the education of these men, on plantations" proved the courage of the officers who acted against them. The only white man he blamed was General Lorenzo Thomas, "who, by a well-meaning, but indiscreet speech, gave the negroes very exalted ideas of their position, and, no doubt, indirectly helped to provoke this trouble."[163] The account's rapid circulation was astounding.

Because of the publicity and his persistent efforts to undermine Black soldiers, Banks ordered a commission to discover the cause of the mutiny and punish those responsible. The commission was run by Major General Francis J. Herron, the youngest major general in the army. Herron chose not to call a single Black soldier as a witness when he investigated the incident.[164] The commission concluded that, upon hearing the disturbance on the parade grounds, Colonel Drew had done the right thing when he had approached the

Major General Francis Herron
(Library of Congress, Prints and Photographs Division)

angry and armed soldiers and attempted to calm them. Drew admitted "that Lieutenant-Colonel Benedict had done wrong," but he also said "that they were doing a greater wrong, and that, if they would go to their quarters, justice should be done them." Drew did not order his officers or other soldiers to quell the insurrection; he relied instead on his promise to give them justice and their own morals as soldiers. The commission found that Drew and his officers had acted appropriately and "that the means resorted to were, perhaps, the best that could have been adopted under the circumstances." According to the members of the commission, "All the witnesses express a belief that an attempt to quiet the disturbance by force would have resulted fatally to the officers."

The true goal of the commission was to punish Black soldiers, and to that end, its members determined that about half the men had mutinied and the other half were equally guilty for not having stopped them. The commission's report read that "the commission is of opinion that the conduct of the men was more owing to an ignorance of their rights and the proper means of redress than to any preconcerted plan of revolt." It failed to acknowledge the steps the men had taken to hold Benedict accountable for months.[165]

While the commission labeled the regiment mutinous, the men did not engage in a mutiny at Fort Jackson. The actions of the soldiers who followed after Benedict, only fired shots toward Benedict, quelled their anger once it was obvious Benedict left for New Orleans, and then listened to their commanding officer (whom they never shot at) all demonstrate that the 4th Regiment did not engage in a mutiny against the Union or the leadership of Fort Jackson. They were frustrated with the actions of Benedict and a command structure that refused to remove an abusive officer. Despite this, the commission's report gave General Banks the fuel he needed to further punish Black soldiers.

Banks chose Brigadier General William Dwight to serve as commandant of Fort Jackson and to punish all those deemed culpable.[166] On 30 December 1863, the Department of the Gulf published General Orders No. 90, which enumerated the punishment for the leaders and others who were easily identifiable. Banks hoped the publicity would reorient the debate away from his white officers back to the mutineers. Unsurprisingly, nearly all of the men brought for court-martial were found guilty. Although not a single person was injured and the mutiny had only lasted a few hours, the soldiers of the 4th Corps d'Afrique were punished severely. Private Frank Williams, of Company I, was sentenced "to be shot to death with musketry, at such time and place as the commanding general may direct"; Musician Edward S. Smith, of Company B, was sentenced "to be imprisoned at hard labor for one year on such permanent fortification as the commanding general may direct"; Corporal Lewis Candy, of Company K, was "to be imprisoned for the term of two years, at hard labor, on such permanent Government fortification as the commanding general may direct, and to forfeit all pay and allowances, except for prison food and clothing"; Private Charles Taylor, of Company K, was sentenced "to be imprisoned at hard labor for the term of ten years, on such permanent Government fortification as the commanding general may direct"; Private Abraham Victoria, of Company D, was ordered "to be shot to death with musketry"; Private Abram Singleton, of Company F, was sentenced "to be imprisoned at hard labor, for the term of ten years, on such Government fortification as the commanding general may direct and to forfeit all pay and allowances, except for prison food and clothing"; Private Willis Curtis, of Company D, was "to be imprisoned at hard labor, for the term of three years, on such permanent fortification as the commanding general may direct, and to forfeit all pay and allowances, except for prison food and clothing"; Private Julius Boudro, of Company D, was "to be imprisoned at hard labor, for the term of twenty years, on such permanent fortification as the commanding general may direct, and to forfeit all pay and allowance except for prison food and clothing"; and Private James H. Moore, of Company F, received the most lenient sentence, "hard labor for one month under guard." Banks set aside Private Moore's one-month sentence, citing conflicting evidence in his case, and he suspended the death penalty for Williams and Victoria, opting instead to imprison them at Fort Jefferson in Florida.[167] All of the sentences were supposed to be carried out at Fort Jefferson by the direction of the provost marshal general. A few mutineers were acquitted of their charges: Privates Volser Verrett and Jacob Kennedy, both of Company D; Private James Hagan, of Company B; and Corporal Henry Green, of Company G, were the only men brought for court-martial and not punished per General Orders No. 90.[168]

The commission also determined that a few white officers should be punished. Major Nye had disappeared when the men started to get rowdy, and the charge of cowardice was suggested against the major by General Dwight. Colonel Drew's case was the most controversial. The commission found that his abuses of the men in the regiment had been just as bad—if not worse—than Benedict's. While the commission suggested charges, Dwight did not endorse them, hoping Drew would learn from witnessing the consequences of mistreating the men of the Corps d'Afrique. Dwight met with Drew to counsel him on the matter, writing that he attempted to give Drew a chance to "correct his manner of discipline and his acknowledged faults." Afterward, Dwight "called the officers together and advised them to forget that they had preferred charges against their Colonel, and to seek, in unity of action, and strict performance of duty, to efface the remembrance of the late mutiny."[169]

The more pressing and public issue was Benedict. Realizing that the commission had discovered his abuses and fearing that General Thomas would end his career, he attempted to resign. Banks, however, decided that Dwight should punish him, and so Benedict, too, was brought for court-martial.[170] For the crime of "inflicting cruel and unusual punishment, to the prejudice of good and military discipline," Lieutenant Colonel Benedict was found guilty, but his sentence was a slap in the face to the men he had mistreated: he was "dismissed" from service in the U.S. Army.[171] It was a punishment typically given to officers for lesser offenses than those committed by Benedict on so many soldiers.

While many of the Black soldiers involved were severely punished, it seems Banks and the rest of the Union soon realized that the incident was not a sign that Black men were disloyal or mutinous. Banks wrote to Halleck after the incident that the 4th was "among the best disciplined and the best instructed regiments of this class of troops." According to Banks, they had done "nothing to impair the confidence of the Government in the efficiency and reliability of black troops" and that "the want of discretion, of a spirit of justice and of capacity to deal with men of this class manifested by some of the officers, whose conduct was the immediate cause of the outbreak, was such as could hardly be expected to produce any other result."[172] A small mutiny from a white cavalry unit in New England a couple months prior had not raised questions about whether those soldiers were disloyal.[173] General Jason Wadsworth wrote to Lorenzo Thomas that the officers commissioned by Banks were the real problem. According to Wadsworth, many of them had "second or third rate character," and little to no training in commanding soldiers of color.[174] Dwight noted, "The late affair is a warning against trusting foolish and passionate officers in high command over black troops."[175] President Lincoln soon acknowledged the loyalty and capability of Black New Orleanians, especially those serving in the Corps d'Afrique. In turn, they made it clear to the president that they wanted to serve their nation as equals.

Indeed, despite a prevailing culture of racism, Blacks in New Orleans continued to demonstrate support for the federal government. The previous summer, while the Native Guards were sieging Port Hudson, operators of *L'Union* organized a series of meetings meant to enfranchise Black men in New Orleans.[176] Ten veterans of the Battle of New Orleans were elected vice presidents, and large numbers of white residents attended and supported the movement. Organizers indicated that, after the failed promises of 1815, Black New Orleanians would not wait for the military to assist them. Captain Pinchback supported this message, declaring that if the government did not give them the right to vote, then they should not be subject to the draft. Eventually, the convention's attendees drafted a petition to Shepley that was passed along to Banks. It enumerated their service in 1815, their sacrifice at Port Hudson, the amount of money the free class paid in taxes, and the fact that many of them were better educated than whites who were eligible to vote.[177]

Two men, Paul Trévigne and Jean-Baptiste Roudanez, were chosen to go to Washington and present the convention's resolution directly to Lincoln and a few members of Congress.[178] In response, Lincoln sent James A. McKaye, of the American Freedmen's Inquiry Commission, to meet with the emissaries, who were requesting public schools, the abolition of black codes that were reminiscent of the negative aspects of *le Code Noir*, equitable treatment, and, above all, recognition as human beings.[179] When Trévigne and Roudanez arrived with over a thousand signatures, Lincoln listened to their demands but publicly turned them down. In private, he acknowledged that the Black population of Louisiana was both loyal and worthy, and he maneuvered in secret to enfranchise the soldiers of color in the Corps d'Afrique.

In the fall of 1863, Philadelphia native Thomas Jefferson Durant was serving as the leader of the Unionist movement in New Orleans. In Durant's view, the chief impediment to Black voters—and voter registration as a whole—was Banks. Durant supported Black suffrage, while Banks, who hoped to make it into the White House one day, feared that supporting Black voters would make him a political pariah after the war. Thus, he worked to keep African Americans from voting.[180] When Durant informed Lincoln that Banks was impeding his movement, the president was angry. Banks feigned ignorance and blamed Shepley. But, while Banks had succeeded in keeping Black men from voting in the election, the calls from Durant and the loyal men who fought at Port Hudson spurred Lincoln to action.

Despite not voting, the soldiers of color stationed in New Orleans helped with efforts to organize the first elections in their reconstructed state. Louisiana's Republican Party was filled with men who had once officered the Native Guards.[181] On 4 March 1864, Michael Hahn, a moderate Unionist Republican from the state, was sworn into office as the first governor elected from a formerly Confederate state.[182] He was one of the few white southerners who had openly supported the Union early in the war.[183] In 1863, he had helped to coordinate the movement to create a new state constitution and even assisted the government in reconstituting banks in New Orleans that had become insolvent because of the blockade.[184] Letter writers to the *New York Times* thought the election of Hahn "indicates an extraordinary readiness in those who have the most at stake to accept the new order of things."[185] Many hoped that Hahn would write a new state constitution following the president's proclamation that would protect formerly enslaved people in the state.

On 13 March, Lincoln sent a private letter to the newly inaugurated governor suggesting that he push for the enfranchisement of Black men at the state convention. Such a move would have given hundreds of formerly enslaved men who were serving or had served in one of the Native Guard regiments the right to vote. Lincoln expressed to Hahn, "They would probably help in some trying time in the future to keep the jewel of Liberty in the family of freedom," and ended his letter, "This is only a suggestion, not to the public, but to you alone."[186] Banks was nominally open to the suggestion as well, believing that Black men who had served in the military, had taxable property, and had a high level of documented intelligence or education should be allowed to vote.[187] These three conditions were all ostracizing measures meant to create a hierarchy of who was the right type of Black person worthy of voting and who was not. Even with these racist measures, Hahn and the newly elected members of the state convention chose not to give Black men in the military the right to vote in 1864. Instead, Hahn spent much of his time writing petitions to Lincoln on behalf of former rebel soldiers to garner support for Unionism and his own reelection.[188]

Meanwhile, the Department of the Gulf continued to organize Corps d'Afrique regiments and Thomas authorized the 1st, 2d, and 3d Light Artillery Regiments (African Descent) from the Department of the Gulf's vast area of operations. The 1st was activated 6 November, and the 2d on 21 December, both in Mississippi. The 3d was activated on 1 December in Arkansas.[189] However, even as the regiments grew, Denison feared that if Banks remained in command, Louisiana would return to the Confederacy. Denison indicated to Chase that everyone wished for the return of General Butler: "Even if all the accusations against him were true, he would accomplish great things of benefit to the country. He used to do more in three days than Gen. Banks has done since his arrival."[190]

With so many political and social changes occurring, Banks had to reorganize his large number of forces. The Corps d'Afrique had grown so large that he was able to assign the 1st, 2d, and 3d Engineers, along with the 16th Corps d'Afrique Infantry, to the XIII Army Corps. The 2d Corps d'Afrique Infantry Regiment was still stationed at Ship Island, and the 20th and 5th were positioned in the defenses of New Orleans with their artillery batteries. The 4th remained at Fort Jackson with a company from the 1st Corps d'Afrique Heavy Artillery, and the 14th Infantry Regiment was in Pensacola, Florida. However, the majority of the regiments still reported to Ullman and Andrews. The 1st Brigade, 1st Division, had the 1st, 3d, 11th, and 12th Infantry Regiments, the 2d Brigade had the 7th, 8th, 9th, and 10th Infantry Regiments, and the rest were split among the 2d Division.[191]

The Corps d'Afrique still supported the XIX Corps. During the winter, its regiments defeated numerous guerrilla raids in their area of operations and helped Banks push the Confederates out of Alexandria, Louisiana.[192] Because of these efforts, the XIX Corps was finally positioned to make maneuvers against Texas.[193] The XIX Corps' position became a staging ground for future operations, and Banks needed as many Black regiments as he could muster to both hold the Gulf and support his movements into Texas.[194] Banks took a few regiments of the Corps d'Afrique with him into the Rio Grande as he prepared to hold the line between Texas and Mexico by the end of the year.[195] When they captured Brazos Island, Banks acknowledged that the 1st and 16th Corps d'Afrique had secured their first foothold in Texas.[196] He further informed Seward that they would not invade Mexico yet.[197] On 3 January 1864, Major General Francis Herron, who had led the commission investigation at Fort Jackson, was selected as the commander of the ground forces on the Rio Grande.[198] The 16th, along with a few engineer companies of the Corps d'Afrique, remained, as Banks believed they could hold the area with little assistance.[199] Herron used them as builders for Brazos and garrison troops, and did not plan for them to see additional combat.[200] The secretary of state congratulated Banks and his men for doing their part to control civil strife resulting from the foreign war, but he cautioned nonintervention between Mexico and France, as he still feared foreign intervention in the Civil War.[201] Banks assured Herron that the Department of the Gulf would not ignite a war with France or Mexico.[202] Thus, the real fight for the Corps d'Afrique during the winter remained in Louisiana.

Old problems continued to arise in the regiments. Many of the white officers were court-martialed for drunkenness under the charge of "conduct unbecoming an Officer and a Gentleman," and Banks continually replaced inept officers with other ineffectual leaders.[203] Banks found out that some white officers gambled in uniform, hired sex workers, and drank before and during duty.[204] These activities became so widely known that one soldier felt compelled to promise his parents he was not involved in them.[205] Worse, some of Banks's officers were accused of—and some even caught—sexually assaulting the wives of soldiers serving in the Corps d'Afrique. One of the first reports of white soldiers assaulting a Black woman occurred in June 1862. Within weeks of the Department of the Gulf liberating New Orleans, Corporal William Chinock was court-martialed for walking into the home of Mary Ellen DeRiley, ordering her to lie down, and raping her for nearly an hour.[206] Despite DeRiley's emotional testimony before the military court, the officers present still adhered to the old paradigm that Black women always wanted sex and thus could not be raped. Chinock was found not guilty of rape, and was only found guilty of the charge of breaking good order and discipline. Soon after this, Lieutenant Thomas B. Curtis was accused of getting drunk and then beating and raping a woman near Camp Parapet. Though he was found guilty, his only punishment was his dismissal from service.[207]

By the time the Department of the Gulf secured Port Hudson and the Mississippi, officers selected by Banks joined the ranks of Corporal Chinock as rapists. William H. Daly, a captain in the 3d Corps d'Afrique Regiment, stationed at Port Hudson, attempted to assault the wife of one of his soldiers, and it resulted in members of the regiment threatening to revolt if he was not removed.[208] Daly was not alone; many whites in the Department of the Gulf reportedly adopted the practice of walking into the homes of Black women near their camps and openly assaulting with no repercussions for their actions. The result was a clear message that the government would not protect Black women. Many African American men took on that responsibility. White officers learned that their men would revolt to protest sexual assault, so some of them tried to avoid being caught.

The night of 25 January 1864, Captains Charles A. Goff and William H. Knapp and Lieutenants Henry E. Blackeslee and William H. Odell went to the homes of Black laundresses near Fort Jackson, supposedly to inspect their quarters. They first arrived at the home of Keziah Davis, a woman in her fifties who worked for Company F. The men ordered her to have sex with at least one of them, but Davis handled the situation expertly by fending them off with the contents of her chamber pot.[209] The pack of men moved on to additional homes to "inspect." They arrived at the home of Rose Plummer, a much younger woman who worked for Company A. In a clear effort to protect herself from the group and other white men in the camp, Plummer agreed to have sex with Captain Knapp on the promise that the others would leave. The remaining three men went on to the homes of Elizabeth Dallas, Laura Davis, and Emma Smith. Dallas and Smith were both told that if they did not comply, they would both be forced out of the camp, so their choices were to sleep with the men or risk walking alone in the Deep South.

Laura Davis was not even given that choice, as she was sound asleep when the officers arrived, and she did not know what was going on until one of the men was already on top of her. They moved on and attempted to enter Elizabeth Taylor's home. She locked her door and refused to open it for their inspection, but Captain Goff broke it down. Inside, Odell attempted to hold her down so Goff could rape her, but Taylor fought them off. As they were preparing to leave, Goff called her a "bitch." She retorted that he must have come from a similar creature to act as he did, and in retaliation Goff struck her in the face with his saber. The noise attracted the attention of Private Edward Idell, a Black soldier, who told his superior officers to their faces that if he had family in those camps he would have sent them away to escape the abuse of officers like them. Goff ordered Idell arrested in retaliation.

By the next morning, General Dwight was informed of the arrest, and as he listened to the officers in question, he realized that the 4th Regiment's dysfunction extended far beyond Benedict. After speaking with the women who had been attacked, Dwight ordered all four officers arrested, and members of the public learned that Union officers had forced their way into the quarters of laundresses attached to their command with the intention to gang rape them.[210] Dwight wanted to simply remove the officers, but Banks ordered a full court-martial, which brought further publicity. As Dwight moved to investigate the matter, one of his own captains informed him "that it would never do to prosecute such an inquiry as this, for that every officer in the Regiment might by implicated!"[211] These words proved true, as Dwight only found one captain in another unit who was not implicated in at least one assault against a Black woman.

During his full investigation into the rapes that occurred on 25 January, General Dwight discovered that sexual assault was common not only in this regiment but across all of the regiments in the Corps d'Afrique, and he found evidence that prior assaults had contributed to the mutiny against Benedict in December. Only three additional officers were charged: Captains James Miller, George Wentworth, and Charles Merritt, all of whom had helped with the commission that had charged the soldiers with mutiny a month prior. Keziah Davis personally called out Miller during her testimony, and Dwight soon pieced together that the reason so many soldiers had threatened multiple officers—not only Benedict—was that those same officers had raped Black women or at least forced them into sexually coercive relationships, as Knapp had done to Rose Plummer. Davis attested that Private Frank Williams had attempted to bayonet Miller during the mutiny because the captain was a regular abuser of the women in the camp, and Williams was standing up for them. Dwight realized that the officers Banks had placed in the Corps d'Afrique were akin to slave drivers, using their position to abuse Black women and men.[212] Dwight's commission concluded that "scenes similar that of the night of January 25, in which other officers of the Regiment have been equally implicated, have been of not infrequent occurrence."[213] Despite his concerns, there was little he could do to remove personnel without Banks's approval, so Dwight approved the report before sending it off to Banks for his decision.

While he awaited Banks's reply, Colonel Drew—the man who had witnessed the soldiers' anger firsthand—demonstrated that he had not learned any lessons from the mutiny. In January, he oversaw a special court-martial and sentenced every Black man who came before him to harsh sentences; one private received a sentence of death.[214] On 4 February 1864, Dwight felt compelled to arrest Drew for numerous crimes against those in his charge, recognizing that if he did not, "This Regiment will rise in revolt . . . and the next revolt will not be bloodless." In a letter to Banks's chief of staff, Dwight laid out the crimes that had forced his hand. On 24 January, Drew had kicked Private Idell because "he did not move quickly enough to suit him." That same evening, he had taken another soldier outside the fort, hit him in the face, and then "he kicked the Sergt. violently once or twice." Later, on the 30th, he had hit a soldier in the head with a pole, causing a concussion.[215] It was another public spectacle of abuse that had angered the soldiers of the 4th Corps d'Afrique, but it was not the last.

General Dwight's official report to Banks detailed that the most recent incident occurred when a private gave Drew an improper salute. Private Dick Sheldon of Company D was standing guard and he "saluted him, facing inward instead of outward." Drew asked why he had given him the wrong salute and ordered him to report to his quarters. When the soldier replied that he had not been taught the proper way, Drew "picked up a book from his table, and threw it at the private," telling him to give a better answer "or he would break the private's head." After another question and threat to "break his head," Drew sent him to the officer of the guard for punishment. Private Sheldon attempted to explain that he had done nothing wrong, and asked to see General Dwight to explain the situation. In response, "The 'Officer of the Guard' then drew his sword and pistol on Private Sheldon," telling him he could not see the general. Drew heard the commotion and came over. Upon hearing why the officer of the guard had his gun out, Drew "also drew his pistol and said with great anger that if Private Sheldon said anything more he would blow his [Sheldon's] brains out." He informed the private that "he would give his officers orders to shoot down the soldiers if they said they intended to go to the General."[216] Despite Drew's attempts to keep Dwight from learning of these events, eventually Sheldon was able to inform Dwight of the situation.

Dwight mused in his report, "Can such exercise and abuse of power obtain respect? Is this military discipline?" He answered, "It is degrading to the officer who uses it and to those who suffer from it." Dwight realized that the commission had been correct to bring Drew up on charges. He reported, "Seven of its officers including the Colonel, are in arrest and ought never again to exercise command." He continued, "Its whole organization and character and discipline is rotten. It was organized by two young men of little experience, with violent passions and unchastened temper. They were proslavery in their feelings. They selected many of its worst officers. They made its discipline consist in physical terror." Dwight also recognized the effects of their beliefs on their treatment of their men: "With their feelings they saw in the organizing a Regiment of blacks nothing of the beneficence which was to make it a means of education for freedom. To them it was so many negroes placed in their power for them to make soldiers of and they selected as means, those which in the hands of the slaveholder have been pronounced by civilization brutal and degrading." According to Dwight, they were "incapable of any elevated feelings" and "in pursuing this tyranny which they mistook for discipline they acted rather the part of bad and brutal overseers than of the slave-holder himself." Another mutiny, Dwight argued, would be just, as it would represent "resistance to oppression and violence from which they find no means of legitimate appeal and protection."[217]

Despite this scathing report, little changed in the regiment. The captains and lieutenants who had attempted to rape the laundresses were not dismissed from service because the War Department refused their dismissals. A full court-martial convened in September and all the officers involved in the 25 January rapes were found not guilty, which further emboldened the white officers.[218] Instead of correcting the problem as Dwight had called for, Banks ordered the women working in the camps to leave unless they were married to a soldier stationed there or were actively serving a specific unit in some way.[219] Banks refused to remove Colonel Drew from service despite multiple documented abuses against his own men. He also continued to purge the last few remaining Black officers and replace them with inept, often abusive officers who threatened women in the camps. The soldiers serving in the regiment were dissatisfied with their commanders and alarmed by these injustices. The men who rioted in protest to protect themselves and women in the camps made their frustrations known to their officers and to the nation. Reports calling their actions a mutiny spurred coverage of Black traitors, but General Dwight's investigations revealed that they were patriots and protectors.

While the 4th Corps d'Afrique was the unit most widely known to have these problems, as General Dwight realized, the regiment was not an outlier. The other regiments had similar problems of abuse and rape to the degree that Dwight struggled to find a single white officer who was not implicated in a similar charge. Hundreds, possibly thousands, of Black women were assaulted in Union encampments that were supposed to keep them safe, and the only people who consistently fought for them were the Black men in their regiments. For example, on 27 December 1863, soldiers in the 2d Corps d'Afrique nearly mutinied. Private Henry Cornish allegedly refused to be arrested, and his friends in the regiment on Ship Island grabbed bricks and other items to throw at their officers to fight them off before grabbing their muskets. Order was quickly restored when another company formed ranks with their weapons, but the closeness of these two incidents in time was not lost on leaders of the XIX Corps.[220]

How many U.S. officers charged their soldiers with disrespect or insubordination when in reality those troops were standing up to their commanding officers on behalf of Black women, as Private Idell had? It is a gap in the record that can never be filled. The abuses that occurred in the 4th Corps d'Afrique compelled some officers to take more inconspicuous measures to punish African American soldiers. Jack Morris had been among the first to enlist in the 1st Native Guards Infantry Regiment in September 1862. For simply walking away from his corporal while standing guard, he was sentenced to two years of hard labor in June 1864 despite having no prior convictions or punishments on his record.[221] Colonel William H. Dickey, who commanded a brigade that two of the regiments were attached to in March 1864, allegedly ordered the 1st Corps d'Afrique to return its flag to Port Hudson because it was "a damn petticoat and a disgrace to the brigade." Dickey reportedly emphasized his feelings by calling the men who questioned his order "Smart Nigers."[222] Overall, a number of Black soldiers were sentenced to inordinate amounts of time for the simplest of crimes. Some were given death sentences for crimes for which their white counterparts only had to forfeit pay.[223]

Desertion rates in the Corps d'Afrique became much higher than those in New Orleans's home guards and the Union's Native Guards combined. For example, a fourth of Captain Emile Detiége's company deserted after he resigned his commission, and similar occurrences of men abandoning their regiments after losing their officers were rampant.[224] Dozens of cases of desertion were elevated to the level of court-martial because military officials hoped that, by making examples of some of the men, the practice would stop. Despite the issuance of punishments that included, in one instance, a private being sentenced to twenty-one years of hard labor while attached to an iron ball, men continued to desert the Corps d'Afrique.[225] There were even cases of white men being shot for desertion.[226] These men were needed because the regiments were positioned throughout Louisiana, Florida, and Texas, garrisoning every major location in the Department of the Gulf.[227]

Without a doubt, the command climate created by General Banks drove hundreds of men to risk imprisonment or death rather than serve under his leadership. Families had become destitute because of the pay situation, white civilians turned against the soldiers once it became clear that the government would not protect them, their own officers were raping women in the camps, their old Black officers had left the military and could only help from afar, and white officers who were known to abuse them were allowed to remain in command. It is unsurprising that so many soldiers chose to escape military service under General Banks.

By the fall of 1864, Banks had to invoke Congress's conscription act to fill empty roles. He even called for men on government and private plantations to serve in the Corps d'Afrique, but the order was ill-timed, as it was harvest season and Black laborers were in demand. Free men of New Orleans wrote a petition calling for the release of people who had been arrested for conscription.[228] Planters wrote to Banks to reconsider because they needed the personnel, and even his own officers questioned the decision because it could further hurt the unstable economy.[229]

Disenchantment with the military only continued to grow among soldiers in the Corps d'Afrique. On 19 February 1864, Special Order No. 25 authorized all of the units that had helped the U.S. Army secure Port Hudson to list the stronghold on their regimental flag.[230] This order was meant to serve as a source of pride, a way to build *esprit de corps* among the soldiers who had fought and died there. Not a single Black regiment was listed in the order, despite the fact that all of the men in the 1st and 3d Regiment had volunteered for a near-suicide mission in June. The soldiers complained to their officers, and eventually Colonel Quincy and General Andrews petitioned the War Department on behalf of the regiments. The secretary of war had to step in to ensure that the regiments in the Corps d'Afrique were authorized to have the words "Port Hudson" inscribed on their colors.[231]

Despite their dissatisfaction with the U.S. Army, Black men and women continued to prove themselves loyal to the Union cause. As one colonel who worked with the regiments noted, African Americans "willingly accept the condition of labor for their own maintenance, and the musket for their freedom."[232] The *Black Warrior*—a paper started at Camp Parapet—honored the regiments' sacrifices at Port Hudson, the Black men massacred at Battery Wagner and Fort Pillow, and the untold number of enslaved people who were still bound by the Confederacy. The editor ended his piece, "Never Surrender. Be this your motto *Death or Victory.*"[233]

Men continued to join the military, women continued to work in and around army encampments at great personal risk, children continued to attend Catholic churches and schools, and the men in the Corps d'Afrique continued to serve under General Nathaniel Banks. However, they wanted something in return for their service. As they prepared to help the Department of the Gulf in one final large campaign along the Red River, African Americans in Louisiana agitated for more than just freedom; they wanted equality and equity before the law and within the state. During the final year of the Civil War, their voices forced federal officials to recognize what they had to do to remunerate the regiments for their service to the Union army.

Chapter 9

# *WE WILL NEVER STOP*

## THE USCT AND THE END OF THE EXPERIMENT

In September 1863, an anonymous writer left a document signed "A Colored Man" on the streets of New Orleans. It called attention to the challenges Blacks faced in the American military and what the war meant to them. The author wrote that the American Civil War meant little if all African Americans in the South were not guaranteed freedom and equal rights. He invoked Lincoln's 1858 house divided speech and the Bible, writing that the Black population of New Orleans could not have two masters: "a rebel master and a union master that both want our services one wants us to make Cotton and Sugar And the Sell it and keep the money the union masters wants us to fight the battles under white officers and the injoy both money and the union." His reference to "union masters" evokes the Black soldiers tasked with garrisoning forts and conducting backbreaking fatigue duty while white men enjoyed the fruits of citizenship without having to prove their worth. He described the reasons why men chose to fight: southern men fought to retain their slaves, northern men fought for the Union and control of the Mississippi River, and Black men fought for liberty. Enmeshed in these three fights that were divided among two races and three classes, African Americans—members of the "the Blackest and bravest race"—must do what it took to achieve victory, according to the writer.[1] The soldiers serving in the Corps d'Afrique proved willing to answer this call—no matter the personal cost—until the very end of the war.

The final chapter of this book examines what that personal cost entailed during the waning months of the Civil War. Thousands were already dead, many more were wounded, and still, the regiments continued to grow in number as they fought in new locations. Political and social change were important factors to consider as both sides came to realize the war would soon end, and many of the most prominent men in the regiments looked to the future of all

Black people once the war was done. Thus, this chapter demonstrates that even with the end of the Black military regiment experiment in the Gulf, the men who joined had no intention of stopping their fight for Black equality and Black rights in the Deep South.

By the spring of 1864, many Black soldiers in the Corps d'Afrique had become disillusioned with military service. In contrast to the low desertion rates among the Louisiana Native Guards in 1862 under Colonel Spencer Stafford and General Benjamin Butler, the Corps d'Afrique regiments were wholly understaffed. In his scathing report on the 4th Regiment, General William Dwight asked that it be broken up, the officers dismissed, and the "men distributed among the Regiments of the Corps d'Afrique."[2] He hoped this would disrupt the traditions set by the officers Banks had put in place and that it would send a lesson to the other regiments as well. Recognizing that not just the 4th but the whole formation was a failure, General Lorenzo Thomas stepped in to reorganize the Corps d'Afrique into the United States Colored Troops (USCT) with General Orders No. 7 in March 1864.[3] The reorganization changed the regiments; a full infantry regiment was made up of ten companies of a hundred men each, for a total of one thousand men, and a cavalry regiment was composed of twelve companies with a similar number of men.[4] His order heralded a new phase for the soldiers of color in Louisiana.

On 4 April 1864, the four former Native Guards regiments were redesignated the 73d, 74th, 75th, and 76th United States Colored Infantry (USCI) Regiments. The remaining regiments in the Corps d'Afrique followed this progression, occupying the 77th to 99th USCI. The cavalry regiment was designated the 4th United States Colored Cavalry (USCC), and the artillery batteries were designated the 7th and 8th United States Colored Heavy Artillery (USCHA).[5] In July, many of the regiments that Ullman had raised were consolidated with those raised by Banks and Thomas into various USCI regiments, per the orders of the Military Division of West Mississippi. The 73d and 75th USCI were organized at Morganza; the 74th at Fort Pike, Fort Macomb, and Ship Island; the 76th and 77th at Port Hudson; and the 79th, 80th, and 82d in and around New Orleans. The department formed two regiments far away from headquarters: the 78th at Pensacola, Florida, and the 81st at Brazos Santiago, Texas.[6] The 79th, 83d, 88th, 89th, and 90th Regiments were broken up completely by the end of July, and everyone was distributed among the remaining units to bring them up to USCT standards.[7]

Many white officers in the new USCT regiments found that their promotions were in jeopardy, as the consolidated regiments did not need them, and General Orders No. 17 and 29 indicated that they would have to be reexamined to determine whether they were worthy of their ranks. Additionally, companies that had once been part of the Native Guards, Ullman's Brigade, Thomas's African Descent regiments, and the Corps d'Afrique were split or shuffled around and formed into a Division of Corps d'Afrique. The new division consisted of two brigades and nine regiments, and the former Native Guards were among them. For example, the old 4th was now commanded by Major William E. Nye—the other officer besides Benedict who ran during the Fort Jackson incident. The officer initially chosen to lead this division was Colonel Charles W. Drew, whom Dwight and Drew's men had tried to remove from command.[8]

Due to a combination of their move to the USCT and the fact that the Bureau of Colored Troops was enlisting men from all over Louisiana now, there was no longer a distinction between units raised in New Orleans and those constituted in other parts of the state. All of the Corps d'Afrique regiments, including the infantry, engineer, artillery, and cavalry, were shuffled around in the move.[9] The engineer units, for example, were designated as infantry units but still functioned as engineering units. Additionally, new regiments formed from residents of New Orleans were not credited to Louisiana anymore, so the Creole and French flair that had characterized the regiments was no more.[10] James F. Jones, for example, served in the 11th USCHA, which was stationed at Camp Parapet for a time, but the regiment had been formed primarily from northern men, and Jones was from Indiana.[11] Sergeant James Taylor, born in Pennsylvania, joined the 93d USCI and recalled serving alongside French-speaking men who recounted the horrors of enslavement.[12] Even after being assigned to the USCT, the former members of the Native Guards still presented good discipline per their muster rolls.[13] General Daniel Ullman recognized their example, crediting their actions in the early years of the war to the existence of all the regiments raised after them in the South.[14]

The officers Banks selected for command were all reviewed for their worthiness to lead. The soldiers under General George Andrews at Port Hudson were questioned, as it was "thought that few officers of the Volunteer Service have better opportunities than the officers of this command, to learn to perform in a correct and soldierly manner their military duties." Andrews referred specifically to the "officers of colored troops" whose proficiency needed to be "improved to the utmost." He wanted to enhance the "discipline and soldierly appearance" of the men to the level of "white volunteer troops."[15] The events of Fort Jackson had raised questions about white officers of Black regiments, but more recently the commanding officer of Ship Island, Colonel William M. Grosvenor, had also behaved badly in his role. In one instance, he punished a Black soldier so severely that the camp surgeon had to step in. When he did, Grosvenor allegedly told him, "If you or any other medical officer ever again dare to interfere with any punishment that I may order be inflicted, I will punish you or him in the same manner." This incident and others—Grosvenor kept women in his tent and abused his adjutant—resulted in his dismissal from service on 28 May.[16] With multiple colonels removed from the army, Andrews wanted to elevate the quality of leadership in the USCT, but a number of external concerns during the last full year of the war demanded U.S. leaders' attention.

Transnational concerns still dictated military strategy. Confederate leaders hoped that Europe would intervene on their behalf, but by 1864 this seemed unlikely. Military leaders in the Department of the Gulf were aware of these hopes as well, and maneuvered to quash them. After securing Port Hudson, Banks wanted to move his army toward Mobile because he thought liberating the city would be an easy victory. However, General Henry Halleck cautioned against such a move, believing that Banks's men should focus on Texas because of what he called "European complications."[17] Of particular concern was Louis Napoleon Bonaparte III, who controlled Mexico and posed a threat to Texas and Louisiana. In September 1863, Banks sent a small contingent to attack Texas shores and patrol near the Mexican border to curtail transnational concerns in the region. On 26 October, he sent even more men.[18] Multiple regiments from the Corps d'Afrique joined Banks on this expedition, attacking Confederate forts in Texas and building up U.S. positions against their European foes. Banks eventually left the 2d Corps d'Afrique Engineer Regiment to siege and hold Corpus Christi while the rest of his forces prepared for a larger offensive.[19] William Seward maintained a vested interest in the troops in Texas, as they were the first line of defense against Mexico and France intervening in the Civil War.[20] All of these maneuvers put the XIX Corps on a path toward its last engagement in the war: creating a line of defense on the Red River.[21]

Banks was charged with capturing Shreveport, the headquarters of the enemy's Trans-Mississippi Department and the Confederate government of Louisiana. Shreveport was key because there were numerous industrial complexes in the city supplying Confederate forces not only in Louisiana but further west. Most importantly, Seward and Lincoln wanted a military presence in Texas, since France had entered Mexico and installed a new government.[22]

*Banks's Army [XIX Corps] in the Advance of Shreveport, Crossing Cane River* (*Frank Leslie's Illustrated Newspaper,* May 7, 1864)

Making matters worse, federal officials knew that France was supplying Confederate strongholds in Texas, bolstering the southern military.[23] U.S. leaders believed that France was likely to intervene in the war on behalf of the South.[24] Banks was given additional troops from New England to join the forces he already had at his disposal.[25] The plan was to head northwest along the Red River, take Shreveport, penetrate into northern Texas, and completely remove the Confederacy from the region.[26] In total, Banks had nearly twenty thousand men under his direct command, along with forty thousand additional men who were supporting him in less direct ways.[27] He was moving in conjunction with Major General Frederick Steele, Brigadier General Andrew Jackson, and Rear Admiral David Porter.[28] Each was charged with his own avenue of approach and tactical goal to pursue once he reached the city.

Despite the Corps d'Afrique's success at Port Hudson, the thousands of Black troops serving in Louisiana were still seen as less capable than their white counterparts. In his continued bid to use the USCT as little as possible, Banks only brought a small contingent of Black troops—four of his smaller infantry regiments and two engineering regiments—with him on the campaign.[29] He assigned Colonel William H. Dickey as the brigade commander for the unit the USCT was attached to, and his choice to bring engineering regiments foretold his plans for them.[30] A white captain serving in this combined task force noted in his diary upon seeing the men, "What use is to be made of them I cannot conjecture unless it be to garrison this or some other points."[31] Even this far into the war, the idea that Black soldiers were only good for garrison duty to relieve white soldiers was still prevalent in the U.S. Army. Even other generals, such as Major General William T. Sherman, were seen by Secretary Edwin Stanton as "indifferent, if not hostile" to the idea of more Black regiments in the army.[32]

Portents of trouble appeared early during the process of planning to take Shreveport. Initially, Sherman was going to lead the campaign, but Major General Ulysses S. Grant wanted Sherman to lead the Atlanta campaign instead. As the remaining senior general, Banks drew up the strategy, but the other commanders did not trust him. Sherman sent General Jackson and ten thousand men to join Porter because they were concerned that Banks would abandon the fleet if the Department of the Gulf was in any trouble. The result was the largest combined arms task force of the Civil War, with nearly one hundred ships under Porter's command and fifty thousand effective troops in total between Banks, Steele, and Jackson. Confederate troops were thought to come to around twenty-five thousand, and with so many naval ships, it appeared that this would be an easy campaign before the fall election.[33]

However, the other commanders' mistrust of Banks had worsened because the War Department had not assigned a commander for the campaign; even though Banks had created the plan, the others did not have to report to him or even contact him once the attack was under way. Porter, in particular, did not trust Banks because he thought he was too incompetent to lead such a large number of troops into battle. In preparation for such an attack, the Trans-Mississippi Department had been preparing for over a year for a federal invasion, building up fortifications and troops.[34] As he was leaving New Orleans, Sherman warned the other generals involved that he believed Banks was leading the army into a disaster.[35]

The campaign officially commenced early in March, and it reached its first hiccup when one of Porter's strongest ships got stuck on a sandbar.[36] Soon after recommencing their movements, the combined forces arrived in Alexandria—or most of them did.[37] Banks was not present, as he was meeting with political donors in preparation for his presidential run in the fall and speculating in cotton, which disgusted men in the XVI Corps and made some officers want to leave.[38] Banks arrived nearly a week later, well after the army had captured the city and was ready to move on.[39] They still had to secure the town from Confederate cavalry, who wanted to push the XIX Corps out of the area.[40] However, they continued on, and the soldiers of color were positioned in the rear to continue protecting the wagons and reserve artillery.[41] The engineers were key in getting the army into position to take the city, building bridges they needed to cross Louisiana's numerous waterways.[42]

After the embarrassment at Alexandria, Banks wanted to ensure that he reached Shreveport before the rest, so he attempted to use a shortcut given to him by a boat pilot. However, that pilot's shortcut turned out to be the longer route, as the captain had wanted to direct Union forces away from cotton he had stored along the shorter route for personal sale. According to Porter, if Banks had taken the correct route, they would have found wide roads with storehouses full of corn, as his forces did when they moved through the area.[43] However, the circuitous route Banks took to Shreveport led his men directly toward Confederate forces. Nearly a month after the campaign had begun, Banks faced enemy combatants on 8 April outside Mansfield.

Southern troops ripped through the federal lines in the Battle of Mansfield because Banks had not prepared and charged too quickly. Additionally, the defenders had much better positions behind cotton bales, which made it difficult even for the cavalry to attack.[44] When informing Porter of his retreat, Banks admitted that he could not use all of his forces due to the landscape of the battlefield.[45] An officer recalled, "Our thinned and wearied ranks stood up nobly against the masses and murderous fire of the rebels, and cheer after cheer went up, mingled with the almost incessant roll of musketry and roar of cannon."[46] According to an officer from the XIII Corps, Banks's orders exposed the soldiers and officers present, resulting in the injury of General Thomas Ransom.[47] The situation was truly dire, and although he did not want to, Banks was forced to retreat at this first engagement.[48] Admiral Porter compared Banks's retreat to the First Battle of Bull Run—an infamous U.S. defeat—to describe his disastrous planning.[49]

Battle of Mansfield, 8 April 1864
(*Frank Leslie's Illustrated Newspaper*, 1864)

Banks's vanguard was trapped, but General Dwight sent a contingent of troops to support him in the rear. Banks pushed Dickey's Brigade to the rear to protect the trains, leaving the Black soldiers of Louisiana rested and prepared to fight. As Banks retreated toward them and the XIX Army Corps, members of Dwight's corps positioned across a road in Pleasant Grove to form a defensive position. Outnumbered three to one, they held their fire until Confederate troops were close enough to ensure maximum destruction. The men opened fire and devastated the charging Confederate forces as the rest of the troops retreated behind their lines. Black soldiers held their line for over an hour, through multiple charges, until night fell and the rebel forces retreated from the field into the darkness. If it had not been for Dwight's men, Banks's forces would have been captured or killed before they met with the rest of the army.[50] As one soldier put it, they barely staved off a general "skedaddle" of the Union army.[51]

The following day, Confederate forces attacked Banks while he was still in retreat at the Battle of Pleasant Hill. The fighting was ill-timed for the U.S. Army, as its forces were not prepared for successive engagements, and Banks

Artistic rendering of the Battle of Pleasant Hill, 9 April 1864
(Library of Congress, Prints and Photographs Division)

had no strategy going into the battle. The one positive outcome for the men serving under Colonel Lewis Benedict and Dwight was that they held their lines, with a war correspondent for the *New York Times* reporting, "The fighting was terrific—old soldiers say it never was surpassed for desperation. Notwithstanding the terrible havoc in their ranks, the enemy pressed fiercely on, slowly pushing the men of the nineteenth corps back, up the hill, but not breaking their line of battle."[52] A white soldier credited Benedict for leading his brigade to victory, even though it cost him his life to do so.[53] The Black soldiers serving in the department once again displayed valor, bravery, and skill in the heat of battle, and they won the field that day despite Banks's unpreparedness. Banks directed Dickey's USCT regiments to hold the pickets that night, and had troops stationed at every road leading toward their defensive position.[54] However, because the XIX Corps had no follow-on maneuver and his troops had not recovered from Mansfield, once again Banks was forced to retreat and regroup before Confederate troops attacked him again.[55] At Dwight's suggestion, Banks decided it was best to retreat to Grand Ecore, but General A. J. Smith wanted to press on for an attack.[56] Banks overruled him, and they left all of the wounded and dead and retreated farther away from Pleasant Hill, ceding the town to the Confederacy.[57] After this second retreat, Banks's incompetence was becoming increasingly apparent to the men serving under him.[58] An officer wrote in his diary that Banks was at fault for all their dead and likened him to a traitor.[59] Smith never forgave Banks forcing him to leave his wounded behind.

Porter and Steele were not aware of Banks's multiple retreats, and they were continuing on with his plans as scheduled when the two regrouped to wait for Banks.[60] Banks sent word to Steele that he was losing ground. Rebel leader Alfred Mouton was dead—the only highlight in the two battles—but Confederate forces would soon be upon him. A few days later, Banks asked Steele if they could combine their forces, in the hopes that together they could take Shreveport.[61] Porter eventually received word that Banks was fleeing the area. He also found out that Confederate forces had destroyed the dam, which meant the water level was going to get too low for his massive ships to traverse the river back to Alexandria.[62] Thus, Porter began to retreat back to where they expected to meet up with Banks. Over the next few days, a series of attacks and withdrawals took place as southern enemy combatants picked away at the disorganized Union forces. Porter wrote to Sherman that the army was demoralized and "shamefully beaten by the rebels." To Porter, the entire affair was proof that political generals did not belong in the field. He called it "a crying sin to put the lives of thousands in the hands of such men." Porter indicated that all of Banks's forces were in a near mutiny over his handling of the campaign, and it would only get worse before they safely left the area.[63] Banks, however, defended himself by insisting that he was facing "the best troops in the rebel service" and that there was little he could do without more men.[64]

Banks and Porter eventually met and continued their united retreat until they discovered that the water level was too low at Alexandria for the ships to get to safety.[65] The combined forces were trapped on the wrong end of the river unless they were willing to abandon their naval vessels. Luckily, one of the officers, Lieutenant Colonel Joseph Bailey, created plans for a makeshift dam to raise the level enough to escape with their ships.[66] The 97th and 99th USCI, along with multiple white regiments, were charged with building and fortifying the dam, and the 73d USCI was there to support them against enemy fire when they came under attack.[67] Bailey left it to Lieutenant Colonel Uri Pearsall, the commander of the 99th USCI, to select the location of the dam and use his soldiers as he saw fit in its construction.[68] In the interim, Banks called for additional reinforcements after Steele and Sherman refused to support his movements. Banks even called for USCT regiments stationed in Texas, demonstrating just how desperate he was for enough manpower to hold the river.[69]

On 27 April, Banks was recalled to New Orleans and ordered to leave someone else in charge, as Grant feared Banks could jeopardize the mission.[70] The following day, Major General David Hunter reported to Grant that Banks had left them in a situation where the troops had to either remain to protect their ships or scuttle and abandon the campaign.[71] The rest of the troops in the XIX and XIII Corps were ordered to remain while they resolved the issue, and General William Emory was given command of the XIX Corps, with instructions to make no change to the corps and division staffs.[72]

The USCT continued building the dam needed to save the army and the ships General Hunter knew they could not afford to lose.[73] Dickey's units were directed to form defensive lines protecting the position between Red River and Bayou Rapides.[74] By the 6th, they expected most of the infantry soldiers of color to assist the USCT engineers in building the dam, while the rest of the men were still in defensive positions.[75] A colonel from the XIII Corps surveyed their lines and commented that the working parties and those who were protecting them were all well posted and working together effectively to hold the area.[76] They negotiated multiple attacks against their lines, as Confederate forces tested the USCT regiments under the assumption that they would fold the most quickly.[77] During one of numerous small-scale attacks, Colonel Basset was captured on 3 May, and he died on 10 May from wounds sustained in the battle. Despite the constant threat of death, the underappreciated Black soldiers completed the dam by 9 May.[78] Field Orders No. 40 directed the full withdrawal of land and naval forces, but because of the sheer number of both, it was a slow retreat, taking days to implement and complete.[79] On 15 May, the Union navy was finally clear of Red River, but the army was still there; all of the navy's supplies and cannons had been taken off of the ships so they would have a lightened load.[80] This, in turn, encumbered the army. Wanting to capture the retreating forces, Confederate troops attacked in large numbers between 16 and 18 May. The entire effective brigade of USCI troops was pulled up from the rear to the center to hold the line as the rest of the army withdrew.[81] The XVI and XIX Corps relied heavily on Dickey's Brigade, even in offensive operations, such as destroying Confederate defensive works.[82] Once again, they performed well, even in the center of battle, and shortly afterward they were sent to the rear to protect supply lines. Southern forces continued to attack them as they withdrew, and the Union army and navy narrowly escaped.[83] The largest water and ground combined task force ever assembled for battle on American soil had lost against an inferior force that was not nearly as well supplied and did not have a navy.[84]

By the end of May, it was clear that the Trans-Mississippi Department had decisively beat the Department of the Gulf.[85] Unbeknownst to both sides, the Union army would never again attempt to claim Red River or attack Shreveport. What historians have largely neglected to document, however, is that the African American regiments saved Banks's army from total destruction, as he only wrote of the entire division in one official report after the campaign.[86] Even in the general orders in which Banks thanked the men for their service, he referred in general terms to the brigades involved and Bailey, who had led the engineers.[87] The dam's construction was so important that Bailey was awarded the Medal of Honor.[88] To Bailey's credit, he noted in his own report that the USCT regiments had been invaluable in constructing the famed dam, with assistance from small detachments of white units; he called them "the best of men."[89] Colonel George Robinson, the commander of the 97th USCI and the engineer brigade, detailed in his report how the engineers of color had been key in building all of the bridges to and from Red River, building the dam that saved the naval ships and the sailors on them, guarding the wagons from cavalry attack, and supplying the army during the entire campaign.[90] In his report on the 3d Brigade, Colonel Francis Fessenden acknowledged the USCT's involvement in the early combat portions of their campaign, and Colonel Dickey detailed their combat involvement and losses in the latter portion of Red River Campaign.[91] A white soldier who was present throughout the campaign acknowledged that the events of Red River united "the men of Maine, Missouri, Massachusetts, Pennsylvania, New York, Kentucky, Illinois, and Indiana . . . with the Loyal Louisiana Troops," and called them the "heroes of Vicksburg and Port Hudson."[92]

Shortly after the campaign, the *New York Times* reported that Banks had made it back to Alexandria and turned over command of the city to General William Franklin. It was a humiliating moment for Banks.[93] Grant wrote to General Henry Halleck that the reports from Banks and his officers "show all his disasters to be attributable to his incompetency."[94] Grant noted that "the army has undoubtedly lost confidence in him."[95] Halleck told Grant that he had wanted Banks gone months ago because of his lack of "military capacity," but Banks's political connections had always stymied his suggestions to remove him.[96] Sherman characterized the Red River Campaign as "one damn blunder from beginning to end."[97] George Denison wrote, "the army would have done better without any Commanding General at all."[98]

It was not only federal leaders who held these views. A junior soldier wrote to his parents, "The Red River Campaign has been an entire failure," and he remarked that many officers were saying that "they will never fight under [Banks] again."[99] Meanwhile, another wrote in a letter to friends that Banks's actions had resulted in the deaths of many of his fellow soldiers.[100] So many soldiers were openly criticizing Banks that officers had to threaten court-martial to stop the gossip.[101] Banks conceded in his report, "It would have been better that the expedition had never been attempted."[102] General David Hunter, on assignment from General Grant to review New Orleans, wrote to Grant that the entire department was "one great mass of corruption. Cotton and politics, instead of the war, appear to have engrossed the army" under Banks, a commander whom no soldier had trusted as a leader.[103] Many of their sentiments were reminiscent of what African American troops had said about Banks before Port Hudson, but now that his actions had cost the lives of white soldiers, federal officials finally took action to remove him.

Members of Congress wanted to know what had made the battle such a failure when the military had had overwhelming ground forces and naval superiority. A congressional investigation was opened in December. During the investigation, it was discovered that Banks had allowed political backers to move with troops in the hopes of confiscating cotton to use in textile mills in

New England. The investigation concluded that political agendas and military politics had informed communications and use of troops. Banks, in particular, was found at fault for ignoring intelligence from his fellow officers, engaging in cotton speculation, and issuing overly simplistic orders in the field.[104] Even in the midst of disaster, officers in the XIX Corps were ensuring that all sugar and molasses were seized near Alexandria.[105] General Smith had reportedly made it clear to Banks while they were retreating that he was not going to bring back any of the cotton and sugar the XIX Corps collected, nor would he be blamed for it.[106] The campaign was so disastrous that the governor of Arkansas, Isaac Murphy, wrote to the president to express concern that the defeat had jeopardized Little Rock and the rest of the state.[107] The results of the investigation, and the anger from so many generals, ended Banks's presidential aspirations.

The USCT regiments in Louisiana did not hold any meetings or pen any letters extolling Banks's merits as a leader or liberator when he was removed from field command. A war correspondent in New Orleans expressed that the city's inhabitants had begun to turn against him as well; the correspondent called him "a petty despot and totally unequal to the situation, vacillating, weak, and without ideas."[108] William Lloyd Garrison publicly called out Banks for his treatment of freed people and the Black regiments under his command, and for his failed tenure in the Department of the Gulf.[109] One officer wrote that Banks had won no great battle aside from the battle at Port Hudson, which he attributed more to the soldiers' efforts than Banks's skills as a commander.[110] General Grant had repeatedly petitioned the president to remove Banks, but to avoid embarrassing the politically connected general, they had put a different general in charge of a higher command and subsumed the Department of the Gulf within the new organization.[111] The only group who protested this move were planters, who appreciated the overtures Banks made toward them. In September, Banks willingly left Louisiana and did not return until April the following year. He spent months defending his campaign on the Red River and why he thought his labor system in Louisiana made sense.[112] Finally, Lincoln told him his words meant little, and Banks had no choice in serving under another general.[113]

Major General Edward R. S. Canby replaced Banks. Canby was the former commander of the Department of Mexico, but he had spent most of the war as a high-ranking staff officer instead of as a military commander. After his promotion to major general, he was given command of the newly constituted Military Division of West Mississippi on 7 May. This military command en-

Major General Edward Canby
(Library of Congress, Prints and Photographs Division)

compassed all of the Department of the Gulf and the Department of Arkansas.[114] Within a few weeks, the Department of the Missouri was integrated into Canby's forces as well.[115] The new formation allowed the USCT of Louisiana to support multiple new states in the Deep South. Unlike Banks, Canby coordinated with the other generals; one of the first things he did in his command was work with General William T. Sherman to cease federal movements into western Louisiana. With Canby in place, Halleck informed Sherman that the latter could finally focus on his own campaigns, free of worry about the Mississippi and the Gulf.[116] In response, Sherman wrote to Canby, "I am rejoiced that you are to command west of the Mississippi River."[117] Denison told Chase that nearly all of the men were happy with the change.[118]

Though Canby allowed Banks to return to New Orleans, he ensured that the general never commanded troops in the field again.[119] Some federal officials feared that Banks's political connections and position would allow him to become military governor, but instead Banks was relegated out of combat roles in the Department of the Gulf and was instead tasked with daily administrative work, a role he did not do well because he had left the city.[120]

Initially, Canby intended to continue the Red River Campaign, even calling on Banks to report all of his troops and their mission so he could maintain his position at the mouth of the Red River.[121] Canby decided against the action after consulting with his subordinate generals. He also planned to centralize all of the positions in the Department of the Gulf, instead of garrisoning dozens of positions throughout their vast area of operations.[122] Canby soon realized that both the white and Black troops in the department were well trained and had only suffered from poor leadership.[123] The troops stationed at Port Hudson were especially prepared; their region was well garrisoned and those who were not in active use had had months to drill and train.[124] Of the six engineering regiments in the entire XIX Corps, five were from the Louisiana USCT, and they were all experienced in their duties.[125]

Canby headquartered the Division of West Mississippi in Natchez, Mississippi.[126] After making preparations at Simmesport, Louisiana, with the XIX Corps, he made movements into Texas, Georgia, and Florida in conjunction with Admirals Porter and Farragut.[127] Canby's marching orders were similar to those Banks had received months earlier: get the Department of the Gulf into Mobile and eliminate the Confederate presence in the Gulf. Canby carefully planned and reorganized his forces, then prepared to move toward Mobile.[128] He required all soldiers to carry the bare minimum in supplies, clothes, and food.[129] He was directed to send a large amount of troops north to support General Benjamin Butler, who was now commanding the Army of the James in Virginia.[130] With so many moving parts, Canby had to ensure that everyone was in the correct place.

Canby reorganized his large command and made changes to the XIX Corps. He left the 1st and 2d Divisions almost as Banks had structured them, but he reconstituted the 3d from the XIII Corps with seventeen of the best regiments, including the USCT engineering units Banks had provided. General Emory retained command of the XIX Corps in the field, while General Reynolds commanded all forces out of Morganza.[131] Brigadier General Thomas Sherman commanded all of the defenses of New Orleans, and the multiple USCT regiments were stationed there as well.[132] Initially, George Andrews remained headquartered at Port Hudson, and his forces repelled small Confederate incursions near the Mississippi.[133] The 91st USCI and Dickey's Brigade were repositioned to protect New Orleans, since so many troops were covering the new Division of West Mississippi.[134] General John McNeil was given command of Port Hudson in mid-June, after Andrews became the temporary provost marshal for the Department of the Gulf, and Brigadier General Fitz Henry Warren was given command of the Rio Grande border.[135] Following Basset's death, on 3 June 1864, Lieutenant Colonel Henry C. Merriam informally took command of the 73d USCI. Merriam already had some experience leading Black troops, having commanded in the 3d Corps d'Afrique and the 85th USCI. Approximately forty-two hundred men under Emory's command were sent to support Butler and Grant.[136]

Canby seemed ambivalent about Black units. He did not want reports on their movements and numbers sent to his office, opting instead to forward them all to General Emory.[137] Recruitment for additional USCT regiments ceased after Canby took over, and all soldiers who had recently been recruited were used as combat replacements in units that had already been constituted.[138] He even attempted to stop using the military to protect formerly enslaved people living on plantations, something the government did not support.[139] However, Canby continued to utilize members of the USCT in varying ways. While most continued to garrison forts and conduct fatigue duty, a few engaged in combat operations. For example, on a number of occasions troops in Lafourche Parish were used to apprehend guerrillas who were raiding the region.[140] There were so many raids near Port Hudson that the camp assistant surgeon was captured, and Ullman had to trade prisoners to get him back.[141] Eventually, Canby authorized Ullman to "clean the rebels out at Waterloo" in order to decrease the number of raids, and Ullman utilized the USCT at Port Hudson to complete those orders.[142] In the Department of the Gulf alone, USCT troops were protecting Plaquemine; New Orleans; Camp Parapet; Carrollton; Ship Island; Forts Pike, Macomb, St. Philip, and Jackson; and, possibly the most important of all, Port Hudson. They were also sent to offer protection at Barrancas and Fort Myers, Florida, and to build up additional small outposts for future operations.[143] Battery E of the 2d USCLA was sent all the way to Arkansas to support their operations.[144] Naturally, with such a large command, Canby had dozens of USCT regiments across multiple states at his disposal, and he employed them in numerous ways.[145]

The first Black regiment that had been raised in the Civil War, the 73d USCI, was part of his plans for Florida and Alabama. The former 1st Louisiana Native Guards was with Canby's main forces. Canby wanted to avoid attempting another campaign on the Red River and opted to use the Washita and White Rivers rather than travel by land.[146] The West Mississippi Division focused on Arkansas and Alabama, areas just as important to the government's overall mission as Shreveport was. The 73d USCI was assigned to Brigadier General William Anderson Pile and detailed to assist in taking Mobile, Alabama, on 26 February 1865.[147] First stationed in Pensacola, Florida, the regiment prepared to invade Alabama and destroy some of the final vestiges of the Confederacy in the Deep South in December 1864.[148] Federal forces had dispatched all the Confederate forces in Pensacola nearly a year prior, so the area now provided a perfect staging ground for an invasion into Mobile.[149] Their targets were Fort Blakely and Spanish Fort.

The presence of Black troops in the Union army continued to effect sweeping changes throughout Louisiana. When the new state legislature passed the Emancipation Act, the 20th USCI, 4th USCC, and 7th USCHA gathered to march in a place of honor in celebration of a new phase of African American life in Louisiana.[150] In late September, twenty enslaved people fled by boat under armed guard after being forced to build southern fortifications, but only seven survived the journey to U.S. lines. Others were able to elude military authorities and reach the nearby USCT regiment.[151] Enslaved people in Louisiana continued to demonstrate the same zeal for freedom they had exhibited for decades prior to the Civil War. Like Peter—who was still serving in the USCI—they used the presence of the military to shorten a journey that had once been hundreds of miles or a naval voyage to reclaim their freedom. Even those who did not emancipate themselves realized that slavery in Louisiana had changed forever, and many came to believe they would all eventually be free once they learned Black troops were serving in the military. The Division of West Mississippi secured freedom for those in its vast area of operations near the end of the year, promising swift action against planters who threatened to defraud or reenslave anyone in the Gulf.[152]

Service in the USCT had the unintended consequence of giving African American soldiers a chance to unify and commiserate, especially about the pay issue that plagued all Black soldiers in the U.S. Army. Men like Private Isidore Kenney—a soldier in the 73d USCI who was shot and injured during one of their multiple charges on 27 May—hoped their service at Port Hudson proved to the government that they deserved their promised pay, and he recognized that many of the men in his regiment were upset that the issue was unresolved.[153] Colonel Drew theorized that pay issues had contributed to the events at Fort Jackson in December 1863.[154] Broadsides featured headlines like, "Equal State Rights! And Monthly Pay with White Men!!" which had proved to be a lie for years now.[155] Congress's decision to pay Black soldiers a reduced rate meant Black commissioned and noncommissioned officers earned less than half as much as a white private.[156] There were entire regiments whose members refused to draw their pay on the principle that it would appear they had approved it, and some soldiers simply deserted when it became clear the policy would not change.[157] In November, Sergeant William Walker of the 3d South Carolina Infantry Regiment led his fellow Black soldiers in stacking their arms and refusing to perform their duties until they were paid as much as white men. Walker was charged with leading a mutiny and executed to quell expressions of discontent. However, he became a martyr for Black rights in the army. Additional Black soldiers who had fought at Port Hudson, Milliken's Bend, and other battles used their military service as a tool to fight for equality, creating a situation that could not be ignored.[158] Soon after Walker's execution on 29 February, multiple regiments in the USCT, including those in Louisiana, made it clear that they would not tolerate the pay disparity any longer, and Congress was forced to act once again.[159]

For nearly two years, Black soldiers complained that they served "without a cent of bounty, on the written pledge of the War Department, that they should receive the same pay and rations with white soldiers."[160] Many of the men who had enlisted in the Corps d'Afrique had made months' worth of advance payments for their uniforms before they received their first paycheck.[161] Finally, on 15 June 1864, paymasters were ordered to pay African American soldiers the same pay as their white counterparts—but the order was very stigmatizing. Those who had been free prior to the war would receive back pay to the time of their enlistment, while those who had been enslaved before the war started would only receive pay from 1 January 1864.[162] The Louisiana regiments were filled with people in both of these groups, and naturally this caused confusion for the paymaster and anger among the soldiers.[163]

The soldiers channeled their anger toward the government. Thomas Sipple, a Black man who had joined the army in New York but was now serving near New Orleans, wrote to President Lincoln that the pay disparity affected the soldiers and their families, and that they were not being treated as soldiers nor as colleagues. He asked him to correct the order quickly, as the men wanted to serve honorably.[164] Warren Hamelton was among those who deserted the military when it became obvious the pay and bounty he had been promised by General Butler would not be honored. Hamelton was eventually imprisoned for his crime. He appealed to Edwin Stanton that he had had no choice but to leave, because the government was not taking care of him or his family and they needed the money.[165] Joseph Brazile, one of few who had been free prior to the war, was injured in battle and had to leave active military service. When he went to the paymaster to withdraw his final pay and promised bounty, the paymaster scornfully told him that there was no law promising his bounty. Colonel Henry Frisbie, the commander of the 92d USCI and the entire 1st Louisiana Infantry Brigade (Colored), assisted Brazile in appealing to the adjutant general on the grounds that Brazile had served honorably and Congress had already passed laws granting him his pay.[166] One of the soldiers stationed in Port Hudson was not paid his promised bounty until April 1865.[167] Even worse, there were soldiers of color applying for their bounties well after the war.[168] There were even cases of men pursuing bounties they had been promised in 1862 into the Reconstruction period.[169] For example, Louisa D'Aunoy continued to fight the government for her husband's promised bounty late into the century.[170]

The soldiers also wanted a way to save and use their money after the war. The Black soldiers petitioned to General George Andrews for a bank. After a request from Andrews, Banks wrote to Chase that the soldiers of color were requesting a bank in New Orleans just for them. He also told Chase that he had received similar requests from other men, women, and even children who earned wages working on plantations. Banks recognized that a bank would give them the opportunity to save money and avoid being robbed or scammed by unscrupulous people who took advantage of formerly enslaved individuals who were not used to the American banking system.[171] The Free Labor Bank was established in 1864.[172]

While Congress stalled on paying Black soldiers equally, the federal government also remained undecided on the question of colonization. Even this late into the war, Lincoln was still contemplating forcibly deporting free African Americans once all hostilities had settled. The government even sent 450 people to Haiti, but it resulted in many deaths, as the deportees were not prepared for the climate. The navy was forced to send ships to Haiti to rescue the survivors once the debacle became public knowledge in 1864. There were smaller attempts to remove newly freed people from the nation, but they all failed because of poor government planning.

To the editors of *L'Union,* all African Americans earned their citizenship the day Black men had put on the blue Union uniform and held a musket in their hands.[173] They pointed to the deaths of men such as Captain André Cailloux to illustrate Black Americans' desire for citizenship and equality before the law.[174] The author of a June 1864 article wrote, "from the day bayonets were placed in the hands of the blacks" they were citizens. Those not in the military also pursued their own paths toward improving themselves and supporting the federal government. To the editors of *L'Union,* their service, too, demanded equal rights before the law.[175] The wealthy Black populace worked together to form the Union Association, a New Orleans group dedicated to creating a new state constitution that would enfranchise all African Americans in Louisiana. After Lincoln failed to convince Governor Michael Hahn to secure their rights, African Americans in the state continued to agitate for more rights. The editors of *L'Union* even drew on the history of the Louisiana Purchase, in which France and Spain had guaranteed their rights and privileges decades prior. When a white paper called the desire for equality "a sick vanity," *L'Union*'s editors responded that the only sick vanity in America "is the white aristocracy of this country that is in a state of chronic sickness—this aristocracy which arrogates to itself all rights and privileges."[176]

Dr. Louis Charles Roudanez, along with his brother Jean-Baptiste Roudanez and many others, formed the Comitė Central des Natifs, commonly called the Freedmen's Aid Association, in late 1863.[177] The organization's members worked to support formerly enslaved people in Louisiana, and members of the USCT donated their time, money, and resources to support the group. The Freedmen's Aid Association supplied food and housing to the formerly enslaved and worked to include them in enfranchisement discussions.[178] Officers who had once served in the Native Guards took positions as directors and supporters of the Freedmen's Aid Association, and members used their connections to work with other organizations throughout the United States.[179] When Black people were arrested on the streets of New Orleans, these groups petitioned Banks and the provost on their behalf.[180]

The Louisiana constitution did not officially abolish slavery in the state until 1864. Leading up to that point, groups including the Union Association and the Freedmen's Aid Association ensured that African American voices kept the issues of freedom and equality at the forefront of Louisiana politics.[181] Over a thousand Black Louisianans, including hundreds who served in the Native Guards and USCT, signed a petition demanding the right to vote and the abolishment of slavery that landed on Lincoln's desk.[182] The government established the Bureau of Refugees, Freedmen, and Abandoned Lands, more commonly called the Freedmen's Bureau, with the aid of men who supported the cause, including Colonel Daniels.[183] In the fall of 1864, Freedmen's Bureau agents arrived in the Department of the Gulf, and General Orders No. 156 transferred the care and supervision of all freed people to the bureau.[184] With the arrival of the bureau, the Civil War entered a new phase, with the federal government preparing for the end of the war and the liberation and care of enslaved people. Lincoln told military authorities that he expected them to respect the rights of all free people in Louisiana; in response, Canby attested to the army's efforts to support, hire, clothe, and educate all its members.[185] By February 1865, bureau agents were ready to take control of the plantations and labor in Louisiana.[186]

In late 1864, Roudanez closed *L'Union* and opened *La Tribune de la Nouvelle Orléans,* more commonly called the *New Orleans Tribune,* which published in both English and French to open up the publication to more readers. The paper was originally published triweekly and was later published daily, becoming the nation's first daily African American newspaper. Like *L'Union* had been, it was the most effective way for Black men serving in the U.S. Army to communicate with African American civilians in New Orleans. The paper's editors were even more adamant regarding Black rights than *L'Union*'s editors had been, and because it was open to more readers, a larger number of northern abolitionists and formerly enslaved people were able to access the paper.[187] The *Black Republican,* another newspaper started by free people in New Orleans, joined in petitioning the government on behalf of soldiers serving in the Louisiana USCT.[188]

Perhaps because of the work of Roudanez and the free press, the men grew to expect rights and privileges, and they fervently believed the federal government owed them as much for their service in the military. The court-martial of Léonnel Macarty in September 1864 illustrates this influence. Macarty spoke with Sergeant Major John Cage about Cage's latest mission to capture deserters who were hiding in New Orleans. Macarty, who was born free in the city and joined the 1st Louisiana Native Guards Regiment in September 1862 as its sergeant major, did not believe a Black man should follow such an order. Macarty questioned why Cage would support a government that was not paying them or taking care of their families. Allegedly, Macarty ended up threatening to shoot Cage if he attempted to arrest any of Macarty's relatives. Cage reported the incident and Macarty was court-martialed on 19 September. He wrote to Lieutenant Colonel Merriam that he believed men who deserted did so out of need, which was the fault of the government. He believed the government had broken faith with them when they were not given their monthly pay and bonuses, and the failure of the Department of the Gulf to protect their families was egregious. Some of his testimony reflected arguments that had appeared in *L'Union* and the *New Orleans Tribune.* Macarty wrote about Black unity, equal rights, equal pay, what the government owed those who served, and why so many of the soldiers in the USCT were frustrated. It was an impassioned plea for all Black men in the army.[189] He was found guilty and sentenced to six months of hard labor, which he completed before returning to the military and, after the war, public life in New Orleans.

The Native Guards maintained deep connections to the newspapers in New Orleans, and military service pushed many of those who served into the political realm. James Ingram served as a captain in the 1st Corps d'Afrique, replacing André Cailloux after his death at Port Hudson. Born enslaved in Mississippi and later freed by his father, who was also his enslaver, Ingram represented the opportunities that military service afforded. On 4 October 1864, when the National Negro Convention held its last meeting in Syracuse, New York, Ingram reiterated the connection between military service and citizenship and how the sacrifices of men like Cailloux at Port Hudson proved the manhood of all Black men and the humanity of the race. His language indicated that he was well read in the talking points of Black excellence during the war. In a dramatic display, he took out and unfurled for all to see the blood soaked, tattered battle flag of the 1st Regiment from Port Hudson. The flag was hung in the convention hall as a symbol of the importance of Black military service. Frederick Douglass, the president of the convention, led everyone in cheering for Ingram, Cailloux, and the soldiers who had served at Port Hudson.[190]

When Ingram returned to New Orleans, many of his fellow soldiers joined him to demand Black suffrage before the war ended. While many of those who served had been free prior to the war, the language they used to demand equality demonstrated unity. At a meeting scheduled by Ingram and publicized in the *New Orleans Tribune,* Oscar Dunn, another former Black officer of the Native Guards, said that they "regard all black and colored men as fellow sufferers."[191] Most of the delegates were men who had served as officers in the Native Guards, and they emphasized that their sacrifice was communal. Captain Henry Rey had returned to New Orleans a changed man, ready to fight the government to uplift the community of formerly enslaved Blacks with whom he had served in the Native Guards. He fought adamantly for suffrage and Black rights for many years after leaving the military.[192]

The idea that this was a common fight for all African Americans appeared frequently in *L'Union* and the *Tribune.* During the war, officials in the new white government of Louisiana attempted to sow division over class and skin color, since everyone was free. However, these tactics did not work on people who had dealt with the same tricks for decades. *L'Union* called out an 1864 plot to give rights only to the lighter-skinned Creoles as a ploy to divide free African Americans. The editorial ended with the phrase, "United, we stand! Divided, we fall!"[193] When the bill was up for a vote in the legislature, editors of the *Tribune* declared that, though they wanted their rights, they would not accept them if they were not given to all men.[194] Many of the newspapers' editors were lighter-skinned men who were born free and would have benefitted most from such a policy, but they led the charge against new laws that would have created a hierarchy among Black Americans. The Louisiana USCT was a pivotal source of inspiration for African American unity, excellence, and political action. New Orleans's Black press gave the soldiers talking points, organized conventions for them, and informed them about political ideas and rhetoric circulating throughout the nation.

The Department of the Gulf—and the multiple USCT regiments in it—thrived under General Canby. With over one hundred thousand effective troops between the Department of the Gulf, the Department of the Missouri, and the Department of Arkansas, the Military Division of West Mississippi was a force in the Gulf.[195] Because of its size, there were dozens of USCT regiments from the North and South in the Division of West Mississippi.[196] By the end of the year, the XVI and XIX Army Corps were abolished and consolidated into Canby's field forces as well.[197] Two small campaigns at Forts Gaines and Morgan were resounding successes, and Canby coordinated with Admiral Farragut to ensure they controlled all of the Mississippi River. Ullman's forces repelled a small assault near Baton Rouge, helping to secure the town against Confederates.[198] He later used the 78th USCI to drive southern cavalry out of the Department of the Gulf.[199] According to their officers, the members of the artillery battery in Arkansas were reported to fight like veterans, "backed by fearless daring" when facing Confederate troops.[200] Before the war's end, the 79th USCI joined them as well.[201]

Denison described it as a total reversal from Banks's approach.[202] Even the 74th USCI had an opportunity to leave Fort Pike and hunt for Confederate soldiers.[203] However, even when they were deployed, the men were often still used for fatigue duty, as Colonel Henry Frisbie discovered when the 92d and 99th left Morganza for the Atchafalaya River and Morgan's Ferry. Frisbie reported that other units always found something for his USCT regiments to do, and Union officers often lied and cheated his men for their own personal gain, to the shame of all U.S. soldiers.[204]

Despite his initial hesitancy, Canby learned to rely on the USCT. There were even discussions about reinstating former Black officers of the Native Guards to their rightful place in the military. Captain P. B. S. Pinchback had been given permission on 2 October 1863, through special order, to recruit a cavalry company for the Department of the Gulf.[205] However, Banks refused to commission an African American officer.[206] A year later, Canby issued an order halting recruitment for new regiments on 19 October 1864.[207] Days later, however, the Department of the Gulf issued General Orders No. 154, which authorized former officers of the Native Guards to raise companies for two regiments meant to serve one year of service.[208] Soon after, recruitment for a regiment for the USCI was underway as well. Former officer James Lewis was given the chance to raise one of those companies, but after failing the boards a year prior—and hearing about Pinchback's experience after he spent his own money recruiting his company—Lewis feared that his reinstatement would result in his removal and further embarrassment.[209] Instead of rejoining the unit, Lewis went on to work with the Freedmen's Bureau, and he worked in numerous political roles to uplift the Black community of New Orleans.[210] Ultimately, none of the former Black officers returned to the regiments.

By the end of the year, no new regiments had been created. Colonel Frisbie was frustrated by the lack of recruiting, writing to Major George Drake, "The present system of recruiting for colored troops has proved a failure, and does not meet the wants of the service." Frisbie called for keeping officers responsible for recruiting and stopping the practice of taking troops from one regiment in Louisiana to fill another somewhere else in the Division of West Mississippi.[211] Even without additional regiments, the USCT of Louisiana were invaluable to the army. They were stationed at Morganza, New Orleans, Port Hudson, Brashear City, Carrollton, Fort Jackson, Fort Macomb, Fort Pike, Ship Island, Fort Livingston, Baton Rouge, Plaquemine, Gaines' Landing, Pass Manchac, De Sair, and even outside of Louisiana in Florida and Texas. Black soldiers were vital to the federal army throughout the Gulf.[212]

The XIX Corps was doing so well that Confederate leaders in Louisiana maneuvered to utilize free African American labor as the Department of the Gulf had done since 1862. The Trans-Mississippi Department issued General Orders No. 55, authorizing the recruitment of officers to conscript free Blacks and one-fifth of all enslaved males of military age for labor duty. However, those who had been promised freedom per the Treaty of Paris of 1803 and the Treaty of Spain of 1819 were excluded from this order. Officials in the department hoped they could use conscripted Black labor to relieve white soldiers from certain duties and put more men in the field, as Thomas had done, but these maneuvers so late in the war helped little. It should be noted that while the South conscripted African Americans for duty, they were employed not as soldiers but for labor duty, and while their names were listed on descriptive rolls for the department, they never served in combat for the South. Instead, they were all assigned to the Commandant of Negro Labor for fatigue and teamster duty. None were volunteers; rather, they were treated as though they were enslaved even if they were free.[213]

The situation was so dire for the South that the Trans-Mississippi resorted to detailing managers and overseers of plantations for conscription duty as well.[214] Henry Allen wrote to the southern secretary of war, "The time has come for us to put into the army every able-bodied negro man as a soldier. This should be done immediately." He wrote, "We have learned from dear bought experience that negroes can be taught to fight, and that all who leave us are made to fight against us."[215] The South's War Department issued a new order that allowed formerly enslaved people to join the Confederate military as conscripts masquerading as volunteers. However, the orders were issued very late in the war, so the department never received the reinforcements. Thankfully for the enslaved men, those who were forced to begin the process of joining the military never served a day in the Confederate armed forces. By November, the rebel army in Louisiana began dismantling its cavalry for want of more infantrymen.[216] Soon, military operations in Louisiana were reduced to raids and guerrilla attacks, as the Confederates lacked troops who could challenge the vast federal army under Canby.[217]

Canby streamlined the USCT reporting process, organizing each brigade into a separate command with its own headquarters positioned throughout the Gulf. Those seeking promotion had to meet new standards for selection, and relatively fewer officers were retained.[218] Thomas had too many men and was unwilling to constitute more regiments, so he ordered excess troops raised in the Department of the Gulf to report to USCT regiments in need of more men.[219] One of Thomas's colonels informed him that they had stopped training because his troops were on labor duty while the white troops did nothing.[220] Thomas Sipple, a Black soldier in the regiments, complained to the president that constant fatigue duty resulted in some men standing guard and then laboring for over twenty-four hours with no meat or coffee. Sipple wrote that, for the African American men serving in Louisiana, "It is a hard thing to be kept in such a state of misery continually." He concluded by asking the president, "How can we stand them [the rebels] in a weak and starving condition?"[221] Sipple was correct: the members of the USCT stationed in Louisiana were not given enough time or food to be prepared to fight. Colonel Frisbie likened their situation to enslavement, describing officers who behaved as overseers utilizing Black soldiers to build and plow.[222] While George Andrews acknowledged that their constant fatigue duty was detrimental to their overall health, he still expressed a belief that the troops were combat effective.[223] Thankfully, the war was nearing its end.

The Louisiana USCT regiments were dispersed throughout the South during the last few months of the war. In New Orleans, there was talk of redesignating some of the units as engineers, since they were used extensively as engineering units.[224] However, the war ended before any such change could be made. The bulk of the New Orleans USCT forces, well over three thousand men, were stationed at Morganza, followed closely by those at Port Hudson with nearly twenty-five hundred men. Two regiments were at Brashear City; one was dispersed across Ship Island, Bonnet Carré, and Lakeport; three were nearing Mobile, Alabama; two were in Florida; two more were still garrisoned in Brazos; and two were protecting New Orleans proper.[225] Ullman remained in control of the 1st Division and Frisbie the 2d. The regiments were broken up into brigades and commanded by various colonels throughout the vast area of the Division of West Mississippi.

The most important event in this area was the White River Campaign.[226] Close to New Orleans, the Military Division of the Mississippi was divided among Port Hudson, Baton Rouge, and Morganza, and General Francis Herron commanded all of these units through the Northern Division of Louisiana. General Thomas Sherman commanded the defenses of New Orleans and the Southern Division of Louisiana.[227] Canby made no distinction between Louisiana's USCT and troops from other states; for example, he stationed the 84th and 92d with the 67th USCI in Morganza. Thus, by the end of the war, Black soldiers from all over the country were intermingling with the Louisiana units that had been there from the start.[228] Small patrols were sent throughout the region, some along with the navy, and while they did not always encounter Confederate troops, they ensured that Louisianans remained aware of the African American soldiers in the military.[229] USCT forces in the field continued to find men who wanted to fight, and offered them chances to join the Union army even as the war neared its end. As Colonel Frisbie phrased it, "They will fight and sell their lives dearly."[230]

During this time, Lincoln remained committed to the abolishment of slavery. Reportedly, he told Alexander W. Randall, "There have been men who have proposed to me to return to slavery the black warriors of Port Hudson & Olustee to their masters to conciliate the South. I should be damned in time & in eternity for so doing. The world shall know that I will keep my faith to friends & enemies, come what will."[231] When speaking to foreign dignitaries, he had a gift for making it clear that the aim of the government was both to save the Union and to end slavery in the nation.[232] At the risk of hurting his reelection campaign, Lincoln expressed that Black regiments made the Civil War a war for abolition.

Lincoln received criticism from both conservatives and liberals who believed he was not doing enough to support Black Americans. A writer for the *New Orleans Tribune* wrote that the nation needed a different president—one who was committed to equality for African Americans. The writer even accused Lincoln of being a secret conservative for supporting stringent measures against the government's greatest supporters.[233] Nevertheless, due to Hahn's failure to enfranchise Black voters, New Orleanians had no power to change who was elected, and with General George McClellan as the alternative, Lincoln was seen by many Americans as the lesser of two evils. Lincoln was reelected and the United States moved into the final phase of the war.

Northerners began to contemplate what the end of the war would mean. Democrats frequently invoked "honorable peace," the idea that the South should be reabsorbed into the nation without violence or surrender. A *New York Times* article parsed the implications of this idea: "The rebels are not fighting for their honor, but to be 'let alone' in their crime."[234] Democrats' and southerners' only hope for this approach was if Lincoln were not reelected, as he had said he would not allow slavery to continue in any form after the war. Banks had been an advocate of honorable peace, attempting to work with rebel leadership in Richmond to end the war on generous terms for the South.[235] His actions sowed further distrust among Black soldiers, who saw him as a traitor to everything they fought for. Members of the USCT did not support a policy of honorable peace and were determined to fight until the Confederacy was defeated.

Lincoln's reelection reignited calls for additional USCT regiments, with the aim being to raise enough men to decisively end the war. In New Orleans, a large number of noncommissioned officers signed a petition calling for the secretary of war to commission them as officers so they could raise regiments as they had in 1862. They wanted the regiments to be officered exclusively by Black men and reminded Stanton that they had already proved themselves as officers in 1862 and 1863. The only impediment to their serving as officers, they argued, was arbitrary rules that Banks had put in place. They continued, "We confidently believe that the removal of this bar to a soldier's ambition would result in an uprising of the colored people, unsurpassed even by the enthusiastic response to the President's first call." They concluded their petition by writing that all of the noncommissioned officers had studied war extensively, and that they were trained and ready to enter service.[236] Illustrating Union leaders' persistent aversion to allowing Black men to serve as officers, Stanton did not commission the men in new USCT regiments.

Governor Hahn gave an address to the new state legislature imploring its members to take care of all of Louisiana's soldiers. He noted that thousands—both white and Black—had joined as early as 1862 and had gone on to serve in campaigns including the Teche, the Siege of Port Hudson, and the disastrous Red River expedition. No matter the location, they served with what he called "conspicuous bravery." Thus, the government had a responsibility to take care of their wives and children, and to support the men themselves after their service. Hahn called on the legislature to declare foreign nationals citizens and subject them to conscription, as Butler had tried to do years earlier. Finally, Hahn pronounced that children of formerly enslaved people would be enrolled in public schools, saying, "Knowledge, which has heretofore been granted only to the white children of our State, will now be diffused among all children, without distinction of race or color." After summarizing these plans for the future, he concluded, "The rebellion everywhere is at its last grasps."[237]

On 9 April 1865, Lee was surrounded, his men downtrodden and starving, and he was forced to surrender his army to General Ulysses S. Grant. Confederate soldier Robert Tarleton wrote to his wife, "The surrender of Lee is not doubted here and our cause is looked upon as gone."[238]

A month before Lee surrendered, the 73d and 76th USCI, along with a five thousand-man division led by General John P. Hawkins, were detailed to Florida before moving to capture Fort Blakely near Mobile, Alabama.[239] The city had reportedly been abandoned by Confederates, but U.S. officers soon discovered that those reports were false.[240] Canby credited the USCT—which suffered a number of casualties—with repulsing Confederate soldiers from Spanish Fort on 2 April.[241] Soon after that, the Union army began encircling Fort Blakely in preparation for a siege to capture the fort and Mobile.[242] While they prepared, they learned about the 1864 massacre of Black troops at Fort Pillow. According to a soldier who witnessed their response, "They sprang to their guns and called unanimously for 'revenge.'"[243] Between 2 and 9 April, the USCT continued to face skirmishers in various numbers as they aided the military in preparing for the siege of Fort Blakely.[244] Around 3:00 p.m. on 9 April, the 73d and 76th charged toward the fort, echoing their charge at Port Hudson. While Banks had not given his troops adequate support, Canby did: the 82d, 86th, 96th, and 97th USCI supported the regiments that were once designated the 1st and 4th Louisiana Native Guards, and all the soldiers in the division held their lines.[245] Together, the division approached *en masse* and attacked the fort, and they quickly overwhelmed the defenders. The 73d USCI was the first to breach Confederate defenses, the first to plant their flag, and the first to enter the fort. It was poetic that the first regiment of Black soldiers successfully constituted in the army was there on the last day of the Civil War, once again defeating a Confederate foe while proving that African American soldiers were more than capable to serve on the battlefield.

Allegedly, the Confederate troops were terrified that Black soldiers would commit the same atrocities that southern soldiers had perpetrated against other USCT units, so they purposely fled toward the white attackers, planning to surrender to them and save their own lives.[246] There were no reports of the Black soldiers acting in that way, and their job securing Mobile became easier after the Confederates fled.[247] Colonel Drew acknowledged in his report that the African Americans in his division had marched through enemy fire, many at the cost of their own lives. He continued, "Notwithstanding the numerous obstacles in the way, there was scarcely a break in the line in the whole distance."[248] As one officer noted, "Great God! They had their revenge, sure enough!"[249] The first regiment of Black soldiers successfully constituted in the Union army was there on the last day of the Civil War, once again demonstrating that African American soldiers were capable of great heroism. The editors of the *New Orleans Tribune* honored the members of the 73d in its French section, calling attention to the long history of the Native Guards fighting in the Gulf.[250] The Native Guards were publicly lauded in other outlets throughout the nation for their actions on 9 April.[251]

Around the time the news became public, Lincoln was assassinated.[252] While the soldiers' achievements received less press in the aftermath of Lincoln's death, Stanton congratulated Canby and his forces on Lincoln's behalf for the siege and liberation of Mobile from Confederate forces.[253] Colonel Merriam, who had led the 73d, was awarded the Medal of Honor for his courage. Although their general recommended a few of Merriam's soldiers for recognition, none of the Black soldiers who followed him into battle received the same honor.[254] Instead, despite having sacrificed twenty-seven casualties in the final assault of the Civil War, they returned to labor and fatigue duty; while they were the heroes who secured Mobile, they were still Black men to their white officers. Soon after the battle, the members of the 73d were back to building fortifications, digging ditches, building bridges, and performing guard duty, and the white soldiers did little to assist them. The soldiers called on government officials to change this status, as they feared it would last long after the war was over.

In short order, the military campaigns in Louisiana came to an end. On 6 May 1865, the Confederate Headquarters Department of Alabama, Mississippi, and East Louisiana issued General Orders No. 54, which surrendered all of their forces under Richard Taylor to Major General Canby.[255] After receiving word of Taylor's surrender, Edmund Smith wrote to his superiors, "At least one half have already or will desert their colors. They say 'we are whipped.'"[256] Smith called for a conference of the three governors who supplied troops for his army, and they agreed that surrender was their only option.[257] Soon after, Canby accepted Smith's surrender of west Louisiana and all his men.[258] The *Liberator* was happy to report that there was no rebel army left west of the Mississippi.[259] Union cavalry in Georgia captured Jefferson Davis.[260] On 2 June 1865, Henry Allen finally left office, declaring, "The contest ended, the soldiers are disbanded . . . and now there is in Louisiana no opposition whatever to the Constitution and laws of the United States."[261] Allen's words reinforced the official end to the Civil War in Louisiana.

While the war ended on 2 June in Louisiana, guerrilla forces in the state and in Texas continued to pester the Department of the Gulf for months. Upon surrendering his office to the lawful governor of the state, Allen advised white Louisianans to "form yourselves into companies and squads for the purpose of protecting your families from outrage and insult and your property from spoliation."[262] Guerrilla attacks were already a norm in Louisiana. For example, the 75th USCI sent multiple units out looking for six men who were causing trouble on a plantation near Brashear.[263] Similar patrols took place all summer long. Algernon Badger wrote to his father that, by September, the former Confederates among them were out of funds and clothes, and had no fighting spirit to speak of anymore.[264]

As the war came to an end, the Native Guards were doing what they had done for the majority of the war: fatigue and labor duty. The 74th USCI, formerly the 2d Louisiana Native Guards, was stationed at Ship Island, with a few of its companies positioned at Fort Pike and Fort Macomb.[265] General Thomas Sherman called out troops in Lafourche for not working hard enough. He wrote, "A complete renovation is required in the system of duties at Brashear."[266] Departments that had men stationed with the Louisiana regiments often had to recall their Black soldiers because they were used too extensively for fatigue duty.[267] Despite these circumstances, soldiers in the 74th USCI continued to impress their senior officers and officials in the War Department with their discipline and skill. Sherman reported as much when he called the regiments "superior to any Volunteer Regiment he ever inspected, and in many important points it is equal to that of the best instructed Regular Troops."[268] In August, as the 73d USCI, formerly the 1st Louisiana Native Guards, was preparing to muster out of service, the *New Orleans Tribune* called for and helped organize a celebration of their heroism as the first and finest Black regiment in the army.[269] Another celebration was held at Port Hudson for those who had fought to end slavery and uplift Louisiana's African American community.[270]

One of the benefits the end of the war brought—in addition to an end to armed combat—was a reevaluation among War Department officials of why so many U.S. soldiers were being held in government prisons. Men who had been sentenced for inordinate periods of time in military prison for trivial crimes were let go and camps were shut down. This new policy applied to men who had served in the Native Guards and Corps d'Afrique, and who now returned to USCI regiments.[271] Peacetime, however, also afforded time to adjudicate numerous cases free of any distractions, and there were days when dozens of men were tried and convicted for various crimes, ranging from murder to sleeping on post in New Orleans.[272]

John Schuyler Crosby reviewed the number of men who fought under the Department of the Gulf. The four regiments raised by Butler—the 1st–4th Native Guards that were later redesignated the 73d–76th USCI—totaled over three thousand men for the Union cause. The five regiments raised by General Ullman, first absorbed into Banks's Corps d'Afrique and then redesignated the 78th–82d USCI, totaled over four thousand men. Finally, Crosby counted over eight thousand men in the nine regiments raised by Banks and Andrews, which is a gross exaggeration given that their regiments were only made up of five hundred men when filled, and very few were fully manned. Banks's regiments were designated the 83d–90th and 99th USCI by the end of the war. An additional fifteen hundred men served in the artillery and cavalry units, and nearly two thousand joined for sixty days as temporary volunteers. Crosby estimated that the Department of the Gulf recruited nearly nineteen thousand men alone for the U.S. Army, not counting the units raised by Thomas. However, that number seems too high, given the size of Banks's formations during much of the war. Crosby's numbers do show that Black men served in every facet of the Department of the Gulf because of the number of regiments raised in New Orleans and Port Hudson.[273] General Lorenzo Thomas was later recognized for recruiting about 40 percent of all African American soldiers for the USCT by the end of the war, a credit he deserved for all of his work touring the Deep South and fighting for Black soldiers to gain a place in the U.S. Army.[274] All told, Louisiana's forces made a significant contribution to the United States' war effort.

By the end of the war, one of Banks's goals had been realized: only about one hundred of the original Native Guards who had joined the federal army in 1862 remained in the military, largely due to miserable conditions born of racism. Despite his efforts, however, Banks had failed to stop Black men in New Orleans—and all of Louisiana—from demonstrating that they wanted to fight to end slavery. Of the 120 USCI regiments raised in the federal army, thirty-four were from Louisiana; and, of the twenty-two heavy and light artillery regiments raised, three were from the state. Only seven Black cavalry regiments were raised in the entire army, and soldiers from New Orleans supplied one of them.[275] According to an official study conducted by the U.S. Army over a century later, Louisiana supplied 24,052 African American soldiers, the most documented in any state.[276] That study, however, missed the dozens, possibly hundreds, of men who were able to join a white regiment by passing as white or European because of their light skin and knowledge of foreign languages. Hundreds more were combat replacements; as Joseph Wilson attested, it was common for officers to replace dead soldiers with new recruits who were instructed to respond to the dead men's names on the roles.[277] Additionally, because General Butler commissioned so many African American line officers for the first three regiments of the Native Guards, the majority of Black officers in the U.S. Army were from those original regiments.[278]

While not in the military, thousands more supported the army in the Gulf. There were thousands of enslaved people captured while preparing to join the military in Brashear. Thousands more assisted the military but made up often overlooked groups that remain impossible to quantify. Black women, for example, worked as washerwomen, nurses, servants, barbers, sex workers, and many other valuable positions vital to a moving army. Men of color worked extensively in similar roles, but they were also employed directly by military commands as teamsters and aides. For example, General William B. Franklin, the field commander for the XIX Corps in late 1863, ordered all of his artillery batteries to use Black civilians as drivers and wagon pullers to free up white soldiers from that work, and the only limit on their number was that they could not exceed the number of enlisted men in the same battery.[279] There were also men too old or disabled to serve, but they recruited for and aided the regiments during the war.[280] These logistical roles were invaluable to the United States' war effort in the Gulf, and the twenty-four thousand men accounted for by the military severely undercounts the true impact of People of Color in Louisiana who ensured the government's success in the Deep South.

Very few Black and Creole officers were willing to suffer the abuses from Banks, white southerners, and fellow soldiers. Captain Charles Sauvenet, the former translator for the Department of the Gulf who had worked with Butler in August 1862 to reorganize the Native Guards, served longer than any other. He was promoted to captain in 1863 when Banks was removing other officers, and he served as the assistant quartermaster for the 2d Regiment, a role that may have protected him from dismissal since he was not a line officer commanding troops.[281] Captain Louis A. Snear commanded Company B, 2d Corps d'Afrique Infantry Regiment, and he remained in that position when the unit was redesignated the 73d United States Colored Infantry Regiment. He commanded in that role through the beginning of the Reconstruction period.[282] The majority of the former officers became more involved with Louisiana politics as the nation moved into Reconstruction.

Thousands of enlisted men remained in service until well after the war. The army needed them for occupation duty and to combat guerrillas.[283] The men in the first few regiments were the first to muster out as they approached the end of their three years of service, while the majority of those in the USCT still had some time left to serve. The 73d USCI mustered out all of its enlisted men on 23 September 1865, and all of the white officers who had been selected by Banks in 1863 and 1864 were sent to the 96th USCI, since their contracts were not yet fulfilled.[284] The 74th mustered out on 11 October, and the 75th followed a month later on 25 November. The 76th, formerly the 4th Louisiana Native Guards, was the last, with its disbandment scheduled for 31 December. By the end of 1865, the four original regiments that General Butler had constituted in the federal army were out of the military. Many of the additional regiments raised by Generals Banks, Andrews, Ullman, and Thomas soon joined them in 1866.[285] However, the transnational nature of the Civil War meant that European intervention in Latin America was ongoing.[286] The French had invaded Mexico and installed Archduke Maximilian of Austria the previous year, and there was the possibility of an invasion into Texas from the French. Thus, fifty-two thousand men—almost half of whom were serving in USCT regiments—were sent to Texas to defend the country's southern border.[287] Men from Louisiana, Mississippi, and other areas of the Deep South were positioned in Texas to help the government hold the line against possible European invasion.[288] Within two years, Spain abandoned Cuba and France slowly withdrew from Mexico.[289] The high number of Black soldiers in the Gulf slowly reduced after transnational conflicts ceased.

Those who remained in the military going into Reconstruction were stationed throughout the vast area under the Department of the Gulf's control. While some things had improved over the years, overly harsh punishment in the USCT remained consistent, as dozens of men were court-martialed, often for minor offenses.[290] In one case, Private Prince Albert appealed directly to the president when he was punished for not fetching oysters for his commanding officers at Fort Livingston, Louisiana. Private Albert expressed that he had joined the army to do military work, not to fetch oysters for his officers.[291] An anonymous soldier from Company A, 99th USCI, wrote to Stanton in 1866 that their officers were still mistreating them as they had done prior to Port Hudson, and their only task in Florida was fatigue duty from seven in the morning until five at night, with only a one-hour break for lunch.[292] Their treatment did not improve, and in response to repeated requests, in 1866 General Grant decided to move Black troops out of urban areas in the Deep South.[293] Slowly, Black troops were removed from New Orleans, as white soldiers were seen as more palatable to white residents of the city.

"Reconstructed Louisiana" poster (Library of Congress, Prints and Photographs Division)

All People of Color had their own visions of Reconstruction at the end of the war, and the soldiers of New Orleans were no different.[294] In 1865, Reverend Thomas Conway, a former chaplain of the New Orleans USCT, printed a report titled *The Freedmen of Louisiana* detailing what the Department of the Gulf had done and what it still needed to do for the formerly enslaved.[295] Those who had served in the Native Guards worked tirelessly to reform Louisiana after the war.[296] Soldiers of color mustering out of the regiments were not allowed to purchase their weapons for personal use, while white soldiers were.[297] Nevertheless, the 1st Native Guards Regiment, now out of service, formed the 1st District Emancipation Club, with a mission to secure citizenship and equality for African Americans during Reconstruction.[298] Many of the men not in groups such as the Emancipation Club still remained in New Orleans after they were discharged and attempted to effect change on smaller levels.[299] Captain James Ingraham led multiple equal rights conventions and fought for equality and equity for African Americans during Reconstruction.[300] Ingraham, Cailloux, and other former members of the Native Guards were celebrated as leaders in spearheading equal rights organizations in New Orleans both during and after the war.[301] Other former officers, including Emile Detiége, Robert Isabelle, Ernest Morphy, and William Barrett, joined this fight, using their wealth and education to build the movement.[302] Oscar Dunn declared, "We regard all Black and colored men . . . as fellow sufferers" in the contest for Black suffrage.[303] The unity that had emerged before the war had come full circle; Black New Orleanians were once again united against the city's white residents.

Abraham Lincoln's final speech, which he gave at the White House the day he received word that the war had ended, encapsulates what the Native Guards meant to the nation militarily and politically. Lincoln called out the new Louisiana government for not enfranchising African American men, saying, "It is also unsatisfactory to some that the elective franchise is not given to the colored man. I would myself prefer that it were now conferred on the very intelligent, and on those who serve our cause as soldiers."[304] Allegedly, these words convinced John Wilkes Booth that Lincoln intended to enfranchise all Black voters, and that he had to assassinate the president if he wanted to prevent Black men from voting across the nation.[305]

Reconstruction was a painful and traumatic time for Black and Creole people in Louisiana. While there were political gains, such as the right to vote for a time, and social gains that included integrated schools and public transportation, there were also numerous massacres.[306] An 1866 massacre in New

Orleans was so severe that Congress investigated and enacted policies aimed at assuaging racial violence, to compensate for President Andrew Johnson's lack of action.[307] Men who had served as commissioned officers in the Louisiana Native Guards made their way into the state legislature and governor's mansion thanks to a new state constitution that enfranchised Black voters.[308] However, congressional aid came to an end, Black men were slowly removed from office through legal and illegal means, and, by 1873, New Orleans was considered to be the center of what the *New York Times* called the "War of Races" because of the atrocities committed against Black people there by white mobs.[309] By the 1890s, retaliation by white New Orleanians had undone nearly all of the gains for which the Native Guards had fought and died.[310] It represented a failure of the federal government to protect those who had sacrificed to ensure the military's success in Louisiana.

As we look back at the Native Guards, the Corps d'Afrique, and their multiple USCT descendants, we have to remember that these regiments were always an experiment to the federal government. Because they were the first test case for a number of policies, they were analyzed more than other regiments, and the results of these trials were often held up as proof of either Black loyalty or disloyalty. Wilson wrote, "In the light of history and of their own deeds, it can be said that in courage, patriotism and dash, they were second to no troops, either in ancient or modern times." He went on, "They were enlisted after rigid scrutiny, and the examination of every man by competent surgeons. Their acquaintance with the country in which they marched, encamped and fought, made them in many instances superior to the white troops."[311]

For a time, these Louisiana regiments were the most significant group of African American units raised in the U.S. Army. Initially constituted in the New Orleans home guards, their presence spurred Black children to hope for equality and a home in 1861. In that role, they made the federal government question the army's policy on Black soldiers. Their reconstitution in the U.S. Army in 1862 showed President Abraham Lincoln that Black men would volunteer in large numbers if given the chance. The general in chief, Henry Halleck, told Ulysses S. Grant that if Black soldiers were given a chance to prove themselves, the army would be filled with Black regiments. He was correct; after Port Hudson, the War Department immediately constituted dozens more regiments across the nation. Undoubtedly, the USCT would not have grown to the size it did if it had not been for the Native Guards. This impact allowed African Americans to secure numerous rights from the federal government.

To the people of Louisiana, these regiments were their liberators and protectors. The men who served in the Native Guards actively freed enslaved people, including themselves, and they fought against the system of oppression as best they could during and after the Civil War. Those who officered and served in any iteration of these regiments contributed to the uplift of African Americans in Louisiana for decades after the war. Their fight—even though not fully successful in the long term—supported thousands. Funds were raised, communities were formed, labor contracts were disputed, and lives were saved. Richard C. Baylor, a former soldier in the regiments, led a large meeting of the Freedmen's Aid Association attended by hundreds of former members of the regiments. At the meeting, he declared, "We will never stop until we get every right that belongs to us as citizens."[312]

When Wendell Phillips asked Major Francis Dumas why he joined the military, Dumas responded, "I only wish to spend what I have, and fight as long as I can, if only my boy may stand in the street equal to a white boy when the war is over."[313] His wish for a better life for the next generation was shared by nearly every man who joined the Native Guards and woman who assisted the U.S. Army in the Deep South. In large measure, they realized that goal: because of the efforts of every member of the Native Guards, Corps d'Afrique, and Louisiana USCT, thousands of children were born free and afforded rights that their ancestors had been deprived of prior to the Civil War. Their sacrifices have not been forgotten.

Conclusion

# *THE MAN FALLS! THE PRINCIPLE LIVES!*

## THE MEMORY OF THE LOUISIANA NATIVE GUARDS

When the 73d United States Colored Infantry returned home, they did so as heroes—soldiers of color who had fought in every major battle of the Department of the Gulf since September 1862. A poem penned under the pseudonym Palmetto and dedicated to the regiment shows what they meant to residents of New Orleans and to African Americans in Louisiana:

Welcome ye sable heroes!
With swords and bayonets bright;
Plumed in war's regalias—
Ye victors of the fight.
Then welcome home, ye gallant boys,
Ye sable boys in blue.
With bayonets bright,
You've won the fight.
We gladly welcome you.

What though the flag be tattered,
Fling it to the breeze.
What though your ranks are shattered,
They tell of victories.
Thrice welcome home, ye gallant boys,
Ye sable boys in blue.
Right shoulder shift with bayonets bright,
We gladly welcome you.

Port Hudson's blood-stained hills,
And labyrinthine bayous,
And brooks and streams and murmuring rills,
All wait the brave Cailloux.
Then welcome home, ye gallant boys,
Ye sable boys in blue.
Charge left, charge right,
We gladly welcome you.

The brazen guns are muzzled now,
The bugle blasts no more.
In the distant sky the promised bow
Of peace is bending o'er.
Thrice welcome home, ye gallant boys,
Ye sable boys in blue.
With bayonets bright
You've won the fight;
We gladly welcome you.[1]

From their initial constitution in the United States' volunteer forces, the Native Guards were a test for the federal government. General Benjamin Butler knew this, and Salmon P. Chase praised the regiments for demonstrating their validity in 1862.[2] However, the true test for the Native Guards was not simply to show that they could be soldiers, but that they were men equal to everyone else in the army. A former lieutenant of the 1st Regiment, Ernest Longpre, wrote, "Had these two regiments failed, or destiny betrayed their courage, the colored troops would have been universally condemned, and would not have been employed as soldiers, but used as servants, drivers, and laborers on fortifications, bridges, and ditches."[3] Halleck, Stanton, and Lincoln all came to recognize the competence and determination of African American soldiers. They helped to secure service for nearly 200,000 Black men during the American Civil War, and their impact on Louisiana and African American history cannot be overstated. From their constitution in the Department of the Gulf to the last day of the Civil War, the Native Guards participated in every major engagement in Louisiana.[4] They fought for Black autonomy and citizenship, struggling until they died for Black society and a country that was extremely racist against them. In 1955, the U.S. Army published a study about the use of manpower and mobilization during war. The officers who conducted the study wrote, "The question of whether Negroes should serve in the armed forces of the United States was settled affirmatively during the Civil War."[5] The authors of the study acknowledged that the first soldiers of color in the federal army were recruited in Louisiana, and the authors credited the Louisiana Native Guards with setting the foundation for all Black service members who continue to serve the United States of America today.

At a séance in 1872, Captain Henry Louis Rey invoked Captain André Cailloux's spirit: "The man falls! The principle lives!"[6] The memory of the Louisiana Native Guards has indeed lived on in New Orleans in one form or another since the Civil War. African Americans, more than any other group, have worked to preserve the accuracy and significance of that memory. As early as May 1865, the *New Orleans Tribune* corrected a Tennessee newspaper when it reported that Major Martin R. Delany was the army's first Black major, noting that Major Francis Dumas was serving in the 2d Regiment well before Delaney donned the uniform.[7] Shortly after the victory of the 73d USCI at Fort Blakely, one writer reflected, "The services of the 73d will be recorded for ever on the pages of American history. They will be mentioned for centuries to come."[8] For the remainder of the nineteenth century, those who fought

Emancipation Memorial
(Library of Congress, Prints and Photographs Division)

in the federal army kept the memory of the Native Guards alive. After the Civil War, Black men continued to be recruited in New Orleans to join the Regular Army, albeit in fewer numbers; and they served in various roles during Reconstruction.[9] Former soldiers of the Native Guards and their families remained friends and worked with one another against a white populace that wanted to curtail the rights they had fought for during the war.[10] After the failures of Reconstruction, Black people in New Orleans remembered who had fought for them. Today, the history of the regiments is included in some high school curricula, and many people from Louisiana are aware of their history. However, their impact remains relatively unknown outside of Louisiana and the field of Civil War historiography. A notable exception are historians of the Lost Cause who invoke the Native Guards as proof of loyal Black Confederates—a false idea that recent research, including this book, has debunked.[11]

Today, we must actively discuss and celebrate the contributions and legacies of these units in order to ensure that their sacrifices occupy an appropriately prominent place in our ever-evolving narratives of the events that have shaped U.S. history. The actions of the Native Guards were profound, not simply because of their victories in battle but because they fought to show that Black people deserved full rights of citizenship in the United States. Recall that President Lincoln ended the first year of the war with a request to Congress to appropriate funds and land for the relocation and colonization of free Blacks living in the South. When he made that address, Lincoln knew that Butler and Farragut were poised to liberate New Orleans. There was a justified fear that he planned to use the military to force free African Americans out of the city in 1862. However, the conviction and economic power of the members of the city's African American society were too strong for such a maneuver; they were deeply entrenched in every facet of Louisianan life. Once members of that same society were authorized to join the military, their place in the United States was all but secured. Butler came to believe that men of color deserved to serve, even volunteering to command other USCT regiments during the war. After the war, Butler argued that Black soldiers should be integrated into the military and not put in segregated units, as the Reconstruction government did.[12] In Lafourche and Port Hudson, the Native Guards also demonstrated to skeptics—Banks, other officials in the War Department, and northerners more broadly—that African Americans were not fearful of whites or combat.

In February 2022, Senator Cory Booker introduced a bill titled the United States Colored Troops Congressional Gold Medal Act.[13] If the act passes, all soldiers of color will be posthumously awarded the Congressional Gold Medal for their service to the U.S. Army. The members of the Native Guards are also long overdue for more specific praise and recognition from the state of Louisiana and the U.S. Congress. It is one of the aims of this book to provide source material that paves the way toward these forms of formal recognition.

The Louisiana Native Guards were the most significant military experiment undertaken by the federal government during the Civil War. Federal authorities recognized the value of the regiments as early as 1862, and President Abraham Lincoln acknowledged that value when he advised the Louisiana governor to grant the men serving in the regiments the right to vote. This would have made them the first African Americans to be granted the right to vote in a former Confederate territory. Despite the refusal of state legislators to enfranchise the soldiers, Lincoln continued to push to grant them suffrage because he recognized their historic significance, and he made his calls for their enfranchisement public knowledge at the end of the war.

Perhaps most important of all, the officers and soldiers who served in these regiments knew that they had fought to create a better country for their descendants. During the war, Major Francis Dumas expressed a fervent desire to give the nation's Black children opportunities that African Americans had never been afforded. He and every soldier who served in the Native Guards, Corps d'Afrique, African Descent Regiments, and United States Colored Troops achieved that dream through their service.

Louisiana Heritage monument
(Photo by A. J. Cade)

# *APPENDIX*

## AFRICAN AMERICAN UNITS OF LOUISIANA

While researching the Louisiana Native Guards, I often had to reread sources to clarify the numerous designations and locations of the regiments and their sister units. I therefore created a table of all the USCT units raised in Louisiana by time period and location. The table on the following pages details every unit, beginning with the Louisiana Native Guards, followed by the Corps d'Afrique and General Lorenzo Thomas's African Descent regiments. The official designation of each unit is followed by the date each organization was completed and the location of the organization. Some units were redesignated multiple times. An examination of all these units was necessary, as this book is not only about the Native Guards but their transformation of African American society during the war. Every single regiment raised in Louisiana after them was based on the foundation created by the first four regiments. Taken with the preceding pages, this appendix serves to complete the history of the African American regiments of New Orleans and the surrounding areas.

African American Units of Louisiana

| Designation | Organization in the Army | Location | Redesignation | Date of Redesignation | 2nd Redesignation | Date of Redesignation | 3rd Redesignation | Date of Redesignation | End of Active Service | List of Battles Credited to Members | Page in Army Register |
|---|---|---|---|---|---|---|---|---|---|---|---|
| 1st Infantry Regiment Louisiana Native Guards (Colored) | 27 September 1862 | New Orleans, LA | 1st Infantry Regiment, Corps d'Afrique | 6 June 1863 | 73d Regiment Infantry, USCT | 4 April 1864 | — | — | Consolidated with 96th USCI, 23 September 1865 | Port Hudson, Jackson, Bayou Tunica, On Steamer, City Belle, Morganza, Fort Blakely | 246–247 |
| 2d Infantry Regiment Louisiana Native Guards (Colored) | 12 October 1862 | New Orleans, LA | 2d Infantry Regiment, Corps d'Afrique | 6 June 1863 | 74th Regiment Infantry, USCT | 4 April 1864 | — | — | Consolidated with 91st USCI, 7 July 1864 | East Pascagoula | 248–249 |
| 3d Infantry Regiment Louisiana Native Guards (Colored) | 24 November 1862 | New Orleans, LA | 3d Infantry Regiment, Corps d'Afrique | 6 June 1863 | 75th Regiment Infantry, USCT | 4 April 1864 | — | — | 25 November 1865, end of three-year service | Jackson, Port Hudson, Pleasant Hill, Waterloo | 250–251 |
| 4th Infantry Regiment Louisiana Native Guards (Colored) | 10 February–6 March 1863 | New Orleans, LA | 4th Infantry Regiment, Corps d'Afrique | 6 June 1863 | 76th Regiment Infantry, USCT | 4 April 1864 | — | — | 31 December 1865, end of three-year service | Fort Blakely | 252 |

| | | | | | | | | | | | |
|---|---|---|---|---|---|---|---|---|---|---|---|
| 5th Infantry Regiment, Corps d'Afrique | 8 December 1863 | Fort St. Philip | 77th Regiment Infantry, USCT | 4 April 1864 | — | — | — | — | Consolidated with the 10th USHA, 1 October 1865 | Amite River | 253 |
| 6th Infantry Regiment, Corps d'Afrique | 4 September 1863 | Port Hudson | 78th Regiment Infantry, USCT | 4 April 1864 | — | — | — | — | 6 January 1866, end of eervice (early) | Port Hudson, Jackson | 254 |
| 7th Infantry Regiment, Corps d'Afrique | 31 August 1863 | Port Hudson | 79th Regiment Infantry, USCT | 4 April 1864 | — | — | — | — | Broken up 28 July 1864; all soldiers and officers sent to other New Orleans USCT units | Port Hudson | 255 |
| 8th Infantry Regiment, Corps d'Afrique | 1 September 1863 | Port Hudson | 80th Regiment Infantry, USCT | 4 April 1864 | — | — | — | — | 1 March 1867, one of the few that completed more than three years of service | Port Hudson | 257–258 |

*continued*

| Designation | Organization in the Army | Location | Redesignation | Date of Redesignation | 2nd Redesignation | Date of Redesignation | 3rd Redesignation | Date of Redesignation | End of Active Service | List of Battles Credited to Members | Page in Army Register |
|---|---|---|---|---|---|---|---|---|---|---|---|
| 9th Infantry Regiment, Corps d'Afrique | 2 September 1863 | Port Hudson | 81st Regiment Infantry, USCT | 4 April 1864 | — | — | — | — | 30 November 1866, end of three-year service | Port Hudson | 259 |
| 10th Infantry Regiment, Corps d'Afrique | 1 September 1863 | Port Hudson | 82d Regiment Infantry, USCT | 4 April 1864 | — | — | — | — | 10 September 1866, end of three-year service | Port Hudson, Barrancas, Mariana, Mitchell's Creek, Pine Barren Ford, Fort Blakely | 260 |
| 11th Infantry Regiment, Corps d'Afrique | 17 August 1863 | Port Hudson | 83d Regiment Infantry, USCT | 4 April 1864 | — | — | — | — | Broken up 28 July 1864; all soldiers and officers sent to other New Orleans USCT units | None | 261 |
| 12th Infantry Regiment, Corps d'Afrique | 24 Septeber–16 October 1863 | Port Hudson | 84th Regiment Infantry, USCT | 4 April 1864 | — | — | — | — | 14 March 1866, end of three-year service | Morganza | 263–264 |

| | | | | | | | | | | | |
|---|---|---|---|---|---|---|---|---|---|---|---|
| 13th Infantry Regiment, Corps d'Afrique | 11 March 1864 | New Orleans, LA | 85th Regiment Infantry, USCT | 4 April 1864 | — | — | — | — | Consolidated with the 77th USCI, 24 March 1864, after failure to complete organization | None | 265 |
| 14th Infantry Regiment, Corps d'Afrique | 12 August–3 September 1863 | New Orleans, LA | 86th Regiment Infantry, USCT | 4 April 1864 | — | — | — | — | 10 April 1866, end of three-year service | Fort Blakely | 266 |
| 15th Infantry Regiment, Corps d'Afrique | 27 August 1863 | New Orleans, LA | 5th Regiment Engineers, Corps d'Afrique | 10 February 1864 | 99th Regiment Infantry, USCT | 4 April 1864 | — | — | Consolidated into a battalion in December 1865, mustered out 23 April 1866, end of three-year service | Natural Bridge, Steamer Alliance | 280 |
| 16th Infantry Regiment, Corps d'Afrique | 8–16 October 1863 | New Orleans, LA | 87th Regiment Infantry, USCT | 4 April 1864 | — | — | — | — | Consolidated with the 95th USCI to form the 81st and 87th USCI, 26 November 1864 | None | 267 |

*continued*

| Designation | Organization in the Army | Location | Redesignation | Date of Redesignation | 2nd Redesignation | Date of Redesignation | 3rd Redesignation | Date of Redesignation | End of Active Service | List of Battles Credited to Members | Page in Army Register |
|---|---|---|---|---|---|---|---|---|---|---|---|
| 81st Infantry Regiment, USCT | 26 November 1864 | New Orleans, LA | 87th Regiment Infantry, USCT | 19 December 1864 | — | — | — | — | Consolidated with the 84th USCI, 31 August 1865 | None | 268 |
| 17th Infantry Regiment, Corps d'Afrique | 24 September 1863 | Port Hudson | 88th Regiment Infantry, USCT | 4 April 1864 | — | — | — | — | Broken up 28 July 1864; all soldiers and officers sent to other New Orleans USCT units | None | 269 |
| 18th Infantry Regiment, Corps d'Afrique | 9 October–8 November 1863 | Port Hudson | 89th Regiment Infantry, USCT | 4 April 1864 | — | — | — | — | Broken up 28 July 1864; all soldiers and officers sent to other New Orleans USCT units | None | 271 |
| 19th Infantry Regiment, Corps d'Afrique | 11 February 1864 | Madi-sonville, LA | 90th Regiment Infantry, USCT | 4 April 1864 | — | — | — | — | Broken up 28 July 1864; all soldiers and officers sent to other New Orleans [illegible] | None | 272 |

| | | | | | | | | | | | |
|---|---|---|---|---|---|---|---|---|---|---|---|
| 20th Infantry Regiment, Corps d'Afrique | 1 September 1863 | Fort Pike, LA | 91st Regiment Infantry, USCT | 4 April 1864 | — | — | — | — | Consolidated with the 74th USCI, 7 July 1864 | Bayou St. Louis | 273 |
| 22th Infantry Regiment, Corps d'Afrique | 30 September–24 October 1863 | New Orleans, LA | 92d Regiment Infantry, USCT | 4 April 1864 | — | — | — | — | 31 December 1865, end of three-year service | Red River Expedition | 274 |
| 25th Infantry Regiment, Corps d'Afrique | 21 November 1863 | New Iberia, LA | 93d Regiment Infantry, USCT | 4 April 1864 | — | — | — | — | Broken up 23 June 1865 because of incompetent officers, enlisted men; transferred to 81st and 82d USCI | Ash Bayou | 275 |
| | | | | | | | | | | | |
| 1st Regiment Louisiana Heavy Artillery, African Descent | 29 November 1862 | New Orleans, LA | 1st Regiment Heavy Artillery, Corps d'Afrique | 19 November 1863 | 7th Regiment, USCHA | 4 April 1864 | 10th Regiment, USCHA | 21 May 1864 | 22 February 1867, served the longest of the 1862 regiments | Pass Manchac | 157–1586 |

*continued*

| Designation | Organization in the Army | Location | Redesignation | Date of Redesignation | 2nd Redesignation | Date of Redesignation | 3rd Redesignation | Date of Redesignation | End of Active Service | List of Battles Credited to Members | Page in Army Register |
|---|---|---|---|---|---|---|---|---|---|---|---|
| 1st Regiment Cavalry, Corps d'Afrique | 12 September 1863 | New Orleans, LA | 4th Regiment Cavalry, USCC | 4 April 1864 | — | — | — | — | 20 March 1866, end of three-year service | Clinton | 144 |
| | | | | | | | | | | | |
| 1st Regiment Engineers, Corps d'Afrique | 28 April 1863 | Camp Parepet | 95th Regiment Infantry, USCT | 4 April 1864 | — | — | — | — | Split to form 3d Engineers Regiment, 26 August 1863; 95th USCI consolidated with 87th USCI, 26 November 1864 | Port Hudson | 276 |
| 2d Regiment Engineers, Corps d'Afrique | 15 August 1863 | New Orleans, LA | 96th Regiment Infantry, USCT | 4 April 1864 | — | — | — | — | 29 January 1866, end of three-year service | Fort Gaines | 277 |
| 3d Regiment Engineers, Corps d'Afrique | 26 August 1863 | New Orleans, LA | 97th Regiment Infantry, USCT | 4 April 1864 | — | — | — | — | 6 April 1866, end of three-year service | Pine Barren Creek | 278 |

| | | | | | | | | | | | |
|---|---|---|---|---|---|---|---|---|---|---|---|
| 4th Regiment Engineers, Corps d'Afrique | 3 September 1863–3 March 1864 | Camp Parepet | 98th Regiment Infantry, USCT | 4 April 1864 | — | — | — | — | Consolidated with the 78th USCI, 26 August 1865; excess men sent to 92d USCI | Berwick and Natchez | 279 |
| | | | | | | | | | | | |
| 5th Regiment Louisiana Volunteers, African Descent | — | New Orleans, LA | — | — | — | — | — | — | Failed to complete organization due to recruiting problems | — | — |
| 6th Regiment Louisiana Volunteers, African Descent | 4 July 1863 | New Orleans, LA | — | — | — | — | — | — | 13 August 1863, mustered in for 60 days to protect Department of the Gulf during the summer | None | 317 |
| 7th Regiment Louisiana Volunteers, African Descent | 10 July 1863 | New Orleans, LA | — | — | — | — | — | — | 6 August 1863, mustered in for 60 days to protect Department of the Gulf during the summer | None | 318 |

*continued*

| Designation | Organization in the Army | Location | Redesignation | Date of Redesignation | 2nd Redesignation | Date of Redesignation | 3rd Redesignation | Date of Redesignation | End of Active Service | List of Battles Credited to Members | Page in Army Register |
|---|---|---|---|---|---|---|---|---|---|---|---|
| 7th Regiment Louisiana Volunteers, African Descent | 1 December 1863 | Holly Springs, MS and Island No. 10, TN | 64th Regiment Infantry, USCT | 11 March 1864 | — | — | — | — | 13 March 1866, end of three-year service | Ashwood Landing, Point Pleasant, Pine Bluff, Davis' Bend, Helena | 237 |
| 8th Regiment Louisiana Volunteers, African Descent | 5 May 1863 | Lake Provi-dence, LA | 47th Regiment Infantry, USCT | 11 March 1864 | — | — | — | — | 5 January 1866, end of three-year service | Lake Providence, Liverpool Heights, Yazoo City, Fort Blakely | 220 |
| 9th Regiment Louisiana Volunteers, African Descent | 7 August 1863–7 January 1864 | Vicks-burg, MS | 1st Regiment Mississippi Heavy Artillery, African Descent | 26 September 1863 | 4th Regiment, USCHA | 11 March 1864 | 5th Regiment, USCHA | 26 April 1864 | 20 May 1866, end of three-year service | Milliken's Bend and Vicksburg | 152–153 |
| 9th Regiment Louisiana Volunteers, African Descent | 19 November–14 December 1863 | Vicks-burg, MS and Good-rich's Landing, LA | 63d Regiment Infantry, USCT | 11 March 1864 | — | — | — | — | 9 January 1866, end of three-year service | Waterproof, Ashwood, Camp Marengo | 236 |

| | | | | | | | | | | | |
|---|---|---|---|---|---|---|---|---|---|---|---|
| 10th Regiment Louisiana Volunteers, African Descent | 6 May–8 August 1863 | Lake Provi-dence and Good-rich's Landing, LA | 48th Regiment Infantry, USCT | 11 March 1864 | — | — | — | — | 4 January 1866, end of three-year service | Bayou Tensas, Vicksburg, Fort Blakely | 221 |
| 11th Regiment Louisiana Volunteers, African Descent | 23 May–22 August 1863 | Mil-liken's Bend, LA | 49th Regiment Infantry, USCT | 11 March 1864 | — | — | — | — | 22 March 1866, end of three-year service | Milliken's Bend and Waterproof | 222 |
| 12th Regiment Louisiana Volunteers, African Descent | 23 May–22 August 1863 | Vicks-burg, MS | 50th Regiment Infantry, USCT | 11 March 1864 | — | — | — | — | 20 March 1866, end of three-year service | Fort Blakely | 223 |
| | | | | | | | | | | | |
| 1st Battery Louisiana Light Artillery, African Descent | 6 November 1863 | Hebron's Planta-tion, MS | Battery A, 2d Regiment, USCLA | 11 March 1864 | Battery C, 2d Regiment, USCLA | 26 April 18684 | — | — | 28 December 1865, end of service (early) | None | 165 |

*continued*

| Designation | Organization in the Army | Location | Redesignation | Date of Redesignation | 2nd Redesignation | Date of Redesignation | 3rd Redesignation | Date of Redesignation | End of Active Service | List of Battles Credited to Members | Page in Army Register |
|---|---|---|---|---|---|---|---|---|---|---|---|
| 2d Battery Louisiana Light Artillery, African Descent | 21 December 1863 | Black River, MS | Battery B, 2d Regiment, USCLA | 11 March 1864 | Battery D, 2d Regiment, USCLA | 26 April 18684 | — | — | 28 December 1865, end of service (early) | None | 166 |
| 3d Battery Louisiana Light Artillery, African Descent | December 1, 1863 | Helena, AK | Battery C, 2d Regiment, USCLA | 11 March 1864 | Battery E, 2d Regiment, USCLA | 26 April 18684 | — | — | 26 September 1865, end of service (early) | Island No. 76 and Big Creek | 166 |

Source: *Official Army Register of the Volunteer Force of the United States Army for the Years 1861, '62, '63, '64, '64*, Part VIII (Washington, DC: Adjunct General's Office, 1867).

# *NOTES*

### *Abbreviations*

| | |
|---|---|
| CMSR | Compiled Military Service Records of Volunteer Union Soldiers Who Served the United States Colored Troops: 56th–138th USCT |
| FWP | Federal Writers' Project: Slave Narrative Project |
| HNOC | The Historic New Orleans Collection |
| LLL | Law Library of Louisiana |
| LOC | Library of Congress |
| LSA | Louisiana State Archives |
| LSU | Louisiana State University |
| MHS | Massachusetts Historical Society |
| NARA | National Archives and Records Administration |
| *OR* | *The War of the Rebellion: A Compilation of the Official Records of the Union and Confederate Armies* |
| *ORN* | *Official Records of the Union and Confederate Navies in the War of Rebellion* |
| TU | Tulane University |
| UNO | University of New Orleans |
| USCC | United States Colored Cavalry |
| USCHA | United States Colored Heavy Artillery |
| USCI | United States Colored Infantry |
| USCLA | United States Colored Light Artillery |
| USCT | United States Colored Troops |

### *Introduction*

1. "Frederick Douglass on the War: An Interesting Meeting at the Cooper Institute," *New York Times*, 13 February 1862.

2. Hall, *Africans in Colonial Louisiana*, 29.

3. Section LIV, Le Code Noir, ou Édit du Roi, Servant de Règlement pour le Gouvernement et l'administration de la Justice, Police, Discipline et le Commerce des Esclaves Nègres dans la Province et Colonie de la Loüisianne, 14 March 1724, LLL.

4. Bonnefoy, "Colonial Militia, Color and Local Forms of Urban Belonging," 7–8.

5. Hilton, "Spanish Louisiana in Atlantic Contexts," 77.

6. Cooper, *The Militia and the National Guard in America Since Colonial Times*, 51, 64.

7. "Address from the Free People of Color," January 1804, in MacGregor and Nalty, eds., *Blacks in the United States Armed Forces*, 1:198.

8. Berry, "Negro Troops in Blue and Gray," 166.

9. "Corps of Militia Act," 6 September 1812, *Acts of the General Assembly of Louisiana*, first session, 1812, in Nalty and MacGregor, eds., *Blacks in the United States Armed Forces*, 1:207.

10. "Proclamation to the Free Colored Inhabitants of Louisiana," 21 September 1814, *Niles Weekly Register*, 3 December 1814, in Nalty and MacGregor, eds., *Blacks in the Military*, 16.

11. Brady, *Chained to History*, 21.

12. Pierce, *Making the White Man's West*, 231.

13. Cooper, *The Militia and the National Guard in America Since Colonial Times*, 43.

14. Quarles, *Black Abolitionists*, 83.

15. "An Act to Prohibit the Emancipation of Slaves," Act of 6 March 1857, *Louisiana Acts*, 1857, LLL, 55.

16. "The Great Rebellion—The Beginning of the End," *New York Times*, 15 April 1861.

17. Ibid.; "The Great Conflict," *New York Times*, 20 April 1861.

18. "The Freedmen of the South—What Shall Be Done with Them?" *New York Times*, 6 March 1862.

19. Hollandsworth, *The Louisiana Native Guards.*

20. Trouillot, *Silencing the Past*, 26.

21. Weaver, ed., *Thank God my Regiment an African One*, xx.

22. Trouillot, *Silencing the Past*, 29.

23. For more information, see Johnson, *Soul by Soul*, 10–12.

24. Irwin, *History of the Nineteenth Army Corps.* It is quite shocking how well Irwin removed Black regiments from the history of the Department of the Gulf. He has an extensive appendix that shows all the white units in the corps every few months, but the Native Guards are only mentioned once. After the summer of 1863, he does not list any of the nearly two dozen Black regiments in the corps even though they served in all of the major campaigns of the department.

25. Pinheiro, *The Families' Civil War;* Mendez, *A Great Sacrifice.*

26. Burton, *Melting Pot Soldiers;* Jacobson, *Whiteness of a Different Color.* For more information on the varying forms of white identity and the use of military service in the Civil War to bring them together, see both of these works.

27. See Blyden, *African Americans and Africa*, for an excellent discussion on the power of these terms for those of African descent in the United States.

28. Hall, *Africans in Colonial Louisiana*, 158.

29. "Slaves Burned in Louisiana—Testimony of a European Savant," *National Anti-Slavery Standard* (New York), 2 August 1862.

30. For more information about the historical use of the phrase "People of Color," see Milteer, *Beyond Slavery's Shadow*, 9–10.

31. Wilson, *The Black Phalanx*, dedication, 96.

### *1. The Black Mantle of Slavery*

1. Quoted in Daggett, "Spiritualism Among Creoles of Color in Nineteenth-Century New Orleans," 431.

2. "Fort Sumpter Fallen" [*sic*], *New York Times*, 15 April 1861.

3. "The Great Rebellion—The Beginning of the End," *New York Times*, 15 April 1861.

4. Section 9.4, Constitution of the Confederate States of America, in Richardson, *A Compilation of the Messages and Papers of the Confederacy . . .*, Lilian Goldman Law Library, Yale University.

5. Alexander H. Stephens, 21 March 1861, in Cleveland, *Alexander H. Stephens*, 717–729. Stephens was elected vice president of the Confederacy at the time he gave this speech.

6. Doyle, *The Cause of All Nations*, 36.

7. "Our Washington Correspondence," *National Anti-Slavery Standard* (New York), 5 January 1861.

8. "The Black Mantle of Slavery," *National Anti-Slavery Standard* (New York), 2 August 1862.

9. *West Indian* (Bridgetown, Barbados), 6 December 1861.

10. Multiple bills of sale and purchase in the Thomas O. Moore Papers, Mss. 305, 893, 1094, LSU (hereafter cited as Moore Papers).

11. Thomas Moore Speech to the Louisiana Legislature, 23 January 1860, Moore Papers.

12. Untitled manuscript in the Moore Papers, Mss. 305, 893, 1094.

13. "Meeting of the Louisiana Legislature—The Governor's Message," *Royal Gazette* (Hamilton, Bermuda), 14 February 1860.

14. Draft of Governor Moore's Speech to the Secession Convention, Moore Papers.

15. Militia Summoning Document, No. 3331, 30 October 1860, Moore Papers.

16. John A. Winston to Governor Andrew B. Moore, 2 January 1861, *OR*, Ser. 4, vol. 1, 1.

17. Thomas Moore to Joseph A. Haskin, 10 January 1861, *OR*, Ser. 1, vol. 1, 490.

18. "The Surrender and Recapture of the Arsenal," *New York Herald*, 18 August 1862.

19. "Summary of the Principal Events," *OR*, Ser. 1, vol. 1, 489.

20. "Message of the Governor of Louisiana to the State Legislature," 22 January 1861, *OR*, Ser. 1, vol. 1, 494.

21. "Arrangements for the Inauguration of Mr. Lincoln at Washington," *New York Herald*, 5 February 1861.

22. "The Convention Election," *Weekly Delta* (New Orleans), 23 February 1861, LSA.

23. Ward, *Garden of Ruins*, 15.

24. "Independent Louisiana," *Gazette and Sentinel* (Iberville, Louisiana), 2 February 1861.

25. "The Feeling in New Orleans," *New Orleans Daily Crescent*, reprinted in *Gazette and Sentinel* (Iberville, Louisiana), 2 February 1861.

26. "Louisiana Legislature," *New Orleans Daily Crescent*, 25 January 1861.

27. Eliot, Shellabarger, and Boyer, *Report of the Select Committee on the New Orleans Riots*, 35.

28. "Dispatch to the New York Associated Press," *Royal Gazette* (Hamilton, Bermuda), 5 February 1861.

29. Casso, *Louisiana Legacy*, 65. See Casso for additional information regarding the early years of Louisiana's militias.

30. Clara Solomon, 6 July 1861, in Ashkenazi, ed., *The Civil War Diary of Clara Solomon*, 58.

31. "A Tennessee Politician on the Crisis," *Nashville Union and American*, 6 December 1860.

32. See Winters, *The Civil War in Louisiana*, 15–17, for the varying number and designations of militia units that formed early in Louisiana.

33. Berry, "Negro Troops in Blue and Gray," 166.

34. Hepworth, *The Whip, Hoe, and Sword*, 78.

35. "New Orleans and Pensacola," *Christian Recorder* (Philadelphia), 15 June 1861.

36. "Reorganization of the Ancient Volunteer Companies," *New Orleans Daily Crescent*, 25 January 1861.

37. *Daily Picayune* (New Orleans), 21 April 1861.

38. "Military Notices," *New Orleans Daily Crescent,* 27 April 1861.

39. *Daily True Delta* (New Orleans), 23 April 1861.

40. Berry, "Negro Troops in Blue and Gray," 166–167.

41. Thomas Moore to The State of Louisiana, May 1861, Butler Papers, LOC.

42. *New Orleans Daily Crescent,* 29 May 1861.

43. Proclamation by the Governor, 21 April 1861, *OR,* Ser. 4, vol. 1, 748.

44. For further information, see Levin, *Searching for Black Confederates,* 45.

45. Berry, "Negro Troops in Blue and Gray," 167.

46. "Military Items," *New Orleans Daily Crescent,* 27 April 1861.

47. *Daily True Delta* (New Orleans), 23 April 1861. Chalmette is a reference to the Battle of New Orleans battle site.

48. Daggett, "Spiritualism Among Creoles of Color in Nineteenth-Century New Orleans," 410–414.

49. Berry, "Negro Troops in Blue and Gray," 168.

50. Nystrom, *New Orleans After the Civil War,* 19–20.

51. Winters, *The Civil War in Louisiana,* 39.

52. Josephine B. Lewis testimony, 23 April 1919, in Emma Barrett Pension File, 1119719, NARA.

53. Daggett, "Spiritualism Among Creoles of Color in Nineteenth-Century New Orleans," 416.

54. Ochs, *A Black Patriot and a White Priest,* 68.

55. Winters, *The Civil War in Louisiana,* 34.

56. Wilson, *The Black Phalanx,* 482.

57. Special Order No. 281, 18 March 1862, Williamsburg, 494, Mss. 83434, box 5, Gladstone Collection, LOC.

58. "The Way It Works," *Pomeroy Weekly Telegraph* (Ohio), 20 December 1861.

59. "Carry Arms," *Weekly Trinity Journal* (Weaverville, Calif.), 2 February 1861.

60. Receipt of Slave to Work on Fortifications, 129, Mss. 83434, box 1, Gladstone Collection, LOC.

61. Milteer, *Beyond Slavery's Shadow,* 227.

62. Glatthaar and Crowder, "The Civil War Through the Eyes of a Sixteen-Year-Old Black Officer," 203–204.

63. "River News, &c." *Des Arc Semi-Weekly Citizen* (Arkansas), 31 May 1861.

64. "American Sketches from the South," *Antigua Observer* (St. John's, Antigua), 26 July 1861.

65. Dinah Watson, "Slave Narratives," 145, FWP, vol. 16, Texas, part 4, LOC.

66. "American Sketches from the South," *Antigua Observer* (St. John's, Antigua), 26 July 1861.

67. *Opelousas Patriot* (Louisiana), 21 September 1861.

68. Quoted in Quarles, *The Negro in the Civil War,* 51, 63.

69. *Daily Picayune* (New Orleans), 8 January 1862.

70. Before the Union army liberated the city of New Orleans, the Native Guards militia unit reported thirty-six officers and 870 enlisted men; however, not all of those officers were Black.

71. Testimony of Charles W. Gibbons, 25 December 1866, quoted in Hollandsworth, *The Louisiana Native Guards,* 4.

72. Ward, *Garden of Ruins,* 41.

73. Quoted in Pierson, *Mutiny at Fort Jackson,* 38.

74. Russell, *My Diary North and South,* 250.

75. Pierson, *Mutiny at Fort Jackson,* 38.

76. Bell Griffith to his family, 21 April 1861, Bell Griffith Letters, Mss. 2428, LSU.

77. Russell, *My Diary North and South,* 250.

78. Quoted in Pierson, *Mutiny at Fort Jackson,* 54.

79. "Terrible Despotism in the South-West," *National Anti-Slavery Standard* (New York), 8 June 1861.

80. Pierson, *Mutiny at Fort Jackson,* 55. For more information about how widespread white Unionists were in the Deep South, see Butler, *True Blue.*

81. Elizabeth Ross Hite, Slave Narratives, N1976-018, microfilm, LSA.

82. "A Negro Preacher Hung," *National Anti-Slavery Standard* (New York), 15 June 1861.

83. Testimony of General Benjamin Butler, "Report of the Freedmen's Inquiry Commission, May 15, 1864," in Woodward, comp., *The Negro in the Military Service of the United States, 1639–1886,* 2552, Microfilm-858, Records of the Adjutant General's Office, 1780s–1917, RG 94, NARA.

84. Orders No. 1147, Adjutant General's Office, Louisiana Militia, 28 September 1861, in *Opelousas Patriot* (Louisiana), 12 October 1861 (emphasis added).

85. Ward, *Garden of Ruins,* 27.

86. "The Black List," *New Orleans Daily Crescent,* 24 October 1861.

87. "Hayti and Immigration Thither," *Daily Picayune* (New Orleans), 16 July 1859.

88. Quoted in Hollandsworth, *Louisiana Native Guards,* 4–5.

89. Horne, *Negro Comrades of the Crown,* 167.

90. "The Free Blacks of America," *Antigua Observer* (St. John's, Antigua), 16 August 1860.

91. East Pascagoula Hotel advertisement, May 1861, John S. Billiu Letters, Mss. 4941, LSU.

92. John Billiu to his wife, 15 June 1861, John S. Billiu Letters, Mss. 4941, LSU.

93. Proclamation by the Governor, 21 April 1861, *OR,* Ser. 4, vol. 1, 748.

94. M. Grivot to Thomas Moore, 22 November 1861, *OR,* Ser. 4, vol. 1, 752.

95. Earl F. Niehaus, "The Irish in New Orleans," 391, LSA.

96. "Colored Soldiers—Fears of Insurrection," *National Anti-Slavery Standard* (New York), 8 June 1861.

97. Ochs, *A Black Patriot and a White Priest,* 72.

98. Wilson, *The Black Phalanx,* 96.

99. "The Views of Massachusetts," *Christian Recorder* (Philadelphia), 19 January 1861.

100. "Will the Negroes Rise?," *National Anti-Slavery Standard* (New York), 8 June 1861, reprinted from the *New York Tribune.*

101. Pierson, *Mutiny at Fort Jackson,* 74.

102. Quoted in ibid., 75.

103. "Search Your Negro Quarters," *National Anti-Slavery Standard* (New York), 15 June 1861.

104. Duganne, *Camps and Prisons,* 49.

105. Wilson, *The Black Phalanx,* 100.

106. N. Lyon to Simon Cameron, 29 June 1861, *OR,* Ser. 1, vol. 6, 386.

107. William W. Richmond to Mary Todd Lincoln, 8 August 1861, Lincoln Papers, General Correspondence, LOC. See H. J. Pucket letter to Abraham Lincoln on 21 January 1861, for a more local example of Unionist men asking for appointments from the federal government.

108. "A Tennessee Politician on the Crisis," *Nashville Union and American,* 6 December 1860.

109. "Foreign Views of Our Constitution," *New Orleans Daily Crescent,* 2 May 1861.

110. R. M. Davis to J. B. Gladney, Esq., 14 January 1862, *OR,* Ser. 4, vol. 1, 892.

111. "Important if True," *New York Times,* 8 November 1861.

112. Sainlaude, *France and the American Civil War,* 177.

113. "Arming of Negroes," *New York Herald,* 21 June 1861.

114. "Who are in Favor of it?" *Smoky Hill and Republican Union* (Junction City, Kans.), 26 December 1861.

115. "Arming of Negroes," *Burlington Weekly Hawk-Eye* (Iowa), 29 June 1861.

116. "The Slavery Question—The Necessity for Some Uniform Policy," *New York Times,* 9 November 1861.

117. "Black Men for the Army," *National Anti-Slavery Standard,* 3 August 1861.

118. "Frederick Douglass on the War—An Interesting Meeting at the Cooper Institute," *New York Times,* 13 February 1862.

119. Brady, *Chained to History,* 154.

120. "The Administration and the Fugitive Slave Law," *New York Times,* 2 September 1861.

121. "Conditions of the Rebels at Manassas Junction," *New York Herald,* 15 June 1861.

122. Williams, *A History of the Negro Troops in the War of the Rebellion,* 71.

123. "Florida . . . Negro Colony," *Smoky Hill and Republican Union* (Junction City, Kans.), 26 December 1861.

124. "The Freedmen of the South—What Shall Be Done with Them?" *New York Times,* 6 March 1862.

125. "Important from Missouri—Proclamation of Gen. Frémont," *New York Times,* 2 September 1861.

126. Quoted in Quarles, *The Negro in the Civil War,* 68.

127. "Slavery and the War—A Blow That Will Be Felt," *New York Times,* 2 September 1861.

128. Quoted in McClaughry, "John Wolcott Phelps," 277.

129. Order Regarding Enlistment of Contrabands, Sec. of the Navy Gideon Welles to Flag Officer Louis M. Goldsborough, in Nalty and MacGregor, eds., *Blacks in the Military,* 34.

130. *The Liberator* (Boston, Mass.), 13 December 1861.

131. Kahan, *Amiable Scoundrel,* 175, 203.

132. "Military Items," *Indiana State Sentinel* (Indianapolis), 18 December 1861.

133. "The Situation," *New York Herald,* 22 March 1862; Quarles, *Lincoln and the Negro,* 72.

134. Quoted in Quarles, *The Negro in the Civil War,* 111.

135. "How It Works," *Council Bluffs Bugle* (Iowa), 16 July 1862.

136. Quoted in Quarles, *The Negro in the Civil War,* 76.

137. "Remarkable Speech of Lincoln on the 'Nigger Question,' &c.," *Shreveport Semi-Weekly News,* 2 September 1862.

138. Postmaster General Montgomery Blair to General Benjamin Butler, 29 May 1861, in Butler, *Private and Official Correspondence,* 1:117.

139. "England," *Royal Gazette* (Hamilton, Bermuda), 8 November 1861.

140. "The Free Blacks of America," *Antigua Observer* (St. John's, Antigua), 16 August 1860.

141. "The Lesson of St. Domingo—How to Make the War Short and the Peace Righteous," *Douglass' Monthly* (Rochester, N.Y.), August 1861.

142. "The Great Method of Peace," *National Anti-Slavery Standard* (New York), 18 November 1861.

143. "City of St. John: Friday, July 12, 1861," *Antigua Observer* (St. John's, Antigua), 12 July 1861.

144. "American Sketches from the South," *Antigua Observer* (St. John's, Antigua), 26 July 1861.

145. "Miscellaneous Items," *Douglass' Monthly* (Rochester, N.Y.), April 1861.

146. "Colored Soldiers—Fears of Insurrection," *National Anti-Slavery Standard* (New York), 8 June 1861.

147. "A Happy Negro," *National Anti-Slavery Standard* (New York), 22 June 1861.

148. "Services of the Contrabands," *National Anti-Slavery Standard* (New York), 6 July 1861.

149. Quarles, *The Negro in the Civil War*, 84.

150. Ibid. For more information on formerly enslaved people using their knowledge of the South as spies, see Quarles, *The Negro in the Civil War.*

151. Ibid., 92.

152. Major General O. M. Mitchel to Secretary of War Edwin Stanton, 4 May 1862, in Nalty and MacGregor, eds., *Blacks in the Military*, 23.

153. "Abolition Aspect of the War," *Christian Recorder* (Philadelphia), 21 September 1861.

## 2. *The Backbone of the Rebellion*

1. David D. Porter, "The Opening of the Lower Mississippi," 25, Jean Lafitte National Historical Park Collection, Mss. 144, series III, 144–330, Earl K. Long Library, UNO.

2. Browning, *Lincoln's Trident*, 7.

3. "The Blockade of Southern Ports," *New York Times*, 14 April 1861.

4. William McBean to Abraham Lincoln, 28 April 1861, Lincoln Papers, General Correspondence, LOC.

5. "America—The Wealth and Population of the Conflicting States," *Antigua Observer* (St. John's, Antigua), 5 July 1861.

6. "Naval and Military Movements," *New York Herald*, 10 April 1861.

7. "The News," *New York Herald*, 9 April 1861.

8. Abraham Lincoln, Proclamation, 19 April 1861, in Lincoln, *Collected Works of Abraham Lincoln*, 4:339–340; see also Abraham Lincoln, Proclamation, 12 May 1862, in Lincoln, *Collected Works of Abraham Lincoln*, 5:211.

9. Browning, *Lincoln's Trident*, 9.

10. "Address to the Cotton Planters," 17 July 1861, circular, folder 01–30, 1861–1865, Jean Baptiste Meullion Papers, Manuscripts Collection 713, TU.

11. Browning, *Lincoln's Trident*, 15.

12. "The Situation of Affairs," *New York Herald*, 7 June 1861.

13. "Rebel Testimony to the Efficiency of the Blockade," *New York Times*, 9 January 1862.

14. "Grand Split in the Southern Confederacy," *National Anti-Slavery Standard* (New York), 26 October 1861.

15. Clara Solomon, 24 June 1861, in Ashkenazi, ed., *The Civil War Diary of Clara Solomon*, 35.

16. "England Versus the Union," *Smoky Hill and Republican Union* (Junction City, Kans.), 26 December 1861.

17. Message of President James Monroe at the commencement of the first session of the 18th Congress, 12/02/1823, Presidential Messages of the 18th Congress, ca. 12/02/1823–ca. 03/03/1825, RG 46, NARA.

18. "The Island of St. Domingo in Possessions of Spain," *Royal Gazette* (Hamilton, Bermuda), 9 April 1861.

19. John Norris Jr. to F. H. Morse, Esq., 12 July 1861, *OR*, Ser. 3, vol. 1, 446–447.

20. H. S. Sanford to William Seward, 12 November 1861, *OR*, Ser. 3, vol. 1, 632.

21. R. W. Shufeldt to William Seward, 16 January 1862, *OR,* Ser. 3, vol. 1, 871.

22. Gideon Welles to Captain W. W. McKean, 4 May 1861, Enclosure from William Seward, 3 May 1861, *ORN,* Ser. 1, vol. 4, 155–156.

23. "France and England in Favor of the Confederacy," *Royal Gazette* (Hamilton, Bermuda), 7 May 1861.

24. "Admiral Milne and the British Squadron in the Gulf of Mexico," *Royal Gazette* (Hamilton, Bermuda), 17 September 1861.

25. "European Intelligence," *Weekly Delta* (New Orleans), 23 February 1861, LSA.

26. "Letter from London," 18 January 1861, *Weekly Delta* (New Orleans), 26 April 1862, LSA.

27. "The Proclamation of the British Government," *New York Times,* 28 May 1861.

28. "The English Mail of the 18th Ultimo," *Royal Gazette* (Hamilton, Bermuda), 11 June 1861.

29. "Reign of Terror in New Orleans," *Antigua Observer* (St. John's, Antigua), 12 July 1861.

30. G. B. Wood to Abraham Lincoln, 3 July 1860, Lincoln Papers, General Correspondence, LOC.

31. *Burlington Free Press* (Vermont), reprinted in *New York Evening Post,* 15 May 1862.

32. "Will New Orleans Be Defended?," *New Orleans Daily Crescent,* 2 May 1861.

33. Obert and Mattiacci, "Keeping Vigil," 606.

34. Grimsted, *American Mobbing,* 226.

35. "A Bloody Affair in Louisiana," *New York Times,* 16 September 1859.

36. "Everyday Life in New Orleans," *New York Herald,* 26 April 1862.

37. "Some Still Left," *New York Times,* August 19, 1861. The article cites reports of the New Orleans vigilance committee published by the *New Orleans Delta* on 7 August 1861.

38. Obert and Mattiacci, "Keeping Vigil," 607.

39. Horne, *Negro Comrades of the Crown,* 167.

40. Catherine Rossvally to J. P. Benjamin, 13 December 1861, *OR,* Ser. 2, vol. 2, 1405.

41. Memoranda of Various Political Arrests—From Reports of Confederate Commissioners, *OR,* Ser. 2, vol. 2, 1433.

42. Clara Solomon, 10 September 1861, in Ashkenazi, ed., *The Civil War Diary of Clara Solomon,* 102.

43. "How Unanimity Is Secured in the South," *Antigua Observer* (St. John's, Antigua), 26 July 1861.

44. "Reign of Terror in New Orleans," *Antigua Observer* (St. John's, Antigua), 12 July 1861.

45. Malone, *Sweet Chariot,* 40

46. "Rebel Testimony to the Efficiency of the Blockade," *New York Times,* 9 January 1862.

47. Winters, *The Civil War in Louisiana,* 46.

48. "Rebel Testimony to the Efficiency of the Blockade," *New York Times,* 9 January 1862.

49. Clara Solomon, 29 June 1861, in Ashkenazi, ed., *The Civil War Diary of Clara Solomon,* 45.

50. "The South, as Seen by a Resident," *National Anti-Slavery Standard* (New York), 20 July 1861.

51. Clara Solomon, 27 June 1861, 29 September 1861, in Ashkenazi, ed., *The Civil War Diary of Clara Solomon,* 42, 154.

52. "A Great Battle Expected," *Antigua Observer* (St. John's, Antigua), 25 October 1861.

53. Petition of Citizens of Carondelet, St. Louis County, Mo., 1862, Lincoln Papers, General Correspondence, LOC.

54. CSA Major General Lovell, 20 March 1862, in General Orders No. 90, Department of the Gulf, *OR,* Ser. 1, vol. 15, 589.

55. Quoted in Pierson, *Mutiny at Fort Jackson,* 38–39.

56. Ochs, *A Black Patriot and a White Priest,* 73

57. Malone, *Sweet Chariot,* 42.

58. Daggett, "Spiritualism Among Creoles of Color in Nineteenth-Century New Orleans," 416.

59. Dessens, "Louis Charles Roudanez, a Creole of Color of Saint-Domingue Descent," 34.

60. Clara Solomon, 5 October 1861, in Ashkenazi, ed., *The Civil War Diary of Clara Solomon,* 173.

61. *New Orleans True Delta,* quoted in Pierson, *Mutiny at Fort Jackson,* 51.

62. "Unique Treatment," *New Orleans Daily Crescent,* 25 September 1861.

63. JNO. G. Devereux to J. L. Lewis, 29 September 1861, *OR,* Ser. 4, vol. 1, 625.

64. Woodward, comp., *The Negro in the Military Service of the United States, 1639–1886,* 1027.

65. Clara Solomon, 25 September 1861, in Ashkenazi, ed., *The Civil War Diary of Clara Solomon,* 144. The Union prisoners transported to New Orleans were not treated that well. Twiggs reported in the late fall that they were "destitute of clothing—many without blankets," but he also made it clear he had no intention of giving them clothes or blankets as the winter began. He had to be ordered to issue them clothing and covering by his superiors in Richmond. For the exchange, see Twiggs to J. P. Benjamin, 10 October 1861, and J. P. Benjamin to Twiggs, 11 October 1861, *OR,* Ser. 2, vol. 1, 90. While it was understood the prisoners were not treated well, and many thought they would die of yellow fever in the parish prisons, there was nothing to be done at this point in the war. See McClintock Young to William Seward, 24 September 1861, *OR,* Ser. 2, vol. 1, 598.

66. Browning, *Lincoln's Trident,* 16.

67. Bielski, *A Mortal Blow to the Confederacy,* 37.

68. Porter, "The Opening of the Lower Mississippi," 23.

69. Charles L. Huntington to John G. Nicolay, 10 December 1861, Lincoln Papers, General Correspondence, LOC.

70. Porter, "The Opening of the Lower Mississippi," 23.

71. Major General George B. McClellan to the Honorable E. M. Stanton, 31 January 1862, Lincoln Papers, General Correspondence, LOC.

72. Clara Solomon, 18 September 1861, in Ashkenazi, ed., *The Civil War Diary of Clara Solomon,* 125.

73. "The Lagoons of the Mississippi," *Charleston Mercury* (South Carolina), 28 September 1861.

74. D. E. Twiggs to L. P. Walker, 12 September 1861, *OR,* Ser. 1, vol. 6, 729.

75. Clara Solomon, 18 September 1861, in Ashkenazi, ed., *The Civil War Diary of Clara Solomon,* 125.

76. D. E. Twiggs to the Confederate Secretary of War, 17 September 1861, *OR,* Ser. 1, vol. 6, 739.

77. "The Traitor Twiggs," *New York Herald,* 26 April 1862.

78. Bielski, *A Mortal Blow to the Confederacy,* 32–33.

79. Braxton Bragg to [Thomas] Moore, 31 October 1861, Moore Papers.

80. J. P. Benjamin to Thomas Moore, 13 October 1861, *OR,* Ser. 1, vol. 6, 751.

81. "News by Telegraph," *Charleston Mercury* (South Carolina), 12 October 1862.

82. Examination of Maj. Gen. Mansfield Lovell, 7 April 1863, 9 April 1863, *OR,* Ser. 1, vol. 6, 558, 564.

83. Braxton Bragg to [Thomas] Moore, 31 October 1861, Moore Papers.

84. "Secret Revolutionary Conspiracy in New York," *New York Herald,* 11 October 1861.

85. "The Rebellion in Its Dying Agonies—Dreadful Condition of the South," *New York Herald,* 21 April 1862.

86. Everett, "Ben Butler and the Louisiana Native Guards, 1861–1862," 203.

87. "The Union Sentiment in the City, and How It Is Treated," *New York Herald*, 26 April 1862.

88. Thomas Moore to Jefferson Davis, 20 September 1861, *OR*, Ser. 1, vol. 6, 740.

89. Mansfield Lovell to J. B. Benjamin, 19 November 1861, *OR*, Ser. 1, vol. 6, 769. See also J. B. Benjamin to Mansfield Lovell, 23 December 1861, in ibid.

90. Report of EWD Fontaine, 17 December 1861, *OR*, Ser. 1, vol. 6, 783.

91. Quoted in Quarles, *The Negro in the Civil War*, 39.

92. Irwin, *History of the Nineteenth Army Corps*, 11.

93. Pierson, *Mutiny at Fort Jackson*, 7.

94. Clara Solomon, 5 October 1861, in Ashkenazi, ed., *The Civil War Diary of Clara Solomon*, 173.

95. Adjutant and Inspector General of Louisiana's Report, 25 November 1861, *OR*, Ser. 4, vol. 1, 755.

96. *Daily Picayune* (New Orleans), 24 November 1861.

97. Nystrom, *New Orleans After the Civil War*, 20.

98. Quarles, *The Negro in the Civil War*, 38.

99. Testimony of Maj. Gen. Lovell, 20 June 1863, *OR*, Ser. 1, vol. 6, 637.

100. Adjutant and Inspector General of Louisiana's Report, 25 November 1861, *OR*, Ser. 4, vol. 1, 755.

101. Clara Solomon, 17 November 1861, in Ashkenazi, ed., *The Civil War Diary of Clara Solomon*, 264 (emphasis in the original).

102. Mansfield Lovell to Jefferson Davis, 31 October 1861, *OR*, Ser. 1, vol. 6, 760.

103. Abstract from Return of Department No. 1, January 1862, *OR*, Ser. 1, vol. 6, 819.

104. Browning, *Lincoln's Trident*, 72.

105. Mansfield Lovell to J. P. Benjamin, 5 December 1861, *OR*, Ser. 1, vol. 6, 776.

106. Fiske, *The Mississippi Valley in the Civil War*, 115–116.

107. For further information regarding Farragut's early life and background, see Mahan, *Admiral Farragut*.

108. Mahan, *Admiral Farragut*, 122–123.

109. Browning, *Lincoln's Trident*, 53–54.

110. Gideon Welles to Captain David Farragut, 23 December 1861, 9 January 1862, *ORN*, Ser. 1, vol. 18, 4–5.

111. "American News," *Antigua Observer* (St. John's, Antigua), 16 August 1861.

112. "Letter from the United States," *Royal Gazette* (Hamilton, Bermuda), 20 August 1861.

113. Gideon Welles to Flag Officer Farragut, 25 January 1862, *ORN*, Ser. 1, vol. 18, 9.

114. "The War News," *Royal Gazette* (Hamilton, Bermuda), 3 December 1861.

115. Gideon Welles to Flag Officer Farragut, 23 January 1862, *ORN*, Ser. 1, vol. 18, 8.

116. General Butler to the Adjutant General of the U.S. Army, 2 December 1861, in Butler, *Private and Official Correspondence*, 1:294–296.

117. Alfred A. Parmenter to his family, 21 November 1861, Parmenter Papers, TU.

118. Ripley, *Slaves and Freedmen in Civil War Louisiana*, 106.

119. General Butler was a complicated man and an even more complicated leader while in New Orleans. For information regarding his time before and during New Orleans, see Leonard, *Benjamin Franklin Butler*, and Hearn, *When the Devil Came Down to Dixie*.

120. "A Federal Victory: Capture of Forts Clark and Hatteras, and 730 Prisoners-Fifteen Confederates Killed and Thirty Wounded," *Daily Exchange* (Baltimore, Md.), 2 September 1861 (emphasis in the original).

121. General Orders No. 1, Headquarters, Department of New England, *OR,* Ser. 3, vol. 1, 823.

122. Hearn, *When the Devil Came Down to Dixie,* 48.

123. General Orders No. 20, Headquarters of the Army, 23 February 1862, in Butler, *Private and Official Correspondence,* 1:360.

124. War Department, Adjunct General's Office, General Order No. 98, 1862, Butler Papers, LOC; "The Situation," *New York Herald,* 22 March 1862.

125. Major General McClellan to Major General B. F. Butler, 23 February 1862, in Butler, *Private and Official Correspondence,* 1:360. McClellan makes it clear in a previous letter to Butler that Weitzel was already aware of their intended destination. General McClellan to Maj. Gen. B. F. Butler, 19 February 1862, in Butler, *Private and Official Correspondence,* 1:359.

126. De Forest, *A Volunteer's Adventures,* 1.

127. P. H. Watson to Benjamin Butler, 17 February 1862, *OR,* Ser. 1, vol. 6, 687–688.

128. Irwin, *History of the Nineteenth Army Corps,* 8.

129. General Benjamin F. Butler to President Abraham Lincoln, 8 May 1862, Lincoln Papers, General Correspondence, LOC.

130. Major General McClellan to Major General B. F. Butler, 23 February 1862, in Butler, *Private and Official Correspondence,* 1:360.

131. Sarah Butler to Mrs. Heard, 25 February 1862, in Butler, *Private and Official Correspondence,* 1:364.

132. "Local Intelligence," *New Orleans Daily Crescent,* 9 December 1861.

133. General Orders No. 1, Headquarters 1st Division LA. V. Troops, 3 January 1862, *Daily Picayune* (New Orleans), 5 January 1862, LSA.

134. General Order No. 5, Headquarters 1st Division LA. V. Troops, 21 January 1862, *New Orleans Daily Crescent,* 25 January 1862.

135. "Local Intelligence," *New Orleans Daily Crescent,* 28 January 1862.

136. Ochs, *A Black Patriot and a White Priest,* 70–71, footnote 4.

137. Berry, "Negro Troops in Blue and Gray," 169.

138. Testimony of D. W. Brickell, 17 April 1863, *OR,* Ser. 1, vol. 6, 575.

139. Testimony of Lt. Col. W. S. Lovell, 27 April 1863, *OR,* Ser. 1, vol. 6, 598.

140. Act to reorganize the militia, 23 January 1862, *OR,* Ser. 4, vol. 1, 869.

141. Hollandsworth, *The Louisiana Native Guard,* 8.

142. General Orders No. 1, Headquarters Louisiana Troops, Mayor General's Office, 15 February 1862, LSA.

143. See E. G. Randolph Collection, 1861–1863, Louisiana Adjutant General Office Library Civil War Manuscripts, N314-7-3, microfilm, reel #6, LSA.

144. Mansfield Lovell to J. B. Benjamin, 12 February 1862, *OR,* Ser. 1, vol. 6, 825.

145. J. P. Benjamin to Thomas Moore, 1 March 1862, *OR,* Ser. 1, vol. 6, 837.

146. Governor Thomas Moore, General Orders No. 426, 24 March 1862, *OR,* Ser. 4, vol. 1, 1020.

147. Misc. Register of Officers, Louisiana State Troops, 1861–1862, chapter 8, vol. 168:94–95, 174–175, LSA.

148. "The Confederate Soldiery," *New York Herald,* 26 April 1862.

149. General J. W. Phelps to General Lorenzo Thomas, 3 February 1862, *OR,* Ser. 1, vol. 6, 680.

150. Frances Dunn testimony, 17 June 1919, Emma Barrett Pension File, 1119719, NARA.

151. De Forest, *A Volunteer's Adventures,* 3.

152. Pierson, *Mutiny at Fort Jackson,* 9–10.

153. Parton, *General Butler in New Orleans,* 209.

154. Alfred A. Parmenter to his family, 6 March 1862, Parmenter Papers, TU.

155. Pierson, *Mutiny at Fort Jackson,* 9–10.

156. Wormeley, *The United States Sanitary Commission,* 201–202.

157. George (no last name) to his brother, 9 March 1862, Lippman Collection, TU.

158. General J. W. Phelps to General Lorenzo Thomas, 9 March 1862, *OR,* Ser. 1, vol. 6, 696.

159. Clara Solomon, 10 April 1862, in Ashkenazi, ed., *The Civil War Diary of Clara Solomon,* 324.

160. Duncan to J. G. Pickett, 30 April 1862, *OR,* Ser. 1, vol. 6, 523.

161. Mansfield Lovell to General George Randolph, 15 April 1862, *OR,* Ser. 1, vol. 6, 877.

162. Report on Forts Jackson and Saint Philip, Inclosure No. 1, First Lieutenant John C. Palfrey to Lieutenant G. Weitzel, 16 May 1862, *OR,* Ser. 1, vol. 15, 428.

163. Dinah Watson, "Slave Narratives," 145, FWP, vol. 16, Texas, part 4, LOC.

164. Charles O'Neil diary, 18 April 1862, in Charles O'Neil Papers, LOC.

165. Everett T. Manter to Eben Sherman, April 1862, quoted in Pierson, *Mutiny at Fort Jackson,* 11.

166. Wormeley, *The United States Sanitary Commission,* 203.

167. "The Attack on Fort Jackson," *New York Herald,* 26 April 1862.

168. "Commander Duncan telegram," *Daily Picayune* (New Orleans), 23 April 1862.

169. Clara Solomon, 22 April 1862, in Ashkenazi, ed., *The Civil War Diary of Clara Solomon,* 340.

170. Mahan, *Admiral Farragut,* 135.

171. Browning, *Lincoln's Trident,* 80.

172. Major General Benjamin Butler to Edwin Stanton, 29 April 1862, *OR,* Ser. 1, vol. 6, 504.

173. Browning, *Lincoln's Trident,* 98.

174. "Latest from Fort Jackson," *Weekly Delta* (New Orleans), 26 April 1862, LSA.

175. Bielski, *A Mortal Blow to the Confederacy,* 108.

176. George Davis to his brother and sister, 3 May 1862, George H. Davis Letters, LSU.

177. Alfred A. Parmenter to his family, 1 May 1862, Parmenter Papers, TU.

178. Major General Benjamin Butler to Edwin Stanton, 29 April 1862, *OR,* Ser. 1, vol. 6, 504.

179. "The News from New Orleans," *Charleston Mercury* (South Carolina), 25 April 1862.

180. W. P. Moore letter, 3 May 1862, reprinted in *Beloit Journal and Courier* (Wisconsin), 12 June 1862.

181. Mansfield Lovell to S. Cooper, 22 May 1862, 26 April 1862, *OR,* Ser. 1, vol. 6, 517, 511.

182. "Our Great Disaster and Humiliation," *Weekly Delta* (New Orleans), 26 April 1862, LSA.

183. Mayor John Monroe to Flag Officer Farragut, 26 April 1862, *OR,* Ser. 2, vol. 3, 613.

184. "Hostile Fleet," *Weekly Delta* (New Orleans), 26 April 1862, LSA.

185. George Hamilton Perkins letter, 27 April 1862, in Belknap, ed., *Letters of Captain Geo. Hamilton Perkins,* 69.

186. "Our Great Disaster and Humiliation," *Weekly Delta* (New Orleans), 26 April 1862, LSA.

187. Jones, ed., *The Civil War Memoirs of Captain William J. Seymour,* 32.

188. Confederate General Duncan's Report, *OR,* Ser. 1, vol. 6, 531.

189. Jones, ed., *The Civil War Memoirs of Captain William J. Seymour,* 33.

190. Major General Benjamin Butler to Edwin Stanton, 29 April 1862, *OR,* Ser. 1, vol. 6, 505.

191. Hollandsworth, *The Louisiana Native Guards,* 9.

192. "The Militia of New Orleans and Their Lack of Arms," *New York Herald,* 26 April 1862.

193. "Our Proper Demeanor," *Weekly Delta* (New Orleans), 26 April 1862, LSA.

194. Major General Benj. F. Butler to Brig. Gen. Thomas Williams, 1 June 1862, *OR,* Ser. 1, vol. 15, 25.

195. A. Battle to G. W. Randolph, 29 April 1862, *OR,* Ser. 4, vol. 1, 1101.

196. "The Capture of New-Orleans," *New York Times,* 28 April 1862.

197. "The Surrender and Recapture of the Arsenal," *New York Herald,* 18 August 1862.

198. Examination of Maj. Gen. Mansfield Lovell, 10 April 1863, *OR,* Ser. 1, vol. 6, 567.

199. S. L. James Testimony, 11 April 1863, *OR,* Ser. 1, vol. 6, 568.

200. "Letter to the Editor," *L'Union,* 15 October 1862.

201. Hollandsworth, *The Louisiana Native Guards,* 17.

202. Eliot, Shellabarger, and Boyer, *Report of the Select Committee on the New Orleans Riots,* 307.

### *3. They Will Be Loyal*

1. "What shall we do with the Negroe," *Daily Green Mountain Freeman* (Montpelier, Vt.), 9 December 1861.

2. General Order No. 1, 1 May 1862, Butler Papers, LOC.

3. Butler, *Butler's Book,* 308.

4. General Orders No. 24, Department of the Gulf, 10 May 1862, *OR,* Ser. 1, vol. 6, 724.

5. "Slaves Burned in Louisiana—Testimony of a European Savant," *National Anti-Slavery Standard* (New York), 2 August 1862.

6. Bielski, *A Mortal Blow to the Confederacy,* 134.

7. Major General Benjamin Butler to Edwin Stanton, 8 May 1862, *OR,* Ser. 1, vol. 6, 506.

8. Telegraph of Mansfield Lovell to George Randolph, 4 May 1862, *OR,* Ser. 1, vol. 6, 885.

9. General Orders No. 36, Headquarters, Department of the Gulf, 31 May 1862, *OR,* Ser. 2, vol. 3, 616.

10. Ochs, *A Black Patriot and a White Priest,* 89.

11. Dessens, "Louis Charles Roudanez, a Creole of Color of Saint-Domingue Descent," 26–38.

12. "The First Louisiana Colored Regiment," *New York Times,* 5 November 1862 (emphasis added).

13. For more information on Dr. Louis Charles Roudanez and his effect on New Orleans, see Anthony J. Cade II, "Dr. Louis Charles Roudanez and the African American Community of New Orleans during the Civil War," *Black Perspectives,* African American Intellectual History Society, 19 October 2022, https://www.aaihs.org/dr-louis-charles-roudanez-and-the-african-american-community-of-new-orleans-during-the-civil-war/.

14. Hollandsworth, *The Louisiana Native Guards,* 18.

15. General Butler to Edwin Stanton, 25 May 1862, Butler Papers, LOC.

16. Berry, "Negro Troops in Blue and Gray," 172.

17. Butler's testimony before the American Freedmen's Inquiry Commission, 28 November 1863, in Woodward, comp., *The Negro in the Military Service of the United States, 1639–1886,* 2558.

18. Testimony of Charles W. Gibbons, 25 December 1866, quoted in Hollandsworth, *The Louisiana Native Guards,* 4 (emphasis added).

19. "Dinner to Citizens of Louisiana," *The Liberator* (Boston, Mass.), 15 April 1864.

20. Butler's testimony before the American Freedmen's Inquiry Commission, 28 November 1863, in Woodward, comp., *The Negro in the Military Service of the United States, 1639–1886,* 2558.

21. Alfred A. Paramater to his family, 1 May 1862, Parmenter Papers, TU.

22. Report of Brigadier General Johnson K. Duncan, C.S. Army, of the bombardment and surrender of Forts Jackson and Saint Philip, *OR,* Ser. 1, vol. 6, 533.

23. Pierson, *Mutiny at Fort Jackson,* 147.

24. Quoted in ibid., 124.

25. Winters, *The Civil War in Louisiana,* 142.

26. Clara Solomon, 4 May 1862, in Ashkenazi, ed., *The Civil War Diary of Clara Solomon,* 348.

27. Governor Moore to Jefferson Davis, 2 June 1862, in *OR,* Ser. 1, vol. 15, 748.

28. Charles C. Fulton to the War Department, 30 April 1862, Lincoln Papers, General Correspondence, LOC.

29. Clara Solomon, 4 May 1862, in Ashkenazi, ed., *The Civil War Diary of Clara Solomon,* 343.

30. Abraham Lincoln, Proclamation, 12 May 1862, in Lincoln, *Collected Works of Abraham Lincoln, 1809–1865,* 5:211.

31. Regulations Relating to Trade with Ports Opened by Proclamation, Salmon P. Chase, 12 May 1862, *OR,* Ser. 3, vol. 2, 32.

32. Butler, *Butler's Book,* 383–384.

33. General Butler to Hon. Edwin M. Stanton, 29 June 1862, in Butler, *Private and Official Correspondence,* 2:14.

34. Ibid.

35. George Denison to his mother, 6 July 1863, quoted in Winters, *The Civil War in Louisiana,* 126.

36. Special Order No. 166, 1862, Butler Papers, LOC; "Governor Moore's Address to the People of Louisiana," 18 June 1862, in Butler, *Private and Official Correspondence,* 2:18.

37. Winters, *The Civil War in Louisiana,* 126.

38. Testimony of Gen. P. G. T. Beauregard, 27 April 1863, *OR,* Ser. 1, vol. 6, 601.

39. Butler, *Butler's Book,* 393–394.

40. Wormeley, *The United States Sanitary Commission,* 204.

41. Alfred A. Paramater to his family, 14 June 1862, Parmenter Papers, TU.

42. George (no last name) to his brother, 25 May 1862, Lippman Collection, TU.

43. John H. Guild to his mother, 21 June 1862, Guild Letters, LSU.

44. John H. Guild to his sister, 2 July 1862, Guild Letters, LSU.

45. Isaac Hazelhurst to President Abraham Lincoln, 6 May 1862, Lincoln Papers, General Correspondence, LOC. See also Joshua F. Speed to President Abraham Lincoln, 6 May 1862, Lincoln Papers, General Correspondence, LOC.

46. Clara Solomon, 10 May 1862, 11 May 1862, in Ashkenazi, ed., *The Civil War Diary of Clara Solomon,* 358, 360.

47. Benj. F. Butler to CSA General Richard Taylor, 10 September 1862, *OR,* Ser. 1, vol. 15, 567.

48. The Historic New Orleans Society has a broadside that depicts the order with the headline "INFAMOUS!" Similar broadsides were circulated throughout Louisiana following the order. General Order No. 28 Broadside, Department of the Gulf, 1862, 99-276-RL, HNOC.

49. General Orders No. 28, 15 May 1862, General Orders, Department of the Gulf, Records of the U.S. Army Continental Commands, RG 393, NARA (hereafter cited as Department of the Gulf Records).

50. Ibid.

51. General Butler to Mr. J. G. Carney, 2 July 1862, in Butler, *Private and Official Correspondence,* 2:36.

52. Clara Solomon, 15 May 1862, in Ashkenazi, ed., *The Civil War Diary of Clara Solomon,* 370.

53. Hearn, *When the Devil Came Down to Dixie,* 131–132.

54. *Daily Picayune* (New Orleans), 21 May 1862.

55. General Butler to Hon. Edwin M. Stanton, 29 June 1862, in Butler, *Private and Official Correspondence,* 2:15.

56. Diary of Lieutenant Roe, 17 May 1862, *ORN,* Ser. 1, vol. 18, 772.

57. Butler to Mr. J. G. Carney, 2 July 1862, in Butler, *Private and Official Correspondence,* 2:36.

58. Clara Solomon, 8 May 1862, in Ashkenazi, ed., *The Civil War Diary of Clara Solomon,* 355.

59. De Forest, *A Volunteer's Adventures,* 31.

60. Clara Solomon, 26 May 1862, in Ashkenazi, ed., *The Civil War Diary of Clara Solomon,* 384, 26–27.

61. Frances Doby, Slave Narratives, N1976-018, microfilm, LSA.

62. Secretary of War to Major General B. F. Butler, 3 July 1862, in Butler, *Private and Official Correspondence,* 2:41–42.

63. General Butler to General Arnold, Comdg. U.S. Forces, Pensacola, 10 July 1862, in Butler, *Private and Official Correspondence,* 2:54.

64. Pierson, *Mutiny at Fort Jackson,* 150.

65. Haskins, *Pinckney Benton Stewart Pinchback,* 23.

66. Pierson, *Mutiny at Fort Jackson,* 150.

67. De Forest, *A Volunteer's Adventures,* 26.

68. Ward, *Garden of Ruins,* 78.

69. For more information regarding Black women working in Union encampments to their detriment, see Feimster, "Rape and Mutiny at Fort Jackson," 11–31.

70. "New Orleans," *Douglass' Monthly* (Rochester, N.Y.), August 1862.

71. "Cruelty to Contrabands," *National Anti-Slavery Standard* (New York), 8 November 1862.

72. "New Orleans," *Douglass' Monthly* (Rochester, N.Y.), August 1862.

73. Ripley, *Slaves and Freedmen in Civil War Louisiana,* 43–45. Butler remembered this lesson for the remainder of the war. When he was given another commander in Virginia, Butler ensured that every single formerly enslaved laborer was paid, and he punished those who cheated their laborers out of wages. See Butler's autobiography for how impactful his time in New Orleans was to his military career and life.

74. *Daily Picayune* (New Orleans), 9 July 1862.

75. Benj. F. Butler to Maj. Gen. Halleck, 1 September 1862, *OR,* Ser. 1, vol. 15, 558.

76. CSA Major General R. Taylor to CSA Secretary of War George Randolph, 21 November 1862, *OR,* Ser. 1, vol. 15, 872.

77. M. Mithoff to General Butler, 20 May 1862, Butler Papers, LOC.

78. Parton, *General Butler in New Orleans,* 547–548, 432.

79. "The Situation in New Orleans," *Semi-Weekly Shreveport News* (Louisiana), 30 September 1862.

80. "The Guerillas," *National Anti-Slavery Standard* (New York), 27 September 1862.

81. Butler, *Butler's Book,* 476.

82. General Orders No. 60, 16 August 1862, Department of the Gulf, General Orders, Department of the Gulf Records.

83. "Misplaced Confidence," *National Anti-Slavery Standard* (New York), 27 September 1862.

84. Hearn, *When the Devil Came Down to Dixie,* 210.

85. "Insubordination Among Slaves," *National Anti-Slavery Standard* (New York), 27 September 1862.

86. "The Situation in New Orleans," *Semi-Weekly Shreveport News* (Louisiana), 30 September 1862.

87. "The Army and the Negroes," *National Anti-Slavery Standard* (New York), 27 September 1862.

88. Jonathan Allen to sister, 20 June 1862, quoted in Pierson, *Mutiny at Fort Jackson,* 183.

89. Martin L. Williston to Annie Williston, 28 December 1862, Martin L. Williston Papers, TU.

90. Carpenter, *History of the Eighth Regiment Vermont Volunteers,* 41–42.

91. "Butler and the Contrabands—Equivocal Conduct of the General—Fate of the Negroes Employed Within Our Lines," *New York Times,* 3 July 1862.

92. Ripley, *Slaves and Freedmen in Civil War Louisiana,* 28.

93. Quoted in McClaughry, "John Wolcott Phelps," 263.

94. Fuller, *Men of Color, to Arms!,* 28.

95. Quoted in McClaughry, "John Wolcott Phelps," 263. For further information regarding Phelps's background and his connection to the Native Guards, see Dobak, *Freedom by the Sword,* 94–97.

96. Benjamin Butler to Montgomery Blair, 23 July 1861, in Butler, *Private and Official Correspondence,* 1:177.

97. McClaughry, "John Wolcott Phelps," 268.

98. Benjamin Butler to Simon Cameron, 13 November 1861, *OR,* Ser. 3, vol. 1, 637.

99. General John Phelps to Major George C. Strong, 30 April 1862, *OR,* Ser. 1, vol. 6, 509.

100. Phelps's Declaration, in Berlin et al., eds., *Free at Last,* 22–25. See this source for the full text of Phelps's declaration.

101. *New York Tribune,* 17 December 1861.

102. General Benj. F. Butler to the Adjutant General of the Army, 19 December 1861, in Butler, *Private and Official Correspondence,* 1:299.

103. McClaughry, "John Wolcott Phelps," 273.

104. Ripley, *Slaves and Freedmen in Civil War Louisiana,* 31.

105. Quoted in Winters, *The Civil War in Louisiana,* 143.

106. Captain Edward Page Jr. to General Butler, 27 May 1862, in Berlin et al., eds., *Free at Last,* 49–50.

107. Quoted in Quarles, *The Negro in the Civil War,* 115.

108. "The Emancipation Question in New Orleans," *National Anti-Slavery Standard* (New York), 5 July 1862. His name is listed as Le Blanche in the article cited, but in official correspondence between Phelps and Butler his name is spelled LaBlanche.

109. J. W. Phelps to Gen. Butler, 16 June 1862, Butler Papers, LOC.

110. "The Emancipation Question in New Orleans," *National Anti-Slavery Standard* (New York), 5 July 1862.

111. Ripley, *Slaves and Freedmen in Civil War Louisiana,* 30.

112. Hollandsworth, *The Louisiana Native Guards,* 27.

113. "Gen. Phelps Proclamation," *National Anti-Slavery Standard* (New York), 16 August 1862.

114. De Forest, *A Volunteer's Adventures,* 38.

115. John C. P. Wederstrandt to General George Shepley, 19 September 1862, in Berlin et al., eds., *Free at Last,* 72–73.

116. Fuller, *Men of Color, to Arms!,* 30.

117. Glatthaar, *Forged in Battle,* 62.

118. "Deposition of Octave Johnson, Corporal Co. C, 15th Regiment Corps d'Afrique," in Berlin et al., eds., *Free at Last,* 51.

119. Section 11, Public Law No. 160, 17 July 1862. This was a constant debate in Congress during 1862, and there was a slowly growing group within who agreed that the military should employ African Americans as soldiers. "Senate Debate on Arming Slaves," *New York Times,* 10 July 1862.

120. Wilson, *The Black Phalanx,* 115.

121. "Two Important Points of Military Policy Settled," *New York Times,* 23 July 1862.

122. General Phelps to Capt. R. S. Davis, A.A.A. General, 30 July 1862, in Butler, *Private and Official Correspondence,* 2:125.

123. Daniel Ruggles to Earl Van Dorn, 22 July 1862, 25 July 1862, *OR,* Ser. 1, vol. 15, 785.

124. "The Situation in New Orleans," *Semi-Weekly Shreveport News,* 30 September 1862.

125. R. E. Lee to Maj. Gen. Halleck, 2 August 1862, *Douglass' Monthly* (Rochester, N.Y.), September 1862.

126. "Arming Negroes," *New York Journal of Commerce,* reprinted in the *Wilmington Journal,* 14 August 1862.

127. Ibid.

128. "Negroes Makes Good Soldiers—Testimony of a French Officer," *National Anti-Slavery Standard* (New York), 19 July 1862.

129. "War and General News of the Week," *Urbana Union* (Ohio), 6 August 1862.

130. De Forest, *A Volunteer's Adventures,* 39–40.

131. "Shall the Negro Be Permitted to Fight? Speech of Major-Gen. Lew. Wallace," *National Anti-Slavery Standard* (New York), 19 July 1862.

132. "Negro Regiments," *National Anti-Slavery Standard* (New York), 19 April 1862.

133. "New to 'Use' the Negroes" *Daily Gate City* (Keokuk, Iowa), 9 June 1862.

134. Winters, *The Civil War in Louisiana,* 144.

135. General Phelps to Capt. R. S. Davis, 31 July 1862, in Butler, *Private and Official Correspondence,* 2:126.

136. Wilson, *The Black Phalanx,* 184.

137. General Phelps to Capt. R. S. Davis, 31 July 1862, in Butler, *Private and Official Correspondence,* 2:126.

138. General Butler to Hon. Edwin M. Stanton, 2 August 1862, in Butler, *Private and Official Correspondence,* 2:142.

139. General Butler to Brig. Gen. Phelps, 2 August 1862, in Butler, *Private and Official Correspondence,* 2:143.

140. General Shepley to Major General B. F. Butler, 2 August 1862, in Butler, *Private and Official Correspondence,* 2:147.

141. Salmon P. Chase to General Butler, 31 July 1862, in Butler, *Private and Official Correspondence,* 2:132–134 (emphasis in original text); Abraham Lincoln to Reverdy Johnson, 26 July 1862, Lincoln Papers, General Correspondence, LOC.

142. General Butler to Hon. Edwin M. Stanton, 2 August 1862, in Butler, *Private and Official Correspondence,* 2:142.

143. General Butler to Secretary Stanton, 25 May 1862, *OR,* 15:441.

144. General Butler to Brig. Gen. J. W. Phelps, 2 August 1862, in Butler, *Private and Official Correspondence,* 2:143.

145. General Butler to Mrs. Butler, 2 August 1862, in Butler, *Private and Official Correspondence,* 2:148.

146. George Denison to Salmon P. Chase, 26 August 1862, in Butler, *Private and Official Correspondence,* 2:229.

147. General Phelps to Maj. Gen. B. F. Butler, 2 August 1862, in Butler, *Private and Official Correspondence,* 2:145.

148. Gen. J. W. Phelps to Gen. Lorenzo Thomas, 2 August 1862, in "Shall the Black Unionists of the South Be Permitted to Fight?" *National Anti-Slavery Standard* (New York), 23 August 1862.

149. Gen. Benjamin Butler to Brig.-Gen. Phelps, 5 August 1862, in "Shall the Black Unionists of the South Be Permitted to Fight?" *National Anti-Slavery Standard* (New York), 23 August 1862.

150. General Phelps to Maj. Genl. B. F. Butler, 2 August 1862, in Butler, *Private and Official Correspondence,* 2:145–146.

151. "Chronicles of the War," *National Anti-Slavery Standard* (New York), 30 August 1862.

152. "Slave-Catching Business in New Orleans," *National Anti-Slavery Standard* (New York), 23 August 1862.

153. Ibid.

154. General Butler to Mrs. Butler, 25 July 1862, in Butler, *Private and Official Correspondence,* 2:109.

155. Mrs. Butler to General Butler, 8 August 1862, in Butler, *Private and Official Correspondence,* 2:164.

156. "James Madison on the Use of Negroes," *Rutland Weekly Herald* (Vermont), 31 July 1862.

157. "Gen. Phelps, the Curtins of Emancipation," *New York Times,* 27 September 1862.

158. Thomas Moore to Secretary of War George W. Randolph, 8 July 1862, Moore Papers.

159. Butler to Gen. Thomas Williams, 6 June 1862, *OR,* Ser. 1, vol. 15, 25–26.

160. Report of CSA Maj. Gen. John C. Breckinridge, 30 September 1862, *OR,* Ser. 1, vol. 15, 76–77.

161. Headquarters, Louisiana Militia, Adjutant General's Office, 10 May 1862, Misc. LA Volunteer Regiments, LSA.

162. Irwin, *History of the Nineteenth Army Corps,* 38.

163. "News from New Orleans," *New York Herald,* 6 September 1862.

164. Major General Butler to Honorable Edwin Stanton, 16 August 1863, *OR,* Ser. 1, vol. 15, 552.

165. Hollandsworth, *The Louisiana Native Guards,* 14.

166. Colonel Deming to General Butler, 4 August 1862, in Butler, *Private and Official Correspondence,* 2:151.

167. War Department, Adjutant General's Office, General Orders No. 98, 8 August 1862, *OR,* Ser. 1, vol. 15, 561.

168. General Phelps to Maj. Gen. B. F. Butler, 2 August 1862, in Butler, *Private and Official Correspondence,* 2:145.

169. Weaver, ed., *Thank God My Regiment an African One,* 10.

170. Quoted in Quarles, *The Negro in the Civil War,* 116–117.

171. Ibid. (emphasis added).

172. Quoted in Berry, "Negro Troops in Blue and Gray," 172.

173. Weaver, ed., *Thank God My Regiment an African One*, 10–11.

174. General Butler to Hon. Edwin M. Stanton, 14 August 1862, in Butler, *Private and Official Correspondence*, 2:192.

175. Butler, *Butler's Book*, 421 (emphasis added).

176. General Butler to Hon. Edwin M. Stanton, 14 August 1862, in Butler, *Private and Official Correspondence*, 2:192.

### *4. Hasten All, Our Blood Only Is Demanded*

1. "The Army, the Nigger Question, and the Coming Election," *New York Herald*, 28 November 1861.

2. General Orders No. 63, Department of the Gulf, 22 August 1862, *OR*, Ser. 1, vol. 15, 557.

3. George Denison to Salmon P. Chase, 9 September 1862, in Butler, *Private and Official Correspondence*, 2:270.

4. General Orders No. 63, Department of the Gulf, 22 August 1862, *OR*, Ser. 1, vol. 15, 557.

5. "Aux Native Guards," *L'Union* (New Orleans), 8 October 1862.

6. The Touro Building was built through the will of Judah Touro, a white citizen of New Orleans who had considerable wealth. He left behind money to aid the lower classes of the city. The building operated as an asylum for some time. Originally intended for widows and orphans, it had many rooms and open fields for drill, which allowed the men to sleep and train in one area. See "Butler's Black Soldiers," *National Anti-Slavery Standard* (New York), 27 September 1862, for more information.

7. Quarles, *The Negro in the Civil War*, 117; see *L'Union* (New Orleans), 25 October 1862, for one of the many examples.

8. Ochs, *A Black Patriot and a White Priest*, 75.

9. General Butler to Hon. E. M. Stanton, 1 September 1862, in Butler, *Private and Official Correspondence*, 2:243.

10. "Negro Regiments Not Accepted," *Christian Recorder* (Philadelphia), 6 September 1862.

11. Spurgeon, *Soldiers in the Army of Freedom*, 156.

12. General Halleck to Major Gen. B. F. Butler, 26 August 1862, in Butler, *Private and Official Correspondence*, vol. 2.

13. Benjamin Butler to General Halleck, 27 August 1862, *OR*, Ser. 1, vol. 15, 556.

14. H. W. Halleck to Maj. Gen. Benjamin Butler, 20 November 1862, *OR*, Ser. 1, vol. 15, 601.

15. General Butler to General Henry Halleck, in Weaver, ed., *Thank God My Regiment an African One*, 10.

16. Weaver, ed., *Thank God My Regiment an African One*, 12.

17. General Butler to Capt. Stafford, 19 July 1862, in Butler, *Private and Official Correspondence*, 2:88.

18. Wilson, *The Black Phalanx*, 195.

19. Quoted in Ochs, *A Black Patriot and a White Priest*, 85.

20. George Denison to Salmon P. Chase, 9 September 1862, in Butler, *Private and Official Correspondence*, 2:271.

21. "Gen. Butler Raising a 'Colored' Regiment," *The Liberator* (Boston, Mass.), 12 September 1862.

22. "Colored Troops in New Orleans," *Portland Daily Press*, 11 September 1862.

23. "Negro Regiments Authorized by Gen. Butler," *Chicago Daily Tribune,* 6 September 1862 (emphasis in original text).

24. "Butler's Black Soldiers," *National Anti-Slavery Standard* (New York), 27 September 1862.

25. "Free Negroes Enrolled in New Orleans," *Burlington Weekly Hawk-Eye* (Iowa), 13 September 1862.

26. "The Negro Enlistment Scheme," *Daily Picayune* (New Orleans), 30 July 1862.

27. "Aux Native Guards," *L'Union* (New Orleans), 8 October 1862.

28. "Gen Butler Organizing a Negro Battalion," *Daily Green Mountain Freeman* (Montpelier, Vt.), 5 September 1862.

29. "Free Negroes Enrolled in New Orleans," *Burlington Weekly Hawk-Eye* (Iowa), 13 September 1862.

30. "Gen Butler Organizing a Negro Battalion," *Daily Green Mountain Freeman* (Montpelier, Vt.), 5 September 1862.

31. "Butler Organizing Negro Regiments," *Daily Green Mountain Freeman* (Montpelier, Vt.), 5 September 1862.

32. Ochs, *A Black Patriot and a White Priest,* 76.

33. Ibid., 112.

34. Hollandsworth, *The Louisiana Native Guards,* 18.

35. Wilson, *The Black Phalanx,* 195.

36. According to Stephen J. Ochs, 19 percent of the original Native Guards joined the 1st Regiment, 14 percent joined other Union regiments, and 18 percent of the men who were in the original regiment had family members who joined the Union army, demonstrating that the younger generation, more willing to fight outside of New Orleans than the older, wealthier generation, joined the new unit. Ochs, *A Black Patriot and a White Priest,* 76–77.

37. Ochs, *A Black Patriot and a White Priest,* 87.

38. John W. Phelps diary, 15 August 1862, quoted in Ripley, *Slaves and Freedmen in Civil War Louisiana,* 104.

39. From Mrs. Butler to General Butler, September 1862, in Butler, *Private and Official Correspondence,* 2:321.

40. Ibid.

41. Butler to Halleck, 1 September 1862, in *OR,* Ser. 1, vol. 4, 549, 5.

42. Parton, *General Butler in New Orleans,* 581.

43. George Denison to Salmon P. Chase, 9 September 1862, in Butler, *Private and Official Correspondence,* 2:270.

44. "President Davis's Message," *Royal Gazette* (Hamilton, Bermuda), 9 September 1862.

45. "From the United States," *Royal Gazette* (Hamilton, Bermuda), 28 October 1862.

46. De Forest, *A Volunteer's Adventures,* 43.

47. Rush C. Hawkins, "John W. Phelps," in *Annual Reunion,* 12 June 1885, 85–86, quoted in McClaughry, "John Wolcott Phelps," 290.

48. "General Phelps," *National Anti-Slavery Standard* (New York), 6 September 1862.

49. "Personal," *National Anti-Slavery Standard* (New York), 13 December 1862.

50. Quoted in Wilson, *The Black Phalanx,* 93.

51. *Vermont Watchman* (Montpelier, Vt.), 17 October 1862.

52. Irwin, *History of the Nineteenth Army Corps,* 43.

53. From General Butler to Mrs. Butler, 13 September 1862, in Butler, *Private and Official Correspondence,* 2:287.

54. For more information on General Weitzel, see Quatman, *A Young General and the Fall of Richmond.*

55. De Forest, *A Volunteer's Adventures,* 47–48, 50–51.

56. "The Negro in New England," *National Anti-Slavery Standard* (New York), 6 September 1862.

57. Colonel Charles Paine to his father, quoted in Hollandsworth, *The Louisiana Native Guards,* 29.

58. George S. Denison to Salmon P. Chase, 26 August 1862, in Butler, *Private and Official Correspondence,* 2:228.

59. "Butler's Black Soldiers," *National Anti-Slavery Standard* (New York), 27 September 1862.

60. "Outline Plan for Proposed Expedition for the Recapture of New Orleans," Daniel Ruggles to S. Cooper, 11 September 1862, *OR,* Ser. 1, vol. 15, 806–807. While the Native Guards were helpful, additional factors, such as not having enough weapons and men, also deterred a fall attack on New Orleans.

61. "General Butler's Black Soldiers—New Orleans," *National Anti-Slavery Standard* (New York), 4 October 1862. The letter is dated 19 September 1862, weeks after the Native Guards were constituted in the army.

62. "The Negro Brigade," *Daily Gate City* (Keokuk, Iowa), 15 November 1862.

63. Commission of Lt. Isidore Honoré, 12 October 1812, in MacGregor and Nalty, eds., *Blacks in the United States Armed Forces,* 1:209.

64. Ochs, *A Black Patriot and a White Priest,* 79.

65. "The Black Guards at Fort McComb, LA.," *National Anti-Slavery Standard* (New York), 14 February 1863.

66. John Crowder to his mother, 23 April 1863, Glatthaar and Crowder, "The Civil War Through the Eyes of a Sixteen-Year-Old Black Officer," 212.

67. Weaver, ed., *Thank God My Regiment an African One,* 13.

68. Ochs, *A Black Patriot and a White Priest,* 68–72.

69. Berry, "Negro Troops in Blue and Gray," 173.

70. Eliot, Shellabarger, and Boyer, *Report of the Select Committee on the New Orleans Riots,* 105.

71. Hollandsworth, *The Louisiana Native Guards,* 27.

72. John Gould to his mother, 28 April 1862, John H. Gould Letters 1862–1864, Mss. 3204, LSU.

73. Hollandsworth, *The Louisiana Native Guards,* 24. Hollandsworth also shows that the other companies in the regiments followed similar patterns of differing heights, skin tones, and trade backgrounds. The only commonality among the various regiments, other than their race, was groups of laborers. This, of course, was expected, as laborer was the general term that the formerly enslaved used when questioned about their employment when they wanted to claim to be freemen. It allowed them to easily explain their lack of skill or literacy, as neither was needed of a general laborer.

74. Ochs, *A Black Patriot and a White Priest,* 84.

75. Glatthaar, *Forged in Battle,* 30–31, 36, 81.

76. "The Colored Regiment," *Tipton Advertiser* (Iowa), 25 September 1862.

77. "DEPARTMENT OF THE GULF," *New York Times,* 7 February 1863.

78. Preliminary Emancipation Proclamation, LOC, https://www.loc.gov/resource/lprbscsm.scsm0950/.

79. See the appendix.

80. "A Proclamation by the President of the United States—A Decree of Emancipation," *New York Times*, 23 September 1862.

81. "Emancipation," *Burlington Weekly Hawk-Eye* (Iowa), 15 November 1862.

82. Quoted in Ochs, *A Black Patriot and a White Priest*, 112.

83. Mrs. Butler to General Butler, 28 September 1862, in Butler, *Private and Official Correspondence*, 2:333.

84. General Orders No. 88, Headquarters, Department of the Gulf, 1 November 1862, *OR*, Ser. 1, vol. 15, 588.

85. "The Emancipated Slaves," *Orleans Independent Standard* (Irasburgh, Vt.) 26 December 1862.

86. Mrs. Butler to General Butler, 28 September 1862, in Butler, *Private and Official Correspondence*, 2:334.

87. General Butler to Major General Henry W. Halleck, 1 September 1862, in Butler, *Private and Official Correspondence*, 2:242.

88. General Butler to General Phelps, 2 September 1862, in Butler, *Private and Official Correspondence*, 2:245.

89. Dwight Foster to General Butler, 11 September 1862, in Butler, *Private and Official Correspondence*, 2:284

90. General Orders No. 60, 16 August 1862, Department of the Gulf Records.

91. Department of the Gulf, General Orders No. 71, 14 September 1862, *OR*, Ser. 1, vol. 15, 571.

92. From Acting French Consul Charles Foster Fauconnet to Major General Butler, 15 September 1862, in Butler, *Private and Official Correspondence*, 2:296.

93. Acting French Consul Charles Foster Fauconnet to Major General B. F. Butler, 3 October 1862, in Butler, *Private and Official Correspondence*, 2:351.

94. There were a few cases of soldiers in the Native Guards attacking their former masters, although those examples were in self-defense. See Cade, "A Free Man, *Fortiori* a Soldier." The article is one example of a soldier stabbing a former enslaver and being released by Butler afterward.

95. General Butler to Senor Don Juan Callejon, 27 September 1862, in Butler, *Private and Official Correspondence*, 2:331.

96. H. W. Halleck to General Butler, 28 August 1862, *OR*, Ser. 1, vol. 15, 557. Halleck made it clear in the message that the letter was sent at the direction of the secretary of war.

97. General Butler to Dr. W. N. Mercer, 27 September 1862, in Butler, *Private and Official Correspondence*, 2:332.

98. General Butler to Hon. E. M. Stanton, 21 October 1862, in Butler, *Private and Official Correspondence*, 2:387–388.

99. Ochs, *A Black Patriot and a White Priest*, 112.

100. General Butler to Hon. E. M. Stanton, 21 October 1862, in Butler, *Private and Official Correspondence*, 2:387–388.

101. Butler's testimony, quoted in Hollandsworth, *The Louisiana Native Guards*, 21.

102. Hollandsworth, *The Louisiana Native Guards*, 21.

103. "A Pro-Slavery Man Converted," *National Anti-Slavery Standard* (New York), 27 September 1862.

104. *L'Union* (New Orleans), 25 October 1862.

105. Captain Henry Louis Rey, *L'Union* (New Orleans), 16 October 1862.

106. Quoted in Wilson, *The Black Phalanx*, 526.

107. Butler, *Butler's Book,* 494. Butler wrote these words as a compliment, which demonstrates just how ingrained the image of the domesticated Negro was in the northern psyche.

108. "Progressing," *Pomeroy Weekly Telegraph* (Ohio), 26 September 1862.

109. General Orders No. 17, War Department, 21 January 1863, Mss. 83434, 39, box 1, Gladstone Collection, LOC.

110. *Official Army Register . . . ,* part 8, 246.

111. G. S. Denison to Salmon P. Chase, 24 September 1862, in Butler, *Private and Official Correspondence,* 2:328.

112. General Butler to Maj. Gen'l Halleck, 24 October 1862, in Butler, *Private and Official Correspondence,* 2:401.

113. Letter from Chaplain J. Colby, quoted in "General Butler's Colored Regiments," *Portland Daily Press,* 11 November 1862.

114. G. S. Denison to Salmon P. Chase, 24 September 1862, in Butler, *Private and Official Correspondence,* 2:328.

115. Letter from Chaplain J. Colby, quoted in "General Butler's Colored Regiments," *Portland Daily Press,* 11 November 1862.

116. "Progressing," *Pomeroy Weekly Telegraph* (Ohio), 26 September 1862.

117. General Butler to M. Fauconnet, 11 October 1862, in Butler, *Private and Official Correspondence,* 2:360.

118. General Butler to Hon. E. M. Stanton, 19 October 1862, 12 October 1862, in Butler, *Private and Official Correspondence,* 2:365; General Butler to Hon. E. M. Stanton, 12 October 1862, in Butler, *Private and Official Correspondence,* 2:384–385, 369. Two separate letters from Butler to Stanton, both sent the same day, argued the amount of foreign interference that was transpiring in New Orleans.

119. General Butler to Hon. E. M. Stanton, 21 October 1862, in Butler, *Private and Official Correspondence,* 2:390.

120. Selected Letters, Portions from St. John Richardson Liddell's "Record of the Civil War," pages 23–46, 56–101, Daniel C. Govan Papers, #1000, Miscellaneous Civil War Letters, Duke University, N88-20, microfilm, reel #7, LSA.

121. Sainlaude, *France and the American Civil War,* 82.

122. "'A Degrading Spectacle'—White Men Working Negro Help to Save the Union," *London Morning Post,* reprinted in *Dollar Weekly Bulletin* (Maysville, Ky.), October 1862 (emphasis and capitalization in original text).

123. "Letter to the editor," *L'Union* (New Orleans), 1 October 1862.

124. "'A Degrading Spectacle'—White Men Working Negro Help to Save the Union," *London Morning Post,* reprinted in *Dollar Weekly Bulletin* (Maysville, Ky.), October 1862.

125. G. S. Denison to Salmon P. Chase, 14 November 1862, in Butler, *Private and Official Correspondence,* 2:428.

126. General Butler to Brig. Gen. Weitzel, 2 November 1862, in Butler, *Private and Official Correspondence,* 2:439.

127. Weaver, ed., *Thank God My Regiment an African One,* 14.

128. Ibid., 15.

129. Colonel N. W. Daniels to Major General Butler, 29 September 1862, Butler Papers, LOC.

130. Weaver, ed., *Thank God My Regiment an African One,* 15; Glatthaar, *Forged in Battle,* 9; Willis, *The Black Civil War Soldier,* 85. Dr. Alexander Thomas Augusta was made a major in 1863 in the medical corps, and he was breveted to lieutenant colonel before the end of the war. Major

Martin Delany was the third African American major, but he was a recruiting officer and saw no combat while he held the rank.

131. Haskins, *Pinckney Benton Stewart Pinchback,* 5–8.

132. P. B. S. Pinchback papers, Howard University, quoted in Weaver, ed., *Thank God My Regiment an African One,* 15. Pinchback would briefly serve as governor of Louisiana, and similar to Dumas, he demonstrated the education and sophistication that existed in the officer corps of the Louisiana Native Guards regiments.

133. Berry, "Negro Troops in Blue and Gray," 176.

134. Ochs, *A Black Patriot and a White Priest,* 86.

135. "Hannibal's Retreat," *The Appeal* (St. Paul, Minn.), 25 July 1891.

136. "Hannibal C. Carter," *New National Era* (Washington, D.C.), 28 March 1872.

137. Declaration for Original Invalid Person, William Barrett Pension File, 715669, NARA.

138. Joseph T. Wilson Pension File, Federal Pension Application Files, Certificates 78,530 and 324,127, Records of the Veterans Administration, RG 15, NARA; Joseph T. Wilson, CMSR, NARA. For a general overview of Joseph Wilson, see Penn, *The Afro-American Press and Its Editors,* 174–175; Cook, "The Glory of the Nation," 17–18.

139. "Native Africans Enlisting," *Douglass' Monthly* (Rochester, N.Y.), 27 February 1863.

140. "Letter to the editor," *L'Union* (New Orleans), 15 October 1862.

141. "Patriotic Work for Women," *New York Times,* 12 October 1862.

142. Quoted in Ochs, *A Black Patriot and a White Priest,* 94.

143. "The First Louisiana Colored Regiment," *New York Times,* 5 November 1862.

144. "News from Along the Coast," *New York Herald,* 16 November 1862.

145. Berry, "Negro Troops in Blue and Gray," 180.

146. July–August Muster Roll, 1st U.S. Infantry Regiment of LA. Volunteer Corps D'Afrique, Company II Muster Roll, folder 1, Mss. 5379, LSU.

147. Ochs, *A Black Patriot and a White Priest,* 114.

148. General Butler to Brig. Gen. Weitzel, 30 October 1862, in Butler, *Private and Official Correspondence,* 2:430.

### *5. Woe to Any Man Who Flinches*

1. "Donaldsonville, Louisiana," *Frank Leslie's Illustrated Newspaper* (New York), 29 August 1863, 360, LSA.

2. General Butler to Brig. Gen. Weitzel, 30 October 1862, in Butler, *Private and Official Correspondence,* 2:430.

3. Hollandsworth, *The Louisiana Native Guards,* 32.

4. General Butler to Maj. Gen'l Halleck, 24 October 1862, in Butler, *Private and Official Correspondence,* 2:401.

5. Berry, "Negro Troops in Blue and Gray," 177.

6. G. S. Denison to Salmon P. Chase, 27 October 1862, in Butler, *Private and Official Correspondence,* 2:412.

7. Harding, *The Miscellaneous Writings of George C. Harding,* 317–322. Harding describes a campaign he thought would be quite easy. His assumption proved wrong, as he was captured and sent to Camp Pratt on the Bayou Teche.

8. Berry, "Negro Troops in Blue and Gray," 177.

9. General Butler to Maj. Gen'l Halleck, 24 October 1862, in Butler, *Private and Official Correspondence,* 2:401.

10. Special Orders No. 30, Executive Department, 24 September 1862, Executive Department Special Orders, 1862–1864, Military Governor Shepley, 456-5-3, microfilm, reel #1, LSA.

11. Captain James H. Ingraham, "Letter to the Editor," *National Anti-Slavery Standard* (New York), 29 November 1862.

12. Hollandsworth, *The Louisiana Native Guards,* 33.

13. General Butler to Maj. Gen'l Halleck, 18 November 1862, in Butler, *Private and Official Correspondence,* 2:490–491.

14. Irwin, *History of the Nineteenth Army Corps,* 47.

15. "The Battle of Labadieville," *Freemont Journal* (Ohio), 28 November 1862.

16. Carpenter, *History of the Eighth Regiment Vermont Volunteers,* 70.

17. Report of CSA General Alfred Mouton, 4 November 1862, *OR,* Ser. 1, vol. 15, 177.

18. Carpenter, *History of the Eighth Regiment Vermont Volunteers,* 70.

19. Headquarters, Louisiana Militia, Orders No. 881, 30 September 1862, *OR,* Ser. 1, vol. 15, 819. The E. G. Randolph Collection, located in the Louisiana State Archives, holds dozens of letters from men who were once in the Louisiana militia acknowledging they were now mustered into military service. Louisiana Adjutant General Office Library Civil War Manuscripts, N314-7-3, microfilm, reel #6, LSA.

20. "Military Operations in Louisiana," *National Intelligencer* (Washington, D.C.), 20 November 1862.

21. S. P. Chase to Major General B. F. Butler, 29 October 1862, in Butler, *Private and Official Correspondence,* 2:423.

22. Annie Flowers, Slave Narratives, N1976-018, microfilm, LSA.

23. Adjutant Colonel Charles Paine to Maj. Gen. B. F. Butler, 15 September 1862, in Butler, *Private and Official Correspondence,* 2:296.

24. Alexander F. Pugh diary, Pugh Family Papers, LSU.

25. Henrietta Butler, Slave Narratives, N1976-018, microfilm, LSA.

26. From F. H. Knapp to General Weitzel, 14 September 1862, in Butler, *Private and Official Correspondence,* 2:297.

27. From G. S. Denison to Salmon P. Chase, 24 September 1862, in Butler, *Private and Official Correspondence,* 2:328.

28. William T. Gay to Ned, 3 December 1862, Edward Gay Family Papers, LSU.

29. General Butler to Brig. Gen. Weitzel, 30 October 1862, in Butler, *Private and Official Correspondence,* 2:430.

30. Weaver, ed., *Thank God My Regiment an African One,* 18.

31. General Butler to Brig. Gen. Weitzel, 2 November 1862, *Butler Correspondence,* 439.

32. General Weitzel to Genl. Butler, 2 November 1862, *OR,* Ser. 1, vol. 15, 162.

33. "General Weitzel and the Negroes," *Daily National Republican* (Washington, D.C.), 21 November 1862.

34. General Butler to Brig. Gen. Weitzel, 30 October 1862, in Butler, *Private and Official Correspondence,* 2:430.

35. "Highly Interesting from New Orleans," *New York Herald,* 19 December 1862.

36. Odel Jackson, Slave Narratives, N1976-018, microfilm, LSA.

37. "Explosion of an Ammunition Car—List of the Sufferers," *New York Herald,* 26 November 1862.

38. John Crowder to his mother, letter undated but signed from Lafourche Crossing, Louisiana, in Glatthaar and Crowder, "The Civil War Through the Eyes of a Sixteen-Year-Old Black Officer," 207.

39. Weaver, ed., *Thank God My Regiment an African One,* 16.

40. Hollandsworth, *The Louisiana Native Guards,* 30.

41. Trudeau, *Like Men of War,* 31.

42. Colonel Stafford to Gen. Butler, 14 October 1862 (with endorsements), Letters Received, Department of the Gulf Records.

43. Colonel Stafford to Lt. Col. R. B. Irwin, 4 January 1863, Letters Received, Department of the Gulf Records.

44. Public Law No. 166, 17 July 1862, Memorandum Index, Officers of the Pay Department, 5, NARA. Colloquially referred to as the Militia Act of 1862.

45. D298, Pay Voucher, Thomas Stillwell, Surgeon, 10 August 1862, Mss. 83434, box OV 1, Gladstone Collection, LOC. The pay voucher demonstrates that even Black surgeon aides were affected by the congressional law, as their pay was fixed at $13, but they were also charged for the cost of their clothing, while the white surgeon and his white surgeon aides were not.

46. General Orders No. 323, War Department, 28 September 1863, Mss. 83434, 16, box 1, Gladstone Collection, LOC.

47. Colonel Stafford to Lt. Col. R. B. Irwin, 4 January 1863, Letters Received, Department of the Gulf Records.

48. Hollandsworth, *The Louisiana Native Guards,* 30.

49. Weaver, ed., *Thank God My Regiment an African One,* 16.

50. Pinheiro, *The Families' Civil War,* 50, 99.

51. Department of the Gulf, General Orders No. 90, *OR,* Ser. 1, vol. 15, 589.

52. Ochs, *A Black Patriot and a White Priest,* 93.

53. *L'Union* (New Orleans), 25 October 1862.

54. "Letter from New Orleans," *National Republican* (Washington, D.C.), 22 October 1862.

55. *L'Union* (New Orleans), 25 October 1862. There are two advertisements for joining the Native Guards, and both have the same advance pay and monthly pay, despite there being a letter in a previous issue complaining that the soldiers had not been paid their bounty.

56. G. S. Denison to Salmon P. Chase, 14 November 1862, in Butler, *Private and Official Correspondence,* 2:428.

57. General Butler to Brig. Gen. Weitzel, 2 November 1862, *Butler Correspondence,* 439.

58. CSA General R. Taylor to CSA General J. C. Pemberton, 21 November 1862, *OR,* Ser. 1, vol. 15, 873.

59. CSA General G. T. Beauregard to CSA General S. Cooper, 24 September 1862, *OR,* Ser. 1, vol. 15, 811. There are multiple letters between southern leadership involving increasing their defenses at both Vicksburg and Port Hudson, as the proximity of the Union army made it clear the federal government intended to take the entire Mississippi River.

60. Robert Patrick to his sister, 20 November 1862, Robert Patrick Letters, Mss. 893, LSU.

61. General Butler to Brig. Gen. Weitzel, 2 November 1862, in Butler, *Private and Official Correspondence,* 2:439–440.

62. Weitzel to George Strong, 5 November 1862, 5 November 1862, *OR,* Ser. 1, vol. 15, 171–172. These are two separate letters with the same date.

63. Geo. C. Strong to Brig. Gen'l Weitzel, 6 November 1862, in Butler, *Private and Official Correspondence,* 2:455–456, 458. Interestingly, Butler never really had approval. He wrote to General Halleck the next day that he never received any communication directly related to constituting

or not creating the Native Guards, so he would assume it was approved. However, he would prefer "distinct orders on this subject." From General Butler to Maj. General H. W. Halleck, 7 November 1862, in Butler, *Private and Official Correspondence,* 2:459.

64. Quoted in Ochs, *A Black Patriot and a White Priest,* 118.

65. "Organizing Troops in the Southwest," *Freemont Journal* (Ohio), 12 December 1862.

66. General Weitzel to Maj. George C. Strong, 1 November 1862, *OR,* Ser. 1, vol. 15, 170.

67. "Organizing Troops in the Southwest," *Freemont Journal* (Ohio), 12 December 1862.

68. General Butler to Henry Wilson, 12 November 1862, Butler Papers, LOC.

69. *Official Army Register . . . ,* part 8, 157.

70. *L'Union* (New Orleans), 25 October 1862.

71. "Interesting from New Orleans," *New York Herald,* 10 December 1862.

72. General Butler to President Abraham Lincoln, 28 November 1862, in Butler, *Private and Official Correspondence,* 2:450.

73. The first white line officer to serve in the Native Guards was William S. Peabody. He was an enlisted man in the 8th Vermont Volunteer Infantry Regiment who replaced Samuel Lawrence as the second lieutenant for Company A, 2d Louisiana Native Guards Volunteer Infantry Regiment. However, Lawrence did not receive his commission, and Peabody replaced him. A month later, Lawrence was commissioned, but as a captain instead, in the 3d. It angered Peabody when he found out a Black man was commissioned over him when initially they were both vying for the same position.

74. "Local Intelligence," *New Orleans Daily Crescent,* 9 December 1862.

75. Quoted in Ochs, *A Black Patriot and a White Priest,* 113.

76. Quoted in Hollandsworth, *The Louisiana Native Guards,* 31.

77. Colonel Spencer H. Stafford to Butler, 11 October 1862, in Woodward, comp., *The Negro in the Military Service of the United States, 1639–1886,* 974.

78. Quoted in Ochs, *A Black Patriot and a White Priest,* 93.

79. Berry, "Negro Troops in Blue and Gray," 179.

80. "Later from New Orleans," *Alexandria Gazette* (Alexandria, Va.), 11 December 1862.

81. Quoted in Ochs, *A Black Patriot and a White Priest,* 91.

82. Hollandsworth, *The Louisiana Native Guards,* 37–38.

83. U.S. Army, Department of the Gulf, *General Court Martial Orders.* Multiple boards were convened in 1862, and none shows rampant criminality among the Native Guards.

84. U.S. Bureau of the Census, *Population of the United States in 1860,* 195. The census reports that there were 18,467 free Blacks and 331,720 enslaved people in the state. New Orleans recorded 10,698 free people, nearly 80 percent of them of mixed birth, and 13,385 enslaved people.

85. Quoted in Quarles, *The Negro in the Civil War,* 55.

86. General Benjamin F. Butler to Hon. E. M. Stanton, 14 November 1862, *OR,* Ser. 1, vol. 15, 592.

87. General Butler to Salmon P. Chase, 14 November 1862, in Butler, *Private and Official Correspondence,* 2:425–426.

88. "Letter from a Colored Soldier," *National Anti-Slavery Standard* (New York), 29 November 1862.

89. President Lincoln to Maj. Genl. Butler, 6 November 1862, in Butler, *Private and Official Correspondence,* 2:447.

90. James Durnin to Ann, 25 September 1862, in James and John Durnin Papers, Mss. 697, LSU.

91. General Butler to President Abraham Lincoln, 28 November 1862, in Butler, *Private and Official Correspondence,* 2:447.

92. General Butler to President Abraham Lincoln, 28 November 1862, in Butler, *Private and Official Correspondence,* 2:450.

93. "Letter to the editor," *L'Union* (New Orleans), 1 October 1862.

94. *L'Union* (New Orleans), 18 October 1862.

95. Butler, *Butler's Book,* 493.

96. 74th USCT, December 1862, Compiled Records of Service of Military Units in Volunteer Union Organizations, P81–526, microfilm, reel 213, Series 594, LSA.

97. Carded Record of Events, 1st, 2d and 3d Louisiana Native Guard Infantry Regiments, RG 94, Adjutant General's Office, NARA.

98. "DEPARTMENT OF THE GULF.; Trip to Fort Macombe. The First Louisiana Native Guards Origin of the Regiment Gen. Butler's Order No. 63 Condition and Efficiency of the Native Guards State of Things at Fort Macombe Contrabands School for the Children," *New York Times,* 7 February 1863.

99. "The Emancipated Slave," *Orleans Independent Standard* (Irasburgh, Vt.), 26 December 1862.

100. Quartermaster General's Annual Report to Edwin Stanton, 18 November 1862, *OR,* Ser. 3, vol. 2, 809.

101. "Immigration from United States at Demerara: Speech of the American Consul," *Antigua Observer* (St. John's, Antigua), 19 September 1862. In the speech, the mayor of Demerara and the American consul spoke of equality and a better way of life for African Americans if they left the United States. In a follow-up article, "Emigration from Barbados," published 24 October 1862, the editors note that Demerara was especially keen on capturing the attention of the free and wealthy of Louisiana; however, few from New Orleans considered this offer by the fall of 1862.

102. "The Emancipated Slave," *Orleans Independent Standard* (Irasburgh, Vt.), 26 December 1862.

103. G. S. Denison to Salmon P. Chase, 14 November 1862, in Butler, *Private and Official Correspondence,* 2:427–428.

## *6. Prove Themselves Worthy of You*

1. David Glasgow Farragut's Comments on Gen. B. F. Butler, in Butler, *Private and Official Correspondence,* 2:543.

2. "The Banks Expedition," *New York Herald,* 17 December 1862. Within the article, the correspondent discussed the fact that many in the city, "both loyalists and secessionists," were surprised by the arrival of Banks, and even more surprised when it was declared he was there to supersede Butler.

3. "Organizing Troops in the Southwest," *Freemont Journal* (Ohio), 12 December 1862.

4. G. S. Denison to Salmon P. Chase, 27 October 1862, in Butler, *Private and Official Correspondence,* 2:412.

5. Dobak, *Freedom by the Sword,* 99.

6. George Denison to Salmon P. Chase, August 25, 1862, 9 September 1862, October 10, 1862, in Butler, *Private and Official Correspondence,* 2:228, 270, 356.

7. General Butler to Salmon P. Chase, 14 November 1862, in Butler, *Private and Official Correspondence,* 2:424.

8. George Denison to Salmon P. Chase, 10 October 1862, in Butler, *Private and Official Correspondence,* 2:358–359. While General Butler and his closest friends claimed that the general

had no connection to his brother's business dealings, one letter between Richard S. Fay Jr. and the general shows that the merchant knew that if he could not turn in the $33,000 owed to Colonel Butler, he was supposed to give it to General Butler. Richard S. Fay Jr. to Major General B. F. Butler, 4 December 1862, in Butler, *Private and Official Correspondence,* 2:518–519.

9. General Butler to Mrs. Butler, 2 August 1862, in Butler, *Private and Official Correspondence,* 2:149.

10. "The Banks Expedition," *New York Herald,* 21 December 1862.

11. Ripley, *Slaves and Freedmen in Civil War Louisiana,* 46–48; Dobak, *Freedom by the Sword,* 99.

12. Charles S. Bartles to Major General Butler, 13 December 1862, in Butler, *Private and Official Correspondence,* 2:533.

13. Warner, *Generals in Blue,* 18.

14. H. W. Halleck to Maj. Gen. Benjamin Butler, 14 September 1862, in Butler, *Butler's Book,* 529.

15. Honorable Salmon P. Chase to Major General Butler, 14 December 1862, in Butler, *Private and Official Correspondence,* 2:542.

16. General Orders No. 106, Department of the Gulf, 15 December 1862, *OR,* Ser. 1, vol. 15, 610.

17. Colonel Stafford to General Butler, quoted in Leonard, *Benjamin Franklin Butler,* 120.

18. *L'Union* (New Orleans), 24 December 1862.

19. Quoted in Hearn, *When the Devil Came Down to Dixie,* 224.

20. General Orders No. 5, War Department, 5 January 1863, *OR,* Ser. 1, vol. 15, 636. There were numerous staff changes as well, which Lieutenant Colonel Richard Irwin documents in Irwin, *History of the Nineteenth Army Corps,* 60.

21. Abraham Lincoln to Major General Banks, 24 December 1863, in Lincoln, *Collected Works of Abraham Lincoln, 1809–1865,* 7:89–90.

22. Henry Halleck to Banks, 9 November 1862, *OR,* Ser. 1, vol. 15, 590.

23. Butler, *Butler's Book,* 536.

24. Sainlaude, *France and the American Civil War,* 229.

25. N. P. Banks to E. M. Stanton, 14 February 1863, *OR,* Ser. 1, vol. 15, 676.

26. "Important from New Orleans—Butler Superseded by Banks," *Charleston Mercury* (South Carolina), 29 December 1862.

27. Butler, *Butler's Book,* 542–546.

28. Letter from Citizens of New Orleans Thanking the President of the United States for the Removal of Maj. Gen. Butler from That City, 16 December 1862, Lincoln Papers, General Correspondence, LOC.

29. Ullman, *Address by Daniel Ullman,* 8, Daniel Murray Pamphlet Collection, E540.N3 U4, LOC.

30. "Important from New Orleans—Butler Superseded by Banks," *Charleston Mercury* (South Carolina), 29 December 1862.

31. Hollandsworth, *The Louisiana Native Guards,* 38.

32. Pierre Soniat to General Banks, 20 December 1862, in Berlin et al., eds., *Free at Last,* 85.

33. *L'Union* (New Orleans), 24 December 1862.

34. *National Anti-Slavery Standard* (New York), 13 December 1862.

35. "The President's Proclamation," *National Anti-Slavery Standard* (New York), 29 November 1862.

36. James Bowen, Office of the Provost Marshal, 25 April 1863, Letters Sent, Department of the Gulf Records.

37. Quoted in Ochs, *A Black Patriot and a White Priest,* 115.

38. "Fred. Douglass on the Proclamation—He Pronounces It a Mighty Event for the Colored Race, the Nation and the World," *New York Times,* 7 February 1863.

39. "Emancipation in Louisiana," *New York Times,* 2 February 1863.

40. "Emancipation in Louisiana—The Effect of the President's Proclamation," *New York Times,* 2 February 1863.

41. Doyle, *The Cause of All Nations,* 223, 237, 243.

42. "Emancipation Proclamation—The Negroes to Be Received into the Armed Service of the United States," *New York Times,* 3 January 1863.

43. "The Use of Negroes as Soldiers," *New York Times,* 16 February 1863. All counterarguments are the opinion of the author, Anthony J. Cade II, and not the *New York Times.* The counterpoints are based on the historical information presented in the previous two chapters. These points are there not to change what the *New York Times* was presenting, but to show that the Native Guards were changing the Union army in ways that many did not recognize in 1863.

44. Quoted in Quarles, *The Negro in the Civil War,* 118.

45. Spurgeon, *Soldiers in the Army of Freedom,* 111.

46. General Henry Halleck to General Ulysses S. Grant, 31 March 1863, in Berlin et al., eds., *Free at Last,* 101.

47. *New York Herald,* 4 February 1863.

48. Henry Martyn Cross to his family, 4 May 1863, quoted in Hollandsworth, *The Louisiana Native Guards,* 29.

49. Ohio soldier's letter to his brothers, 28 January 1863, Mss. 83434, 501, box 5, Gladstone Collection, LOC.

50. Lieutenant Dana W. King, quoted in Hollandsworth, *The Louisiana Native Guards,* 37.

51. *L'Union* (New Orleans), 29 January 1863.

52. Banks to Henry Halleck, 24 December 1862, *OR,* Ser. 1, vol. 15, 618.

53. "Condition and Efficiency of the Native Guards State of Things at Fort Macombe," *New York Times,* 7 February 1863.

54. Jefferson Davis, 23 December 1862, quoted in Wilson, *The Black Phalanx,* 316.

55. Confederate States Congress, Joint Resolutions Adopted on the Subject of Retaliation, 1 May 1863, in Nalty and MacGregor, eds., *Blacks in the Military,* 39.

56. Abraham Lincoln to Major General Banks, 23[?] January 1863, in Lincoln, *Collected Works of Abraham Lincoln,* 6:73. Stanton wrote to Lincoln earlier that day calling for Butler to return to New Orleans as well, demonstrating that in a month both men had already changed their mind on the general (76).

57. J. C. to his family, 6 April 1863, Lippman Collection, TU.

58. Charles Kennedy to Kate, 3 May 1863, in Steers, ed., *From Port Hudson to Cedar Creek,* 76.

59. There are numerous reports from Richard Irwin, his assistant adjutant general, in regard to all the steps they took correcting administration issues in the city. Irwin to Banks, 15 January 1863, *OR,* Ser. 1, vol. 15, 653–654, is one of many examples.

60. General Orders No. 48, Headquarters, Department of the Gulf, 9 June 1863, U.S. Army, Department of the Gulf, *General Court Martial Orders,* 4.

61. General Banks to Mary Banks, 24 January 1863, box 2, Family Correspondence, 1841–1911, Banks Papers, Mss. 11734, LOC.

62. Ward, *Garden of Ruins,* 174–175.

63. "Employment of Slaves in Louisiana," *National Intelligencer* (Washington, D.C.), 20 February 1863.

64. Inclosure of Banks declaration, N. P. Banks to Major General Halleck, 24 December 1862, *OR*, Ser. 1, vol. 15, 616.

65. Hollandsworth, *Pretense of Glory*, 93. For a more pessimistic view of how Banks's new labor system affected Louisiana, see Roland, *Louisiana Sugar Plantations During the American Civil War.*

66. Hepworth, *The Whip, Hoe, and Sword*, 27.

67. Flinn, *Campaigning with Banks in Louisiana*, 12.

68. Yarbrough, *Choctaw Confederates*, 179.

69. Ripley, *Slaves and Freedmen in Civil War Louisiana*, 94–95.

70. George Denison to Salmon P. Chase, 31 March 1865, General Correspondence, 1810–1898, Mss. 15610, Chase Papers, LOC.

71. Department of the Gulf, General Orders No. 12, 29 January 1863, *OR*, Ser. 1, vol. 15, 667. The order made it clear that officers and soldiers in the Department of the Gulf were not supposed to go onto plantations and entice people toward freedom; however, the Native Guards and many white abolitionists in the military continued to do so. This made Banks issue General Orders No. 17 on 18 February (678), which mandated only officers from headquarters could authorize such movements, and still the Native Guards and others freed enslaved people under his administration.

72. Ripley, *Slaves and Freedmen in Civil War Louisiana*, 95.

73. Lt. Colonel A. W. Leoiliss to General Banks, 16 April 1863, Letters Sent, Department of the Gulf Records.

74. William A. Smith to Caroline Smith, 7 January 1863, 11 February 1863, Smith Family Papers, TU.

75. J. A. Pickens to General Banks, 5 January 1863, in Berlin et al., eds., *Free at Last*, 256–257.

76. De Forest, *A Volunteer's Adventures*, 97.

77. Hepworth, *The Whip, Hoe, and Sword*, 160.

78. Irwin, *History of the Nineteenth Army Corps*, 455.

79. "The Army and the Negroes," *National Anti-Slavery Standard* (New York), 25 April 1863.

80. Butler, *Butler's Book*, 493.

81. Ochs, *A Black Patriot and a White Priest*, 84–85.

82. Doyle, *The Cause of All Nations*, 260.

83. Colonel Spencer Stafford to General Hoffman, 23 February 1863, Letters Received, Department of the Gulf Records.

84. Colonel S. B. Holabird to Major General Banks, 22 December 1862, in Berlin et al., eds., *Freedom, Series II*, 638.

85. Hollandsworth, *The Louisiana Native Guards*, 39.

86. Weaver, ed., *Thank God My Regiment an African One*, 22.

87. Unnamed Civil War Officer Letter to his sister Rosa, 30 March 1863, Civil War Officer Letter, Mss. 3941, LSU.

88. Nathan Daniels, 12 January 1863, in Weaver, ed., *Thank God My Regiment an African One*, 47.

89. Nathan Daniels, 16 February 1863, in Weaver, ed., *Thank God My Regiment an African One*, 49.

90. "The Expedition to Pascagoula: Exploits of the 2d Regiment of Native Guards," *L'Union* (New Orleans), 14 April 1863.

91. "First Engagement of the Native Guards," *L'Union* (New Orleans), 14 April 1863.

92. Nathan Daniels Report, quoted in Wilson, *The Black Phalanx*, 211.

93. Nathan Daniels, 12 April 1863, in Weaver, ed., *Thank God My Regiment an African One,* 86–87.

94. Seventy-Fourth Regiment, Casualties, *Official Army Register . . . ,* part 8, 249.

95. Diary of Henry Rust, quoted in Weaver, ed., *Thank God My Regiment an African One,* 27.

96. Nathan Daniels, 19 April 1863, in Weaver, ed., *Thank God My Regiment an African One,* 92–93.

97. "Prejudice Against Colored Soldiers," *The Liberator* (Boston, Mass.), 13 March 1863.

98. "Anti-Negro Epidemic," *National Anti-Slavery Standard* (New York), 7 March 1863.

99. "Our Baton Rouge Correspondent," *New York Herald,* 4 February 1863.

100. Hollandsworth, *Pretense of Glory,* 149.

101. Haskins, *Pinckney Benton Stewart Pinchback,* 24.

102. Quoted in Ochs, *A Black Patriot and a White Priest,* 80.

103. General Orders No 48, Headquarters, Department of the Gulf, 9 June 1863, U.S. Army, Department of the Gulf, *General Court Martial Orders,* 3.

104. "Letter from Louisiana," *The Liberator* (Boston, Mass.), 27 March 1863.

105. S. W. Ringgold to Nathaniel Banks, 7 July 1863, in Samuel W. Ringgold, CMSR, 300398, RG 94, NARA.

106. P. B. S. Pinchback to Nathaniel Banks, 2 March 1863, in Berlin et al., eds., *Freedom, Series II,* 321–323.

107. Weaver, ed., *Thank God My Regiment an African One,* 33.

108. Court Martial Proceedings of First Lieutenant Edgar A. Peek, Company A, 3d Louisiana Native Guards, General Orders No. 48, Headquarters, Department of the Gulf, 9 June 1863, U.S. Army, Department of the Gulf, *General Court Martial Orders,* G.O. 48, 18–19.

109. President Abraham Lincoln to Governor Andrew Johnson, 26 March 1863, in Lincoln, *Collected Works of Abraham Lincoln,* 6:150–151.

110. Ullman, *Address by Daniel Ullman,* 2, 7, Daniel Murray Pamphlet Collection, E540.N3 U4, LOC.

111. Berlin, Fields, Miller, Reidy, and Rowland, "The Black Military Experience, 1861–1867," 200.

112. *New Orleans Tribune,* 25 September 1866. After the war, the *New Orleans Tribune* regularly referred to the regiments Ullman raised as the 5th, 6th, and 7th Louisiana Native Guards Regiment. While these were never their official designations, it shows how connected the people of New Orleans felt to the regiments, since so many of the soldiers came from either in or around the city. Even the mustering officer in 1866 referred to them as continuations of the Native Guards.

113. Bvt. Maj. Gen. Daniel Ullman to Gen. Richard C. Drum, 16 April 1887, in Woodward, comp., *The Negro in the Military Service of the United States, 1639–1886.*

114. Ullman, *Address by Daniel Ullman,* 3.

115. Daniel Ullman to Lorenzo Thomas, 19 May 1863, in Berlin et al., eds., *Freedom, Series II,* 145–146.

116. A. E. Berey to President Abraham Lincoln, 18 February 1863, in Woodward, comp., *The Negro in the Military Service of the United States, 1639–1886,* 1103.

117. Hepworth, *The Whip, Hoe, and Sword,* 39–40.

118. Free Military School Broadside, D301, box 3, Gladstone Collection, LOC.

119. General Orders No, 125, War Department, Adjutant General's Office, 29 March 1864, 14, box 1, Gladstone Collection, LOC.

120. Provisional Commission, Private Augustus Bretts Promoted to Captain, 2 September 1863, D481, box 5, Gladstone Collection, LOC.

121. John H. Taggart, *Free Military School for Applicants for Commands of Colored Troops,* 4, box 2, Gladstone Collection, LOC.

122. John F. Marsh to family friend, 28 March 1864, 240, box 3, Gladstone Collection, LOC.

123. Lieutenant Colonel W. Babcock to Richard Irwin, 5 January 1863, Lansing Porter Family Papers, Manuscripts Collection 1065, box 2, TU.

124. Bvt. Maj. Gen. Daniel Ullman to Gen. Richard C. Drum, 16 April 1887, in *The Negro in the Military Service of the United States, 1639–1886.*

125. Ullman, *Address by Daniel Ullman,* 3

126. Wilson, *The Black Phalanx,* 169.

127. Ullman, *Address by Daniel Ullman,* 3.

128. Edwin Stanton to Brigadier General Ullman, 24 March 1863, in Woodward, comp., *The Negro in the Military Service of the United States, 1639–1886,* 1134.

129. Wilson, *The Black Phalanx,* 120.

130. Court Martial Proceedings of 2d Lieutenant Thomas Wiseburne, 133d Regiment New York Volunteers, Headquarters, Department of the Gulf, General Orders No. 33, 25 April 1863, U.S. Army, Department of the Gulf, *General Court Martial Orders,* G.O., 32, 3–4.

131. General Orders No. 18, Headquarters, Department of the Gulf, 24 February 1863, in Woodward, comp., *The Negro in the Military Service of the United States, 1639–1886,* 1105–1106.

132. Ullman, *Address by Daniel Ullman,* 4

133. Glatthaar, *Forged in Battle,* 177. Glatthaar expands further into the alliances that formed between some white line officers and their men during the war.

134. Hepworth, *The Whip, Hoe, and Sword,* 178–179.

135. Ullman, *Address by Daniel Ullman,* 4

136. Capers, *Occupied City,* 219.

137. "Employment of Slaves in Louisiana," *National Intelligencer* (Washington, D.C.), 20 February 1863.

138. "A Typical Negro," *National Anti-Slavery Standard* (New York), 4 July 1863.

139. Escaped slave Gordon, also known as "Whipped Peter," showing his scarred back at a medical examination, Baton Rouge, Louisiana, 4 April 1863, LOT 14043-2, no. 606, Prints and Photographs Division, LOC.

140. "The Realities of Slavery," *American Citizen* (Butler, Pa.), 23 December 1863.

141. "Native Africans Enlisting," *Douglass' Monthly* (Rochester, N.Y.), April 1863.

142. Colonel Stafford to N. P. Banks, 3 January 1863, Regimental Papers, USCT, box 44, RG 94, NARA.

143. Irwin, *History of the Nineteenth Army Corps,* 162.

144. Rowland and Croxall, eds., *The Journal of Julia LeGrand,* 168.

145. Black Officers in a Louisiana Black Regiment, in Berlin et al., eds., *Freedom, Series II,* 316.

146. Ibid.

147. Captain Leon Forstall, CMSR, 3d Louisiana Native Guard Infantry Regiment.

148. Weaver, ed., *Thank God My Regiment an African One,* 160.

149. Joseph G. Parker to Edwin Stanton, 30 May 1863, in Woodward, comp., *The Negro in the Military Service of the United States, 1639–1886,* 1273.

150. Petition from the Officers of the 3d Native Guards Infantry Regiment, in Berlin et al., eds., *Free at Last,* 438 (emphasis added).

151. "Native Africans Enlisting," *Douglass' Monthly* (Rochester, N.Y.), April 1863.

152. John Crowder to his mother Martha, 23 April 1863, in Glatthaar and Crowder, "The Civil War Through the Eyes of a Sixteen-Year-Old Black Officer," 212.

153. Hepworth, *The Whip, Hoe, and Sword,* 92.

154. Charles C. Nott Report on the Potts' Plantation, 5 April 1863, in Berlin et al., eds., *Free at Last,* 259.

155. Lewis Rosslyn to his mother, March 21, (undated year, but the references to Port Hudson leads me to believe it is 1863), Mss. 83434, box 5, Gladstone Collection, LOC.

156. General Orders No. 143, War Department, Adjutant General's Office, 22 May 1863, *OR,* Ser. 3, vol. 3, 215.

157. Kreidberg and Henry, *History of Military Mobilization in the United States Army,* 113.

158. Michael T. Meier, "Lorenzo Thomas and the Recruitment of Blacks in the Mississippi Valley, 1863–1865," in Smith, ed., *Black Soldiers in Blue,* 252–253.

159. General Banks to General Lorenzo Thomas, 12 February 1863, *OR,* Ser. 3, vol. 3, 47.

160. Bvt. Maj. Gen. Daniel Ullman to Gen. Richard C. Drum, 16 April 1887, in Woodward, comp., *The Negro in the Military Service of the United States, 1639–1886.*

161. Sam White to Amice, 22 May 1863, Civil War Soldiers' Letters, Mss. 3188, LSU.

162. 1st Louisiana Colored Troops Muster Roll 1863, U.S. Army 6th Infantry Regiment Muster Roll, Mss. 4695, LSU.

### *7. We Prove Ourselves Men!*

1. *Christian Recorder* (Philadelphia), 27 June 1863.

2. Quoted in Gallman, "In Your Hands That Musket Means Liberty," in Waugh and Gallagher, eds., *Wars within a War,* 96–97.

3. *L'Union* (New Orleans), 13 January 1863.

4. George Denison to Salmon P. Chase, 14 November 1862, 25 December 1862, in Butler, *Private and Official Correspondence,* 2:428, 551.

5. Butler, *Butler's Book,* 532.

6. N. P. Banks to General Halleck, 16 February 1863, *OR,* Ser. 1, vol. 15, 678.

7. Mahan, *Admiral Farragut,* 232.

8. Henry Halleck to Nathaniel Banks, 11 May 1863, *OR,* Ser. 1, vol. 15, 725–726.

9. Fiske, *The Mississippi Valley in the Civil War,* 232–233.

10. Berlin et al., eds., *Freedom, Series II,* 441–442.

11. Hepworth, *The Whip, Hoe, and Sword,* 180.

12. Berry, "Negro Troops in Blue and Gray," 182.

13. N. P. Banks to Col. Holabird, 12 May 1863, *OR,* Ser. 1, vol. 15, 728.

14. N. P. Banks to General Dwight, 22 April 1863, *OR,* Ser. 1, vol. 15, 706–707.

15. Elisha Smith to Richard Irwin, 24 April 1863, *OR,* Ser. 1, vol. 15, 709.

16. Organization of the Troops in the Department of the Gulf (XIX Army Corps), 30 April 1863, *OR,* Ser. 1, vol. 15, 711–713.

17. N. P. Banks to Major General Grant, 13 May 1863, *OR,* Ser. 1, vol. 15, 732.

18. *New York Tribune,* 1 May 1863.

19. Berry, "Negro Troops in Blue and Gray," 183.

20. "The Banks Expedition—The Reopening of the Mississippi," *New York Herald,* 30 December 1862.

21. Browning, *Lincoln's Trident*, 276.

22. "The Port Hudson Report," *New York Times*, 19 March 1863.

23. Algernon Badger to John Badger, 22 March 1863, Badger Family Papers, Manuscripts Collection 1080, box 1, TU.

24. Winters, *The Civil War in Louisiana*, 216–217.

25. "A Picture for the Times," *The Liberator* (Boston, Mass.), 3 July 1863.

26. "Gallant Work at Vicksburgh," *New York Times*, 22 April 1863.

27. Winters, *The Civil War in Louisiana*, 230–231.

28. Sprague, *History of the 13th Infantry Regiment of Connecticut Volunteers*, 102 (emphasis in original).

29. Colonel Spencer H. Stafford, CMSR.

30. Captain J. P. Garland to Colonel E. P. Chapin, 14 May 1863, Colonel Spencer H. Stafford, CMSR.

31. Colonel Stafford to General Banks, 4 June 1863, Colonel Spencer H. Stafford, CMSR.

32. Nathan Daniels, 22 August 1863, in Weaver, ed., *Thank God My Regiment an African One*, 47. Daniels was first arrested on 3 May, and his prolonged imprisonment gave the impression that he was being punished more for supporting the 2d Regiment than for the crime for which he was charged.

33. Williams, *A History of the Negro Troops in the War of the Rebellion*, 216.

34. Ochs, *A Black Patriot and a White Priest*, 140; Blassingame, *Black New Orleans*, 41.

35. George Denison to Salmon P. Chase, 8 January 1863, in Butler, *Private and Official Correspondence*, 2:573.

36. Returns of Casualties in the Union Forces at Port Hudson, *OR*, Ser. 1, vol. 26, 67–68.

37. Report of Major General Banks on the Siege of Port Hudson, 30 May 1863, *OR*, Ser. 1, vol. 26, 44.

38. General T. W. Sherman to Brigadier General Andrews, 25 May 1863, *OR*, Ser. 1, vol. 26, 505.

39. Irwin, *History of the Nineteenth Army Corps*, 166–168.

40. Special Orders No. 123, Headquarters, Department of the Gulf, 26 May 1863, *OR*, Ser. 1, vol. 26, 508–509.

41. Browning, *Lincoln's Trident*, 315; Wilson, *The Black Phalanx*, 212–213.

42. Williams, *A History of the Negro Troops in the War of the Rebellion*, 216–217.

43. Hollandsworth, *The Louisiana Native Guards*, 52.

44. John Ogee, "Slave Narratives," 155–156, FWP, vol. 16, Texas, part 3, LOC.

45. Williams, *A History of the Negro Troops in the War of the Rebellion*, 217.

46. Major General Banks Report on the XIX Corps, 6 April 1865, *OR*, Ser. 1, vol. 26, 13. Banks admits in his own report that if the attacks had been unified, it is possible they could have taken Port Hudson that day. His failure to properly coordinate the attack against a well-defended enemy cost the lives of hundreds on 27 May 1863.

47. William A. Smith to Caroline Smith, 9 June 1863, William A. Smith Letters, Manuscripts Collection, M-1102, TU.

48. Sprague, *History of the 13th Infantry Regiment of Connecticut Volunteers*, 151.

49. Lawrence L. Hewitt, "An Ironic Route to Glory," in Smith, ed., *Black Soldiers in Blue*, 90.

50. "They Stand Vindicated," *The Liberator* (Boston, Mass.), 12 June 1863.

51. Quarles, *The Negro in the Civil War*, 219.

52. Flinn, *Campaigning with Banks in Louisiana*, 74.

53. Returns of Casualties in the Union Forces at Port Hudson, *OR*, Ser. 1, vol. 26, 70.

54. "They Stand Vindicated," *The Liberator* (Boston, Mass.), 12 June 1863.

55. Williams, *A History of the Negro Troops in the War of the Rebellion*, 220.

56. "The Attack upon Port Hudson," *Boston Daily Advertiser*, 8 June 1863.

57. Hollandsworth, *The Louisiana Native Guards*, 55.

58. Irwin, *History of the Nineteenth Army Corps*, 174.

59. Daniel Ullman to Edwin Stanton, 6 June 1863, in Woodward, comp., *The Negro in the Military Service of the United States, 1639–1886*, 1298.

60. Dwight had a tendency to order drunken charges, even before Port Hudson. One of his most infamous was the "Whisky Charge," which resulted in numerous casualties and forever tarnished Dwight's reputation after the Civil War. For more information, see Blount, *The Longest Siege*, 120–130.

61. Lawrence L. Hewitt, "An Ironic Route to Glory," in Smith, ed., *Black Soldiers in Blue*, 92.

62. Hollandsworth, *The Louisiana Native Guards*, 56–57.

63. Wilson, *The Black Phalanx*, 217.

64. "The Battles at Port Hudson," *Milwaukee Daily Sentinel*, 17 June 1863.

65. John Wesley Dixon to his family, 6 April 1864, Dixon Papers. Mss. 3423, LSU.

66. William Dixon diary, illegible date in 1863, 1863–1864, vol. 2, Dixon Papers, LSU.

67. Browning, *Lincoln's Trident*, 316.

68. *Bahama Herald* (Nassau, New Providence), 6 June 1863.

69. "Battle at Port Hudson," *National Intelligencer* (Washington, D.C.), 8 June 1863.

70. Telegram concerning news from New Orleans, New York City Associated Press, 2–3 June 1863, Lincoln Papers, General Correspondence, LOC.

71. "Address of Jefferson Davis to the Confederate States," *St. Christopher Advertiser* (Basseterre, St. Kitts and Nevis), 9 June 1863.

72. Elias D. Strunke letter, 29 May 1863, Berlin, Reidy, and Rowland, eds., *Freedom's Soldiers*, 95.

73. 73d, 74th, and 75th USCT Company Muster Rolls, Compiled Records of Service of Military Units in Volunteer Union Organizations, P81–526, microfilm, reel 213, Series 594, LSA. The muster rolls demonstrate that that every company cited at Port Hudson during the summer reported either wounded or dead soldiers after the battle.

74. Company K, 75th USCT, June 1863, Compiled Records of Service of Military Units in Volunteer Union Organizations, P81–526, microfilm, reel 213, Series 594, LSA.

75. J. Harvey Brown to Catherine Brown, 25 June 1863, J. Harvey Brown Papers, Manuscripts Collection 967, TU.

76. "From the Confederate States," *Royal Gazette* (Hamilton, Bermuda), 16 June 1863.

77. Dobak, *Freedom by the Sword*, 106.

78. Algernon Badger to Sarah and George Badger, 14 July 1864, Badger Family Papers, Manuscripts Collection 1080, TU.

79. J. M. Wiswell to Orissa Wiswell, 25 June 1863, Lippman Collection, TU.

80. Wilson, *The Black Phalanx*, 214. In *History of the Nineteenth Army Corps* (174), Richard Irwin recalls no repeated charges. Rather, he thought they were reforming for an attack that never came. However, there are numerous accounts—from both the Union and the Confederacy—of multiple charges by the Native Guards.

81. Wilson, *The Black Phalanx*, 217.

82. Daggett, "Spiritualism Among Creoles of Color in Nineteenth-Century New Orleans," 418.

83. Glatthaar and Crowder, "The Civil War Through the Eyes of a Sixteen-Year-Old Black Officer," 206.

84. Organization of the Troops in the Department of the Gulf (XIX Army Corps), 31 May 1863, *OR,* Ser. 1, vol. 26, 531–532.

85. Confederate Major General Taylor to Confederate Brigadier General Boggs, 27 June 1863, *OR,* Ser. 1, vol. 26, 211.

86. Richard Irwin to General Emory, 31 May 1863, *OR,* Ser. 1, vol. 26, 524.

87. Irwin, *History of the Nineteenth Army Corps,* 218–219.

88. Organization of the Troops in the Department of the Gulf (XIX Army Corps), 31 May 1863, *OR,* Ser. 1, vol. 26, 529.

89. "A Picture for the Times," *The Liberator* (Boston, Mass.), 3 July 1863.

90. Irwin, *History of the Nineteenth Army Corps,* 186, 201.

91. Wilson, *The Black Phalanx,* 218.

92. Roland C. McConnell, "Louisiana's Black Military History, 1729–1865," in Macdonald, Kemp, and Haas, eds., *Louisiana's Black Heritage,* 57–58.

93. General Daniel Ullman to General Lorenzo Thomas, 30 June 1863, *OR,* Ser. 1, vol. 26, 609.

94. Major General Banks Report on the XIX Corps, 6 April 1865, *OR,* Ser. 1, vol. 26, 14.

95. Major General Banks to Admiral Farragut, 13 June 1863, *OR,* Ser. 1, vol. 26, 117.

96. De Forest, *A Volunteer's Adventures,* 38.

97. P. D. Montgomery to his cousin, 14 June 1863, P. D. Montgomery Letters, 1857–1864, Mss. 4763, LSU.

98. General Orders No. 49, Headquarters, Department of the Gulf, 15 June 1863, *OR,* Ser. 1, vol. 26, 59. The 1st and 3d Native Guards are the only regiments that have a signifier showing that the entire regiment volunteered for the storming column.

99. Irwin, *History of the Nineteenth Army Corps,* 493–494. Irwin has a list of every soldier who volunteered to attack.

100. Irwin, *History of the Nineteenth Army Corps,* 213.

101. De Forest, *A Volunteer's Adventures,* 38.

102. Ochs, *A Black Patriot and a White Priest,* 151.

103. Henry (no last name), 4 June 1863, Union Soldier Henry Civil War Letter, Mss. 4870, LSU.

104. Sherman, *In the Lowlands of Louisiana in 1863,* 19.

105. Quoted in Hollandsworth, *The Louisiana Native Guards,* 97. Hollandsworth also shows that hundreds of men were sick each month because of this racist belief, and many died of preventable cases as a result.

106. Declaration for Original Pension, Louisa D'Aunoy Pension Application, 209889, NARA.

107. Stearns, *Reminiscence of the Late War,* 17.

108. Captain Albert Stearns to James Bowen, 19 June 1863, *OR,* Ser. 1, vol. 26, 191–192.

109. Richard Irwin to Genial Paine, 5 June 1863, *OR,* Ser. 1, vol. 26, 127.

110. David Farragut to James Alden, 19 June 1863, *ORN,* Ser. 1, vol. 20, 240.

111. *New York Times,* 9 August 1863.

112. "Capture of Brashear City," *Milwaukee Daily Sentinel,* 14 July 1863.

113. Major General Banks to Major General Henry Halleck, 6 July 1863, *OR,* Ser. 1, vol. 26, 48.

114. Major General Banks Report on the XIX Corps, 6 April 1865, *OR,* Ser. 1, vol. 26, 15.

115. Duganne, *Camps and Prisons,* 189–193.

116. James P. Major to Luis Bush, 30 June 1863 *OR,* Ser. 1, vol. 26, 217–220.

117. "Affairs at Port Hudson—Statement of Deserters," *New York Herald,* 29 June 1863.

118. John Merritt to his parents, 27 June 1863, Mss. 4674, box 1, John Merritt Letters, 1861–1874, LSU.

119. Brigadier General Emory to General Banks, 4 July 1863, *OR,* Ser. 1, vol. 26, 51.

120. General Banks to Major General Halleck, 4 June 1863, *OR,* Ser. 1, vol. 26, 535–536.

121. Richard Irwin to General Emory, 5 July 1863, *OR,* Ser. 1, vol. 26, 51.

122. "The Gunboat *Winona,*" *New York Times,* 4 February 1864.

123. General Godfrey Weitzel to Major General Benjamin Butler, 5 August 1863, in Butler, *Private and Official Correspondence,* 3:103.

124. Anne J. Bailey, "A Texas Cavalry Raid: Reaction to Black Soldiers and Contrabands," in Urwin, ed., *Black Flag over Dixie,* 19–33.

125. *New York Times,* 19 July 1863.

126. Banks to his wife, 30 May 1863, Banks Papers, box 2, Family Correspondence, 1841–1911, LOC.

127. General Nathaniel Banks to General Henry Halleck, 20 May 1863, in MacGregor and Nalty, eds., *Blacks in the United States Armed Forces,* 2:66–67.

128. General George Leonard Andrews to his wife, 8 July 1863, George Andrews Papers Mss. 3067, LSU.

129. "The Black Braves at Port Hudson," *National Anti-Slavery Standard* (New York), 20 June 1863.

130. "The Army and the Negroes," *National Anti-Slavery Standard* (New York), 20 June 1863.

131. Ochs, *A Black Patriot and a White Priest,* 152–153.

132. George H. Boker, *The Second Louisiana: May 27th, 1863,* Broadside Mss. 83434, 320, box 4, Gladstone Collection, LOC. Boker wrote the poem attributing it to the 2d Native Guards Infantry Regiment, unaware the regiment was at Ship Island during the Siege of Port Hudson.

133. Wilson, *The Black Phalanx,* 218.

134. John H. Gould to his brother, 10 August 1863, John H. Gould Letters 1862–1864, Mss. 3204, LSU.

135. Bvt. Maj. Gen. Daniel Ullman to Gen. Richard C. Drum, 16 April 1887, in *The Negro in the Military Service of the United States, 1639–1886.*

136. "How They Fought," *New York Tribune,* reprinted in the *Prescott Journal* (Wisconsin), 27 June 1863. It was an exaggeration that the Native Guards charged six times; however, they did assault Port Hudson more than once, as even a few Confederate accounts attest. Authors of numerous reports began exaggerating the heroics of the Native Guards once it became clear that this battle would serve at the litmus test for all African American men in the Union army.

137. "Negro Soldiers—The Question Settled," *New York Times,* 11 June 1863.

138. "The Rebels and the Negro Question" and "Will the Negro Fight," *L'Union* (New Orleans), 14 July 1863. Both articles appear on page 2 of the English language version of the paper.

139. Hepworth, *The Whip, Hoe, and Sword,* 190.

140. Daniel Ullman to William C. Bryant, 7 March 1864, in Woodward, comp., *The Negro in the Military Service of the United States, 1639–1886,* 2412.

141. Wilson, *The Black Phalanx,* 218.

142. "Colored Regiments," *La Crosse Republican* (Wisconsin), reprinted in the *Prescott Journal* (Wisconsin), 27 June 1863.

143. *Christian Recorder* (Philadelphia), 13 June 1863.

144. Quarles, *The Negro in the Civil War,* 223.

145. Moore, *Women of the War,* 275; Richard Lowe, "Battle on the Levee: The Fight at Milliken's Bend," in Smith, ed., *Black Soldiers in Blue,* 110.

146. Wilson, *The Black Phalanx,* 203–204.

147. Richard Lowe, "Battle on the Levee: The Fight at Milliken's Bend," in Smith, ed., *Black Soldiers in Blue,* 121.

148. Muster Roll of the 49th USCT, 22 March 1866, in Woodward, comp., *The Negro in the Military Service of the United States, 1639–1886,* 2142.

149. Admiral David Porter to General Grant, 7 June 1863, in Woodward, comp., *The Negro in the Military Service of the United States, 1639–1886,* 2147.

150. Captain Miller letter quoted in Wilson, *The Black Phalanx,* 205–207. See also Elias S. Dennis letter, 12 June 1863, in Berlin et al., eds., *Free at Last,* 441–444.

151. "Important from New Orleans," *New York Herald,* 1 July 1863.

152. "Men of Color" recruitment broadside by Frederick Douglass, Object Number 2012.133, in Collection of the Smithsonian National Museum of African American History and Culture.

153. "Copperhead Democracy Illustrated," *National Anti-Slavery Standard* (New York), 15 August 1863.

154. "Black Troops in Louisiana," *National Intelligencer* (Washington, D.C.), 4 June 1864.

155. "The Negro Union Soldiers," *The Times* (London, UK), quoted in Wilson, *The Black Phalanx,* 395–396.

156. Glatthaar, *Forged in Battle,* 124–135.

157. "The Fight at Port Hudson," *Morning Post* (London, UK), 22 June 1863.

158. Quoted in Richard Lowe, "Battle on the Levee: The Fight at Milliken's Bend," in Smith, ed., *Black Soldiers in Blue,* 127.

159. "The Opposing Press," *L'Union* (New Orleans), 22 September 1863.

160. See *L'Union* (New Orleans), 14 July 1863.

161. Rear Admiral David D. Porter to Gustavus V. Fox, 1863 [specific date unknown], Lincoln Papers, General Correspondence, LOC.

162. General Orders No. 40, Headquarters, Department of the Gulf, 1 May 1863, Department of the Gulf Records.

163. General Orders No. 47, Headquarters, Department of the Gulf, 6 June 1863, Department of the Gulf Records.

164. Irwin, *History of the Nineteenth Army Corps,* 261.

165. Hunt, *Colonels in Blue,* 3.

166. Noah A. Trudeau, "Proven Themselves in Every Respect to Be Men: Black Cavalry in the Civil War," in Smith, ed., *Black Soldiers in Blue,* 278–280.

167. Butler, *Butler's Book,* 495.

168. Hepworth, *The Whip, Hoe, and Sword,* 180.

169. *L'Union* (New Orleans), 2 June 1863.

170. General Orders No. 7, Headquarters, Brigadier General Ullman, 10 June 1863, in Woodward, comp., *The Negro in the Military Service of the United States, 1639–1886,* 1314.

171. "A Black Cloud," *Bangor Daily Whig and Courier* (Bangor, Maine), 19 August 1863.

172. "The Surrender of Vickburgh," *New York Times,* 8 July 1863.

173. J. E. Johnston to William Mackall, 7 June 1863, Mackall Papers, #1299, Duke University, N88-20, M 7, LSA.

174. Henry (no last name), 4 June 1863, Union Soldier Henry Civil War Letter, Mss. 4870, LSU; Frank Gardner to Major General Banks, 13 June 1863, *OR,* Ser. 1, vol. 26, 553.

175. Articles of Capitulation between the Commissioners on the part of the Garrison of Port Hudson, LA, and the Forces of the United States before said place, 8 July 1863, *OR*, Ser. 1, vol. 26, 54.

176. Major General Banks Report on the XIX Corps, 6 April 1865, *OR*, Ser. 1, vol. 26, 16.

177. Malone, *Sweet Chariot*, 90.

178. Governor Moore's Last Speech to the General Assembly, 18 January 1864, Moore Papers.

179. General Banks to Maj. Gen. U. S. Grant, 8 July 1863, *OR*, Ser. 1, vol. 26, 624.

180. Quoted in Wilson, *The Black Phalanx*, 219.

181. Report of Major General Banks on the Siege of Port Hudson, 30 May 1863, *OR*, Ser. 1, vol. 26, 45.

182. N. P. Banks to General Henry Halleck, 12 August 1863, in Woodward, comp., *The Negro in the Military Service of the United States, 1639–1886*, 1478.

183. Richard Irwin to General Banks, report on the Corps d'Afrique, 13 August 1863, in Woodward, comp., *The Negro in the Military Service of the United States, 1639–1886*, 1496–1497.

184. Company I, 1st Louisiana Colored Troops Muster Roll 1863, US Army 6th Infantry Regiment Muster Roll, Mss. 4695, LSU.

185. "General Banks' Visit to Vicksburg," *New York Herald*, 15 August 1863.

186. General Orders No. 41, War Department, 1 February 1864, *OR*, Ser. 1, vol. 26, 911.

187. C. W. Foster to Frederick Douglass, 13 August 1863, Frederick Douglass Papers, LOC.

188. General Lorenzo Thomas to Colonel Isaac F. Shepard, 25 July 1863, in Woodward, comp., *The Negro in the Military Service of the United States, 1639–1886*, 1431.

189. Lorenzo Thomas to Edwin Stanton, 5 October 1863, in Berlin et al., eds., *Freedom, Series II*, 415.

190. Richard Irwin to General Emory, 14 July 1863, *OR*, Ser. 1, vol. 26, 641.

191. Richard Irwin to General George Andrews, 14 July 1863, *OR*, Ser. 1, vol. 26, 641.

192. General George Andrews to Lieut. Colonel Richard Irwin, 15 July 1863, *OR*, Ser. 1, vol. 26, 641.

193. General Charles Stone to Major General Banks, 15 July 1863, *OR*, Ser. 1, vol. 26, 642.

194. Ullman, *Address by Daniel Ullman*, 9.

195. General N. P. Banks to Provost Marshal General, 9 December 1863, Nathaniel P. Banks Letterpress Copybook, 1863–1864, 74, Mss. 2326, box 1, LSU.

196. "Enlisting Soldiers of 'African Descent,'" *Boston Daily Advertiser* (Boston, Mass.), 23 January 1864.

197. W. M. Dixon diary, Dixon Papers, LSU.

198. Governor Moore's Last Speech to the General Assembly, 18 January 1864, Moore Papers.

199. Confederate Major-General Dabney H. Maury to General Samuel Cooper, 7 November 1863, *OR*, Ser. 4, vol. 2, 941.

200. Dabney Maury to Samuel Cooper, indorsed to James Seddon, 20 November 1863, *OR*, Ser. 4, vol. 2, 941.

201. James Seddon indorsement, 24 November 1863, on Dabney Maury to Samuel Cooper, 7 November 1863, *OR*, Ser. 4, vol. 2, 941.

202. Genl Homme, 29 December 1862, Slave Patrol Document, D488, Mss. 83434, box 5, Gladstone Collection, LOC.

203. Reid, *Freedom for Themselves*, xii.

204. Durden, *The Gray and the Black*, 60.

205. J. P. Van Nest to his wife, 31 August 1863, Lippman Collection, TU.

206. "The Coloured Army of the United States," *Daily News* (London, UK), 23 December 1863.

207. "General Banks' Visit to Vicksburg," *New York Herald,* 15 August 1863.

208. Special Orders No. 183, Headquarters, Department of the Gulf, 27 July 1863, *OR,* Ser. 1, vol. 26, 676–679.

209. "Prosperity of New Orleans," *New Orleans Times,* 27 November 1863.

210. M. C. Meigs to William Seward, August 1863, *OR,* Ser. 3, vol. 3, 601.

211. Edwin Stanton to President Abraham Lincoln, 5 December 1863, *OR,* Ser. 3, vol. 3, 1132.

212. General Lorenzo Thomas to Honorable Henry Wilson, 30 May 1864, in Woodward, comp., *The Negro in the Military Service of the United States, 1639–1886,* 2596–2598.

213. Abraham Lincoln to James C. Conkling, 26 August 1863, in Lincoln, *Collected Works of Abraham Lincoln, 1809–1865,* 6:30.

214. Doyle, *The Cause of All Nations,* 126.

215. William Seward to Edwin Stanton, 25 August 1863, in Woodward, comp., *The Negro in the Military Service of the United States, 1639–1886,* 1531.

216. "Heroes of Port Hudson," *Bangor Daily Whig and Courier* (Bangor, Maine), 13 June 1863.

217. "The Negro Volunteer," in Williams, *A History of the Negro Troops in the War of the Rebellion,* 341.

### *8. Dissatisfaction and Discontent*

1. P. B. S. Pinchback to N. P. Banks, 10 September 1863, Pinckney Pinchback, CMSR, NARA.

2. Captain P. B. S. Pinchback to General Banks, 2 March 1863, Pinckney Pinchback, CMSR, NARA.

3. Second Lieutenant Robert. H. Isabelle to Captain Wickham Hoffman, 31 March 1863, Robert H. Isabelle, 74th USCI, CMSR, NARA.

4. Captain Joseph Follin to George Drake, 18 February 1864, Joseph Follin, CMSR, NARA.

5. G. T. Ruby to the editor of the *Liberator,* "Letter from New Orleans," *The Liberator* (Boston, Mass.), 26 February 1864.

6. Benjamin Butler testimony to the American Freedmen's Inquiry Commission, 15 May 1864, in Woodward, comp., *The Negro in the Military Service of the United States, 1639–1886,* 2562.

7. General Benjamin Butler to Salmon P. Chase, 28 February 1863, in Butler, *Private and Official Correspondence,* 3:24.

8. Diary of the 3d Regiment During the Siege of Port Hudson, quoted in Wilson, *The Black Phalanx,* 526.

9. One of the Union Colored Friends to President Lincoln, September 1863, in Berlin et al., eds., *Free at Last,* 458.

10. Warner, *Generals in Blue,* 9.

11. General Orders No. 12, 30 July 1863, General Orders, Port Hudson, Department of the Gulf Records.

12. "New Orleans to Vicksburg," *New Orleans Era,* reprinted in *Daily Richmond Examiner* (Virginia), 4 September 1863.

13. George Denison to Salmon P. Chase, 15 July 1863, General Correspondence, 1810–1898, Mss. 15610, Chase Papers, LOC.

14. General George Leonard Andrews to his wife, 8 July 1863, Andrews Papers, Mss. 3067, LSU.

15. General George Andrews to Lieutenant Colonel R. B. Irwin, 12 August 1863, Letters Sent, Department of the Gulf Records. Years after the war, the War Department realized the folly of Stafford's dismissal, and on 3 January 1871 it changed his dismissal from service to an honorable discharge. See Special Order No. 1, 3 January 1871, in Colonel Spencer H. Stafford, CMSR, NARA.

16. Special Orders No. 200, Headquarters, Department of the Gulf, 15 August 1863, *OR*, Ser. 1, vol. 26, 685.

17. Charles Kennedy to Kate, 21 August 1863, in Steers, ed., *From Port Hudson to Cedar Creek*, 129.

18. General George Andrews to Lt. Col. Samuel M. Quincy, 20 October 1863, Letters Sent, Department of the Gulf Records.

19. Winters, *The Civil War in Louisiana*, 313.

20. Samuel M. Quincy to his grandfather, 8 December 1863, Letters to Family, Samuel M. Quincy Papers, LOC.

21. Quincy, *A Camp and Garrison Manual for Volunteers and Militia.*

22. Samuel Quincy to his grandfather, 5 December 1863, Letters to Family, Samuel M. Quincy Papers, LOC.

23. Lorenzo Thomas to Edwin Stanton, 12 April 1863, in Woodward, comp., *The Negro in the Military Service of the United States, 1639–1886*, 1182.

24. Inspector General's Report to General Banks on the Department of the Gulf, 23 September 1863, Letters Sent, Department of the Gulf Records. The report shows the 1st, 3d, 6th, 7th, 8th, 9th, 10th, and 11th Corps d'Afrique stationed at Port Hudson, along with one of the Black artillery regiments.

25. "Adjt. Gen. Thomas," *Milwaukee Daily Sentinel*, 22 September 1863.

26. "The Negro," *Prescott Journal*, reprinted in the *Polk County Press* (Saint Croix Falls, Wisc.), 27 June 1863.

27. General Orders No. 7, Headquarters, Brigadier General Ullman, 10 June 1863, in Woodward, comp., *The Negro in the Military Service of the United States, 1639–1886*, 1314.

28. C. T. Buddeck to Major General Banks, 5 August 1863, in Berlin et al., eds., *Freedom, Series II*, 150; George H. Hanks to Major General Banks, 5 August 1863, in Berlin et al., eds., *Freedom, Series II*, 152.

29. P. F. Mancosas to Major General Banks, 7 August 1863, in Berlin et al., eds., *Freedom, Series II*, 152.

30. George G. Davis to General James Bowen, 21 August 1863, Letters Received, Department of the Gulf Records.

31. General Orders No. 7, Headquarters, Brigadier General Ullman, 10 June 1863, in Woodward, comp., *The Negro in the Military Service of the United States, 1639–1886*, 1316.

32. Baton Rouge Free Blacks to the Provost Marshal, November 1863, in Berlin et al., eds., *Freedom, Series II*, 159–160.

33. Special Orders No. 166, Headquarters, Department of the Gulf, 10 July 1863, in Woodward, comp., *The Negro in the Military Service of the United States, 1639–1886*, 1382.

34. Special Order No. 50, General Lorenzo Thomas, by Order of the Secretary of War, 3 September 1863, in Woodward, comp., *The Negro in the Military Service of the United States, 1639–1886*, 1553.

35. Ullman's time in the Southern Division was short lived, as his new commander removed

him and sent him back to the Department of the Gulf because he was not a good battlefield commander. Winters, *The Civil War in Louisiana,* 412–413.

36. General George Andrews to Captain James Dwight, 28 October 1863, Letters Sent, Department of the Gulf Records.

37. General Charles P. Stone to Major General N. P. Banks, 21 July 1863, in Woodward, comp., *The Negro in the Military Service of the United States, 1639–1886,* 1421.

38. General George Andrews to Captain James Dwight, 28 October 1863, Letters Sent, Department of the Gulf Records.

39. Lorenzo Thomas to Edwin Stanton, 14 April 1863, in Woodward, comp., *The Negro in the Military Service of the United States, 1639–1886,* 1183–1184.

40. Lorenzo Thomas to Edwin Stanton, 7 November 1864, in Berlin et al., eds., *Freedom, Series II,* 170.

41. Deposition of Charles Franklin Crosby, Civil War Pension File of Frank Nunn, 86th USCI, Frank Nunn, CMSR, NARA.

42. Instructions Issued by General Daniel Ullman, 1 May 1863, in Woodward, comp., *The Negro in the Military Service of the United States, 1639–1886,* 1218.

43. Sergeant Lewis Reed, CMSR, NARA. (His name also appears as Lewis Rede in the CMSR.)

44. General N. P. Banks to his wife, 21 April 1863, and 30 May 1863, box 2, Family Correspondence, Banks Papers, LOC.

45. "Negro Soldiers—The Question Settled," *New York Times,* 11 June 1863.

46. John A. Andrew to Honorable Edwin Stanton, 3 February 1863, in Woodward, comp., *The Negro in the Military Service of the United States, 1639–1886,* 1086.

47. Edwin M. Stanton to Governor Andrew, 13 February 1863, in Woodward, comp., *The Negro in the Military Service of the United States, 1639–1886,* 1102.

48. Edwin Stanton to William F. Adair, 21 March 1863, in Woodward, comp., *The Negro in the Military Service of the United States, 1639–1886,* 1132.

49. Rufus Sibb Jones to Edwin Stanton, 13 May 1862, in Berlin et al., eds., *Freedom, Series II,* 83.

50. C. W. Foster to Colonel H. Van Renssalear, 30 July 1863, in Woodward, comp., *The Negro in the Military Service of the United States, 1639–1886,* 1455.

51. Nathaniel Banks Report on the Native Guards, 12 February 1863, in Woodward, comp., *The Negro in the Military Service of the United States, 1639–1886,* 1094.

52. General Nathaniel Banks to President Abraham Lincoln, 17 August 1863, Lincoln Papers, General Correspondence, LOC.

53. Nathan Daniels, 1 September 1863 and 13 September 1863, in Weaver, ed., *Thank God My Regiment an African One,* 134, 144.

54. Nathan Daniels, 23 September 1863, in Weaver, ed., *Thank God My Regiment an African One,* 152.

55. Berry, "Negro Troops in Blue and Gray," 184.

56. "Liuet-Colonel Henry Finnegass," *Boston Daily Advertiser,* 2 April 1864.

57. Alcide Lewis, CMSR, NARA.

58. Hippolyte St. Louis, CMSR, NARA.

59. Louis A. Thibaut, CMSR, NARA.

60. "The Retreat of Gen. Banks—His Whole Force and Trains Across the Potomac in Safety," *New York Times,* 27 May 1862.

61. Samuel W. Ringgold, CMSR, NARA.

62. Arnold Bertonneau to Wickham Hoffman, 2 March 1863, Arnold Bertonneau, CMSR, NARA.

63. Captain Joseph Follin to General George Drake, 18 February 1864, Service Record Book of Joseph Follin, Joseph Follin CMSR, NARA.

64. Francis Dumas to A. G. Hall, 31 July 1863, Francis E. Dumas, CMSR, NARA.

65. Quoted in Fred Harvey Harrington, "The Fort Jackson Mutiny," *Journal of Negro History* 24, no. 4 (1942): 421.

66. "Officers Wanted for the Corps d'Afrique," *Wisconsin State Register* (Portage, Wisc.), 12 September 1863. One of many examples, this shows the calls were nationwide, not just in the Gulf.

67. Joseph G. Parker to Edwin Stanton, 30 May 1863, in Woodward, comp., *The Negro in the Military Service of the United States, 1639–1886,* 1275.

68. Ibid.

69. Charles Kennedy to Kate, 7 November 1863, in Steers, ed., *From Port Hudson to Cedar Creek,* 158.

70. *New Haven Palladium* (Connecticut), 9 June 1863.

71. Sprague, *History of the 13th Infantry Regiment of Connecticut Volunteers,* 13.

72. Harding, *The Miscellaneous Writings of George C. Harding,* 329.

73. Glatthaar, *Forged in Battle,* 52.

74. Col. John S. Clarke to Maj. Gen. Banks, 13 October 1863, Letters Sent, Department of the Gulf Records.

75. George Andrews to Colonel Dwight, 4 November 1863, Letters Sent, Department of the Gulf Records.

76. Special Orders No. 126, Headquarters, Department of the Gulf, 30 May 1863, General Orders, Department of the Gulf Records.

77. Colonel Alban B. Botsford to Major General N. P. Banks, 13 September 1863, Letters Sent, Department of the Gulf Records.

78. 1st U.S. Infantry Regiment of LA. Volunteer Corps D'Afrique, Company II Muster Roll, folder 1, Mss. 5379, LSU.

79. Company A, 74th USCT, Compiled Records of Service of Military Units in Volunteer Union Organizations, P81–526, microfilm, reel 213, Series 594, LSA. This report shows up on a few of the 2d Corps d'Afrique company rolls, and undoubtedly this would have affected those who wished to join.

80. No. 52, Statement of the Allowance of Clothing to each Soldier, Quartermaster Receipt Roll, James D. Rich Papers, Accounts of Provisions, 1867, Mss. 4783, LSU. According to the statement, soldiers were issued all these things the first year, and many were reissued yearly—or at least they were supposed to be if the quartermaster had them.

81. Colonel Alban B. Botsford to Major General N. P. Banks, 13 September 1863, Letters Sent, Department of the Gulf Records.

82. Special Order No. 6, Recruiting Depot, 20 March 1864, box 32, Banks Papers, LOC.

83. Ochs, *A Black Patriot and a White Priest,* 92.

84. Inspector General's Report on the 6th Michigan Infantry Regiment and Corps d'Afrique to General Banks, 23 September 1863, Letters Sent, Department of the Gulf Records.

85. General Orders No. 4, Headquarters, Defenses of New Orleans, 24 May 1863, attached to Inspector General's Report on 23 September 1863, Letters Sent, Department of the Gulf Records.

86. Norreddin Cowen to Abraham Lincoln, 24 January 1864, Lincoln Papers, General Correspondence, LOC.

87. "From Louisiana," 17 December 1864, *The Sanitary Commission Bulletin* 30 (15 January 1865), 951, Mss. 83434, D261, box 3, Gladstone Collection, LOC.

88. "Testimonials," 10 October 1864, *The Sanitary Commission Bulletin* 30 (15 January 1865), 951, Mss. 83434, D261, box 3, Gladstone Collection, LOC.

89. John Merritt to his parents, 25 August 1863, Mss. 4674, box 1, John Merritt Letters, LSU.

90. Approved Pension Application File for Amy Lee Webb, Application #WC85563, folder 3, Case Files of Approved Pension Applications of Widows and Other Dependents of the Army and Navy Who Served Mainly in the Civil War and the War with Spain, 1861—1934, RG 15, Records of the Department of Veterans Affairs, 1773—2007, NARA.

91. Unsigned letter to Sir, 20 August 1864, in Berlin et al., eds., *Freedom, Series II,* 640.

92. General N. P. Banks to Major C. T. Christensen, 18 July 1864, in Woodward, comp., *The Negro in the Military Service of the United States, 1639-1886,* 2694.

93. "The Campaign in Louisiana-Late and Interesting Details," *Milwaukee Daily Sentinel,* 5 April 1864.

94. "Local News," *L'Union* (New Orleans), 9 July 1864.

95. Fischer, *The Segregation Struggle in Louisiana,* 30–31.

96. *Daily Picayune* (New Orleans), 23 October 1862.

97. Parton, *General Butler in New Orleans,* 494–495.

98. *New Orleans Tribune,* 13 January 1865.

99. Mc Laughlin-Stonham, *From Slavery to Civil Rights,* 59–61.

100. Register of Free Colored Persons Entitled to Remain in the State, vol. 4, 1861–1864, AA 430, New Orleans, Office of the Mayor, Louisiana Division/City Archives, New Orleans Public Library. The registry was used less during 1862 and 1863, but it was not until 1864 before the practice completely fell out of favor in Louisiana and the populace.

101. Ochs, *A Black Patriot and a White Priest,* 112–113.

102. *Richmond Enquirer* (Richmond, Va.), 29 May 1863.

103. "Colored Citizens and Our City Railroad Cars," *New York Tribune,* 9 February 1864.

104. "Colorphobia," *National Anti-Slavery Standard* (New York), 20 February 1864.

105. Williams, *A History of the Negro Troops in the War of the Rebellion,* 314–315, 318.

106. "A Lieutenant and Twenty Negroes Hanged," *Newark Advocate* (Newark, Ohio), 27 November 1863.

107. Daniel Ullman to Edwin Stanton, 6 June 1863, in Woodward, comp., *The Negro in the Military Service of the United States, 1639-1886,* 1298.

108. George Andrews to Richard Irwin, 6 August 1863, *OR,* Ser. 1, vol. 26, 239.

109. Ochs, *A Black Patriot and a White Priest,* 204–205.

110. General George Andrews to Colonel R. B. Irwin, 21 August 1863, Letters Received, Department of the Gulf Records.

111. Dobak, *Freedom by the Sword,* 109.

112. Quoted in ibid.

113. Frazier, *Blood on the Bayou,* 323.

114. Colonel James Gleusk to Lt. Colonel R. B. Irwin, 4 July 1863, Letters Sent, Department of the Gulf Records.

115. B. H. G. to Lieutenant Colonel Irwin, 2 July 1863, Letters Sent, Department of the Gulf Records.

116. Inspector General's Report to General Banks on the Department of the Gulf, 23 September 1863, 7 October 1863, Letters Sent, Department of the Gulf Records.

117. 74th USCT, October 1863, Compiled Records of Service of Military Units in Volunteer Union Organizations, P81-526, microfilm, reel 213, Series 594, LSA.

118. Ochs, *A Black Patriot and a White Priest,* 210.

119. Dobak, *Freedom by the Sword,* 99.

120. Lt. Col. David Branson to Lt. Col. Irwin, 7 July 1864, Letters Received, Department of the Gulf Records.

121. General Daniel Ullman to Henry Wilson, 4 December 1863, *OR,* Ser. 3, vol. 3, 1126–1127.

122. Williams, *A History of the Negro Troops in the War of the Rebellion,* 161.

123. Organization of the Department of the Gulf, 31 August 1863, *OR,* Ser. 1, vol. 26, 707.

124. B. H. G. to Lieutenant Colonel Irwin, 2 July 1863, Letters Sent, Department of the Gulf Records.

125. Form for a Medical Certificate, Edward Carter, CMSR, NARA.

126. Joseph T. Wilson Pension File, Federal Pension Application Files, Certificates 78,530 and 324,127, RG 15, Records of the Veterans Administration, NARA.

127. H. Styles Report on Dick Robinson Plantation, quoted in Berlin et al., eds., *Free at Last,* 111.

128. George Davis to General Banks, 21 August 1863, in Berlin et al., eds., *Free at Last,* 112.

129. Minister Prescott to Edwin Stanton, 11 July 1863, in Berlin et al., eds., *Free at Last,* 201.

130. E. E. Camp Report on formerly enslaved working in multiple hospitals, 31 July 1863, in Berlin et al., eds., *Free at Last,* 204–206.

131. Ochs, *A Black Patriot and a White Priest,* 87.

132. Edwin Stanton to Brigadier General George Shepley, 24 August 1863, *OR,* Ser. 1, vol. 26, 695.

133. Abraham Lincoln, Proclamation of Amnesty and Reconstruction, Lincoln Papers, LOC.

134. "The Restoration of Louisiana," *New York Times,* 21 January 1864.

135. George Denison to Salmon P. Chase, 5 March 1864, General Correspondence, 1810–1898, Mss. 15610, Chase Papers, LOC.

136. Winters, *The Civil War in Louisiana,* 317–318.

137. General Orders No. 64, Headquarters, Department of the Gulf, 29 August 1863, Department of the Gulf Records.

138. Fannie to her mother, 12 January 1864, in Berlin et al., eds., *Free at Last,* 287.

139. Frederick Douglass, quoted in McPherson, *The Negro's Civil War,* 130.

140. Wilson, *The Black Phalanx,* 132.

141. Glatthaar, *Forged in Battle,* 118–119.

142. Ochs, *A Black Patriot and a White Priest,* 91.

143. Glatthaar, *Forged in Battle,* 215.

144. Eliot, Shellabarger, and Boyer, *Report of the Select Committee on the New Orleans Riots,* 412.

145. James G. Hollandsworth, "The Execution of White Officers from Black Units by Confederate Forces During the Civil War," in Urwin, ed., *Black Flag over Dixie,* 53–54.

146. "Bravery of Colored Troops. Colored Soldiers and Sailors Vindicated," *The Elevator* (San Francisco, Calif.), 18 March 1870.

147. Captain Emile Detiége, 25 September 1863, Emile Detiége CMSR, NARA.

148. Hollandsworth, *The Louisiana Native Guards,* 77.

149. Isadore John Kinney to his mother, 1 September 1863, Pension Record of Isadore J. Kinney, CMSR, NARA.

150. General Ullman to Senator Wilson, 4 December 1863, *OR*, Ser. 3, vol. 3, 1127.

151. General Orders No. 77, Headquarters, Department of the Gulf, 27 October 1863, Department of the Gulf Records.

152. Testimony by Officers of a Louisiana Black Regiment before a Military Commission, 12 December 1863, in Berlin et al., eds., *Freedom, Series II*, 442–448.

153. Hollandsworth, *Pretense of Glory*, 145.

154. Testimony by Officers of a Louisiana Black Regiment before a Military Commission, 12 December 1863, in Berlin et al., eds., *Freedom, Series II*, 442–448.

155. "A Sketch of Banks' Expedition up the Red River," William Graham Civil War diary, N2013-042, LSU.

156. "The Fort Jackson Affair," *National Anti-Slavery Standard* (New York), 2 January 1864.

157. "The Negro Mutiny in Fort St. Philip an African Account and Apology," *Milwaukee Daily Sentinel*, 31 December 1863.

158. Proceedings of a Military Commission Convened at Fort Jackson, LA., 21 December 1863, *OR*, Ser. 1, vol. 26, 459–476.

159. Harrington, "The Fort Jackson Mutiny," 424.

160. Brigadier General John P. Hawkins to Col. R. H. Ballinger, 24 December 1863, in Berlin et al., eds., *Freedom, Series II*, 449.

161. "The Negro Mutiny in Fort St. Philip an African Account and Apology," *Milwaukee Daily Sentinel*, 31 December 1863.

162. Proceedings of a Military Commission Convened at Fort Jackson, LA., 21 December 1863, *OR*, Ser. 1, vol. 26, 459–476.

163. "The Mutiny at Fort Jackson," *New York Times*, 6 January 1864.

164. Special Orders No. 309, Headquarters, Department of the Gulf, in Woodward, comp., *The Negro in the Military Service of the United States, 1639–1886*, 1839.

165. Proceedings of a Military Commission Convened at Fort Jackson, LA., 21 December 1863, *OR*, Ser. 1, vol. 26, 459–476.

166. General Charles Stone to General William Dwight, 13 December 1863, *OR*, Ser. 1, vol. 26, 848.

167. General Orders No. 90, Headquarters, Department of the Gulf, 30 December 1863, U.S. Army, Department of the Gulf, *General Court Martial Orders*, 1–6.

168. General Orders No. 90, 30 December 1863, Department of the Gulf Records.

169. Brig. Genl Dwight to Brig Genl Charles P. Stone, 4 February 1864, box 31, Banks Papers, LOC.

170. General Nathaniel Banks to General Henry Halleck, 11 December 1863, in Woodward, comp., *The Negro in the Military Service of the United States, 1639–1886*, 1807.

171. General Orders No. 90, 30 December 1863, General Orders, Department of the Gulf Records.

172. N. P. Banks to H. W. Halleck, 17 December 1863, *OR*, Ser. 1, vol. 26, 457–459.

173. Proceedings of a Military Commission Assembled at Thibodeaux, LA., 5 September 1863, *OR*, Ser. 1, vol. 26, 262–268.

174. General Jason Wadsworth to General Lorenzo Thomas, (no date) December 1863, in Woodward, comp., *The Negro in the Military Service of the United States, 1639–1886*, 1811.

175. General Dwight to General Charles P. Stone, 15 December 1863, in Woodward, comp., *The Negro in the Military Service of the United States, 1639–1886*, 1827.

176. *L'Union* (New Orleans), 30 June 1863.

177. Capers, *Occupied City*, 228.

178. Milteer, *Beyond Slavery's Shadow*, 248.

179. Quarles, *The Negro in The Civil War*, 251.

180. Hollandsworth, *Pretense of Glory*, 165–168.

181. Du Bois, *Black Reconstruction in America*, 462.

182. "The Louisiana Election—Secessionism and Copperheadism Spurned," *New York Times*, 5 March 1864.

183. Wetta, *The Louisiana Scalawags*, 27.

184. Michael Hahn to Abraham Lincoln, 6 June 1863, Lincoln Papers, General Correspondence, LOC.

185. "The Louisiana Election—Secessionism and Copperheadism Spurned," *New York Times*, 5 March 1864.

186. Abraham Lincoln to Michael Hahn, 13 March 1864, in Lincoln, *Collected Works of Abraham Lincoln, 1809–1865*, 7:243.

187. Hollandsworth, *Pretense of Glory*, 209. Many, especially African Americans, did not agree with the criteria Banks wanted, as it was too restrictive for most men to ever vote.

188. Michael Hahn Petition, 16 March 1865, Michael Hahn Papers, Mss. 4808, LSU.

189. Lorenzo Thomas to Edwin Stanton, 24 December 1863, *OR*, Ser. 3, vol. 3, *1190–1191*.

190. George Denison to Salmon P. Chase, 20 December 1863, General Correspondence, 1810–1898, Mss. 15610, Chase Papers, LOC.

191. Troops in the Department of the Gulf, Maj. Gen. N. P. Banks, 31 January 1864, *OR*, Ser. 1, vol. 34, part 2, 193–199.

192. Major D. C. Houston to General Nathaniel Banks, 22 January 1864, *OR*, Ser. 1, vol. 34, part 2, 127.

193. Roland, *Violence in the Hill Country*, 134.

194. "Summary of Daily Intelligence," *North American* (Philadelphia), 2 November 1863.

195. Strength and Composition of the Rio Grande Expedition, 31 October 1863, *OR*, Ser. 1, vol. 26, 398.

196. General Banks to General Henry Halleck, 4 November 1863, in Woodward, comp., *The Negro in the Military Service of the United States, 1639–1886*, 2252–2253.

197. General N. P. Banks to Secretary of State W. H. Seward, 11 December 1863, Nathaniel P. Banks Letterpress Copybook, LSU, 80.

198. Major General F. J. Herron to Gen. Charles Stone, 15 January 1864, 7 January 1864, *OR*, Ser. 1, vol. 34, part 2, 84–85.

199. Major General N. J. T. Dana to Brig. Gen. C. P. Stone, 7 January 1864, *OR*, Ser. 1, vol. 34, part 2, 39.

200. Major General F. J. Herron to Gen. Charles Stone, 15 January 1864, 7 January 1864, *OR*, Ser. 1, vol. 34, part 2, 84–85.

201. William Seward to Major General Banks, 23 November 1863, *OR*, Ser. 1, vol. 26, 815.

202. Major General N. P. Banks to Major General Herron, 25 December 1863, Nathaniel P. Banks Letterpress Copybook, LSU, 140–141.

203. For multiple examples, see U.S. Army, Department of the Gulf, *General Court Martial Orders*. The record book demonstrates that the Corps d'Afrique was not the only regiment with this problem, but in terms of officers, more were from Black regiments than from others, such as the New York and Connecticut regiments. There was even the case of a major acting untoward to the degree he had to be dismissed from service (Major Alexander S. Hill, General Orders No. 29, 24 February 1864).

204. General N. P. Banks to General George Shepley, 2 October 1863, Nathaniel P. Banks Letterpress Copybook, LSU, 50–51.

205. John Merritt to his parents, 11 August 1863, Mss. 4674, box 1, John Merritt Letters, LSU.

206. Feimster, "Rape and Mutiny at Fort Jackson," 11.

207. Court Martial Proceedings of First Lieutenant Thomas B. Curtis, 162d Regiment New York Volunteers, General Order No. 26, Headquarters, Department of the Gulf, 6 April 1863, U.S. Army, Department of the Gulf, *General Court Martial Orders,* G.O. 26, 2–3.

208. Wilson, *Campfires of Freedom,* 205.

209. Feimster, "Rape and Mutiny at Fort Jackson," 22–23.

210. *New Orleans Times,* 23 March 1864.

211. General Dwight to General Charles P. Stone, 31 January 1864, MS. N-13, Dwight Family Papers, 1815–1942, MHS.

212. General Dwight to General Charles P. Stone, 31 January 1864, MS. N-13, Dwight Family Papers, 1815–1942, MHS.

213. Military Commission Convened at Fort Jackson, 1 February 1864, NN1332, Records of the Office of the Judge Advocate General, RG 153, NARA.

214. General Orders No. 14, Headquarters, Department of the Gulf, 27 January 1864, U.S. Army, Department of the Gulf, *General Court Martial Orders,* 5–7.

215. Brig. Genl Dwight to Brig Genl C. P. Stone, 4 February 1864, box 31, Banks Papers, LOC.

216. Ibid.

217. Ibid.

218. Trials of G. E. Wentworth, C. A. Goff, W. H. Knapp, H. F. Blakeslee, and W. H. O'Dell, 4th Corps d'Afrique, NN1332 and LL2744, Records of the Office of the Judge Advocate General, RG 153, NARA.

219. *Weekly Times-Democrat* (New Orleans), 26 March 1864.

220. Lieutenant Colonel S. Fellows to Lieutenant Jack Burchmore, 4 January 1864, in Woodward, comp., *The Negro in the Military Service of the United States, 1639–1886,* 2303.

221. Samuel Roosa to President Lincoln, 24 January 1865, in Berlin et al., eds., *Free at Last,* 487–488.

222. 1st Corps d'Afrique Infantry Regiment to General G. Norman Lieber, 28 March 1864, Regimental Papers, 73d USCI, Records of the Adjutant General's Office, RG 94, NARA. The letter was signed by multiple members of the 1st Regiment, and they begged Banks to address their grievance and return their flag.

223. U.S. Army, Department of the Gulf, *General Court Martial Orders.* The year 1864 demonstrates a shift in the courts-martial in the Department of the Gulf, as there was a serious uptick in the number of Black soldiers sentenced to death. The most common crimes were sleeping on post or leaving their guard.

224. Hollandsworth, *The Louisiana Native Guards,* 82.

225. General Orders No. 14, Headquarters, Department of the Gulf, 27 January 1864, U.S. Army, Department of the Gulf, *General Court Martial Orders,* 1.

226. John Merritt to his parents, 27 December 1863, Mss. 4674, box 1, John Merritt Letters, LSU.

227. Returns from the Department of the Gulf, December 1863, *OR,* Ser. 1, vol. 26, 891–900.

228. New Orleans Free Blacks to the Commander of the Department of the Gulf, 17 August 1864, in Berlin et al., eds., *Freedom, Series II,* 165.

229. Bradish Johnson to General Canby, 17 August 1864, and Colonel H. N. Frisbie to Gorge Drake, 24 October 1864, in Berlin et al., eds., *Freedom, Series II,* 167–169

230. Special Order No. 25, Department of the Gulf, 19 February 1864, in Woodward, comp., *The Negro in the Military Service of the United States, 1639–1886,* 2508.

231. General E. D. Townsend to Colonel S. M. Quincy, 11 November 1864, in Woodward, comp., *The Negro in the Military Service of the United States, 1639–1886,* 2822.

232. "The Freedmen of the Lower Mississippi," *National Anti-Slavery Standard* (New York), 23 July 1864.

233. *Black Warrior* (Camp Parapet, La.), 17 May 1864 (emphasis added).

## *9. We Will Never Stop*

1. Statement of A Colored Man, September 1863, in Berlin, Reidy, and Rowland, eds., *Freedom's Soldiers,* 109–111.

2. Quoted in Harrington, "The Fort Jackson Mutiny," 431.

3. General Orders No. 7, by authority of General Lorenzo Thomas, Adjutant General's Office, 11 Mach 1864, in Woodward, comp., *The Negro in the Military Service of the United States, 1639–1886,* 2417.

4. Longacre, *A Regiment of Slaves,* 10.

5. General Orders No. 16, by authority of General Lorenzo Thomas, Adjutant General's Office, 4 April 1864, in Woodward, comp., *The Negro in the Military Service of the United States, 1639–1886,* 2469. The Department of the Gulf later republished the order on 19 April 1864 in General Orders No. 51, *OR,* Ser. 1, vol. 34, part 3, 221–222.

6. General Orders No. 17, Military Division of West Mississippi, 7 July 1864, Mss. 83434, D40, box 1, Gladstone Collection, LOC.

7. General Orders No. 29, Headquarters, Military Division of West Mississippi, 28 July 1864, in Woodward, comp., *The Negro in the Military Service of the United States, 1639–1886,* 2721.

8. Harrington, "The Fort Jackson Mutiny," 431.

9. General Orders No. 29, Headquarters, Military Division of West Mississippi, 28 July 1864, *New Orleans Tribune,* 4 August 1864.

10. General Orders No. 154, Headquarters, Department of the Gulf, 27 October 1864, Department of the Gulf Records.

11. James F. Jones Letter, 8 May 1864, Letter 57, in Redkey, ed., *A Grand Army of Black Men,* 141–142.

12. James C. Taylor Letter, 14 April 1865, Letter 59, in Redkey, ed., *A Grand Army of Black Men,* 147–148.

13. 77th USCT Infantry Regiment Muster Roll 1865, US Army 6th Infantry Regiment Muster Roll, Mss. 4695, LSU.

14. Ullman, *Address by Daniel Ullman before the Soldier's and Sailor's Union . . . ,* 5, Murray Pamphlet Collection, E540.N3 U4, LOC.

15. General Orders No. 9, Headquarters, U.S. Forces Port Hudson, 9 March 1864, Andrews Papers, Mss. 3067, LSU.

16. General Orders No. 62, Headquarters, Department of the Gulf, 28 May 1864, U.S. Army, Department of the Gulf, *General Court Martial Orders,* 6–7.

17. General Henry Halleck to General N. Banks, 10 August 1863, *OR,* Ser. 1, vol. 26, part 1, 673.

18. Irwin, *History of the Nineteenth Army Corps,* 265–266, 275.

19. Dobak, *Freedom by the Sword*, 122.

20. William H. Seward to Maj. Gen. N. P. Banks, 23 November 1863, *OR*, Ser. 1, vol. 41, part 4, 410.

21. General Banks to Edwin Stanton, 6 April 1865, *OR*, Ser. 1, vol. 34, part 1, 194.

22. Johnson, *Red River Campaign*, 35; Browning, *Lincoln's Trident*, 369.

23. Hepworth, *The Whip, Hoe, and Sword*, 274.

24. Eugéne Dumez to Henry Vignaud, 29 January 1864, Henry Vignaud Papers, Mss. 1281, box 1, LSU.

25. Major General Henry Halleck to Major General Banks, 23 May 1863, *OR*, Ser. 1, vol. 26, 500.

26. Sprague, *History of the 13th Infantry Regiment of Connecticut Volunteers*, 191.

27. Returns and Rosters of US Troops Composing Red River Expedition, *OR*, Ser. 1, vol. 34, part 1, 168.

28. "The Red River Expedition. Details of the Recent Battles," *New York Times*, 24 April 1864.

29. Returns and Rosters of US Troops Composing Red River Expedition, *OR*, Ser. 1, vol. 34, part 1, 167. The 73d, 75th, 84th, 92d USCT were the infantry units, and the 97th and 99th USCT were the engineering units brought along on the campaign.

30. General George Andrews to General C. P. Stone, 1 March 1864, *OR*, Ser. 1, vol. 34, part 2, 474.

31. Captain Otis Whitney diary, 23 March 1864, Terry Waxham Collection, Shreveport, Louisiana, quoted in Cuccia, "'Gorillas' and White Glove Gents," 427.

32. Edwin Stanton to Lieutenant General U. Grant, 5 January 1865, in Woodward, comp., *The Negro in the Military Service of the United States, 1639–1886*, 3514.

33. General N. P. Banks to General U. S. Grant, 13 April 1864, *OR*, Ser. 1, vol. 34, part 1, 187.

34. "Naval Operations on Red River—Admiral Porter's Official Report," *New York Times*, 30 April 1864.

35. Joiner, *Through the Howling Wilderness*, 51.

36. For a full summary of the events during the Red River Campaign, see 10 March–22 May 1864, The Red River (Louisiana Campaign), *OR*, Ser. 1, vol. 34, part 1, 162–167.

37. "A Sketch of Banks' Expedition up the Red River," William Graham Civil War diary, N2013-042, Manuscripts Collections, LSU.

38. Itinerary of the 2d Brigade, 3d Division, XVI Army Corps, *OR*, Ser. 1, vol. 34, part 1, 358.

39. Winters, *The Civil War in Louisiana*, 334.

40. George Drake to Brig. Gen. C. Grover, 2 April 1864, *OR*, Ser. 1, vol. 34, part 3, 19.

41. Circular, Headquarters, U.S. Forces in Western Louisiana, 6 April 1864, *OR*, Ser. 1, vol. 34, part 3, 58.

42. "The Red River Expedition, Capture of Fort De Russy," *New York Herald*, 25 March 1864.

43. Rear Admiral David Porter to Major General William T. Sherman, 16 April 1864, *OR*, Ser. 1, vol. 34, part 3, 171.

44. "A Sketch of Banks' Expedition up the Red River," William Graham Civil War diary, N2013-042, Manuscripts Collections, LSU.

45. N. P. Banks to Rear-Admiral David Porter, 9 April 1864, *OR*, Ser. 1, vol. 34, part 3, 98.

46. Flinn, *Campaigning with Banks in Louisiana*, 106.

47. Lieutenant Colonel R. B. Hatch to Major General J. A. McClernand, 19 April 1864, *OR*, Ser. 1, vol. 34, part 3, 223.

48. "The Red River Expedition. Details of the Recent Battles," *New York Times*, 24 April 1864.

49. Rear Admiral David Porter to Major General William T. Sherman, 16 April 1864, *OR*, Ser. 1, vol. 34, part 3, 170.

50. Wilson, *The Black Phalanx*, 200–203. See also "The Red River Expedition. Details of the Recent Battles," *New York Times*, 24 April 1864.

51. "A Sketch of Banks' Expedition up the Red River," William Graham Civil War diary, N2013-042, Manuscripts Collections, LSU.

52. "The Red River Expedition. Details of the Recent Battles," *New York Times*, 24 April 1864.

53. Flinn, *Campaigning with Banks in Louisiana*, 114.

54. George Drake to Colonel W. H. Dickey, 10 April 1864, *OR*, Ser. 1, vol. 34, part 3, 114.

55. "The Victory in Louisiana," *New York Herald*, 25 April 1864.

56. Johnson, *Red River Campaign*, 163.

57. Major General N. P. Banks to Commanding General Forces, C. S. Army, Pleasant Hill, 11 April 1864, *OR*, Ser. 1, vol. 34, part 3, 125. Banks's letter acknowledges his retreat and asks if he can send for supplies for the "large number of wounded officers and men" he left behind.

58. Private Cornelius M. Sammis diary, 8 May 1864, Terry Waxham Collection, Shreveport, Louisiana, quoted in Cuccia, "'Gorillas' and White Glove Gents," 428.

59. Captain Otis Whitney diary, 15 April 1864, Terry Waxham Collection, Shreveport, Louisiana, quoted in Cuccia, "'Gorillas' and White Glove Gents," 420.

60. Grant, *Personal Memoirs of General Ulysses S. Grant in Two Volumes*, 2:591–592.

61. Major General Banks to Major General Steele, 11 April 1864, 15 April 1864, *OR*, Ser. 1, vol. 34, part 3, 132, 162.

62. "Naval Operations on Red River—Admiral Porter's Official Report," *New York Times*, 30 April 1864.

63. Rear Admiral David D. Porter to Major General W. T. Sherman, 14 April 1864, *OR*, Ser. 1, vol. 34, part 3, 153–154.

64. General Nathaniel Banks to General William Sherman, 14 April 1864, *OR*, Ser. 1, vol. 34, part 3, 266.

65. "The Situation," *New York Herald*, 27 April 1864.

66. Johnson, *Red River Campaign*, 249.

67. Irwin, *History of the Nineteenth Army Corps*, 341.

68. Report of Lieutenant Colonel Uri B. Pearsall, 1 August 1864, *OR*, Ser. 1, vol. 34, part 1, 254.

69. George Drake to Brig. Gen. Fitz Henry Warren, 17 April 1864, *OR*, Ser. 1, vol. 34, part 3, 195.

70. Major General Henry Halleck to Major General Banks, 27 April 1864, *OR*, Ser. 1, vol. 34, part 3, 307.

71. Major General D. Hunter to Lieutenant General Grant, 28 April 1864, *OR*, Ser. 1, vol. 34, part 3, 316.

72. General W. Dwight to Brig. Gen. W. H. Emory, 2 May 1864, *OR*, Ser. 1, vol. 34, part 3, 391.

73. Major General N. P. Banks to Rear Admiral D. D. Porter, 29 April 1864, *OR*, Ser. 1, vol. 34, part 3, 333.

74. George Drake to Colonel Dickey, 5 May 1864, *OR*, Ser. 1, vol. 34, part 3, 453.

75. George Drake to Colonel Dickey, 6 May 1864, *OR*, Ser. 1, vol. 34, part 3, 474.

76. Colonel Henry Rust, Jr., to Brigadier General Dwight, 7 May 1864, *OR*, Ser. 1, vol. 34, part 3, 493.

77. Robertson, *The Red River Campaign and Its Toll*, 164.

78. Major General N. P. Banks to Admiral Porter, 9 May 1864, *OR*, Ser. 1, vol. 34, part 3, 513.

79. Field Orders No. 40, Headquarters, Department of the Gulf, 9 May 1864, *OR*, Ser. 1, vol. 34, part 3, 517.

80. Joiner, *Through the Howling Wilderness*, 155–156.

81. George Drake to Colonel W. H. Dickey, 16 May 1864, *OR*, Ser. 1, vol. 34, part 3, 614.

82. C. S. Sargent to General W. H. Emory, 17 May 1864, *OR*, Ser. 1, vol. 34, part 3, 632.

83. Flinn, *Campaigning with Banks in Louisiana*, 146.

84. S. A. Smith to Jefferson Davis, 21 August 1864, *OR*, Ser. 1, vol. 41, part 1, 116.

85. Browning, *Lincoln's Trident*, 427; Ochs, *A Black Patriot and a White Priest*, 213.

86. General Banks to Edwin Stanton, 6 April 1865, *OR*, Ser. 1, vol. 34, part 3, 201.

87. General Orders No. 48, Headquarters, XIX Army Corps, 18 May 1864, *OR*, Ser. 1, vol. 34, part 1, 398.

88. Joiner, *Through the Howling Wilderness*, 156.

89. Lieutenant Colonel J. Bailey to Maj. George B. Drake, 25 May 1864, *OR*, Ser. 1, vol. 34, part 1, 405.

90. Report of Col. George D. Robinson, 13 June 1864, *OR*, Ser. 1, vol. 34, part 1, 248–253.

91. Report of Col. Francis Fessenden, 13 April 1864, *OR*, Ser. 1, vol. 34, part 1, 430; Report of Col. William H. Dickey, 27 May 1864, *OR*, Ser. 1, vol. 34, part 1, 443.

92. Flinn, *Campaigning with Banks in Louisiana*, 116.

93. "The Red River Expedition—The Army Returned to Alexandria," *New York Times*, 12 May 1864.

94. Lieutenant General U. S. Grant to Maj. Gen. Henry Halleck, 25 April 1864, *OR*, Ser. 1, vol. 34, part 3, 279.

95. Lieutenant General U. S. Grant to Major General Halleck, 16 May 1864, *OR*, Ser. 1, vol. 34, part 3, 615.

96. Major General Henry Halleck to Major General Grant, 3 May 1863, *OR*, Ser. 1, vol. 34, part 3, 409.

97. Joiner, *One Damn Blunder from Beginning to End*, xviii.

98. George Denison to Salmon P. Chase, 17 June 1864, General Correspondence, 1810–1898, Chase Papers, LOC.

99. W. C. Littlefield to his parents, 15 April 1864, Terry Waxham Collection, Shreveport, Louisiana, quoted in Cuccia, "'Gorillas' and White Glove Gents," 430.

100. Unknown soldier to John P. Usher, 30 April 1864, Lincoln Papers, General Correspondence. LOC.

101. Rear Admiral David Porter to Major General William T. Sherman, 16 April 1864, *OR*, Ser. 1, vol. 34, part 3, 171.

102. General Banks to Edwin Stanton, 6 April 1865, *OR*, Ser. 1, vol. 34, part 1, 201.

103. General David Hunter to General Ulysses S. Grant, 2 May 1864, *OR*, Ser. 1, vol. 34, part 3, 390.

104. Joiner, *Through the Howling Wilderness*, 173. Joiner shows that the blame for the failures at Red River was not solely on Banks's shoulders, demonstrating there were a number of factors from Porter and other generals regarding their distrust of Banks, and his understanding of the enemy disposition (179–180).

105. H. D. Woodruff to the Quartermaster of Alexandria, 11 April 1864, *OR*, Ser. 1, vol. 34, part 3, 124.

106. Brigadier General A. J. Smith to Brig. Gen. William Dwight, 10 May 1864, *OR*, Ser. 1, vol. 34, part 3, 535.

107. Governor Isaac Murphy to President A. Lincoln, 12 May 1864, *OR,* Ser. 1, vol. 34, part 3, 559.

108. James Parton to General Benjamin Butler, 22 February 1864, in Butler, *Private and Official Correspondence,* 3:447.

109. "Gen. Banks and the Freedmen," *The Liberator* (Boston, Mass.), 24 February 1865.

110. Duganne, *Camps and Prisons,* 363.

111. Irwin, *History of the Nineteenth Army Corps,* 347.

112. "Gen. Banks Defends and Explains His Labor System," *National Anti-Slavery Standard* (New York), 19 November 1864.

113. Abraham Lincoln to Nathaniel P. Banks, 2 December 1864, Lincoln Papers, General Correspondence, LOC.

114. General Orders No. 192, War Department, 7 May 1864, *OR,* Ser. 1, vol. 34, part 3, 490. It was further specified in Special Orders No. 171 that although his command was called the Military Division of West Mississippi, all troops on the eastern bank were to follow his orders as well. Order on same page in *OR.*

115. General Orders No. 203, War Department, 27 May 1864, *OR,* Ser. 1, vol. 34, part 4, 63.

116. General H. W. Halleck to Major General Sherman, 8 May 1864, *OR,* Ser. 1, vol. 34, part 3, 505.

117. Major General W. T. Sherman to Major General Canby, 8 May 1864, *OR,* Ser. 1, vol. 34, part 3, 505.

118. George Denison to Salmon P. Chase, 17 June 1864, General Correspondence, Mss. 15610, Chase Papers, LOC.

119. Major General Canby to Maj. Gen. Banks, 14 May 1864, *OR,* Ser. 1, vol. 34, part 3, 583.

120. "A Puzzle in Philosophy," *The Liberator* (Boston, Mass.), 17 June 1864.

121. Special Orders No. 16, Headquarters, Military Division of West Mississippi, 16 May 1864, *OR,* Ser. 1, vol. 34, part 3, 615.

122. Major C. T. Christensen to Major General Banks, 17 May 1864, *OR,* Ser. 1, vol. 34, part 3, 632.

123. Major General Ed. Canby to General H. W. Halleck, 18 May 1864, *OR,* Ser. 1, vol. 34, part 3, 644.

124. General Thomas Sherman to Major General Reynolds, 14 May 1864, *OR,* Ser. 1, vol. 34, part 3, 649.

125. John C. Palfrey to Major C. T. Christensen, 19 May 1864, *OR,* Ser. 1, vol. 34, part 3, 664.

126. General Orders No. 3, Headquarters, Division of West Mississippi, 23 May 1864, *OR,* Ser. 1, vol. 34, part 4, 3.

127. Browning, *Lincoln's Trident,* 428, 430; Dobak, *Freedom by the Sword,* 127.

128. Major General Ed. Canby to Rear Admiral D. G. Farragut, 1 July 1864, *OR,* Ser. 1, vol. 41, part 2, 3.

129. General Orders No. 4, Headquarters, Division of West Mississippi, 23 May 1864, *OR,* Ser. 1, vol. 34, part 4, 5.

130. Irwin, *History of the Nineteenth Army Corps,* 354.

131. Ibid., 350.

132. Special Orders No. 39, Headquarters, Military Division of West Mississippi, 16 June 1864, *OR,* Ser. 1, vol. 34, part 4, 406.

133. George Andrews to Lieut. Col. R. B. Irwin, 9 April 1864, *OR,* Ser. 1, vol. 34, part 1, 878.

134. Special Orders No. 134, Headquarters, Department of the Gulf, 23 May 1864, and Special Orders No. 116, Headquarters, XIX Army Corps, 23 May 1864, *OR,* Ser. 1, vol. 34, part 4, 6–7.

135. Special Orders No. 151, Headquarters, Department of the Gulf, 9 June 1864, *OR*, Ser. 1, vol. 34, part 4, 276.

136. Irwin, *History of the Nineteenth Army Corps*, 357.

137. J. Schuyler Crosby to Brigadier General W. H. Emory, 24 May 1864, *OR*, Ser. 1, vol. 34, part 4, 19.

138. See the appendix for full details.

139. Major General Ed. Canby to Major General Henry Halleck, 28 May 1864, *OR*, Ser. 1, vol. 34, part 4, 74.

140. General William Dwight to General McNeil, 26 May 1864, *OR*, Ser. 1, vol. 34, part 4, 46.

141. General Daniel Ullmann to General William Dwight, 31 May 1864, *OR*, Ser. 1, vol. 34, part 4, 141.

142. O. O. Matthews to Brigadier General Ullmann, 2 June 1864, *OR*, Ser. 1, vol. 34, part 4, 174.

143. Major D. C. Houston to Major General Nathaniel Banks, 4 June 1864, *OR*, Ser. 1, vol. 34, part 4, 213–215.

144. General N. B. Buford to Lieut. Col. W. D. Green, 11 June 1864, *OR*, Ser. 1, vol. 34, part 4, 310.

145. George Drake Full Unit Report for Department of the Gulf, 9 June 1864, *OR*, Ser. 1, vol. 34, part 4, 277–278.

146. Major General Ed. Canby to Major General H. W. Halleck, 24 May 1864, *OR*, Ser. 1, vol. 34, part 4, 16.

147. Organization of the Union Forces against Mobile, Ala, 17 March–12 April [1865], *OR*, Ser. 1, vol. 49, part 1, 108–109.

148. Bunn, *The Assault on Fort Blakely*, 77; Major General E. R. S. Canby to Major General Halleck, 27 December 1864, *OR*, Ser. 1, vol. 41, part 4, 940.

149. "Seventh Regiment," *Vermont Watchman* (Montpelier, Vt.), 29 April 1864.

150. John Levering to General Roberts, 10 June 1864, *OR*, Ser. 1, vol. 34, part 4, 292.

151. Ripley, *Slaves and Freedmen in Civil War Louisiana*, 16.

152. General Orders No. 82, Headquarters, Military Division of West Mississippi, 11 December 1864, *OR*, Ser. 1, vol. 41, part 4, 828.

153. Isidore John Kenney to his mother, September 1863, Celina Kenney Pension File, 281929, NARA.

154. Proceedings of a Military Commission Convened at Fort Jackson, LA., 21 December 1863, *OR*, Ser. 1, vol. 26, 461.

155. Recruitment broadside for Connecticut and Rhode Island Black regiments, in Berlin et al., eds., *Freedom, Series II*, 103.

156. Berlin et al., "The Black Military Experience, 1861–1867," in Berlin et al., *Slaves No More*, 214.

157. Egerton, *Thunder at the Gates*, 208.

158. Casey, *New Men*, 138–139.

159. Pinheiro, *The Families' Civil War*, 54.

160. "The Pay of Colored Soldiers," *New York Times*, 21 February 1864.

161. Volunteer Descriptive Lists and Account of Pay and Clothing, April 1864, LSU.

162. Section 2 of An Act of 15 June 1864, in Nalty and MacGregor, eds., *Blacks in the Military*, 31.

163. "Congressional Summary," *Weekly National Intelligencer* (Washington, D.C.), 16 June 1864.

164. Thomas Sipple to President Lincoln, August 1864, in Berlin et al., eds., *Free at Last,* 476.

165. Warren D. Hamelton to Edwin Stanton, May 1865, in Berlin et al., eds., *Free at Last,* 485.

166. Colonel H. Frisbie to the Adjutant General, 24 October 1864, Letters Sent, Department of the Gulf Records.

167. Joseph Price to his wife, 14 April 1865, Mss. 83434, D458, box 5, Gladstone Collection, LOC.

168. General Orders No. 23, Bureau of Refugees, Freedmen, and Abandoned Lands, 16 October 1866, Mss. 83434, D120, box 1, Gladstone Collection, LOC.

169. *New Orleans Republican,* 11 May 1867.

170. Louisa D'Aunoy to the Second Auditor, 14 February 1871, Louisa D'Aunoy Pension Application, 209889, NARA.

171. General N. P. Banks to Hon. Salmon P. Chase, 4 April 1864, *OR,* Ser. 1, vol. 34, part 3, 34–35.

172. Fleming, *The Freedmen's Saving Bank,* 20. The establishment of the Free Labor Bank was one of Chase's last acts as Secretary of the Treasury before Lincoln accepted his resignation and later appointed him as chief justice of the Supreme Court in the fall. It is another feature of Louisiana's Black history that is severely understudied.

173. *L'Union* (New Orleans), 13 January 1863.

174. Ochs, *A Black Patriot and a White Priest,* 185.

175. *L'Union* (New Orleans), 21 June 1864.

176. *L'Union* (New Orleans), 30 December 1862.

177. Dessens, "Louis Charles Roudanez, a Creole of Color of Saint-Domingue Descent," 34.

178. "Freedmen's Aid Association," *New Orleans Tribune,* 16 April 1865.

179. Biographical Information on Black Leaders in New Orleans during Reconstruction, in Foner and Lewis, eds., *The Black Worker,* 1:318–321.

180. New Orleans Free Blacks to the Commander of the Department of the Gulf, 17 August 1864, in Berlin et al., eds., *Freedom, Series II,* 165.

181. Foner and Lewis, eds., *The Black Worker,* 1:315.

182. Ochs, *A Black Patriot and a White Priest,* 189.

183. Weaver, ed., *Thank God My Regiment an African One,* 172–173.

184. "Freedmen's Bureau," *New Orleans Tribune,* November 1, 1864.

185. Stephen A. Hurlbut to Abraham Lincoln, 29 November 1864, Lincoln Papers, General Correspondence, LOC. For Lincoln's original letter, see Abraham Lincoln to Stephen Hurlbut, 14 November 1864, Lincoln Papers, General Correspondence, LOC.

186. General Orders No. 7, Headquarters, Department of the Gulf, 8 February 1865, *OR,* Ser. 1, vol. 48, part 1, 774.

187. Mark Charles Roudané, "The New Orleans Tribune: An Introduction to America's First Daily Newspaper," https://roudanez.com/the-new-orleans-tribune/ (accessed 2 August 2022). Roudané is a historian and descendant of Dr. Louis Charles Roudanez who takes great pride in bringing his ancestor's story to the forefront of Civil War historiography.

188. Petition from the Office of the *Black Republican,* 26 May 1865, Caesar C. Antoine, CMSR, NARA.

189. Court-Martial of Leonnel McCarty, 19 September 1864, Records of the Office of the Judge Advocate General's Office (Army), 1809–1890, Court-Martial Case File LL-3106, RG 153, NARA.

190. Ochs, *A Black Patriot and a White Priest,* 223–224.

191. Quoted in Ochs, *A Black Patriot and a White Priest*, 225.

192. Daggett, *Spiritualism in Nineteenth-Century New Orleans*, 60.

193. *L'Union* (New Orleans), 26 May 1864.

194. *New Orleans Tribune*, 10 November 1864.

195. Table of Organization, Military Division of West Mississippi, October 1864, *OR*, Ser. 1, vol. 41, part 4, 360. Canby's forces ended the year with 126,498 effective soldiers, or 165,204 if those absent from duty for various reasons were included. Table of Organization, Military Division of West Mississippi, December 1864, *OR*, Ser. 1, vol. 41, part 4, 972.

196. Organization of Troops in the Military Division of West Mississippi, 31 December 1864, *OR*, Ser. 1, vol. 41, part 4, 973–988. There were USCT regiments in every part of the Military Division of West Mississippi, and not all were from the region of the Gulf.

197. General Orders No. 277, War Department, Adjutant General's Office, 7 November 1864, *OR*, Ser. 1, vol. 41, part 4, 464.

198. Report of Brig. Gen. Henry W. Birge, 3 May 1864, *OR*, Ser. 1, vol. 34, part 1, 906.

199. Report of Brig. Gen. Daniel Ullman, 17 May 1864, *OR*, Ser. 1, vol. 34, part 1, 934.

200. Report of Lieut. Harmon T. Chappell, 29 July 1864, *OR*, Ser. 1, vol. 41, part 1, 23.

201. Report of Col. James M. Williams, 9 February 1865, *OR*, Ser. 1, vol. 48, part 1, 102.

202. George Denison to Salmon P. Chase, 6 September 1864, General Correspondence, 1810–1898, Mss. 15610, Chase Papers, LOC.

203. Report of Lieutenant Colonel Alfred G. Hall, 13 September 1864, *OR*, Ser. 1, vol. 41, part 1, 757; Report of Lieut. Michael Gallagher, 1 February 1865, *OR*, Ser. 1, vol. 48, part 1, 85.

204. Report of Col. Henry N. Frisbie, 24 September 1864, *OR*, Ser. 1, vol. 41, part 1, 808–809.

205. Special Orders No. 8, Headquarters, Department of the Gulf, 2 October 1863, quoted in Haskins, *Pinckney Benton Stewart Pinchback*, 27.

206. Haskins, *Pinckney Benton Stewart Pinchback*, 29.

207. General Orders No. 150, Headquarters, Department of the Gulf, 19 October 1864, *OR*, Ser. 1, vol. 41, part 4, 104.

208. General Orders No. 154, Headquarters, Department of the Gulf, 27 October 1864, in Woodward, comp., *The Negro in the Military Service of the United States, 1639–1886*, 2810.

209. Captain Sheldon Sturgeon to Major George B. Drake, 18 November 1864, with multiple enclosures, James Lewis, CMSR, NARA.

210. Josephine B. Lewis testimony, 23 April 1919, Emma Barrett Pension File, 1119719, NARA.

211. Colonel H. N. Frisbie to Major George B. Drake, 24 October 1864, *OR*, Ser. 1, vol. 41, part 4, 215–216.

212. Organization of Troops in the Department of the Gulf, 31 October 1864, *OR*, Ser. 1, vol. 41, part 4, 361–366.

213. General Orders No. 55, Headquarters, Bureau of Conscription, 20 July 1864, Trans-Mississippi Department General Orders, Special Orders, and Circulars Relating to Conscription, 1863–1865, Louisiana Adjutant General Office Library Civil War Manuscripts, N314-7-3, microfilm, reel #2, LSA.

214. Special Orders No. 121, Headquarters, Bureau of Conscription, 17 May 1864, Trans-Mississippi Department General Orders, Special Orders, and Circulars Relating to Conscription, 1863–1865, Louisiana Adjutant General Office Library Civil War Manuscripts, N314-7-3, microfilm, LSA.

215. Henry Allen to Rebel Secretary of War, 26 September 1864, in General Orders No. 58,

Military Division of West Mississippi, 11 October 1864, Mss. 83434, D492, box 5, Gladstone Collection, LOC.

216. General Orders No. 90, Headquarters, Bureau of Conscription, 25 November 1864, Trans-Mississippi Department General Orders, Special Orders, and Circulars Relating to Conscription, 1863–1865, Louisiana Adjutant General Office Library Civil War Manuscripts, N314-7-3, microfilm, reel #2, LSA.

217. Winters, *The Civil War in Louisiana,* 395.

218. General Orders No. 169, Headquarters, Department of the Gulf, 30 November 1864, General Orders, Department of the Gulf Records.

219. Special Orders No. 48, Headquarters, Department of the Gulf, 20 February 1865, in Woodward, comp., *The Negro in the Military Service of the United States, 1639–1886,* 3575.

220. Lt. Col. Jno. L. Rice to General Lorenzo Thomas, 20 September 1864, in Berlin et al., eds., *Freedom, Series II,* 509.

221. Thomas Sipple to President Lincoln, August 1864, in Berlin et al., eds., *Free at Last,* 477.

222. Report of Col. Henry N. Frisbie, 24 September 1864, *OR,* Ser. 1, vol. 41, part 1, 810.

223. George Andrews to Maj. George Drake, 5 September 1864, *OR,* Ser. 1, vol. 41, part 3, 66.

224. Captain P. C. Chains to Major George Drake, 18 October 1864, *OR,* Ser. 1, vol. 41, part 4, 67.

225. General Lorenzo Thomas to Edwin Stanton, 23 February 1865, in Woodward, comp., *The Negro in the Military Service of the United States, 1639–1886,* 3578.

226. Special Orders No. 282, Headquarters, Department of the Gulf, 18 October 1864, *OR,* Ser. 1, vol. 41, part 4, 68.

227. General Orders No. 8, Headquarters, Department of the Gulf, 9 February 1865, *OR,* Ser. 1, vol. 48, part 1, 787; Special Orders No. 63, Headquarters, Department of the Gulf, 7 March 1865, *OR,* Ser. 1, vol. 48, part 1, 1112.

228. List of Regiments Serving on the Mississippi, 1865, Major General Ed. R. S. Canby to Maj. Gen. Halleck, 7 March 1865, *OR,* Ser. 1, vol. 48, part 1, 1108–1110.

229. Two reports show how small but frequent the patrols were: Report of Col. Simon Jones, 27 March 1865, and Report of Lieut. Col. John L. Rice, *OR,* Ser. 1, vol. 48, part 1, 153, 175.

230. Colonel H. N. Frisbie to Lieutenant Colonel O. A. Rice, 18 December 1864, *OR,* Ser. 1, vol. 41, part 1, 994.

231. Interview with Alexander W. Randall and Joseph T. Mills, 19 August 1864, in Lincoln, *Collected Works of Abraham Lincoln, 1809–1865,* 7:507.

232. Doyle, *The Cause of All Nations,* 281–283.

233. *New Orleans Tribune,* 25 August 1864.

234. "What Is an Honorable Peace?," *New York Times,* 19 August 1864.

235. Hollandsworth, *Pretense of Glory,* 155.

236. *New Orleans Tribune,* 10 February 1865.

237. Hahn, *Message of the Governor of the State of Louisiana: Delivered October 7, 1864,* 7–9, 12, Michael Hahn, Message Delivered 7 October 1864, J87.L82, LSU.

238. Robert Tarleton to Sallie, 27 April 1865, Letters of Sallie Lightfoot Tarleton, LSA.

239. Bunn, *The Assault on Fort Blakely,* 77.

240. "Rejection by the South of President Lincoln's Peace Propositions," *Royal Gazette* (Hamilton, Bermuda), 21 February 1865.

241. Report of Maj. Gen. R. S. Canby, 1 June 1865, *OR,* Ser. 1, vol. 49, part 1, 95; Consolidated Report of Casualties from 25 March to 10 April 1865, Army and Division of West Mississippi, *OR,*

Ser. 1, vol. 49, part 1, 101. Hawkins's Division took forty-two of the seventy-three casualties suffered that day among all of Canby's forces.

242. "The Situation," *New York Herald*, 7 April 1865.

243. E. Longpre to Colonel J. T. Wilson, 18 January 1883, in Wilson, *The Black Phalanx*, 528.

244. Report of Brig. Gen. John P. Hawkins, 8 April 1865, *OR*, Ser. 1, vol. 49, part 1, 287.

245. Organization of the Union Forces against Mobile, Ala, 17 March–12 April, *OR*, Ser. 1, vol. 49, part 1, 108–109. The 47th, 50th, 51st, 48th, and 68th USCT were all part of Hawkins's Division as well.

246. Report of Brig. Gen. William A. Pile, 13 April 1865, *OR*, Ser. 1, vol. 49, part 1, 289.

247. "The Seventy-Third Regiment," *New Orleans Tribune*, 14 July 1865.

248. Quoted in Harrington, "The Fort Jackson Mutiny," 431.

249. E. Longpre to Colonel J. T. Wilson, 18 January 1883, in Wilson, *The Black Phalanx*, 528.

250. "Les Troupes de Couleur au Fort Blakely," *New Orleans Tribune*, 16 April 1865.

251. "L'Assaut du Fort Blakeley et les Native Guards," *New Orleans Tribune*, 21 June 1865; "Le 1er des Native Guards," *New Orleans Tribune*, 14 June 1865.

252. "Chronicles of the War," *National Anti-Slavery Standard* (New York), 22 April 1865.

253. Edwin Stanton to Major General Canby, 16 May 1865, *OR*, Ser. 1, vol. 49, part 1, 104.

254. Report of Brig. Gen. William A. Pile, 13 April 1865, *OR*, Ser. 1, vol. 49, part 1, 290.

255. "Terms of Capitulation," General Orders No. 54, Headquarters, Department of Alabama, Mississippi, and East Louisiana, 6 May 1865, Richard Taylor Papers, 16 October 1863–9 May 1865, Louisiana Adjutant General Office Library Civil War Manuscripts, N314-7-3, microfilm, reel #6, LSA.

256. Edmund Smith to Maj. Gen. Magruder, 19 May 1865, William A. Smith Letters, Manuscripts Collection, M-1102, TU.

257. Winters, *The Civil War in Louisiana*, 422.

258. Edmund Smith to Brigadier General of US Volunteers Davis, 31 May 1865, William A. Smith Letters, Manuscripts Collection, M-1102, TU.

259. "Surrender of Rebel Forces West of the Mississippi," *The Liberator* (Boston, Mass.), 2 June 1865.

260. Algernon Badger to John B. Badger, 10 June 1865, Badger Family Papers, Manuscripts Collection 1080, TU.

261. Henry Allen to the People of Louisiana, 2 June 1865, Moore Papers.

262. Henry Allen to the People of Louisiana, 2 June 1865, Moore Papers.

263. Report of Capt. Eben F. Barker, 7 May 1865, *OR*, Ser. 1, vol. 48, part 1, 49.

264. Algernon Badger to John B. Badger, 8 September 1865, Badger Family Papers, Manuscripts Collection 1080, TU.

265. 74th USCT Muster Roll, Compiled Records of Service of Military Units in Volunteer Union Organizations, P81-526, microfilm, reel 213, Series 594, LSA.

266. P. J. Maloney to Brigadier General Cameron, 10 April 1865, *OR*, Ser. 1, vol. 48, part 2, 63.

267. Edward Augustus Wild to General Weitzel, 16 February 1865, Mss. 83434, 53, box 1, Gladstone Collection, LOC.

268. Ullman, *Address by Daniel Ullman . . .*, 7, Murray Pamphlet Collection.

269. *New Orleans Tribune*, 17 August 1865.

270. "Local Intelligence," *New Orleans Tribune*, 24 October 1865.

271. Special Orders No 199, War Department, Adjutant General's Office, 2 May 1865, Mss. 83434, 459, box 5, Gladstone Collection, LOC.

272. General Orders No. 23, Headquarters, Southern Division of Louisiana, 23 May 1865, Mss. 83434, D486, box 5, Gladstone Collection, LOC. Forty soldiers and three civilians were convicted on 2 May 1865. General Orders No. 28, Headquarters, Southern Division of Louisiana, 17 June 1865, Mss. 83434, D461, box 5, Gladstone Collection, LOC. General Orders No. 32, 5 July 1865, of the same command demonstrates the full extent of the convictions. Another forty-six soldiers were convicted a few weeks later. The most common offense was sleeping on post, a consequence of boredom while on guard as soldiers became complacent regarding the end of the war. Fourteen civilians were convicted on that date as well.

273. J. Schuyler Crosby to Henry Clay Warmouth, 14 November 1865, quoted in Ripley, *Slaves and Freedmen in Civil War Louisiana,* 108.

274. John D. Smith, "Let Us All Be Grateful That We Have Colored Troops That Will Fight," in Smith, ed., *Black Soldiers in Blue,* 25; Michael T. Meier, "Lorenzo Thomas and the Recruitment of Blacks in the Mississippi Valley, 1863–1865," in Smith, ed., *Black Soldiers in Blue,* 268.

275. Report, Provost Marshal General's Bureau, 17 March 1866, in Nalty and MacGregor, eds., *Blacks in the Military,* 32. See the appendix for all units credited to Louisiana.

276. Kreidberg and Henry, *History of Military Mobilization in the United States Army,* 114.

277. Wilson, *The Black Phalanx,* 123.

278. Williams, *A History of the Negro Troops in the War of the Rebellion,* 141.

279. Special Orders No. 49, Headquarters, XIX Army Corps, 28 October 1863, *OR,* Ser. 1, vol. 26, 780.

280. Eliot, Shellabarger, and Boyer, *Report of the Select Committee on the New Orleans Riots,* 105.

281. Captain Charles Sauvenet, 2 September 1863, Charles Sauvenet, CMSR, NARA; see also Hollandsworth, *The Louisiana Native Guards,* 76. Hollandsworth believes Sauvenet remained because his complexation seemed white enough that his presence was palatable to Banks and other white officers, a plausible answer for why Banks would have not worked as vehemently to remove him.

282. Ochs, *A Black Patriot and a White Priest,* 207.

283. For more information regarding how much of a nuisance guerrillas were during and after the war, see Sutherland, *A Savage Conflict.*

284. Special Orders No. 67, Headquarters, Department of the Gulf, 23 September 1864, General Orders, Department of the Gulf Records; *Official Army Register . . . ,* part 8, 246.

285. See the appendix for the muster out date of each unit.

286. "Texas: Affairs in the Lone Star State," *New York Herald,* 9 January 1865.

287. Mendez, *A Great Sacrifice,* 156.

288. For more information regarding the USCT regiments who held Texas for the United States into Reconstruction, see Dobak, *Freedom by the Sword,* 425–454.

289. Doyle, *The Cause of All Nations,* 300; 304.

290. See U.S. Army, Department of the Gulf, *General Court Martial Orders.*

291. Private Prince Albert to Andrew Johnson, 28 January 1866, in Berlin et al., eds., *Freedom, Series II,* 428.

292. Unsigned letter to Edwin Stanton, 7 March 1866, in Berlin et al., eds., *Freedom, Series II,* 515.

293. General Ulysses. S. Grant to General G. H. Thomas, 28 March 1866, in MacGregor and Nalty, eds., *Blacks in the United States Armed Forces,* 3:13.

294. Brown, "Negotiating and Transforming the Public Sphere," 111–112.

295. Conway, *The Freedmen of Louisiana,* Department of the Gulf Records, NARA.

296. Rankin, "The Origins of Black Leadership in New Orleans during Reconstruction," 434. Rankin shows that a large portion of the Black leadership of New Orleans during Reconstruction was made up of those who served in the Native Guards.

297. General Orders No. 62, Headquarters, Department of Louisiana, 28 October 1865, in Woodward, comp., *The Negro in the Military Service of the United States, 1639–1886,* 3728.

298. "The Republican Turn-out on Sunday," *New Orleans Tribune,* 31 October 1865.

299. Deposition of Charles Franklin Crosby, Civil War Pension File of Frank Nunn, 86th USCI, Charles F. Crosby, CMSR, NARA.

300. "The Radical Convention," *New Orleans Tribune,* 11 June 1867.

301. Comminey, "National Black Conventions and the Quest for African American Freedom and Progress, 1847–1867," 10.

302. Hollandsworth, *The Louisiana Native Guards,* 105.

303. Quoted in Foner, *A Short History of Reconstruction,* 30.

304. Abraham Lincoln, "Last Public Address," 11 April 1865, in Lincoln, *Collected Works of Abraham Lincoln, 1809–1865,* 8:400–405.

305. Beard and Makowicki, *Lincoln Assassination,* 4.

306. Eliot, Shellabarger, and Boyer, *Report of the Select Committee on the New Orleans Riots,* 277.

307. Du Bois, *Black Reconstruction in America,* 466. See Eliot, Shellabarger, and Boyer, *Report of the Select Committee on the New Orleans Riots,* for the full report.

308. Vincent, *Black Legislators in Louisiana During Reconstruction,* 226–227.

309. "The War of Races," *New York Times,* 16 April 1873.

310. Hogue, *Uncivil War,* 183.

311. Wilson, *The Black Phalanx,* 200 (emphasis in original).

312. "The Meeting Sunday," *New Orleans Tribune,* 28 November 1865.

313. "The State of the Country," *National Anti-Slavery Standard* (New York), 31 May 1863.

### *Conclusion*

1. "Most Respectfully Dedicated to the 73d Late First Regiments Louisiana Native Guards," *New Orleans Tribune,* 5 September 1865. A testament to how little the populace liked the designation "Corps d'Afrique," it was rarely used after the war. The regiments were almost exclusively referred to as the Native Guards or by their USCT designation. Thus, this conclusion will respect their preference and refer to the regiments by the designations they preferred when possible.

2. S. P. Chase to Major General B. F. Butler, 29 October 1862, in Butler, *Private and Official Correspondence,* 2:423.

3. E. Longpre to Colonel J. T. Wilson, 18 January 1883, in Wilson, *The Black Phalanx,* 528.

4. "Le 1er des Native Guards," *New Orleans Tribune,* 14 June 1865.

5. Kreidberg and Henry, *History of Military Mobilization in the United States Army,* 113.

6. Daggett, *Spiritualism in Nineteenth-Century New Orleans,* 63.

7. "The Colored Tennessean," *New Orleans Tribune,* 19 May 1865.

8. "The Seventy-Third Regiment," *New Orleans Tribune,* 14 July 1865.

9. Dobak and Phillips, *The Black Regulars,* 4–5.

10. Prescella Martin testimony, 17 June 1919, Emma Barrett Pension File, 1119719, NARA.

11. Levin, *Searching for Black Confederates,* 45–46.

12. E. K. Davis to Benjamin F. Butler, 7 December 1876, in MacGregor and Nalty, eds., *Blacks in the United States Armed Forces,* 3:116.

13. "S.3702—United States Colored Troops Congressional Gold Medal Act," 17 February 2022, 117th Congress, https://www.congress.gov/bill/117th-congress/senate-bill/3702/actions (accessed 20 November 2022). The bill is currently referred to the Committee on Banking, Housing, and Urban Affairs.

# *BIBLIOGRAPHY*

### *Primary Sources*

#### ARCHIVES AND MANUSCRIPT COLLECTIONS

Earl K. Long Library, University of New Orleans, New Orleans, Louisiana
Historian's Files, U.S. Army Center of Military History, Washington, D.C.
Law Library of Louisiana, New Orleans, Louisiana
Library of Congress, Washington, D.C.
A Century of Lawmaking for a New Nation: U.S. Congressional Documents and Debates, 1774–1875
Chronicling America: Historic American Newspapers
Federal Writers' Project: Slave Narrative Project
Manuscript Division
Benjamin F. Butler Papers
Salmon P. Chase Papers
Frederick Douglass Papers
William A. Gladstone Afro-American Military Collection
Andrew Johnson Papers
Abraham Lincoln Papers
Charles O'Neil Papers
Nathaniel Prentiss Banks Papers
Samuel M. Quincy Papers
Edwin M. Stanton Papers
Louisiana Slave Database, Whitney Plantation Museum, Edgard, Louisiana
Louisiana State Archives, Baton Rouge, Louisiana
Civil War Letters Collection
Civil War Newspapers
Compiled Records of Service of Military Units in Volunteer Union Organizations
Department of the Gulf Microfilm
Louisiana Adjutant General Office Library Civil War Manuscripts
Louisiana Slave Narratives

Mayor General's Office
Thomas O. Moore Papers
Letters of Sallie Lightfoot Tarleton
Louisiana State University, Baton Rouge, Louisiana, Special Collections
George Andrews Papers
Nathaniel P. Banks Letterpress Copybook
Bell Griffith Letters
John S. Billiu Letters
Civil War Letters, 1861–1866
George H. Davis Letters
Department of the Gulf Files
William Y. Dixon Papers
Fielding Yeager Doke Papers
James and John Durnin Papers
Free People of Color in Louisiana
Greene Family Correspondence
John H. Guild Letters
Michael Hahn Papers
William T. Johnson Family and Memorial Papers
Louisiana Black Newspapers
Louisiana Newspapers Published during the Civil War, 1861–1865
John Merritt Letters
P. D. Montgomery Letters
Thomas O. Moore Papers
Muster Rolls, Corps d'Afrique
James D. Rich Papers
Nicholas John Sandlin Letters
United States Colored Infantry Regiment Descriptive Book Collection
Union Soldiers Civil War Letters
Henry Vignaud Papers
Louisiana Research Collection, Howard-Tilton Memorial Library, Tulane University, New Orleans, Louisiana
Algernon Badger Family Papers
J. Harvey Brown Papers
Alfred S. Lippman Collection of Civil War Letters
Jean Baptiste Meullion Papers
Alfred A. Parmenter Papers
Lansing Porter Family Papers
William A. Smith Letters
Martin L. Williston Papers
Making of America, Cornell University, Ithaca, New York

Making of America, University of Michigan, Ann Arbor, Michigan
Massachusetts Historical Society, Boston, Massachusetts
Dwight Family Papers
William Lloyd Garrison Papers
National Archives and Records Administration, Washington, D.C.
Compiled Military Service Records
Records of the Adjunct General Office
Records of the Colored Troops Division
Records of the Department of Veterans Affairs, 1773–2007
Records of the Record and Pension Office of the War Department
Records of the U.S. Army Continental Commands, Department of the Gulf
United States Colored Infantry, Regimental Papers
New Orleans Public Library, New Orleans, Louisiana
North American Immigrant Letters, Diaries, and Oral Histories, University of Chicago. Chicago, Illinois
Smithsonian, National Museum of African American History and Culture, Washington, D.C.
U.S. Army Sanitary Commission Records, Department of the Gulf, Manuscripts and Archives Division, New York Public Library, New York
Williams Research Center, Historic New Orleans Collection, New Orleans, Louisiana

## AUTOBIOGRAPHIES, LETTERS, AND OTHER PERSONAL ACCOUNTS

Ashkenazi, Elliott, ed. *The Civil War Diary of Clara Solomon: Growing Up in New Orleans, 1861–1862*. Baton Rouge: Louisiana State Univ. Press, 1995.

Belknap, George E., ed. *Letters of Captain Geo. Hamilton Perkins, U.S.N.: Also a Sketch of His Life*. Concord, N.H.: Rumford Press, 1901.

Butler, Benjamin F. *Butler's Book: Autobiography and Personal Reminiscences of Major General Benjamin F. Butler*. Boston: A. M. Thayer, 1892.

——. *Private and Official Correspondence of Gen. Benjamin F. Butler During the Period the Civil War*. Edited by Jessie Ames Marshall. 5 vols. Norwood, Mass.: Plimpton Press, 1917.

Cleveland, Henry. *Alexander H. Stephens, in Public and Private: With Letters and Speeches, Before, During, and Since the War*. Philadelphia: National Publishing Company, 1866.

De Forest, John William. *Volunteer's Adventures: A Union Captain's Record of the Civil War*. Edited by James H. Croushore. New Haven: Yale Univ. Press, 1946.

Duganne, Augustine J. H. *Camps and Prisons: Twenty Months in the Department of the Gulf*. New York: J. P. Robens, Publisher, 1865.

Flinn, Frank M. *Campaigning with Banks in Louisiana, '63 and '64, and with Sheridan in the Shenandoah Valley in '64 and '65*. 2nd ed. Boston: W. B. Clarke, 1889.

Glatthaar, Joseph T., and John H. Crowder. "The Civil War Through the Eyes of a Sixteen-Year-Old Black Officer: The Letters of Lieutenant John H. Crowder of the 1st Louisiana Native Guards." *Journal of the Louisiana Historical Association* 35, no. 2 (Spring 1994): 201–216.

Grant, Ulysses S. *Personal Memoirs of General Ulysses S. Grant in Two Volumes.* New York: Charles L. Webster, 1885.

Harding, George C. *The Miscellaneous Writings of George C. Harding.* Indianapolis: Carlon and Hollenbeck, Printers and Binders, 1882.

Hepworth, George H. *The Whip, Hoe, and Sword; or, the Gulf Department in '63.* Boston: Walker, Wise, 1864.

Houzeau, Jean-Charles. *My Passage at the New Orleans Tribune: A Memoir of the Civil War Era.* Edited by David C. Rankin and translated by Gerard F. Denault. Baton Rouge: Louisiana State Univ. Press, 1984.

Jones, Terry L., ed. *The Civil War Memoirs of Captain William J. Seymour: Reminiscences of a Louisiana Tiger.* El Dorado Hills, Calif.: Savas Beatie, 2020.

Lane, Susan Gilbreath, ed. *Dignity of Duty: The Journals or Erasmus Corwin Gilbreath, 1861–1898.* Chicago: Pritzker Military Museum and Library, 2015.

Lincoln, Abraham. *Collected Works of Abraham Lincoln, 1809–1865.* Edited by Roy P. Basler, Marion Dolores Pratt, and Lloyd A. Dunlap. 9 vols. New Brunswick, N.J.: Rutgers Univ. Press, 1953–1955.

Rowland, Kate M., and Morris L. Croxall, eds. *The Journal of Julia Le Grand: New Orleans, 1862–1863.* Richmond, Va.: Everett Waddey, 1911.

Olmsted, Frederick L. *The Cotton Kingdom: A Traveler's Observation on Cotton and Slavery in the American Slave States.* Bedford, Mass.: Applewood Books, 1861.

——. *A Journey in the Seaboard Slave States: With Remarks on Their Economy.* New York: Dix and Edwards, 1856.

Russell, William Howard. *My Diary North and South.* Boston: T. O. H. P. Burnham, 1863.

Sprague, Homer B. *History of the 13th Infantry Regiment of Connecticut Volunteers During the Great Rebellion.* Hartford, Conn.: Case, Lockwood, 1867.

Stearns, Albert. *Reminiscence of the Late War.* Brooklyn: Self-Published, 1881.

Steers, Edward, Jr., ed. *From Port Hudson to Cedar Creek: The Civil War Letters of Charles Washington Kennedy.* Middletown, Del.: CreateSpace Independent Publishing Platform, 2014.

Weaver, C. P., ed. *Thank God My Regiment an African One: The Civil War Diary of Colonel Nathan W. Daniels.* Baton Rouge: Louisiana State Univ. Press, 1998.

Weld, Theodore Dwight. *American Slavery as It Is.* New York: American Anti-Slavery Society, 1839.

Williams, George W. *A History of the Negro Troops in the War of the Rebellion, 1861–1865: Preceded by a Review of the Military Services of Negroes in Ancient and Modern Times.* New York: Harper and Brothers, Franklin Square, 1888.

Wilson, Joseph T. *The Black Phalanx: A History of the Negro Soldiers of the United States in the Wars of 1775–1812; 1861–'65.* Hartford, Conn.: American Publishing Company, 1897.

Wormeley, Katherine P. *The United States Sanitary Commission: A Sketch of Its Purposes and Its Work.* Boston: Little, Brown, 1863.

GOVERNMENT SOURCES

*Acts of the General Assembly of the State of Arkansas.* Little Rock: General Assembly of the State of Arkansas, 1859.

*Acts Passed by the Fourth Legislature of the State of Louisiana.* New Orleans, 1859.

Eliot, Thomas D., Samuel Shellabarger, and Benjamin M. Boyer. *Report of the Select Committee on the New Orleans Riots.* Washington, D.C.: Government Printing Office, 1867.

Heitman, Francis B. *Historical Register and Dictionary of the United States Army.* Washington, D.C.: Government Printing Office, 1903.

Kreidberg, Marvin A., and Merton G. Henry. *History of Military Mobilization in the United States Army, 1775–1945.* Washington, D.C.: Department of the Army, 1955.

*Journal of the Confederate States of America, 1861–1865.* Washington, D.C.: Government Printing Office, 1904.

*The Laws of Las Siete Partidas, Which Are Still in Force in the State of Louisiana.* Vols. 1–2. Translated by L. Morea Lislet and Henry Carleton. New Orleans: James M'Karaher, 1820.

*The Negro in the Military Service of the United States: 1639–1886.* Washington, D.C.: National Archives and Records Service, General Services Administration, 1973.

*Official Army Register of the Volunteer Force of the United States Army for the Years 1861, '62, '63, '64, '64.* Part 8. Washington, D.C.: Adjunct General's Office, 1867.

*Official Register of the United States, Containing a List of the Officers and Empoyés in the Civil, Military, and Naval Service on the First of July, 1893.* Vol. 1: *Legislative, Executive, Judicial.* Washington, D.C.: Government Printing Office, 1893.

U.S. Army, Department of the Gulf. *General Court Martial Orders: From the Headquarters of the Department of the Gulf 1862–1867.* Washington, D.C.: Government Printing Office, 1868.

U.S. Bureau of the Census. *Population of the United States in 1860; Compiled from the Original Returns of the Eighth Census. . . .* Washington, D.C.: Government Printing Office, 1864.

———. *Statistical Abstract of the United States,* 69th ed. Washington, D.C.: Government Printing Office, 1948.

U.S. Department of State. *French and American Claims Commission: Report from the Secretary of State Concerning Transactions of the French and American Commission.* Washington, D.C.: Government Printing Office, 1885.

U.S. War Department. *Annual Report of the Secretary of War.* Washington, D.C.: Government Printing Office, 1866.

——. *Official Records of the Union and Confederate Navies in the War of Rebellion.* 30 vols. Washington, D.C.: Government Printing Office, 1894–1922.

——. *Revised United States Army Regulations of 1861.* Washington, D.C.: Government Printing Office, 1863.

——. *The War of the Rebellion: A Compilation of the Official Records of the Union and Confederate Armies.* 127 vols. Washington, D.C.: Government Printing Office, 1880–1901.

Woodward, Elon A., comp. *The Negro in the Military Service of the United States: A Compilation of Official Records, State Papers, Historical Extracts, Etc. Relating to His Military Status and Service from the Date of His Introduction into the British North American Colonies.* Washington, D.C.: National Archives and Records Service, General Services Administration, 1963. Microfilm-858, Records of the Adjutant General's Office, 1780s–1917, RG 94, NARA.

## NEWSPAPERS AND PERIODICALS

*Alexandria Gazette* (Alexandria, Virginia)

*Antigua Observer* (St. John's, Antigua)

*The Appeal* (St. Paul, Minnesota)

*Army and Navy Messenger* (Shreveport, Louisiana)

*Bahama Herald* (Nassau, New Providence)

*Bangor Daily Whig and Courier* (Bangor, Maine)

*Beloit Journal and Courier* (Beloit, Wisconsin)

*Black Republican* (New Orleans, Louisiana)

*Black Warrior* (Camp Parapet, Louisiana)

*Burlington Weekly Hawk-Eye* (Iowa)

*Charleston Mercury* (South Carolina)

*Chicago Daily Tribune*

*Christian Recorder* (Philadelphia)

*Council Bluffs Bugle* (Iowa)

*Daily Delta* (New Orleans, Louisiana)

*Daily Gate City* (Keokuk, Iowa)

*Daily Gazette and Comet* (Baton Rouge, Louisiana)

*Daily Green Mountain Freeman* (Montpelier, Vermont)

*Daily Inter Ocean* (Chicago, Illinois)

*Daily National Republican* (Washington, D.C.)

*Daily News* (London, UK)

*Daily Picayune* (New Orleans, Louisiana)

*Daily Register* (Raleigh, North Carolina)

*Des Arc Semi-Weekly Citizen* (Arkansas)

*Detroit Free Press* (Michigan)

*Dollar Weekly Bulletin* (Maysville, Kentucky)

*Douglass' Monthly* (Rochester, New York)

*The Elevator* (San Francisco, California)

*Evening Delta* (New Orleans, Louisiana)

*Evening Star* (Washington, D.C.)

*Frank Leslie's Illustrated Newspaper* (New York)

*Frederick Douglass' Paper* (New York)

*Freemont Journal* (Ohio)

*The Gazette* (United Kingdom)

*Gazette and Sentinel* (Iberville, Louisiana)
*The Liberator* (Boston, Massachusetts)
*London Times*
*Louisiana Democrat* (Alexandria, Louisiana)
*Louisiana Republican* (New Orleans, Louisiana)
*L'Union* (New Orleans, Louisiana)
*Milwaukee Daily Sentinel* (Wisconsin)
*Morning Post* (London, UK)
*Nashville Union and American*
*Natchitoches Union* (Louisiana)
*National Anti-Slavery Standard* (New York)
*National Republican* (Washington, D.C.)
*Newark Advocate* (Newark, Ohio)
*New Haven Palladium* (Connecticut)
*New Orleans Bee*
*New Orleans Daily Crescent*
*New Orleans Democrat*
*New Orleans Louisianan*
*New Orleans Republican*
*New Orleans Times*
*New Orleans Tribune*
*New Orleans Weekly Times*
*New York Herald*
*New York Times*
*New York Tribune*
*Opelousas Patriot* (Louisiana)
*Orleans Independent Standard* (Irasburgh, Vermont)
*Polk County Press* (Saint Croix Falls, Wisconsin)
*Pomeroy Weekly Telegraph* (Ohio)
*Portland Daily Press* (Portland, Maine)
*Prescott Journal* (Wisconsin)
*Richmond Enquirer* (Richmond, Va.)
*Royal Gazette* (Hamilton, Bermuda)
*Rutland Weekly Herald* (Vermont)
*St. Christopher Advertiser* (Basseterre, St. Kitts and Nevis)
*St. Christopher Advertiser and Weekly Intelligencer* (Basseterre, St. Kitts and Nevis)
*St. Christopher Gazette* (Basseterre, St. Kitts and Nevis)
*Semi-Weekly Shreveport News* (Louisiana)
*Smoky Hill and Republican Union* (Junction City, Kans.)
*Tipton Advertiser* (Iowa)
*True Witness* (New Orleans, Louisiana)
*Urbana Union* (Ohio)
*Vermont Watchman* (Montpelier, Vermont)
*Weekly Delta* (New Orleans, Louisiana)
*Weekly Trinity Journal* (Weaverville, California)
*West Indian* (Bridgetown, Barbados)
*Wilmington Journal* (Delaware)
*Wilmington Journal* (North Carolina)
*Wisconsin State Register* (Portage, Wisconsin)

## OTHER PUBLISHED PRIMARY SOURCES

Berlin, Ira, Barbara J. Fields, Steven F. Miller, Joseph P. Reidy, and Leslie S. Rowland, eds. *Free at Last: A Documentary History of Slavery, Freedom, and the Civil War.* New York: New Press, 1992.

Berlin, Ira, Barbara J. Fields, Thavolia Glymph, Joseph P. Reidy, and Leslie S. Rowland, eds. *Freedom: A Documentary History of Emancipation, 1861–1867.* Series 1, vol. 1: *The Destruction of Slavery.* New York: Cambridge Univ. Press, 1986.

Berlin, Ira, Thavolia Glymph, Steven F. Miller, Joseph P. Reidy, Leslie Rowland, and

Julie Saville, eds. *Freedom: A Documentary History of Emancipation, 1861–1867.* Series 1, vol. 3: *The Wartime Genesis of Free Labor: The Lower South.* New York: Cambridge Univ. Press, 1991.

Berlin, Ira, Joseph P. Reidy, and Leslie S. Rowland, eds. *Freedom: A Documentary History of Emancipation, 1861–1867. Series II: The Black Military Experience.* New York: Cambridge Univ. Press, 1982.

——. *Freedom's Soldiers: The Black Military Experience in the Civil War.* New York: Cambridge Univ. Press, 1998.

Brown, William W. *The Negro in the American Rebellion: His Heroism and His Fidelity.* Boston: Lee and Shepard, 1867.

Carpenter, George N. *History of the Eighth Regiment Vermont Volunteers, 1861–1865.* Boston: Press of Deland and Barta, 1886.

Conway, Thomas W. *The Freedmen of Louisiana: Final Report of the Bureau of Free Labor, Department of the Gulf, to Major General E. R. S. Canby.* New Orleans: New Orleans Times Book and Job Office, 1865.

Dyer, Frederick H. *A Compendium of the War of the Rebellion.* New York: Thomas Yoseloff, 1959.

Hahn, Michael. *Message of the Governor of the State of Louisiana: Delivered October 7, 1864.* New Orleans: W. R. Fish, State Printer, 1864.

Irwin, Richard Biddle. *History of the Nineteenth Army Corps.* New York: G. P. Putnam's Sons, 1892.

Livermore, Thomas L. *Numbers and Losses in the Civil War America, 1861–1865.* Boston: Houghton Mifflin, 1901.

Matthews, James M., ed., *Public Laws of the Confederate States of America Passed at the First Session of the First Congress; 1862.* Richmond, Va.: R. M. Smith, Printer to the Congress, 1862.

Moore, Frank, ed. *The Rebellion Record: A Diary of American Events with Documents, Narratives, Illustrative Incidents, Poetry, ETC.*, vol. 1. New York: G. P. Putnam, 1862.

——. *Women of the War: Their Heroism and Self-Sacrifice.* Hartford, Conn.: S. S. Scranton, 1866.

Nalty, Bernard C., and Morris J. MacGregor, eds. *Blacks in the Military: Essential Documents.* Wilmington, Del.: Scholarly Resources, 1981.

——. *Blacks in the United States Armed Forces: Basic Documents,* vols. 1–3. Wilmington, Del.: Scholarly Resources, 1977.

Parton, James. *General Butler in New Orleans: History of the Administration of the Department of the Gulf in the Year 1862.* Boston: Ticknor and Fields, 1866.

Quincy, Samuel M. *A Camp and Garrison Manual for Volunteers and Militia.* New Orleans: Peter O'Donnell, 1865.

Redkey, Edwin S., ed. *A Grand Army of Black Men: Letters from African-American Soldiers in the Union Army, 1861–1865.* New York: Cambridge Univ. Press, 1992.

Richardson, James D. *A Compilation of the Messages and Papers of the Confederacy Including the Diplomatic Correspondence 1861–1865.* Nashville: United States Publishing Company, 1905.

Sherman, Andrew M. *In the Lowlands of Louisiana in 1863: An Address Delivered by Andrew M. Sherman at the Forty-Second Reunion of the Twenty-Third Connecticut.* Morristown, N.J.: Howard Publishing, 1908.

Sideman, Belle Becker, and Lillian Friedman, eds. *Europe Looks at the Civil War: An Anthology.* New York: Orion Press, 1960.

Simpson, Brooks D., ed. *The Civil War: The Third Year Told by Those Who Lived It.* New York: Library of America, 2013.

Taggart, John H. *Free Military School for Applicants for Commands of Colored Troops.* Philadelphia: King and Baird Printers, 1863.

Ullman, Daniel. *Address by Daniel Ullman, L.L.D., before the Soldier's and Sailor's Union of the State of the State of New York, February 5, 1868.* Washington, D.C.: The Great Republic Office, 1868.

### ***Secondary Sources***

#### BOOKS AND ARTICLES

Anbinder, Tyler. *Nativism and Slavery: The Northern Know Nothings and Politics of the 1850s.* New York: Oxford Univ. Press, 1992.

Baptist, Edward E. *The Half Has Never Been Told: Slavery and the Making of American Capitalism.* New York: Basic Books, 2014.

Beard, Joseph A., and Shane D. Makowicki. *Lincoln Assassination.* Washington, D.C.: U.S. Army Center of Military History, 2020.

Beckert, Sven. *Empire of Cotton: A Global History.* New York: Knopf, 2014.

Berlin, Ira. *Many Thousands Gone: The First Two Centuries of Slavery in North America.* Cambridge, Mass.: The Belknap Press of Harvard Univ. Press, 1998.

Berlin, Ira, and Herbert G. Gutman. "Natives and Immigrants, Free Men and Slaves: Urban Workingmen in the Antebellum American South." *American Historical Review* 88, no. 5 (December 1, 1983): 1175–1200.

Berlin, Ira, Barbara J. Fields, Steven F. Miller, Joseph P. Reidy, and Leslie S. Rowland. *Slaves No More: Three Essays on Emancipation and the Civil War.* New York: Cambridge Univ. Press, 1992.

Bennett, Lerone, Jr. "Black Power in Dixie." *Ebony* 17, no. 9 (1962): 84–90.

Bernstein, Iver. *The New York City Draft Riots: Their Significance for American Society and Politics in the Age of the Civil War.* New York: Oxford Univ. Press, 1990.

Berry, Mary F. "Negro Troops in Blue and Gray: The Louisiana Native Guards, 1861–1863." *Louisiana History* 8, no. 2 (Spring 1967): 165–190.

Bielski, Mark F. *A Mortal Blow to the Confederacy: The Fall of New Orleans, 1862.* El Dorado Hills, Calif.: Savas Beatie, 2021.

Blackburn, Robin. *The American Crucible: Slavery, Emancipation and Human Rights.* New York: Verso Books, 2013.

Blair, William A. *The Records of Murders and Outrages: Racial Violence and the Fight over Truth at the Dawn of Reconstruction.* Chapel Hill: Univ. of North Carolina Press, 2021.

Blair, William A., and William Pencak, eds. *Making and Remaking Pennsylvania's Civil War.* University Park: Pennsylvania State Univ. Press, 2001.

Blassingame, John W. *Black New Orleans, 1860–1880.* Chicago: Univ. of Chicago Press, 1973.

Blight, David. *Race and Reunion: The Civil War in American Memory.* Cambridge, Mass.: The Belknap Press of Harvard Univ. Press, 2001.

Blount, Russell W., Jr. *The Longest Siege: Port Hudson, Louisiana, 1863.* Jefferson, N.C.: McFarland, 2021.

Blyden, Nemata Amelia Ibitayo. I. *African Americans and Africa: A New History.* New Haven: Yale Univ. Press, 2019.

Bonnefoy, Baptiste. "Colonial Militia, Color and Local Forms of Urban Belonging (Spanish America, 18th century)." *Revue d'histoire Moderne et Contemporaine* 69, no. 4 (2022): 5–28.

Brady, Steven. *Chained to History: Slavery and US Foreign Relations to 1865.* Ithaca, N.Y.: Cornell Univ. Press, 2022.

Brasseaux, Carl A., and Glenn R. Conrad, eds. *The Road to Louisiana: The Saint-Domingue Refugees, 1792–1809.* Lafayette: Univ. of Louisiana at Lafayette Press, 1992.

Brown, Elsa B. "Negotiating and Transforming the Public Sphere: African American Political Life in the Transition from Slavery to Freedom." *Public Culture* 7, no. 1 (1994): 107–146.

Browning, Robert M. *Lincoln's Trident: The West Gulf Blockading Squadron during the Civil War.* Tuscaloosa: Univ. of Alabama Press, 2015.

Bunn, Mike. *The Assault on Fort Blakely: The Thunder and Lightning of Battle.* Charleston, S.C.: History Press, 2021.

Burton, William L. *Melting Pot Soldiers: The Union's Ethnic Regiments.* Ames: Iowa State Univ. Press, 1988.

Butler, Clayton J. *True Blue: White Unionists in the Deep South During the Civil War and Reconstruction.* Baton Rouge: Louisiana State Univ. Press, 2022.

Butts, Heather. *African American Medicine in Washington, D.C.: Healing the Capital During the Civil War Era.* Charleston, S.C.: History Press, 2014.

Cade, Anthony J., II. "Dr. Louis Charles Roudanez and the African American Community of New Orleans during the Civil War." *Black Perspectives,* African American Intellectual History Society, 19 October 2022. https://www.aaihs.org/dr-louis

-charles-roudanez-and-the-african-american-community-of-new-orleans-during-the-civil-war/.

———. "A Free Man, *Fortiori* a Soldier: Corporal John Andrew vs. Archibald Montgomery and the Transformation of New Orleans." *Journal of Military History* 88, no. 3 (July 2024): 660–681.

———. "Why They Fought: The Initial Motivations of German American Soldiers Who Fought for the Union in the American Civil War." *European Review of History* 27, no. 1–2 (March 2020): 65–87.

Campbell, James T. *Middle Passages: African American Journeys to Africa, 1787–2005.* New York: Penguin Press, 2006.

Capers, Gerald M. *Occupied City: New Orleans under the Federals, 1862–1865.* Lexington: Univ. of Kentucky Press, 1965.

Caplan, Arthur L., James J. McCartney, and Dominic A. Sisti, eds. *Health, Disease, and Illness: Concepts in Medicine.* Washington, D.C.: Georgetown Univ. Press, 2004.

Casey, John A., Jr. *New Men: Reconstructing the Figure of the Veteran in Late-Nineteenth-Century American Literature and Culture.* New York: Fordham Univ. Press, 2015.

Casso, Evans J. *Louisiana Legacy: A History of the State National Guard.* Gretna, La.: Pelican, 1998.

Chadwick, Bruce. *The Creole Rebellion: The Most Successful Slave Revolt in American History.* Albuquerque: Univ. of New Mexico Press, 2022.

Comminey, Shawn C. "National Black Conventions and the Quest for African American Freedom and Progress, 1847–1867." *International Social Science Review* 91, no 1 (2015): 1–18.

Cook, Robert. "'The Glory of the Nation': Black Soldier-Historians and the Continuing African American Struggle for a Usable Past." *Acta Universitatis Carolinae Studia Territorialia* 20, no. 2 (April 2020): 13–38.

Cooper, Jerry M. *The Militia and the National Guard in America Since Colonial Times.* Westport, Conn.: Greenwood Press, 1993.

Cornish, Dudley Taylor. *The Sable Arm: Negro Troops in the Union Army, 1861–1865.* Lawrence: Univ. Press of Kansas, 1987.

Cuccia, Phillip. "'Gorillas' and White Glove Gents: Union Soldiers in the Red River Campaign." *Louisiana History* 36, no. 4 (Autumn 1995): 413–430.

Daggett, Melissa. "Spiritualism Among Creoles of Color in Nineteenth-Century New Orleans: The Life and Times of Henry Louis Rey." *Louisiana History* 55, no. 4 (fall 2014): 409–431.

———. *Spiritualism in Nineteenth-Century New Orleans: The Life and Times of Henry Louis Rey.* Jackson: Univ. Press of Mississippi, 2017.

Davis, Angela. "Reflections on the Black Woman's Role in the Community of Slaves." *Black Scholar* 3, no. 4 (December 1971): 2–15.

Dessens, Nathalie. *Creole City: A Chronicle of Early American New Orleans.* Gainesville: Univ. Press of Florida, 2015.

———. "Louis Charles Roudanez, a Creole of Color of Saint-Domingue Descent: Atlantic Reinterpretations of Nineteenth-Century New Orleans." *South Atlantic Review* 73, no. 2 (Spring 2008): 26–38.

Diouf, Sylviane A. *Slavery's Exiles: The Story of the American Maroons.* New York: New York Univ. Press, 2014.

Dixson Adrienne D., and Celia Roussea Anderson. "Where Are We? Critical Race Theory in Education 20 Years Later." *Peabody Journal of Education* 93, no. 1 (2018): 121–131.

Dobak, William A. *Freedom by the Sword: The U.S. Colored Troops 1862–1867.* Washington, D.C.: U.S. Army Center of Military History, 2011.

Dobak, William A., and Thomas D. Phillips. *The Black Regulars, 1866–1898.* Norman: Univ. of Oklahoma Press, 2001.

Donald, David Herbert. *Lincoln.* New York: Simon and Schuster, 1995.

Dorman, James H. "The Persistent Specter: Slave Rebellion in Territorial Louisiana." *Louisiana History* 18, no. 4 (Autumn 1977): 389–404.

Doyle, Don Harrison, ed. *American Civil Wars: The United States, Latin America, Europe, and the Crisis of the 1860s.* Chapel Hill: Univ. of North Carolina Press, 2017.

———. *The Cause of All Nations: An International History of the American Civil War.* New York: Basic Books, 2015.

Du Bois, W. E. B. *Black Reconstruction in America, 1860–1880.* New York: Free Press, 1935.

Duffy, James P. *Lincoln's Admiral: The Civil War Campaigns of David Farragut.* New York: John Wiley and Sons, 1997.

Durden, Robert F. *The Gray and the Black: The Confederate Debate on Emancipation.* Baton Rouge: Louisiana State Univ. Press, 2000.

Egerton, Douglas R. *Thunder at the Gates: The Black Civil War Regiments That Redeemed America.* New York: Basic Books, 2016.

Eggleston, Michael A. *President Lincoln's Recruiter: General Lorenzo Thomas and the United States Colored Troops in the Civil War.* Jefferson, N.C.: McFarland, 2013.

Eltis, David. *The Rise of African Slavery in the Americas.* Cambridge, UK.: Cambridge Univ. Press, 2000.

Erickson, Charlotte. *Invisible Immigrants: The Adaptation of English and Scottish Immigrants in 19th-Century America.* Ithaca, N.Y.: Cornell Univ. Press, 1990.

Everett, Donald E. "Ben Butler and the Louisiana Native Guards, 1861–1862." *Journal of Southern History* 24, no. 2 (1958): 202–217.

Faust, Drew Gilpin. *The Creation of Confederate Nationalism: Ideology and Identity in the Civil War South.* Baton Rouge: Louisiana State Univ. Press, 1988.

Feimster, Crystal N. "Rape and Mutiny at Fort Jackson: Black Laundresses Testify in Civil War Louisiana." *Labor Studies in Working-Class History* 19, no. 1 (2022): 11–31.

Fischer, Roger A. *The Segregation Struggle in Louisiana, 1862–1877.* Urbana: Univ. of Illinois Press, 1974.

Fiske, John. *The Mississippi Valley in the Civil War.* Boston: Houghton, Mifflin, 1900.

Fleming, Walter L. *The Freedmen's Saving Bank: A Chapter in the Economic History of the Negro Race.* Chapel Hill: Univ. of North Carolina Press, 1927.

Follett, Richard J. *The Sugar Masters: Planters and Slaves in Louisiana's Cane World, 1820–1860.* Baton Rouge: Louisiana State Univ. Press, 2005.

Foner, Eric. *The Fiery Trial: Abraham Lincoln and American Slavery.* New York: Norton, 2010.

———. *Forever Free: The Story of Emancipation and Reconstruction.* New York: Random House, 2005.

———. *Reconstruction: America's Unfinished Revolution, 1863–1877.* New York: Harper & Row, 1988.

———. *A Short History of Reconstruction: 1863–1877.* New York: Harper Perennial, 2015.

Foner, Philip S., and Ronald L. Lewis, eds. *The Black Worker: A Documentary History from Colonial Times to the Present.* Vol. 1: *The Black Worker to 1896.* Philadelphia: Temple University Press, 1978.

Frazier, Donald S. *Blood on the Bayou: Vicksburg, Port Hudson, and the Trans-Mississippi.* Buffalo Gap, Tex.: State House Press, 2015.

Fuller, James R. *Men of Color, to Arms! Vermont African-Americans in the Civil War.* San Jose, Calif.: iUniverse Press, 2001.

Gannon, James P. *Irish Rebels, Confederate Tigers: A History of the 6th Louisiana Volunteers.* New York: Hachette Books, 1998.

Gerteis, Louis S. *From Contraband to Freedom: Federal Policy Toward Southern Blacks, 1861–1865.* Westport, Conn.: Greenwood Press, 1973.

Gladstone, William A. *Men of Color.* Gettysburg, Pa.: Thomas Publications, 1993.

Glatthaar, Joseph T. *Forged in Battle: The Civil War Alliance of Black Soldiers and White Officers.* New York: Free Press, 1990.

Gleeson, David T., and Simon Lewis, eds. *The Civil War as Global Conflict: Transnational Meanings of the American Civil War.* Columbia: Univ. of South Carolina Press, 2014.

Gomez, Michael A. *Exchanging Our Country Marks: The Transformation of African Identities in the Colonial and Antebellum South.* Chapel Hill: Univ. of North Carolina Press, 1998.

Green, Hilary. *Educational Reconstruction: African American Schools in the Urban South, 1865–1890.* New York: Fordham Univ. Press, 2016.

Grimsley, Mark. *The Hard Hand of War: Union Military Policy Toward Southern Civilians, 1861–1865.* Cambridge, UK: Cambridge Univ. Press, 1995.

Grimsted, David. *American Mobbing, 1828–1861: Toward Civil War.* New York: Oxford Univ. Press, 1998.

Hall, Gwendolyn Midlo. *Africans in Colonial Louisiana: The Development of Afro-Creole Culture in the Eighteenth Century.* Baton Rouge: Louisiana State Univ. Press, 1992.

——. *Slavery and African Ethnicities in the Americas: Restoring the Links.* Chapel Hill: Univ. of North Carolina Press, 2005.

Harrington, Fred Harvey. *Fighting Politician: Major General N. P. Banks.* Philadelphia: Univ. of Pennsylvania Press, 1948.

Haskins, James S. *Pinckney Benton Stewart Pinchback.* New York: Macmillan, 1973.

Hearn, Chester G. *Admiral David Dixon Porter: The Civil War Years.* Annapolis, Md.: Naval Institute Press, 1996.

——. *When the Devil Came Down to Dixie: Ben Butler in New Orleans.* Baton Rouge: Louisiana State Univ. Press, 1997.

Hess, Earl J. *The Civil War in the West: Victory and Defeat from the Appalachians to the Mississippi.* Chapel Hill: Univ. of North Carolina Press, 2012.

Hewitt, Lawrence Lee. *Port Hudson: Confederate Bastion on the Mississippi.* 1989; rpr. Baton Rouge: Louisiana State Univ. Press, 1994.

Higham, John. *Strangers in the Land: Patterns of American Nativism, 1860–1925.* New Brunswick, N.J.: Rutgers Univ. Press, 1977.

Hilton, Sylvia. "Spanish Louisiana in Atlantic Contexts: Nexus of Imperial Transactions and International Relations." In *Louisiana: Crossroads of the Atlantic World,* edited by Cecil Vidal. Philadelphia: Univ. of Pennsylvania Press, 2014.

Hogue, James K. *Uncivil War: Five New Orleans Street Battles and the Rise and Fall of Radical Reconstruction.* Baton Rouge: Louisiana State Univ. Press, 2006.

Hollandsworth, James G., Jr. *The Louisiana Native Guards: The Black Military Experience During the Civil War.* Baton Rouge: Louisiana State Univ. Press, 1995.

——. *Pretense of Glory: The Life of General Nathaniel P. Banks.* Baton Rouge: Louisiana State Univ. Press, 1998.

Holt, Michael F. *The Political Crisis of the 1850s.* New York: Norton, 1978.

Horne, Gerald. *Negro Comrades of the Crown: African Americans and the British Empire Fight the U.S. Before Emancipation.* New York: New York Univ. Press, 2012.

Houston, James L. *Calculating the Value of the Union: Slavery, Property Rights, and the Economic Origins of the Civil War.* Chapel Hill: Univ. of North Carolina Press, 2003.

Hunt, Roger D. *Colonels in Blue: U.S. Colored Troops, U.S. Armed Forces, Staff Officers and Special Units.* Jefferson, N.C.: McFarland, 2022.

Jacobson, Matthew F. *Whiteness of a Different Color: European Immigrants and the Alchemy of Race.* Cambridge, Mass.: Harvard Univ. Press, 1998.

Johnson, Ludwell H. *Red River Campaign: Politics and Cotton in the Civil War.* Kent, Ohio: Kent State Univ. Press, 1993.

Johnson, Walter. "The Slave Trader, the White Slave, and the Politics of Racial Determination in the 1850s." *Journal of American History* 87, no. 1 (June 2000): 13–38.

——. *Soul by Soul: Life Inside the Antebellum Slave Market.* Cambridge, Mass.: Harvard Univ. Press, 1999.

Joiner, Gary D. *One Damn Blunder from Beginning to End: The Red River Campaign of 1864.* Wilmington, Del.: SR Books, 2003.

——. *Through the Howling Wilderness: The 1864 Red River Campaign and Union Failure in the West.* Knoxville: Univ. of Tennessee Press, 2006.

Jones, Martha S. *Birthright Citizens: A History of Race and Rights in Antebellum America.* New York: Cambridge Univ. Press, 2018.

Joshi, Monaj K., and Joseph P. Reidy. "'To Come Forward and Aid in Putting Down This Unholy Rebellion': The Officers of Louisiana's Free Black Native Guard During the Civil War Era." *Southern Studies* 21 (1982): 326–342.

Kahan, Paul. *Amiable Scoundrel: Simon Cameron, Lincoln's Scandalous Secretary of War.* Lincoln: Univ. of Nebraska Press, 2016.

Lamphier, Peg A., and Rosanne Welch. *The Civil War on Film: Hollywood History.* Santa Barbara: ABC-CLIO, 2020.

Leonard, Elizabeth D. *Benjamin Franklin Butler: A Noisy, Fearless Life.* Chapel Hill: Univ. of North Carolina Press, 2022.

Levin, Kevin M. *Searching for Black Confederates: The Civil War's Most Persistent Myth.* Chapel Hill: Univ. of North Carolina Press, 2019.

Longacre, Edward G. *A Regiment of Slaves: The 4th United States Colored Infantry, 1863–1866.* Mechanicsburg, Pa.: Stackpole Books, 2003.

Luebke, Frederick C., ed. *Ethnic Voters and the Election of Lincoln.* Lincoln: Univ. of Nebraska Press, 1971.

Lynch, Matthew, ed. *Before Obama: A Reappraisal of Black Reconstruction Era Politicians.* Vol. 1: *Legacies Lost: The Life and Times of John R. Lynch and His Political Contemporaries.* Santa Barbara, Calif.: Praeger, 2012.

Mahan, Alfred T. *Admiral Farragut.* New York: Appleton, 1893.

Malone, Ann Patton. *Sweet Chariot: Slave Family and Household Structure in Nineteenth-Century Louisiana.* Chapel Hill: Univ. of North Carolina Press, 1992.

Manning, Chandra. *What This Cruel War Was Over: Soldiers, Slavery, and the Civil War.* New York: Vintage Books, 2008.

May, Robert E., ed. *The Union, the Confederacy, and the Atlantic Rim: The Pending Conflict.* West Lafayette, Ind.: Purdue Univ. Press, 1995.

McCardell, John. *The Idea of a Southern Nation: Southern Nationalists and Southern Nationalism, 1830–1860.* New York: Norton, 1979.

McClaughry, John. "John Wolcott Phelps: The Civil War General Who Became a Forgotten Presidential Candidate in 1880." *Vermont History* 38, no. 4 (Autumn 1970): 263–290.

McConnell, Roland C. "Louisiana's Black Military History, 1729–1865." In *Louisiana's Black Heritage,* edited by Robert R. Macdonald, John R. Kemp, and Edward F. Haas, 32–62. New Orleans: Louisiana State Museum, 1979.

McCrary, Peyton. *Abraham Lincoln and Reconstruction: The Louisiana Experiment.* Princeton: Princeton Univ. Press, 1978.

McCurry, Stephanie. *Confederate Reckoning: Power and Politics in the Civil War South.* Cambridge, Mass.: Harvard Univ. Press, 2010.

McDonald, Roderick A. *The Economy and Material Culture of Slaves: Goods and Chattels on the Sugar Plantations of Jamaica and Louisiana.* Baton Rouge: Louisiana State Univ. Press, 1993.

McLaughlin-Stonham, Hilary. *From Slavery to Civil Rights: On the Streetcars of New Orleans 1830s–Present.* Liverpool, UK: Liverpool Univ. Press, 2020.

McPherson, James M. *Battle Cry of Freedom: The Civil War Era.* New York: Oxford Univ. Press, 1988.

——. *For Cause and Comrades: Why Men Fought in the Civil War.* New York: Oxford Univ. Press, 1997.

——. *The Negro's Civil War: How American Blacks Felt and Acted During the War for the Union.* New York: Vintage Books, 1965.

Mendez, James G. *A Great Sacrifice: Northern Black Soldiers, Their Families, and the Experience of the Civil War.* New York: Fordham Univ. Press, 2019.

Mills, Gary B. "Patriotism Frustrated: The Native Guards of Confederate Natchitoches." *Louisiana History* 18, no. 4 (Autumn 1977): 437–51.

Milteer, Warren Eugene, Jr. *Beyond Slavery's Shadow: Free People of Color in the South.* Chapel Hill: Univ. of North Carolina Press, 2021.

Nystrom, Justin A. *New Orleans After the Civil War: Race, Politics, and a New Birth of Freedom.* Baltimore: Johns Hopkins Univ. Press, 2010.

Obert, Jonathan, and Eleonora Mattiacci. "Keeping Vigil: The Emergence of Vigilance Committees in Pre-Civil War America." *Perspectives on Politics* 16, no. 3 (2018): 600–616.

Ochs, Stephen J. *A Black Patriot and a White Priest: André Cailloux and Claude Paschal Maistre in Civil War New Orleans.* Baton Rouge: Louisiana State Univ. Press, 2000.

Owens, Emily A. *Consent in the Presence of Force: Sexual Violence and Black Women's Survival in Antebellum New Orleans.* Chapel Hill: Univ. of North Carolina Press, 2023.

Penn, I. Garland. *The Afro-American Press and Its Editors.* Springfield, Mass.: Wiley, 1891.

Pierce, Jason E. *Making the White Man's West: Whiteness and the Creation of the American West.* Boulder: Univ. Press of Colorado, 2016.

Pierson, Michael D. *Mutiny at Fort Jackson: The Untold Story of the Fall of New Orleans.* Chapel Hill: Univ. of North Carolina Press, 2008.

Pinheiro, Holly A., Jr. *The Families' Civil War: Black Soldiers and the Fight for Racial Justice.* Athens: Univ. of Georgia Press, 2022.

Prushankin, Jeffery S. *The Civil War in the Trans-Mississippi Theater, 1861–1865.* Washington, D.C.: U.S. Army Center of Military History, 2015.

Quarles, Benjamin. *Black Abolitionists.* New York: Oxford Univ. Press, 1969.

——. *Lincoln and the Negro.* New York: Oxford Univ. Press, 1962.

——. *The Negro in the Civil War.* Boston: Little, Brown, 1953.

Quatman, G. William. *A Young General and the Fall of Richmond: The Life and Career of Godfrey Weitzel.* Athens: Ohio Univ. Press, 2015.

Rankin, David C. "The Origins of Black Leadership in New Orleans During Reconstruction." *Journal of Southern History* 40, no. 3 (August 1974): 417–440.

Raphael, Morris. *The Battle in the Bayou Country.* Detroit: Harlo Press, 1976.

Reid, Richard M. *Freedom for Themselves: North Carolina's Black Soldiers in the Civil War Era.* Chapel Hill: Univ. of North Carolina Press, 2008.

Rhodes, James F. *History of the Civil War 1861–1865.* New York: Macmillan, 1917.

Richardson, Heather Cox. *The Death of Reconstruction: Race, Labor, and Politics in the Post-Civil War North, 1865–1901.* Cambridge, Mass.: Harvard Univ. Press, 2001.

Ripley, C. Peter. *Slaves and Freedmen in Civil War Louisiana.* Baton Rouge: Louisiana State Univ. Press, 1976.

Robertson, Henry O. *The Red River Campaign and Its Toll: 69 Bloody Days in Louisiana, March–May 1864.* Jefferson, N.C.: McFarland, 2016.

Rodrigue, John C. *Reconstruction in the Cane Fields: From Slavery to Free Labor in Louisiana's Sugar Parishes 1862–1880.* Baton Rouge: Louisiana State Univ. Press, 2001.

Roediger, David R. *Wages of Whiteness: Race and the Making of the American Working Class.* New York: Verso, 1991.

Roland, Charles Pierce. *Louisiana Sugar Plantations During the Civil War.* Leiden, Netherlands: E. J. Brill, 1957.

Roland, Nicholas Keefauver. *Violence in the Hill Country: The Texas Frontier in the Civil War Era.* Austin: Univ. of Texas Press, 2021.

Ross, Michael A. *The Great New Orleans Kidnapping Case: Race, Law, and Justice in the Reconstruction Era.* New York: Oxford Univ. Press, 2015.

Rothman, Adam. *Slave Country: American Expansion and the Origins of the Deep South.* Cambridge, Mass.: Harvard Univ. Press, 2005.

Sacher, John M. *Confederate Conscription and the Struggle for Southern Soldiers.* Baton Rouge: Louisiana State Univ. Press, 2021.

Sainlaude, Stève. *France and the American Civil War: A Diplomatic History.* Chapel Hill: Univ. of North Carolina Press, 2019.

Salter, Krewasky A., I. *The Story of Black Military Officers, 1861–1948.* New York: Routledge, 2014.

Samito, Christian G. *Becoming American Under Fire: Irish Americans, African Americans, and the Politics of Citizenship During the Civil War Era.* Ithaca, N.Y.: Cornell Univ. Press, 2009.

Sandow, Robert M., ed. *Contested Loyalty: Debates Over Patriotism in the Civil War North.* New York: Fordham Univ. Press, 2018.

Schafer, Judith Kelleher. *Becoming Free, Remaining Free: Manumission and Enslavement in New Orleans, 1846–1862.* Baton Rouge: Louisiana State Univ. Press, 2003.

——. *Brothels, Depravity, and Abandoned Women: Illegal Sex in Antebellum New Orleans.* Baton Rouge: Louisiana State Univ. Press, 2009.

Schoeppner, Michael A. *Moral Contagion: Black Atlantic Sailors, Citizenship, and Diplomacy in Antebellum America.* New York: Cambridge Univ. Press, 2019.

Severance, Ben H. *A War State All Over: Alabama Politics and the Confederate Cause.* Tuscaloosa: Univ. of Alabama Press, 2020.

Shaffer, Donald R. *After the Glory: The Struggles of Black Civil War Veterans.* Lawrence: Univ. Press of Kansas, 2004.

Shannon, Fred A. *The Organization and Administration of the Union Army, 1861–1865.* Cleveland, Ohio: Arthur H. Clark, 1928.

Sinha, Manisha. *The Slave's Cause: A History of Abolition.* New Haven: Yale Univ. Press, 2016.

Smith, John David, ed. *Black Soldiers in Blue: African American Troops in the Civil War Era.* Chapel Hill: Univ. of North Carolina Press, 2002.

Smith, John David, and Raymond Arsenault, eds. *The Long Civil War: New Explorations of America's Enduring Conflict.* Lexington: Univ. Press of Kentucky, 2021.

Smith, Timothy B. *The Siege of Vicksburg: Climax of the Campaign to Open the Mississippi River, May 23–July 4, 1863.* Lawrence: Univ. Press of Kansas, 2021.

Spurgeon, Ian Michael. *Soldiers in the Army of Freedom: The 1st Kansas Colored, the Civil War's First African American Combat Unit.* Norman: Univ. of Oklahoma Press, 2014.

Steiner, Bernard C. *Life of Reverdy Johnson.* Baltimore: Norman, Remington, 1914.

Sterling, Dorothy. *The Making of an Afro-American: Martin Robison Delany, 1812–1885.* Garden City, N.Y.: Doubleday, 1971,

Sutherland, Daniel E., ed. *Guerrillas, Unionists, and Violence on the Confederate Home Front.* Fayetteville: Univ. of Arkansas Press, 1999.

——. *A Savage Conflict: The Decisive Role of Guerrillas in the American Civil War.* Chapel Hill: Univ. of North Carolina Press, 2009.

Tansey, Richard. "Out of State Free Blacks in Late Antebellum New Orleans." *Louisiana History* 22, no. 4 (Autumn 1981): 369–386.

Taylor, Amy Murrell. *Embattled Freedom: Journeys Through the Civil War's Slave Refugee Camps.* Chapel Hill: Univ. of North Carolina Press, 2018.

Trethewey, Natasha D. *Native Guard.* Boston: Houghton Mifflin, 2006.

Trouillot, Michel-Rolph. *Silencing the Past: Power and the Production of History.* Boston: Beacon Press, 1995.

Trudeau, Noah Andre. *Like Men of War: Black Troops in the Civil War, 1862–1865.* Boston: Little, Brown, 1999.

Tunnell, Ted. *Crucible of Reconstruction: War, Radicalism, and Race in Louisiana, 1862–1877.* Baton Rouge: Louisiana State Univ. Press, 1984.

Urwin, Gregory J. W., ed. *Black Flag Over Dixie: Racial Atrocities and Reprisals in the Civil War.* Carbondale: Southern Illinois Univ. Press, 2004.

Vandal, Gilles. *The New Orleans Riot of 1866: Anatomy of a Tragedy.* Lafayette: University of Southwestern Louisiana, 1983.

Vincent, Charles. *Black Legislators in Louisiana During Reconstruction.* Baton Rouge: Louisiana Univ. Press, 1976.

Ward, J. Matthew. *Garden of Ruins: Occupied Louisiana in the Civil War.* Baton Rouge: Louisiana State Univ. Press, 2024.

Warner, Ezra J. *Generals in Blue: Lives of the Union Commanders.* Baton Rouge: Louisiana State Univ. Press, 1964.

Waugh, Joan, and Gary W. Gallagher, eds. *Wars within a War: Controversy and Conflict over the American Civil War.* Chapel Hill: Univ. of North Carolina Press, 2009.

Westwood, Howard C. "Benjamin Butler's Enlistment of Black Troops in New Orleans in 1862." *Louisiana History* 26, no. 1 (Winter 1985): 5–22.

Wetta, Frank J. *The Louisiana Scalawags: Politics, Race, and Terrorism During the Civil War and Reconstruction.* Baton Rouge: Louisiana State Univ. Press, 2012.

Williams, David. *I Freed Myself: African American Self-Emancipation in the Civil War Era.* New York: Cambridge Univ. Press, 2014.

Willis, Deborah. *The Black Civil War Soldier: A Visual History of Conflict and Citizenship.* New York: New York Univ. Press, 2021.

Wilson, Keith P. *Campfires of Freedom: The Camp Life of Black Soldiers During the Civil War.* Kent, Ohio: Kent State Univ. Press, 2002.

Winters, John D. *The Civil War in Louisiana.* Baton Rouge: Louisiana State Univ. Press, 1963.

Work, David K. *Lincoln's Political Generals.* Urbana: Univ. of Illinois Press, 2009.

Yarbrough, Fay A. *Choctaw Confederates: The American Civil War in Indian Country.* Chapel Hill: Univ. of North Carolina Press, 2021.

Yosso, Tara J., William A. Smith, Daniel G. Solórzano, and Man Hung. "A Critical Race Theory Test of W. E. B. DuBois' Hypothesis: Do Black Students Need Separate Schools?" *Race Ethnicity and Education* 25, no. 4 (October 2021): 370–388.

## DISSERTATIONS

Dawson, Joseph Green, III. "The Long Ordeal: Army Generals and Reconstruction in Louisiana, 1862–1877. (Volumes I and II)." Ph.D. diss., Louisiana State University, 1978.

Devore, Donald E. "Race Relations and Community Development: The Education of Blacks in New Orleans, 1862–1960." Ph.D. diss., Louisiana State University, 1989.

Everett, Donald E. "Free Persons of Color in New Orleans, 1803–1865." Ph.D. diss., Tulane University, 1952.

Fritz, Karen Elizabeth. "Voices in the Storm: Confederate Rhetoric, 1861–1865." Ph.D. diss., Louisiana State University, 1995.

Gordy, Ruby Nell. "The Irish in New Orleans, 1845–1855." Ph.D. diss., Louisiana State University, 1960.

Highsmith, William Edward. "Louisiana During Reconstruction." Ph.D. diss., Louisiana State University, 1954.

Lebreton, Marietta Marie. "A History of the Territory of Orleans, 1803–1812. (Parts I and II)." Ph.D. diss., Louisiana State University, 1969.

Marshall, David Coughlin. "A History of the Higher Education of Negroes in the State of Louisiana." Ph.D. diss., Louisiana State University, 1956.

Melancon, Kristi Richard. "An African American Discourse Community in Black and White: The *New Orleans Tribune*." Ph.D. diss., Louisiana State University, 2011.

Nguyen, Julia Huston. "Worldly Rites: The Social and Political Significance of Religious Services in Louisiana, 1803–1865." Ph.D. diss., Louisiana State University, 2001.

Rizzuto, Gina M. "Voices from the Coolest Corner of Hell: A Content Analysis of Slave Narratives in the Study of Creolization in the Education of 19th Century African American Slaves." Ph.D. diss., Louisiana State University, 2013.

Roland, Charles Pierce. "Louisiana Sugar Plantations During the Civil War." Ph.D. diss., Louisiana State University, 1951.

Rouzan, Laura Velina. 1989. "A Rhetorical Analysis of Editorials in *L'Union* and the *New Orleans Tribune*." Ph.D. diss., Florida State University, 1989.

Spletstoser, Fredrick Marcel. "Back Door to the Land of Plenty: New Orleans as an Immigrant Port, 1820–1860. (Volumes I and II)." Ph.D. diss., Louisiana State University, 1978.

Taylor, Joe Gray. "Negro Slavery in Louisiana." Ph.D. diss., Louisiana State University, 1952.

Vincent, Charles. "Negro Legislators in Louisiana During Reconstruction." Ph.D. diss., Louisiana State University, 1973.

Wegmann, Andrew N. "Skin Color and Social Practice: The Problem of Race and Class Among New Orleans Creoles and Across the South, 1718–1862." Ph.D. diss., Louisiana State University, 2015.

# INDEX

*Note:* Page numbers in italics indicate images in the text.